Thank you very much for purchasing *Haikyu!!* volume 42! I wish I could eat forever without ever getting full.

HARUICHI FURUDATE began his manga career when he was 25 years old with the one-shot *Ousama Kid* (King Kid), which won an honorable mention for the 14th Jump Treasure Newcomer Manga Prize. His first series, *Kiben Gakuha, Yotsuya Sensei no Kaidan* (Philosophy School, Yotsuya Sensei's Ghost Stories), was serialized in Weekly Shonen Jump in 2010. In 2012, he began serializing *Haikyu!!* in Weekly Shonen Jump, where it became his most popular work to date.

HAIKYU!!

VOLUME 42
SHONEN JUMP Manga Edition

Story and Art by
HARUICHI FURUDATE

Translation **1** **ADRIENNE BECK**
Touch-Up Art & Lettering **2** **ERIKA TERRIQUEZ**
Design **3** **JULIAN [JR] ROBINSON**
Editor **4** **MARLENE FIRST**

HAIKYU!! © 2012 by Haruichi Furudate
All rights reserved.
First published in Japan in 2012 by SHUEISHA Inc., Tokyo.
English translation rights arranged by SHUEISHA Inc.

The stories, characters and incidents mentioned
in this publication are entirely fictional.

Printed in Canada

Published by VIZ Media, LLC
P.O. Box 77010
San Francisco, CA 94107

10 9 8 7 6 5 4 3 2 1
First printing, January 2021

viz.com

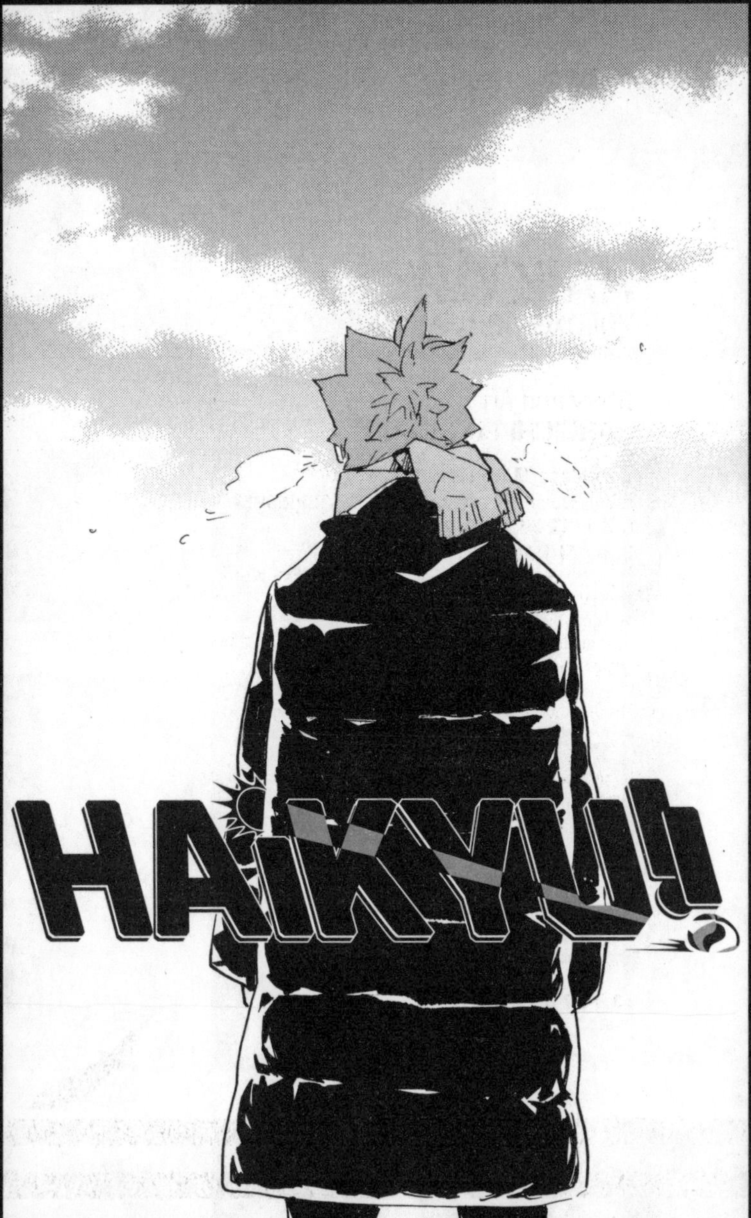
HAIKYU!!

HARUICHI
FURUDATE

BECOMING **42**

Karasuno High School Volleyball Club

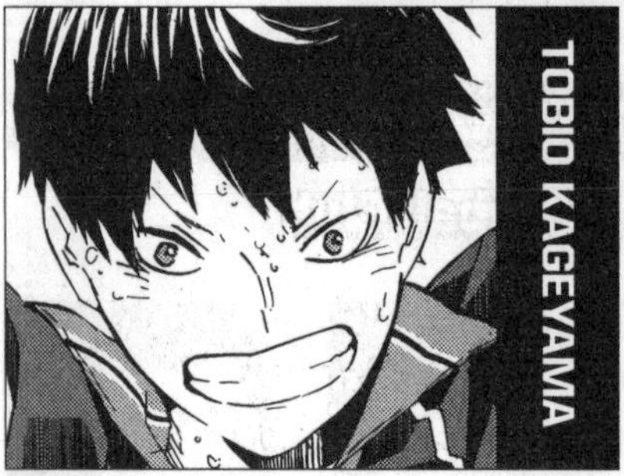
TOBIO KAGEYAMA

1ST YEAR / SETTER

His instincts and athletic talent are so good that he's like a "king" who rules the court. Demanding and egocentric.

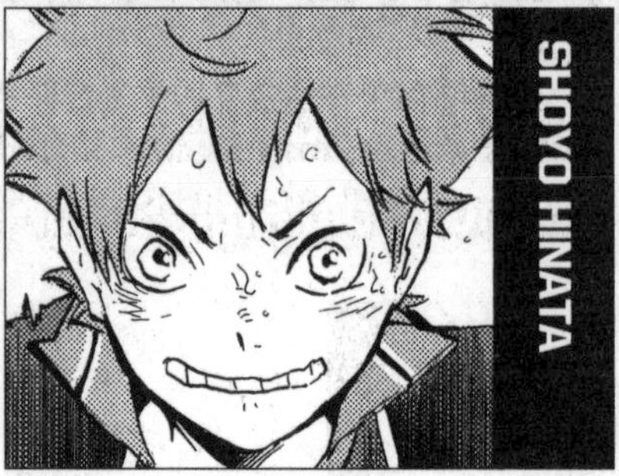
SHOYO HINATA

1ST YEAR / MIDDLE BLOCKER

Even though he doesn't have the best body type for volleyball, he is super athletic. Gets nervous easily.

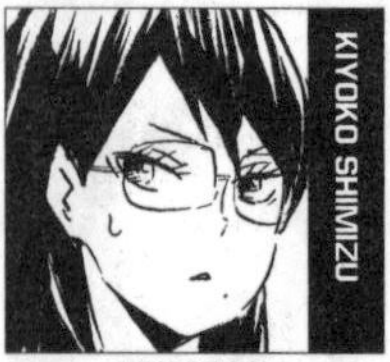
KIYOKO SHIMIZU

3RD YEAR
MANAGER

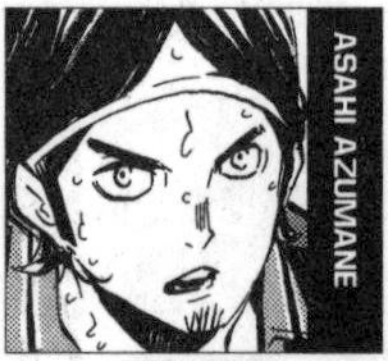
ASAHI AZUMANE

3RD YEAR
WING SPIKER

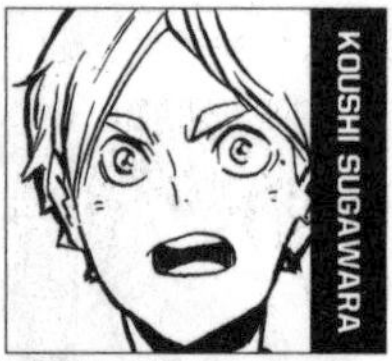
KOUSHI SUGAWARA

3RD YEAR (VICE CAPTAIN)
SETTER

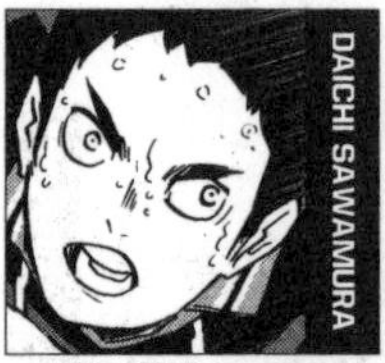
DAICHI SAWAMURA

3RD YEAR (CAPTAIN)
WING SPIKER

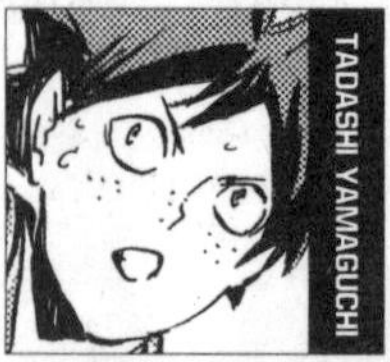
TADASHI YAMAGUCHI

1ST YEAR
MIDDLE BLOCKER

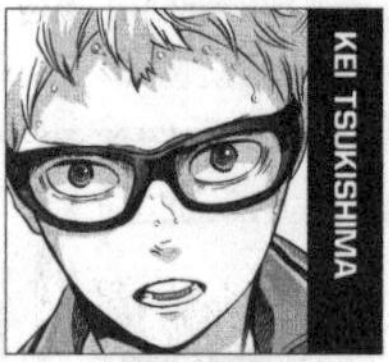
KEI TSUKISHIMA

1ST YEAR
MIDDLE BLOCKER

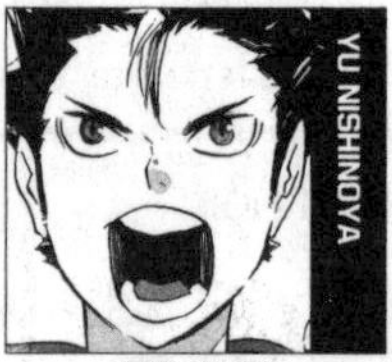
YU NISHINOYA

2ND YEAR
LIBERO

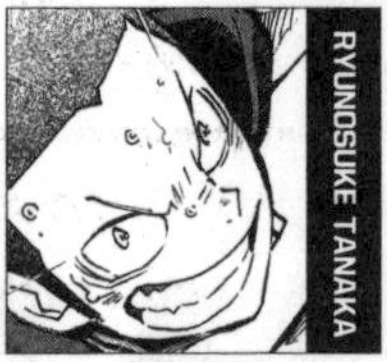
RYUNOSUKE TANAKA

2ND YEAR
WING SPIKER

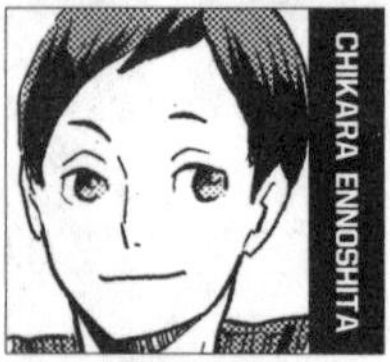
CHIKARA ENNOSHITA

2ND YEAR
WING SPIKER

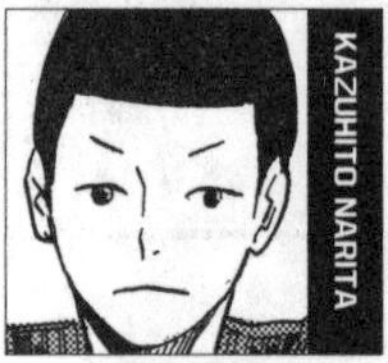
KAZUHITO NARITA

2ND YEAR
MIDDLE BLOCKER

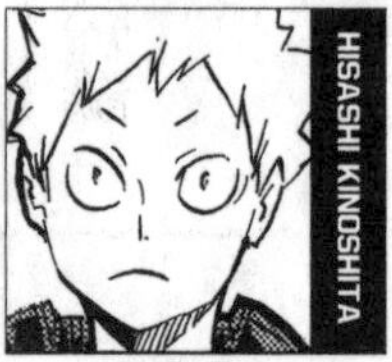
HISASHI KINOSHITA

2ND YEAR
WING SPIKER

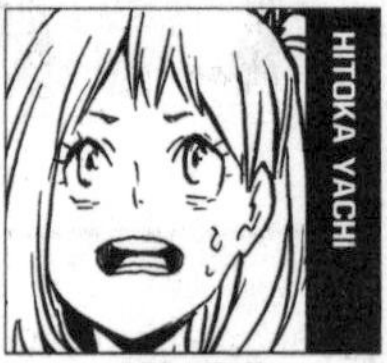
HITOKA YACHI

1ST YEAR
MANAGER

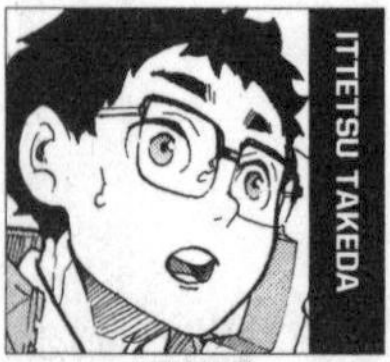
ITTETSU TAKEDA

ADVISER

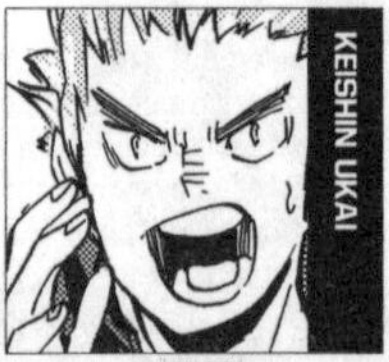
KEISHIN UKAI

COACH

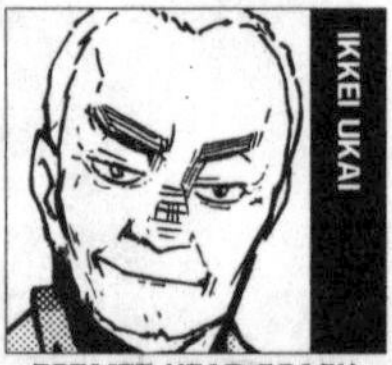
IKKEI UKAI

FORMER HEAD COACH

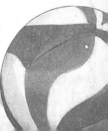

CHARACTERS

NATIONAL SPRING TOURNAMENT ARC

Kamomedai High School Volleyball Club

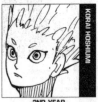

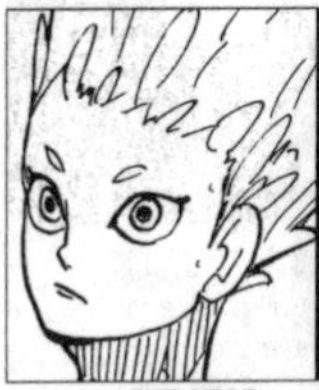
KORAI HOSHIUMI
2ND YEAR
WING SPIKER

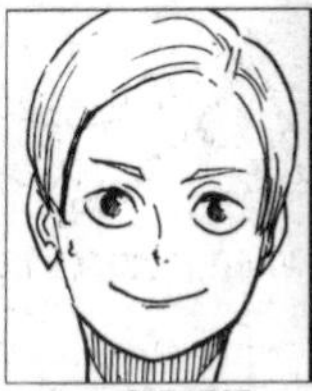
KEIICHIRO UEBAYASHI
3RD YEAR
LIBERO

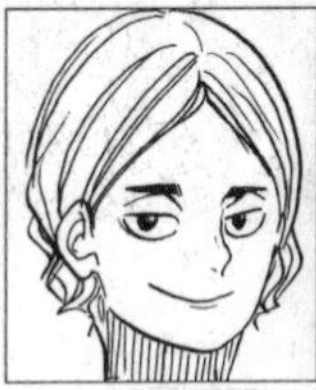
IZURU NOZAWA
3RD YEAR
WING SPIKER

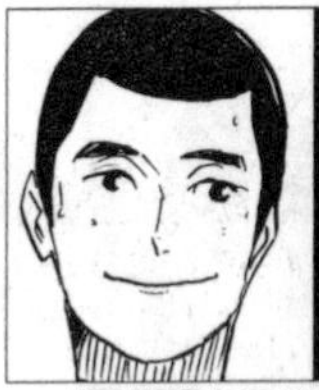
AIKICHI SUWA
3RD YEAR (CAPTAIN)
SETTER

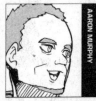

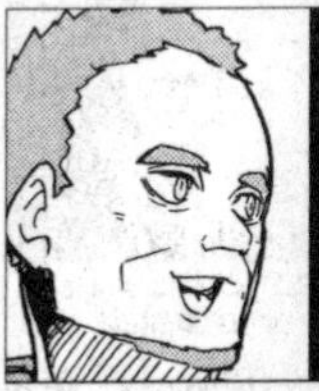
AARON MURPHY
HEAD COACH

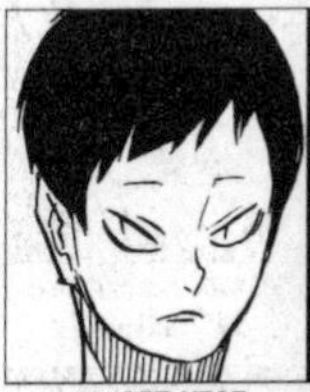
KAZUYOSHI BESSHO
1ST YEAR
MIDDLE BLOCKER

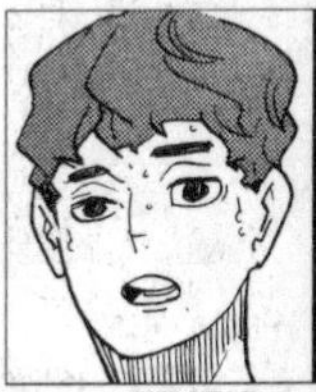
SACHIRO HIRUGAMI
2ND YEAR
MIDDLE BLOCKER

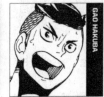

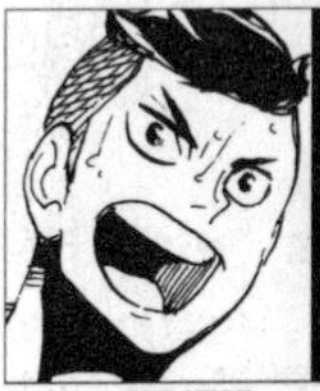
GAO HAKUBA
2ND YEAR
WING SPIKER

Nekoma Volleyball Club

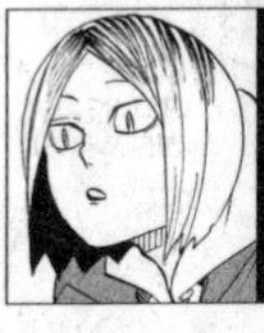
KENMA KOZUME

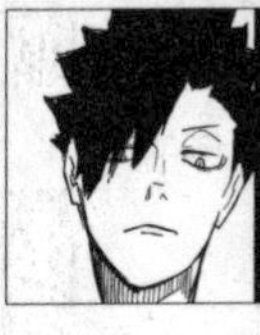
TETSURO KUROO

Karasuno Alumni

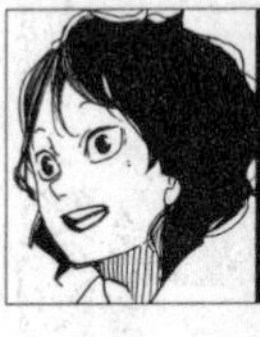
TENMA UDAI

Shiratorizawa Academy

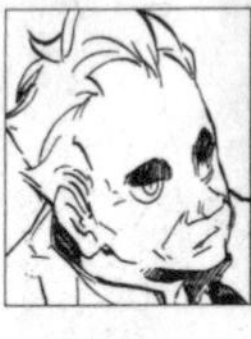
TANJI WASHIJO

Ever since he saw the legendary player known as "the Little Giant" compete at the national volleyball finals, Shoyo Hinata has been aiming to be the best volleyball player ever! He decides to join the volleyball club at his middle school and gets to play in an official tournament during his third year. His team is crushed by a team led by volleyball prodigy Tobio Kageyama, also known as "the King of the Court." Swearing revenge on Kageyama, Hinata graduates middle school and enters Karasuno High School, the school where the Little Giant played. However, upon joining the club, he finds out that Kageyama is there too! The two of them bicker constantly, but they bring out the best in each other's talents and become a powerful combo. It's the final set of the Spring Tournament quarterfinals. Thanks to their training, Kamomedai's blockers remain solid and unshakable, as success is simply a habit for them. Continuing his search for a way to overcome their wall, Hinata makes the most of both his jumping height and speed and finally slams one past them! This starts a chain reaction, splitting Kamomedai's blockers and giving Karasuno a shot at victory. Seeing the effect of his efforts, Hinata finally accepts the title of "Greatest Decoy." But right when he seems at the top of his game, Hinata collapses with a fever. In a painful decision for everyone, he's removed from the game!

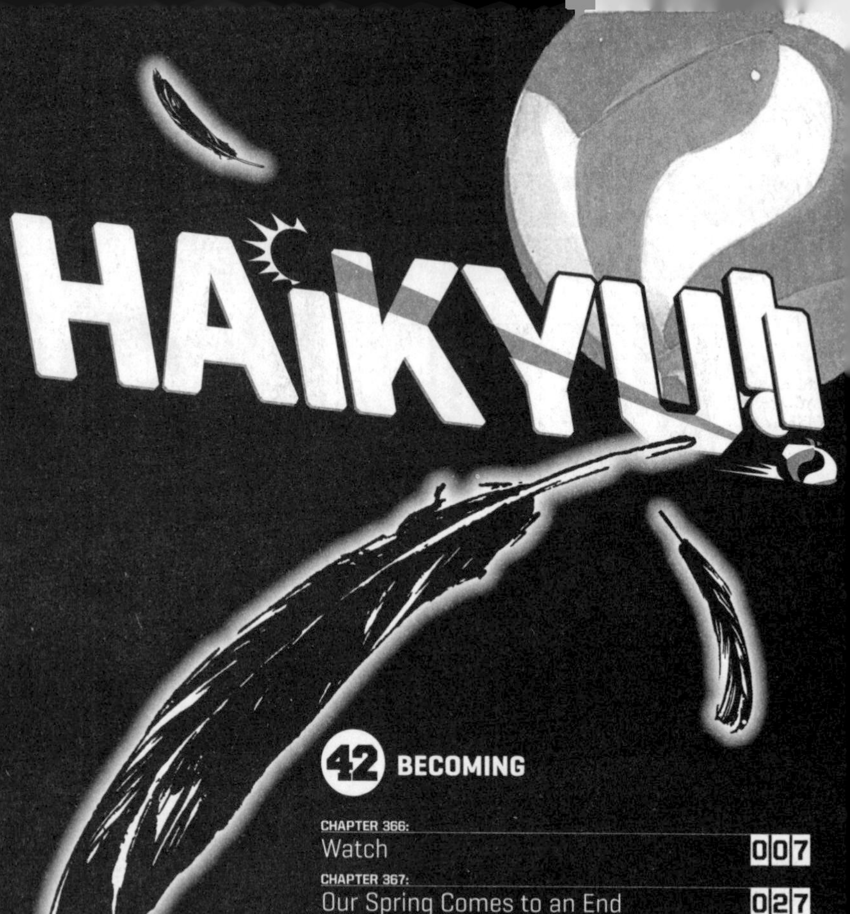
HAIKYU!!

42 BECOMING

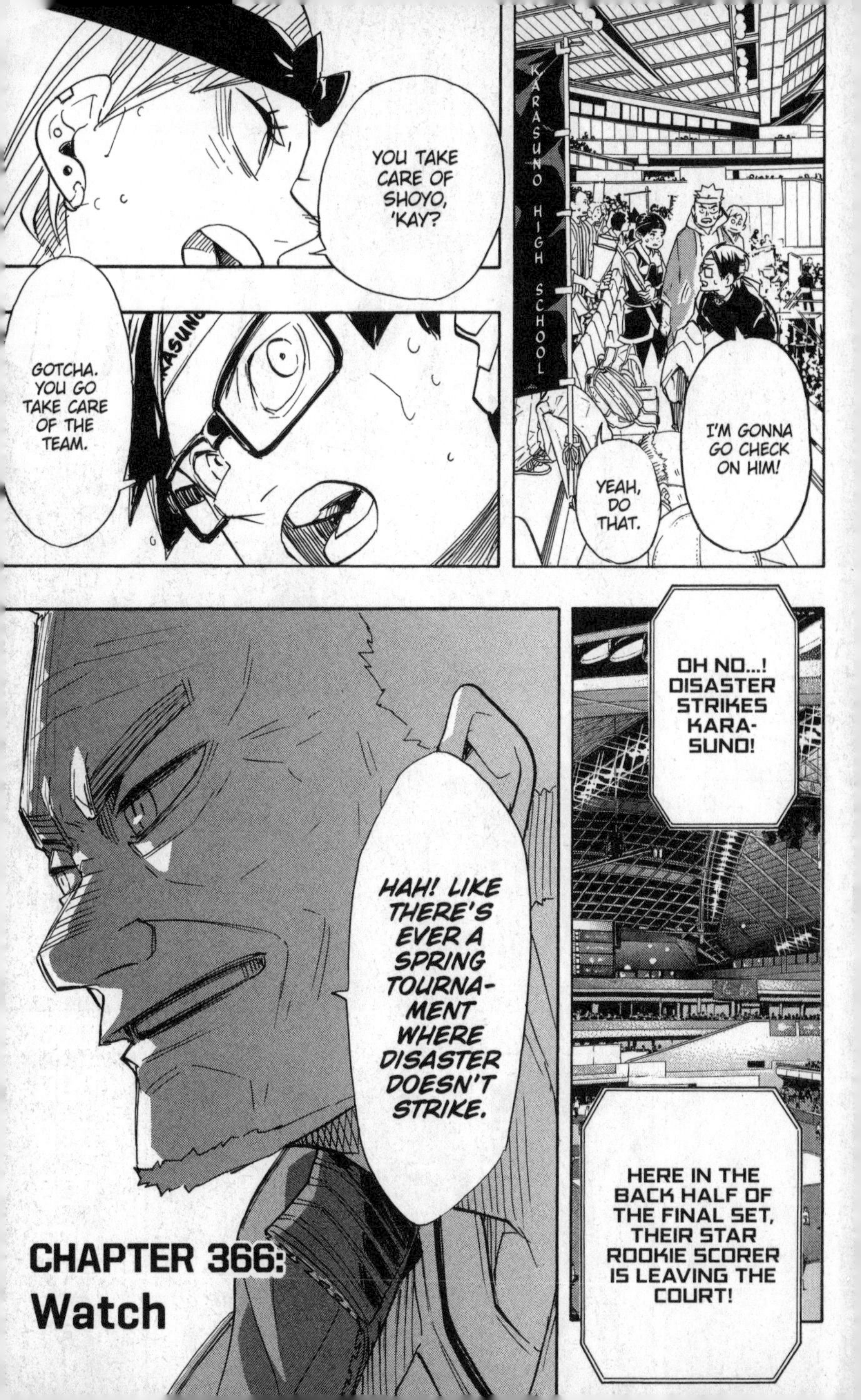
KARASUNO HIGH SCHOOL
I'M GONNA GO CHECK ON HIM!
YEAH, DO THAT.
YOU TAKE CARE OF SHOYO, 'KAY?
GOTCHA. YOU GO TAKE CARE OF THE TEAM.
OH NO...! DISASTER STRIKES KARA-SUNO!
HERE IN THE BACK HALF OF THE FINAL SET, THEIR STAR ROOKIE SCORER IS LEAVING THE COURT!
HAH! LIKE THERE'S EVER A SPRING TOURNA-MENT WHERE DISASTER DOESN'T STRIKE.
CHAPTER 366: Watch

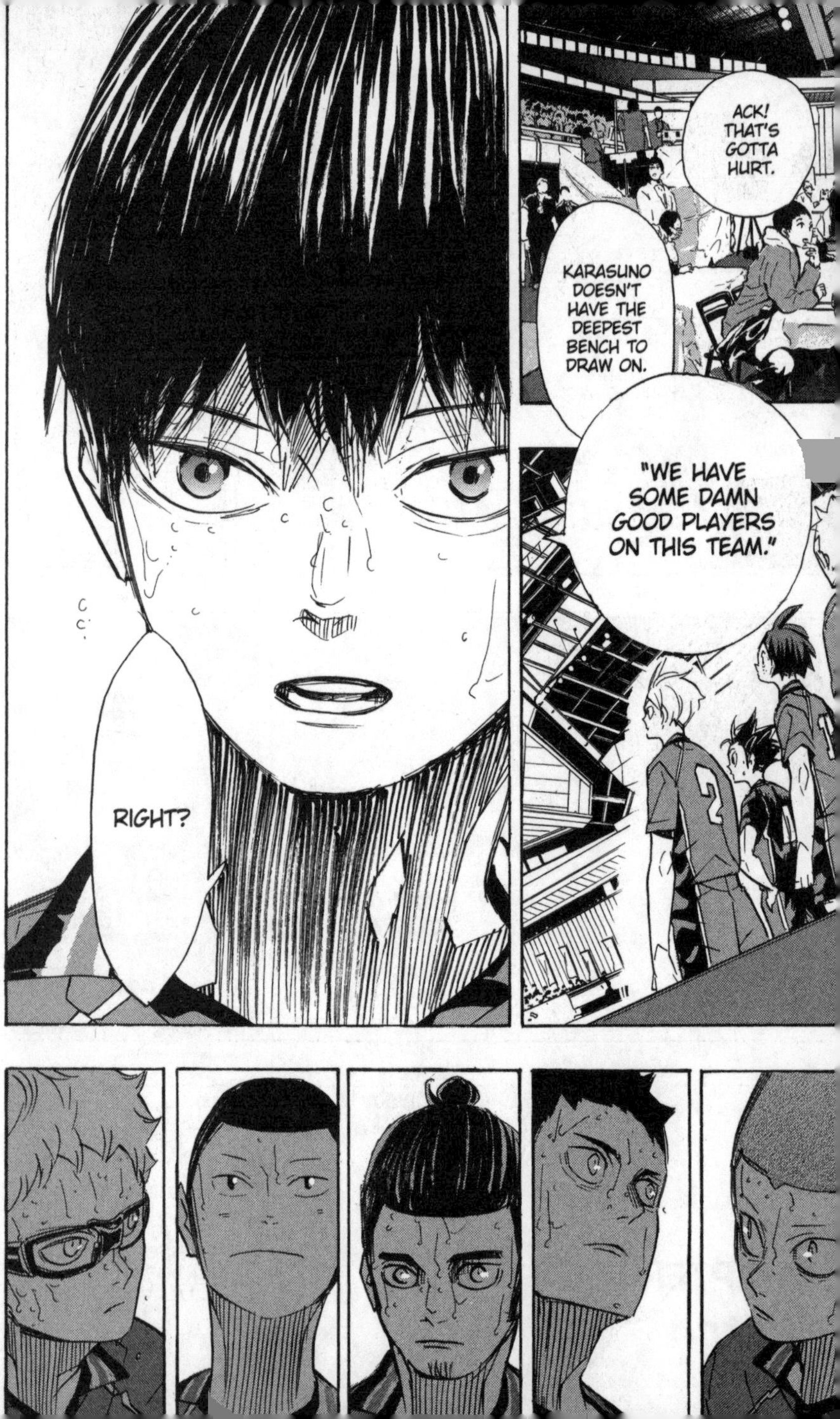
ACK! THAT'S GOTTA HURT.
KARASUNO DOESN'T HAVE THE DEEPEST BENCH TO DRAW ON.
"WE HAVE SOME DAMN GOOD PLAYERS ON THIS TEAM."
RIGHT?

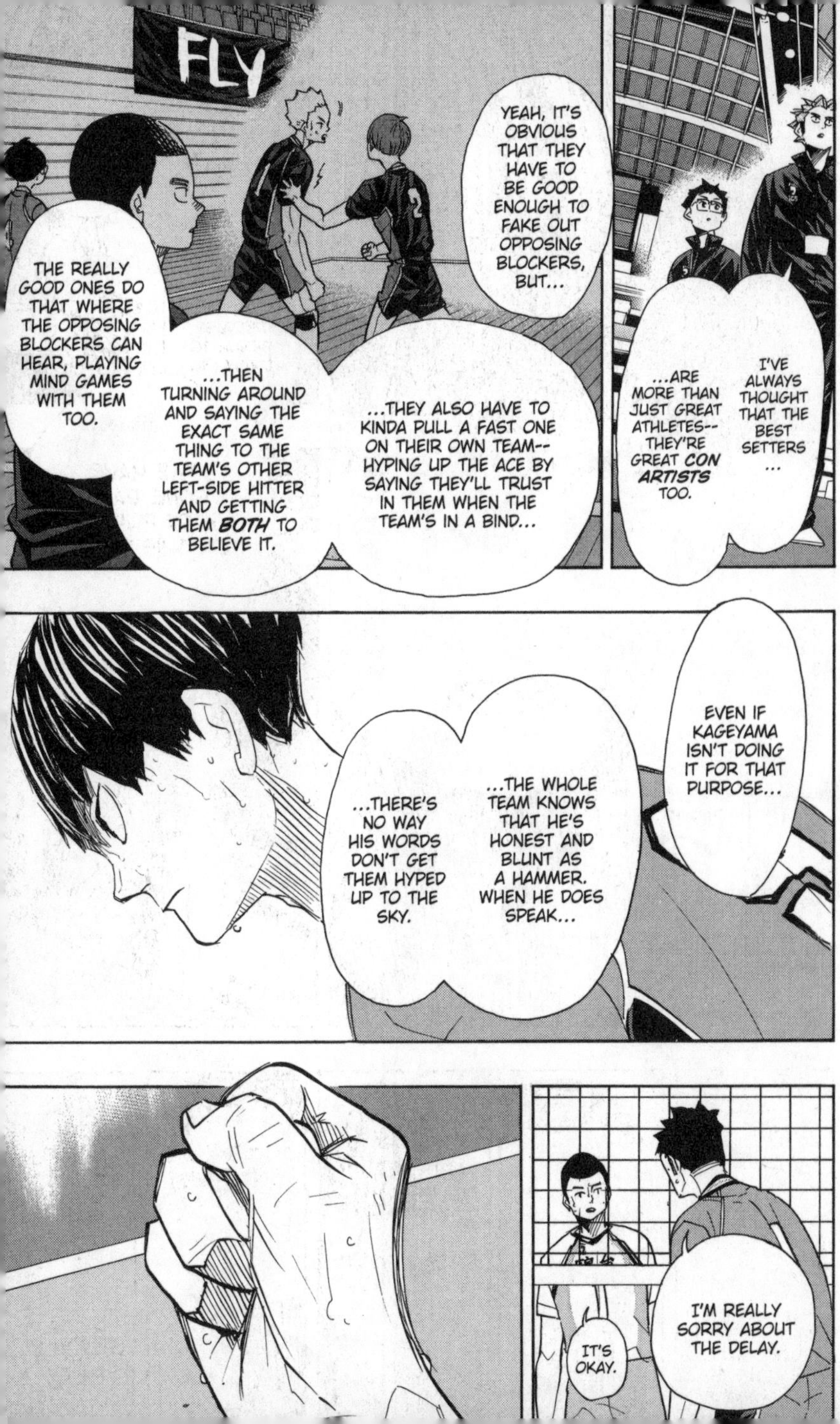

I'VE ALWAYS THOUGHT THAT THE BEST SETTERS ...
...ARE MORE THAN JUST GREAT ATHLETES-- THEY'RE GREAT **CON ARTISTS** TOO.
FLY
YEAH, IT'S OBVIOUS THAT THEY HAVE TO BE GOOD ENOUGH TO FAKE OUT OPPOSING BLOCKERS, BUT...
...THEY ALSO HAVE TO KINDA PULL A FAST ONE ON THEIR OWN TEAM-- HYPING UP THE ACE BY SAYING THEY'LL TRUST IN THEM WHEN THE TEAM'S IN A BIND...
...THEN TURNING AROUND AND SAYING THE EXACT SAME THING TO THE TEAM'S OTHER LEFT-SIDE HITTER AND GETTING THEM **BOTH** TO BELIEVE IT.
THE REALLY GOOD ONES DO THAT WHERE THE OPPOSING BLOCKERS CAN HEAR, PLAYING MIND GAMES WITH THEM TOO.
EVEN IF KAGEYAMA ISN'T DOING IT FOR THAT PURPOSE...
...THE WHOLE TEAM KNOWS THAT HE'S HONEST AND BLUNT AS A HAMMER. WHEN HE DOES SPEAK...
...THERE'S NO WAY HIS WORDS DON'T GET THEM HYPED UP TO THE SKY.
I'M REALLY SORRY ABOUT THE DELAY.
IT'S OKAY.

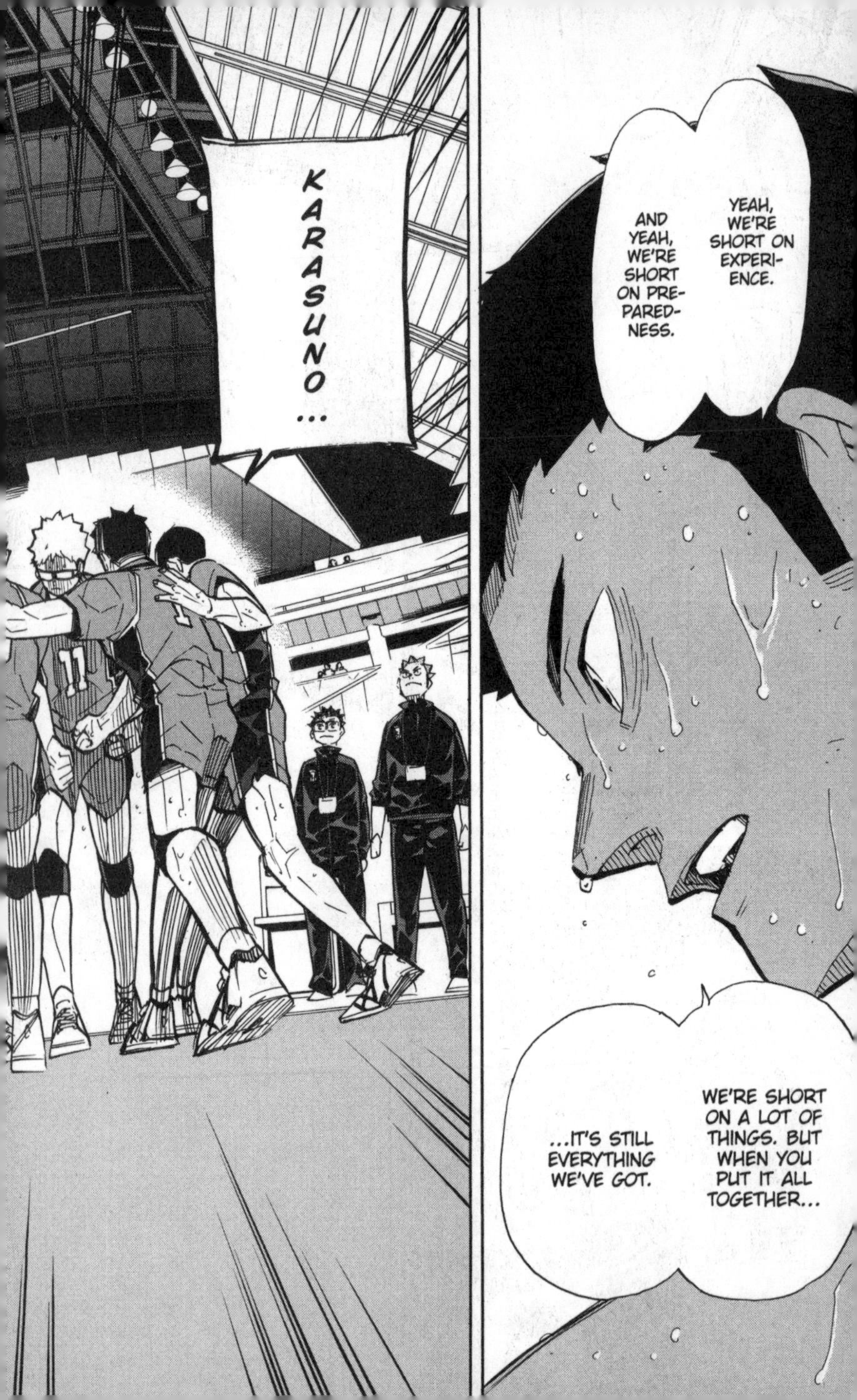
YEAH, WE'RE SHORT ON EXPERIENCE.
AND YEAH, WE'RE SHORT ON PREPAREDNESS.
WE'RE SHORT ON A LOT OF THINGS. BUT WHEN YOU PUT IT ALL TOGETHER...
...IT'S STILL EVERYTHING WE'VE GOT.
KARASUNO...

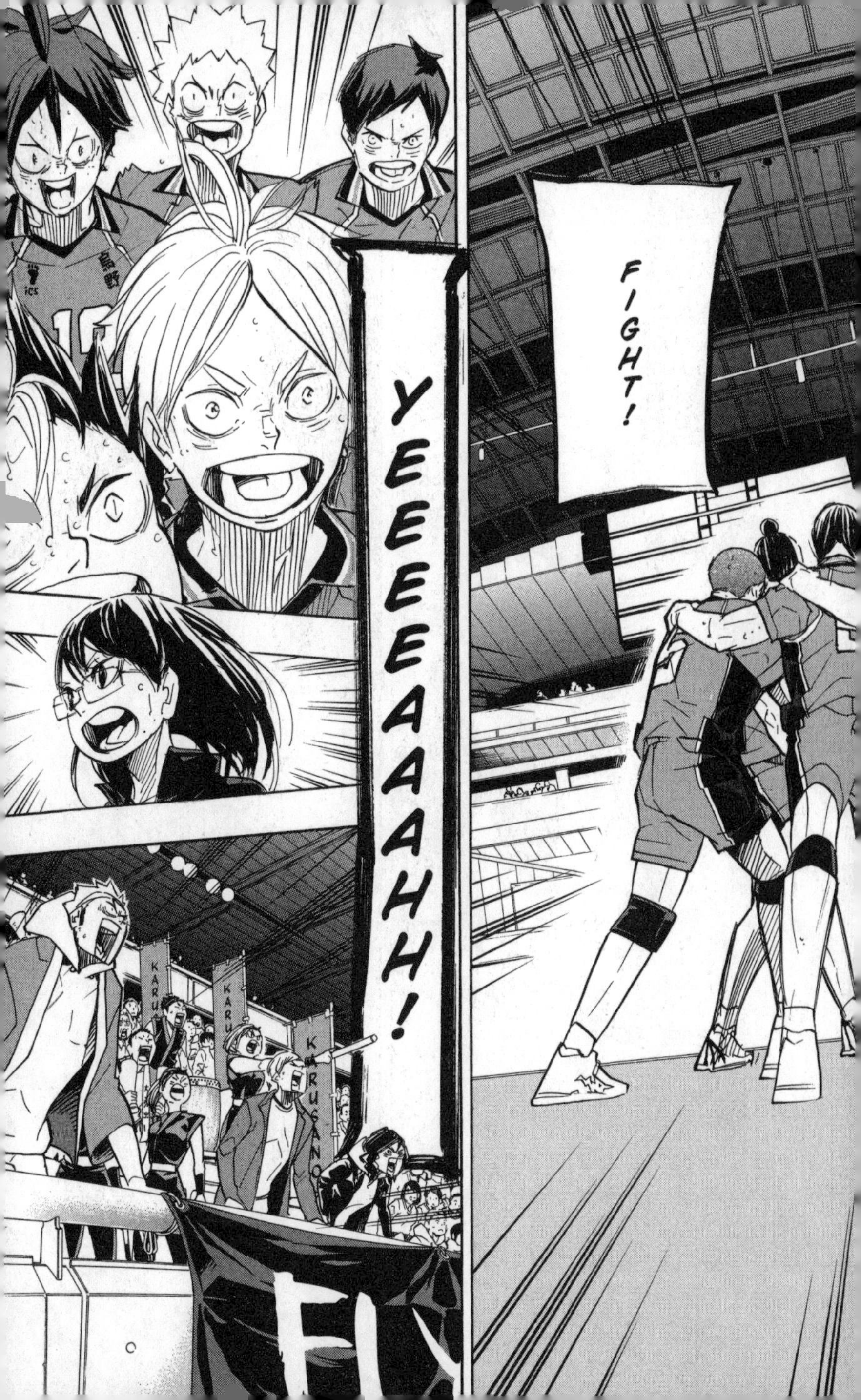
FIGHT!
YEEEEAAAHH!
KARUSANO

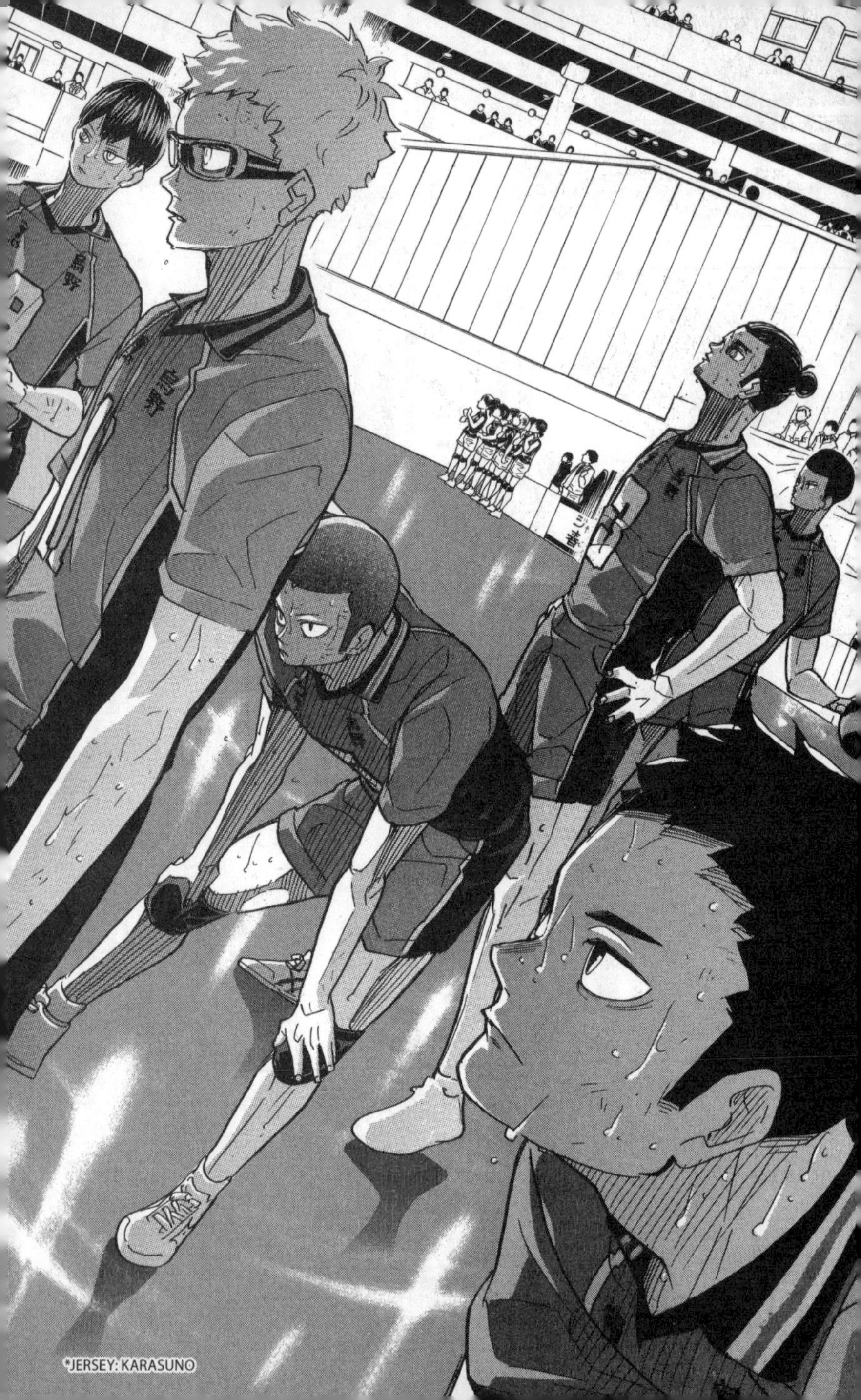
*JERSEY: KARASUNO

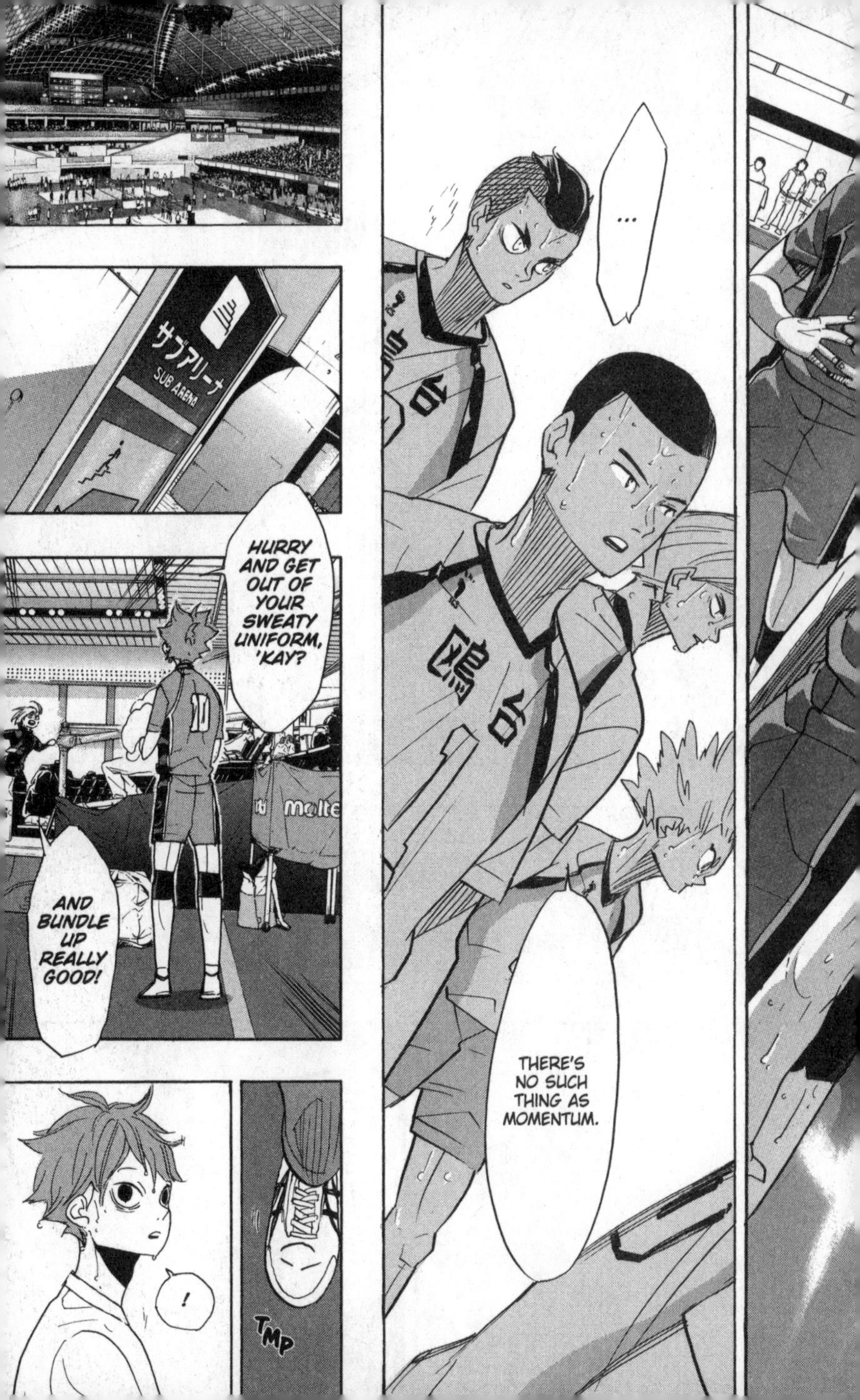
...
THERE'S NO SUCH THING AS MOMENTUM.
サブアリーナ
SUB ARENA
HURRY AND GET OUT OF YOUR SWEATY UNIFORM, 'KAY?
AND BUNDLE UP REALLY GOOD!
TMP
!

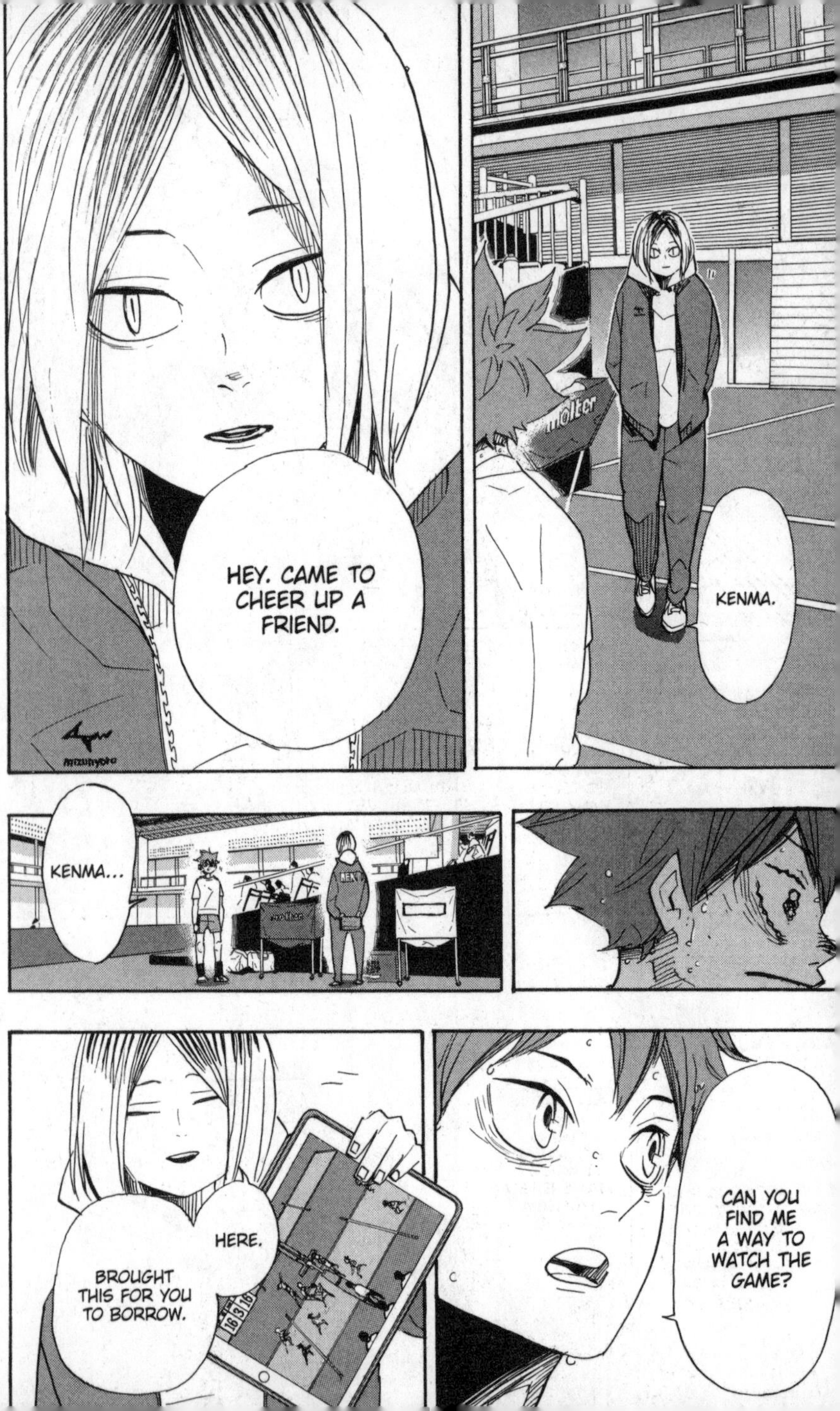
KENMA.
HEY. CAME TO CHEER UP A FRIEND.
KENMA...
CAN YOU FIND ME A WAY TO WATCH THE GAME?
HERE. BROUGHT THIS FOR YOU TO BORROW.

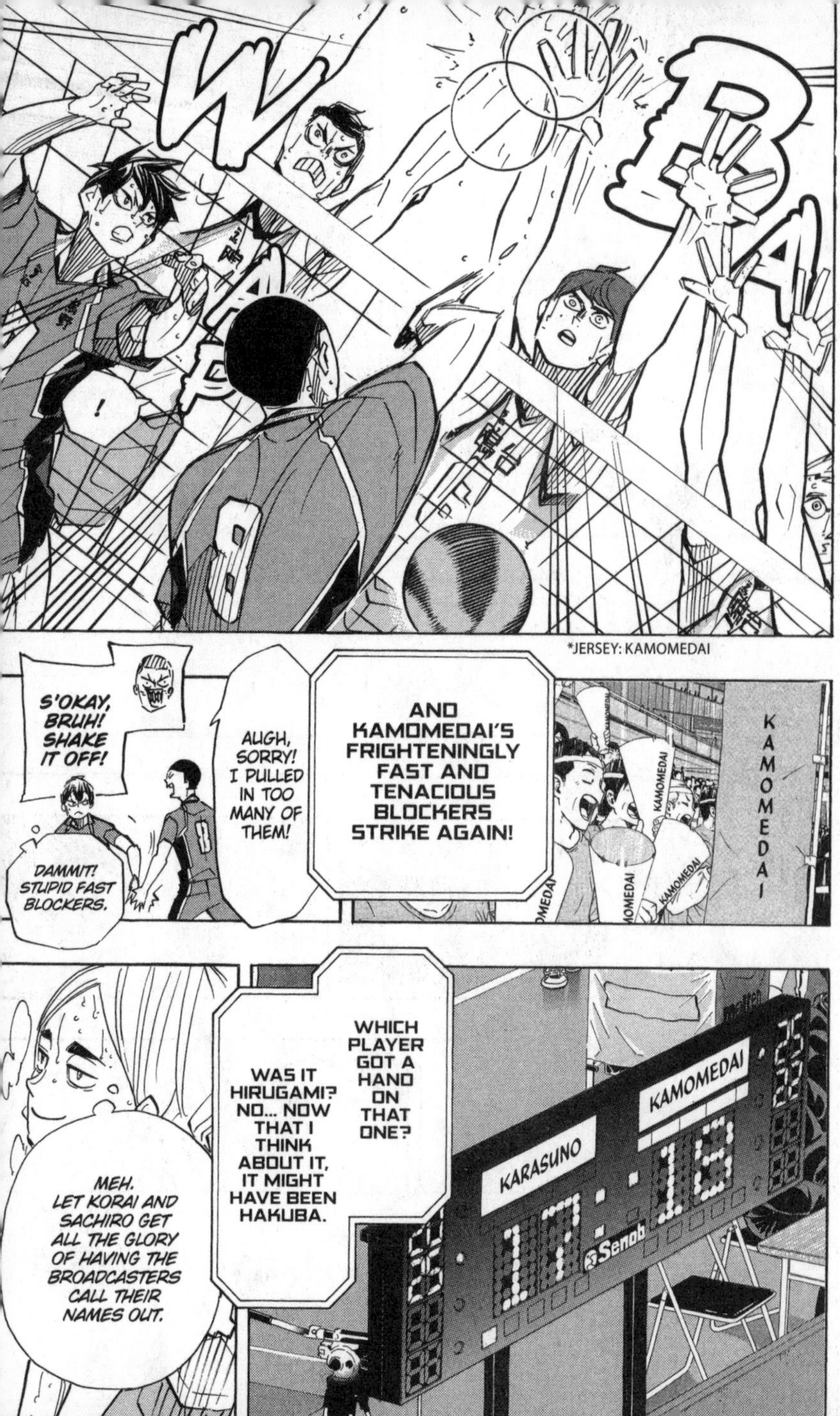
!
*JERSEY: KAMOMEDAI
AND KAMOMEDAI'S FRIGHTENINGLY FAST AND TENACIOUS BLOCKERS STRIKE AGAIN!
KAMOMEDAI
KAMOMEDAI
AUGH, SORRY! I PULLED IN TOO MANY OF THEM!
S'OKAY, BRUH! SHAKE IT OFF!
DAMMIT! STUPID FAST BLOCKERS.
WHICH PLAYER GOT A HAND ON THAT ONE?
WAS IT HIRUGAMI? NO... NOW THAT I THINK ABOUT IT, IT MIGHT HAVE BEEN HAKUBA.
KAMOMEDAI
KARASUNO
17
18
Senob
MEH. LET KORAI AND SACHIRO GET ALL THE GLORY OF HAVING THE BROADCASTERS CALL THEIR NAMES OUT.

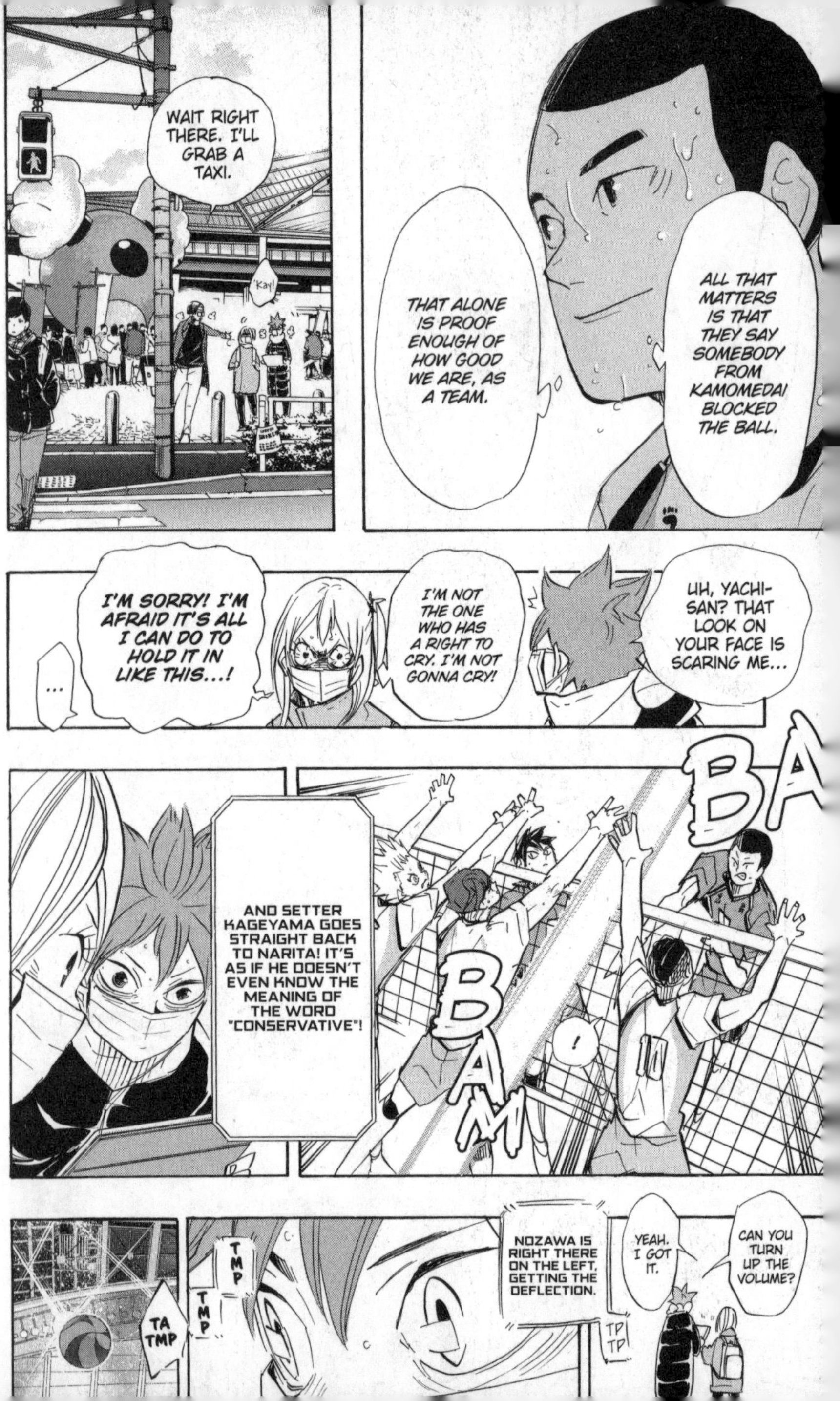
ALL THAT MATTERS IS THAT THEY SAY SOMEBODY FROM KAMOMEDAI BLOCKED THE BALL.
THAT ALONE IS PROOF ENOUGH OF HOW GOOD WE ARE, AS A TEAM.
WAIT RIGHT THERE. I'LL GRAB A TAXI.
'Kay!
UH, YACHI-SAN? THAT LOOK ON YOUR FACE IS SCARING ME...
I'M NOT THE ONE WHO HAS A RIGHT TO CRY. I'M NOT GONNA CRY!
I'M SORRY! I'M AFRAID IT'S ALL I CAN DO TO HOLD IT IN LIKE THIS...!
...
BA
BAM
!
AND SETTER KAGEYAMA GOES STRAIGHT BACK TO NARITA! IT'S AS IF HE DOESN'T EVEN KNOW THE MEANING OF THE WORD "CONSERVATIVE"!
CAN YOU TURN UP THE VOLUME?
YEAH. I GOT IT.
NOZAWA IS RIGHT THERE ON THE LEFT, GETTING THE DEFLECTION.
TP TP
TMP
TMP
TA TMP

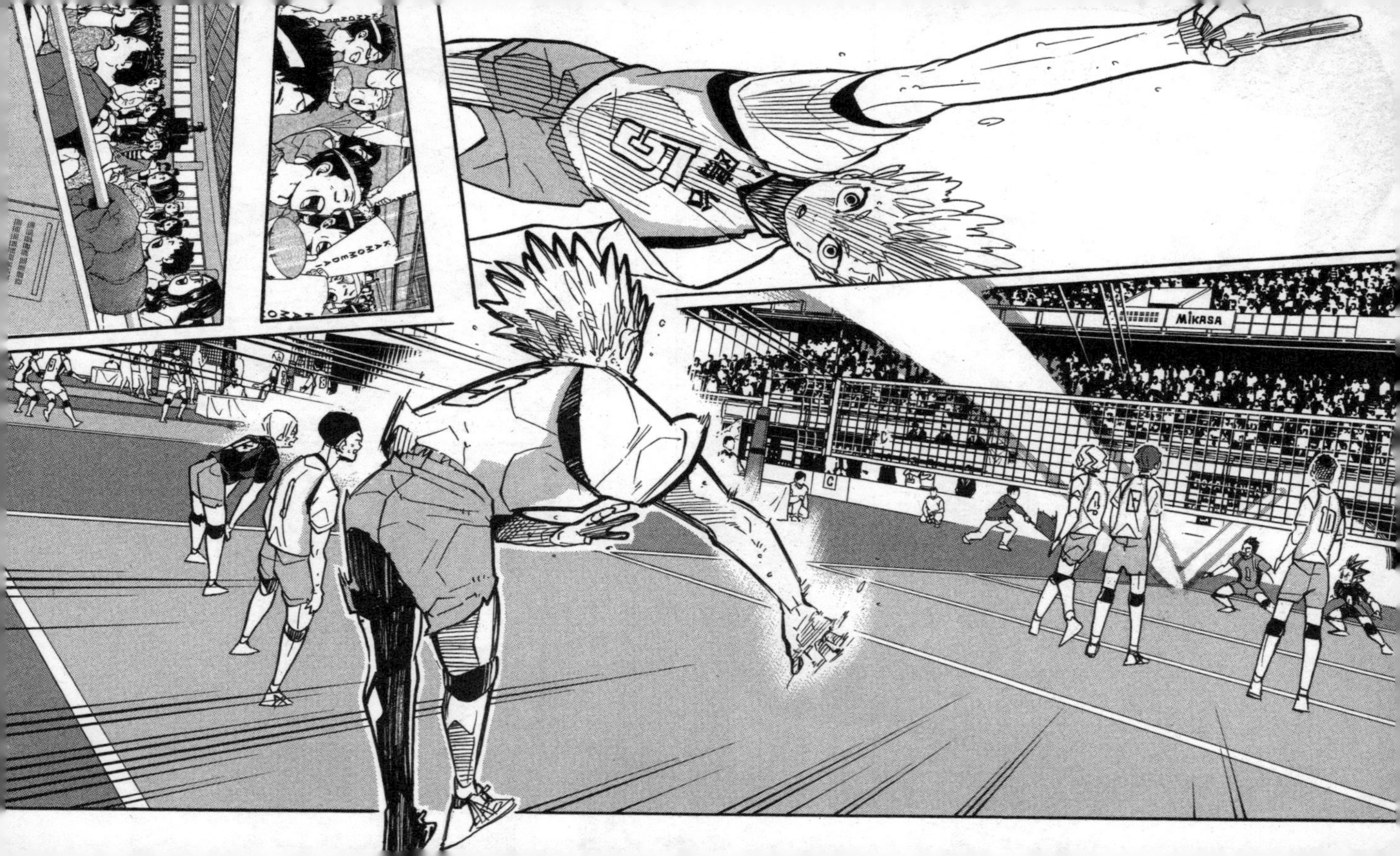
KAMOMEDAI!
MIKASA

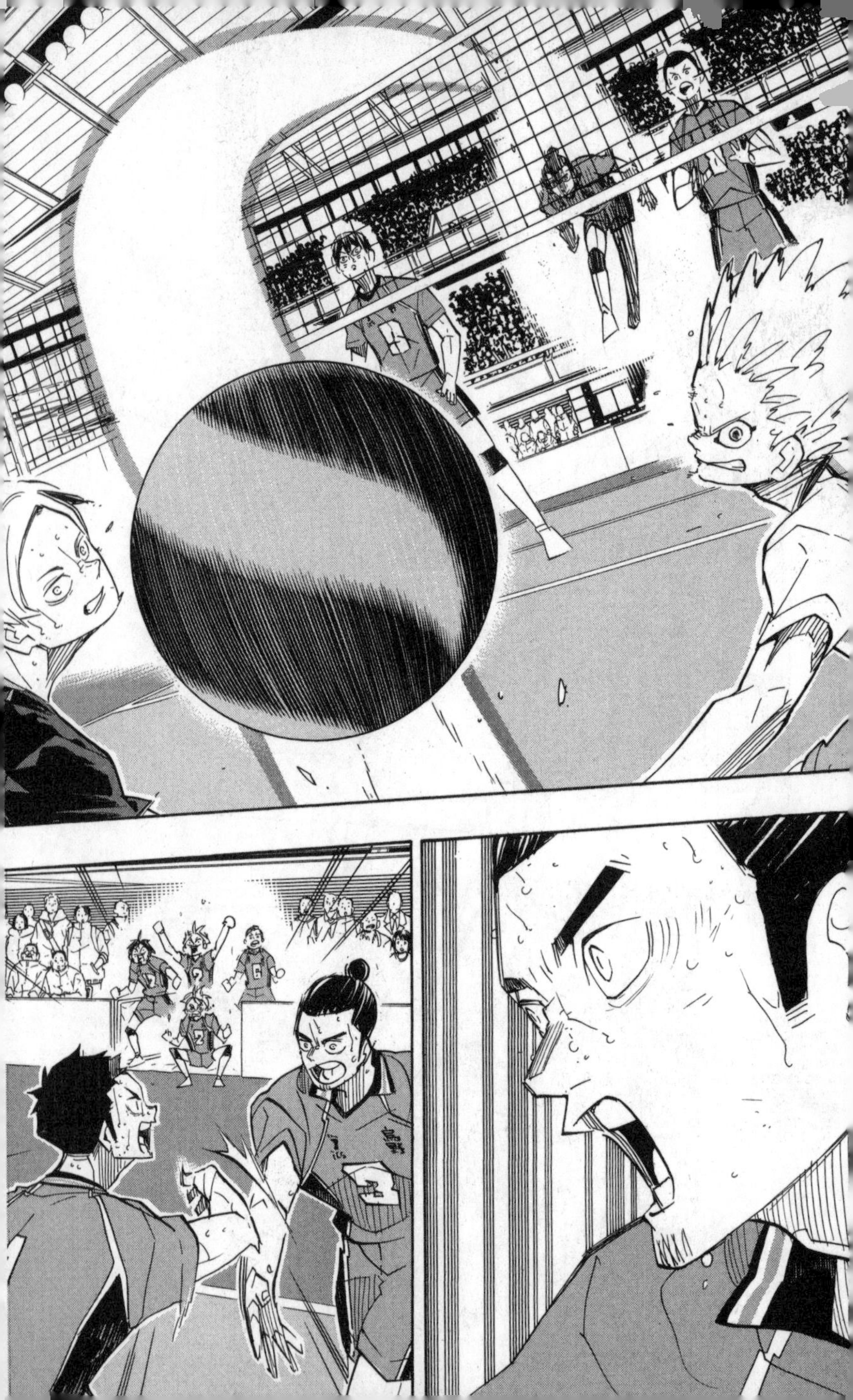

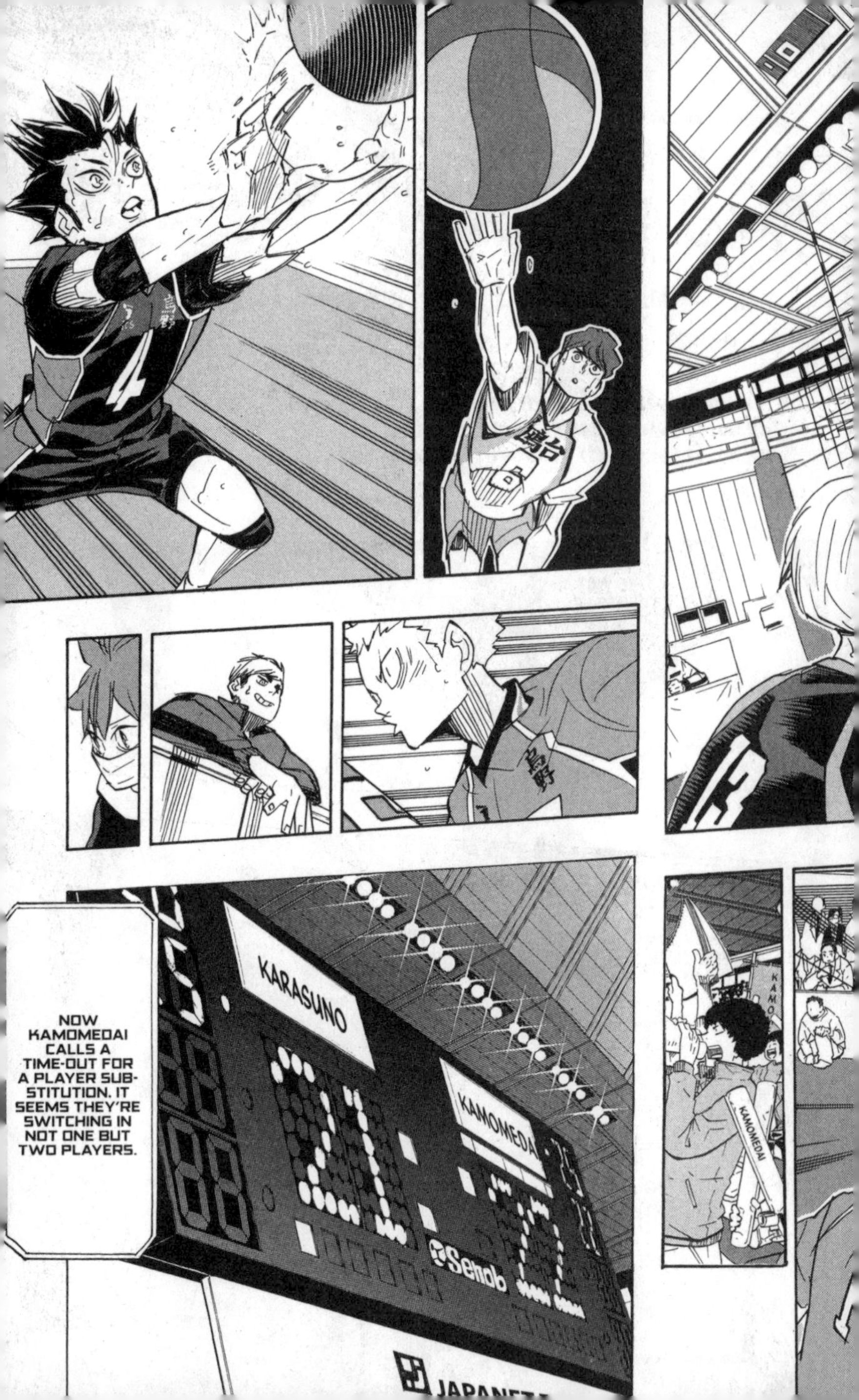
KAMOMEDAI
KARASUNO
NOW KAMOMEDAI CALLS A TIME-OUT FOR A PLAYER SUB-STITUTION. IT SEEMS THEY'RE SWITCHING IN NOT ONE BUT TWO PLAYERS.

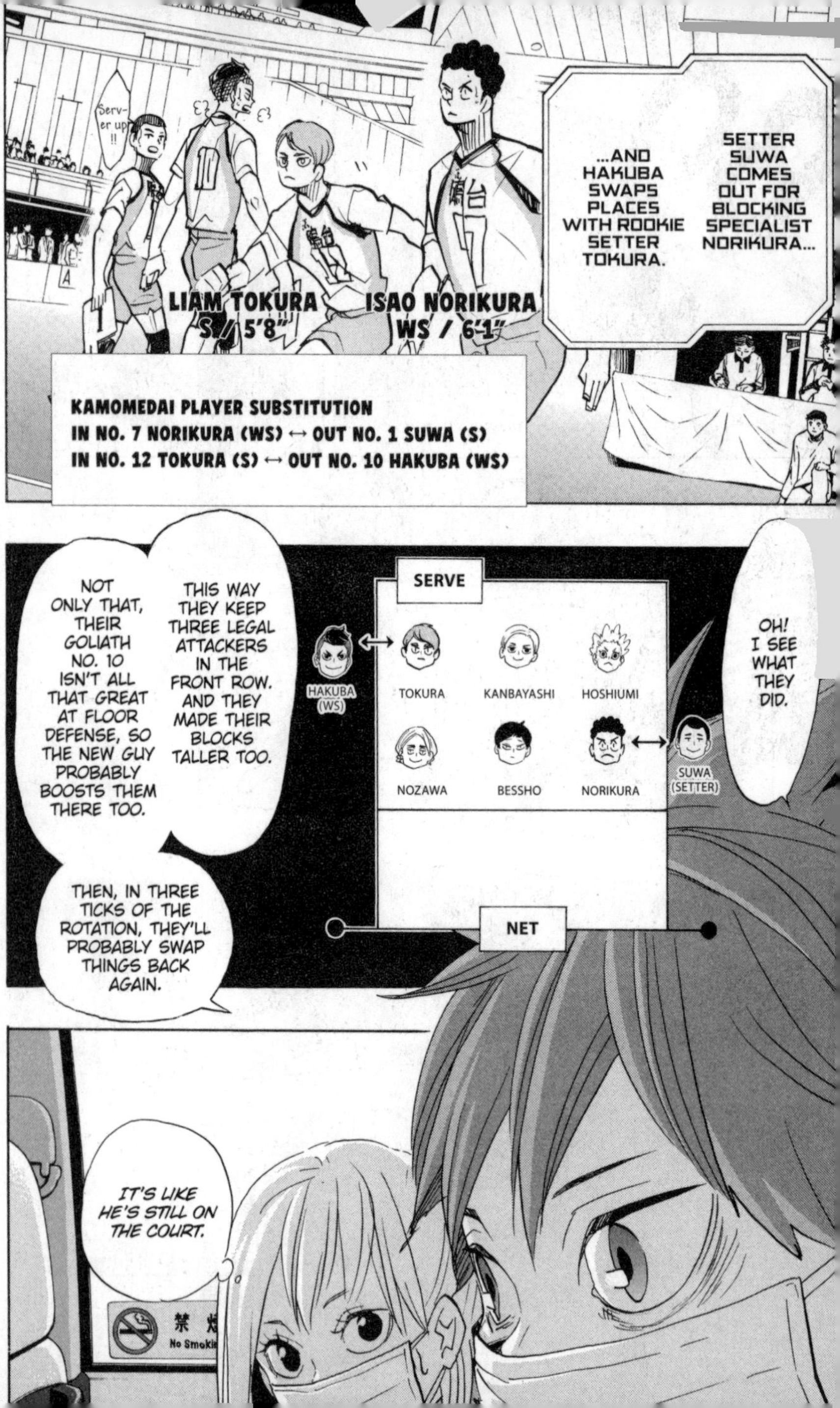
SETTER SUWA COMES OUT FOR BLOCKING SPECIALIST NORIKURA...
...AND HAKUBA SWAPS PLACES WITH ROOKIE SETTER TOKURA.
Serv-er up!!
ISAO NORIKURA WS / 6'1"
LIAM TOKURA S / 5'8"
KAMOMEDAI PLAYER SUBSTITUTION
IN NO. 7 NORIKURA (WS) ↔ OUT NO. 1 SUWA (S)
IN NO. 12 TOKURA (S) ↔ OUT NO. 10 HAKUBA (WS)
OH! I SEE WHAT THEY DID.
SERVE
HAKUBA (WS)
TOKURA
KANBAYASHI
HOSHIUMI
NOZAWA
BESSHO
NORIKURA
SUWA (SETTER)
NET
THIS WAY THEY KEEP THREE LEGAL ATTACKERS IN THE FRONT ROW. AND THEY MADE THEIR BLOCKS TALLER TOO.
NOT ONLY THAT, THEIR GOLIATH NO. 10 ISN'T ALL THAT GREAT AT FLOOR DEFENSE, SO THE NEW GUY PROBABLY BOOSTS THEM THERE TOO.
THEN, IN THREE TICKS OF THE ROTATION, THEY'LL PROBABLY SWAP THINGS BACK AGAIN.
IT'S LIKE HE'S STILL ON THE COURT.

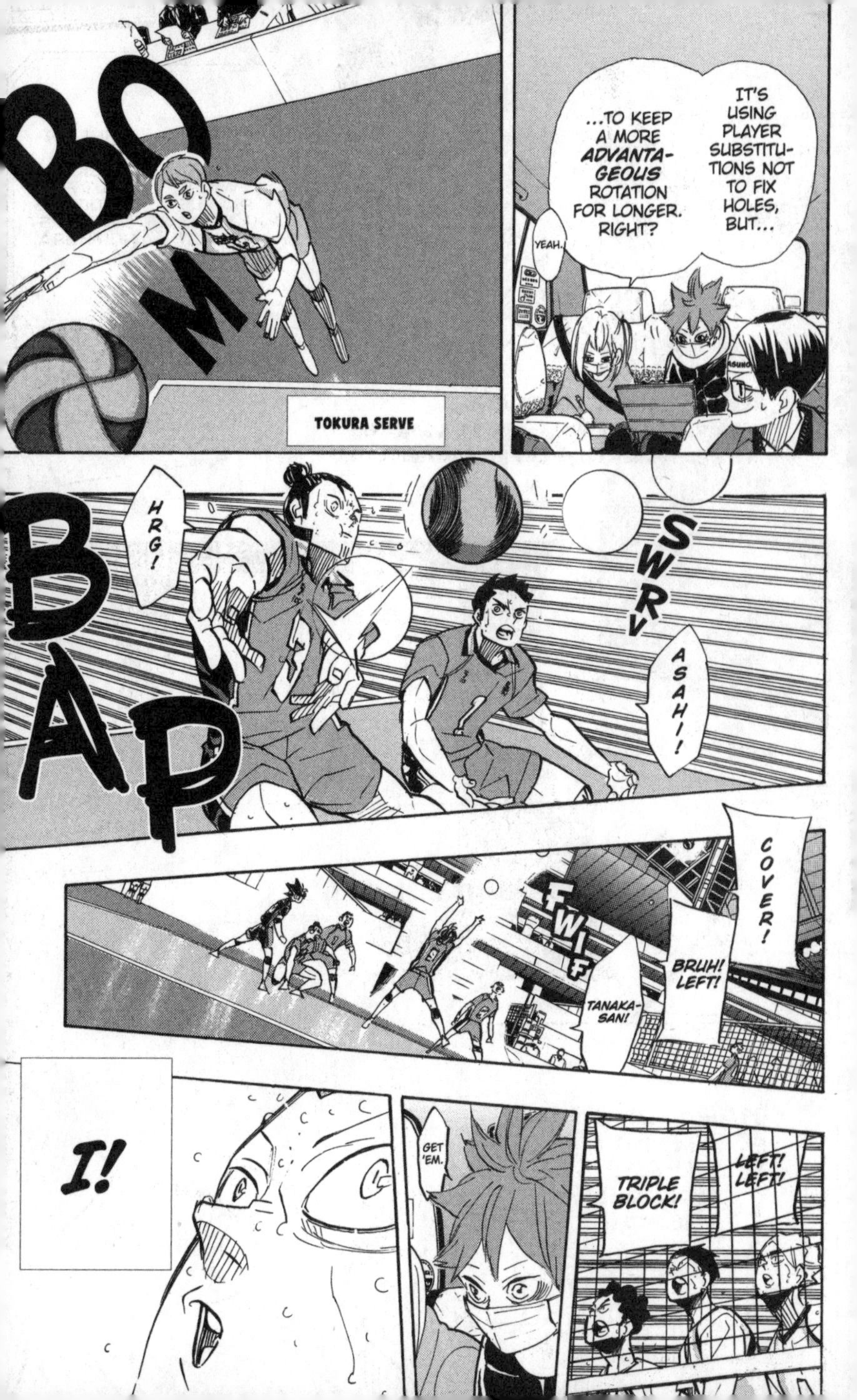
IT'S USING PLAYER SUBSTITUTIONS NOT TO FIX HOLES, BUT...
...TO KEEP A MORE ADVANTAGEOUS ROTATION FOR LONGER. RIGHT?
YEAH.
BOOM
TOKURA SERVE
SWRV
ASAHI!!
HRG!
BAP
COVER!
BRUH! LEFT!
TANAKA-SAN!
FWIF
TRIPLE BLOCK!
LEFT! LEFT!
GET 'EM.
I!

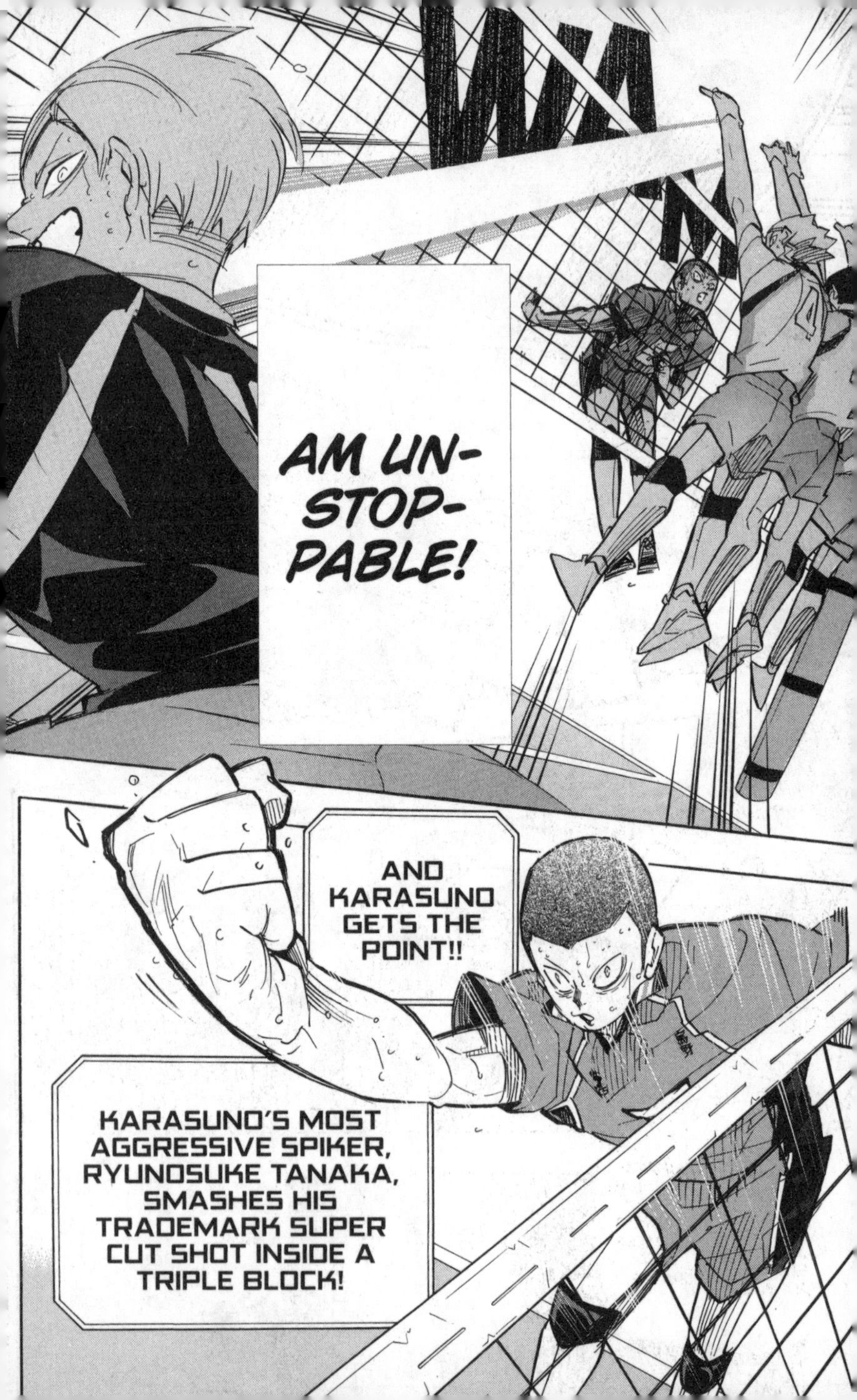
AM UN-STOP-PABLE!
AND KARASUNO GETS THE POINT!!
KARASUNO'S MOST AGGRESSIVE SPIKER, RYUNOSUKE TANAKA, SMASHES HIS TRADEMARK SUPER CUT SHOT INSIDE A TRIPLE BLOCK!

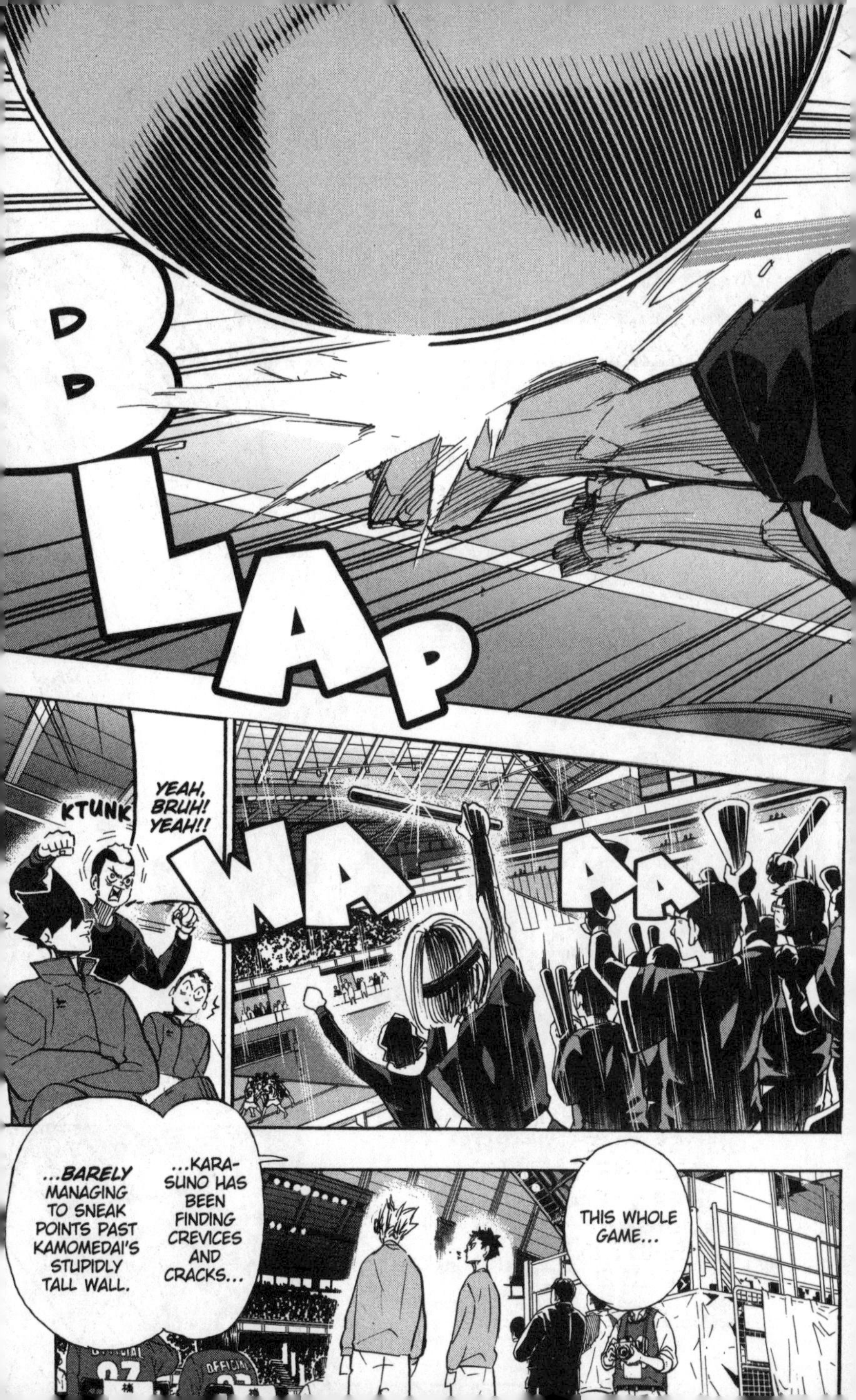
BLAP
WA AA
YEAH, BRUH! YEAH!!
KTUNK
THIS WHOLE GAME...
...KARA-SUNO HAS BEEN FINDING CREVICES AND CRACKS...
...BARELY MANAGING TO SNEAK POINTS PAST KAMOMEDAI'S STUPIDLY TALL WALL.

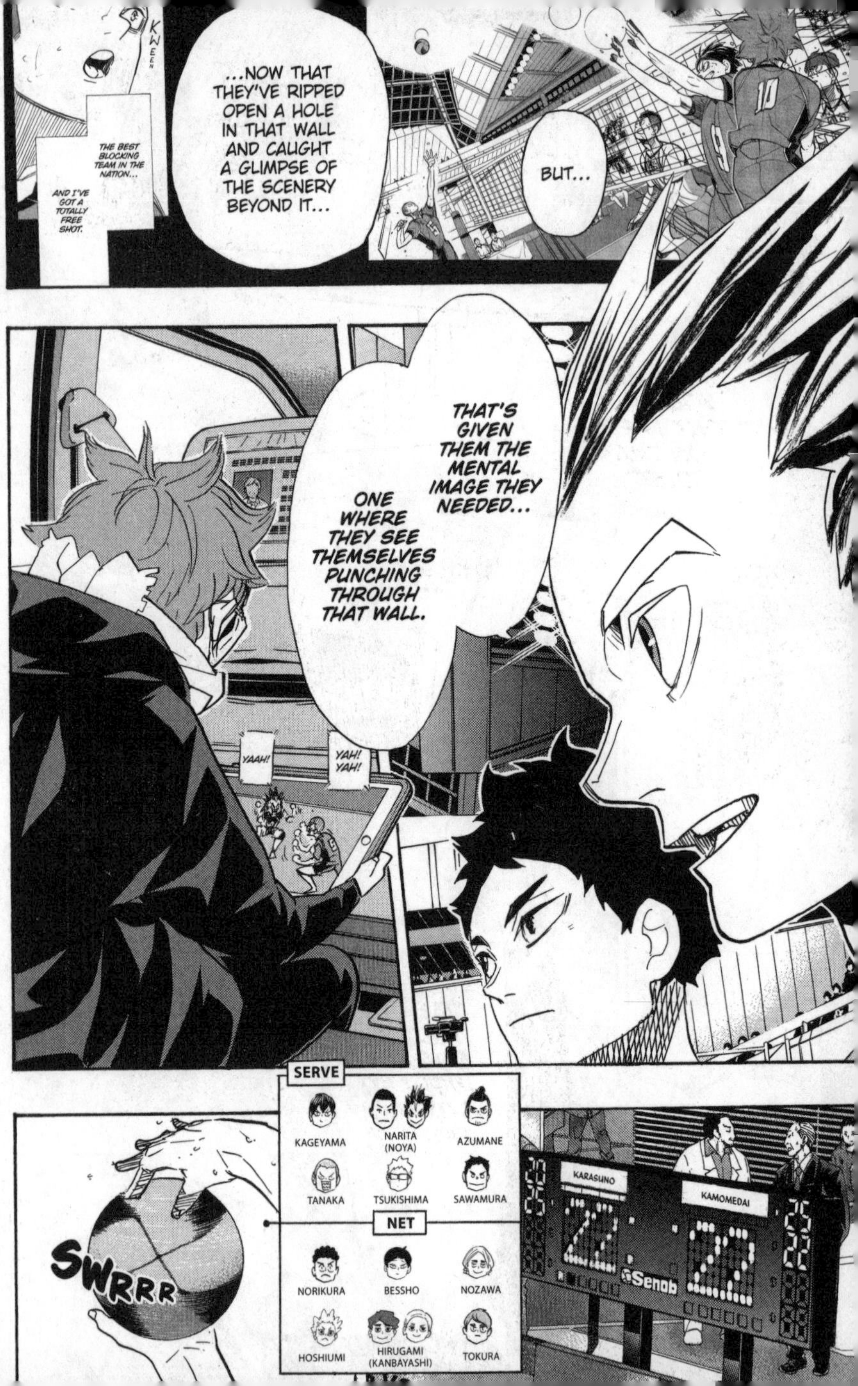
BUT...
...NOW THAT THEY'VE RIPPED OPEN A HOLE IN THAT WALL AND CAUGHT A GLIMPSE OF THE SCENERY BEYOND IT...
KWEEN
THE BEST BLOCKING TEAM IN THE NATION...
AND I'VE GOT A TOTALLY FREE SHOT.
THAT'S GIVEN THEM THE MENTAL IMAGE THEY NEEDED...
ONE WHERE THEY SEE THEMSELVES PUNCHING THROUGH THAT WALL.
YAH! YAH!
YAAH!
KARASUNO
KAMOMEDAI
22
22
Senob
SERVE
KAGEYAMA
NARITA (NOYA)
AZUMANE
TANAKA
TSUKISHIMA
SAWAMURA
NET
NORIKURA
BESSHO
NOZAWA
HOSHIUMI
HIRUGAMI (KANBAYASHI)
TOKURA
SWRRR

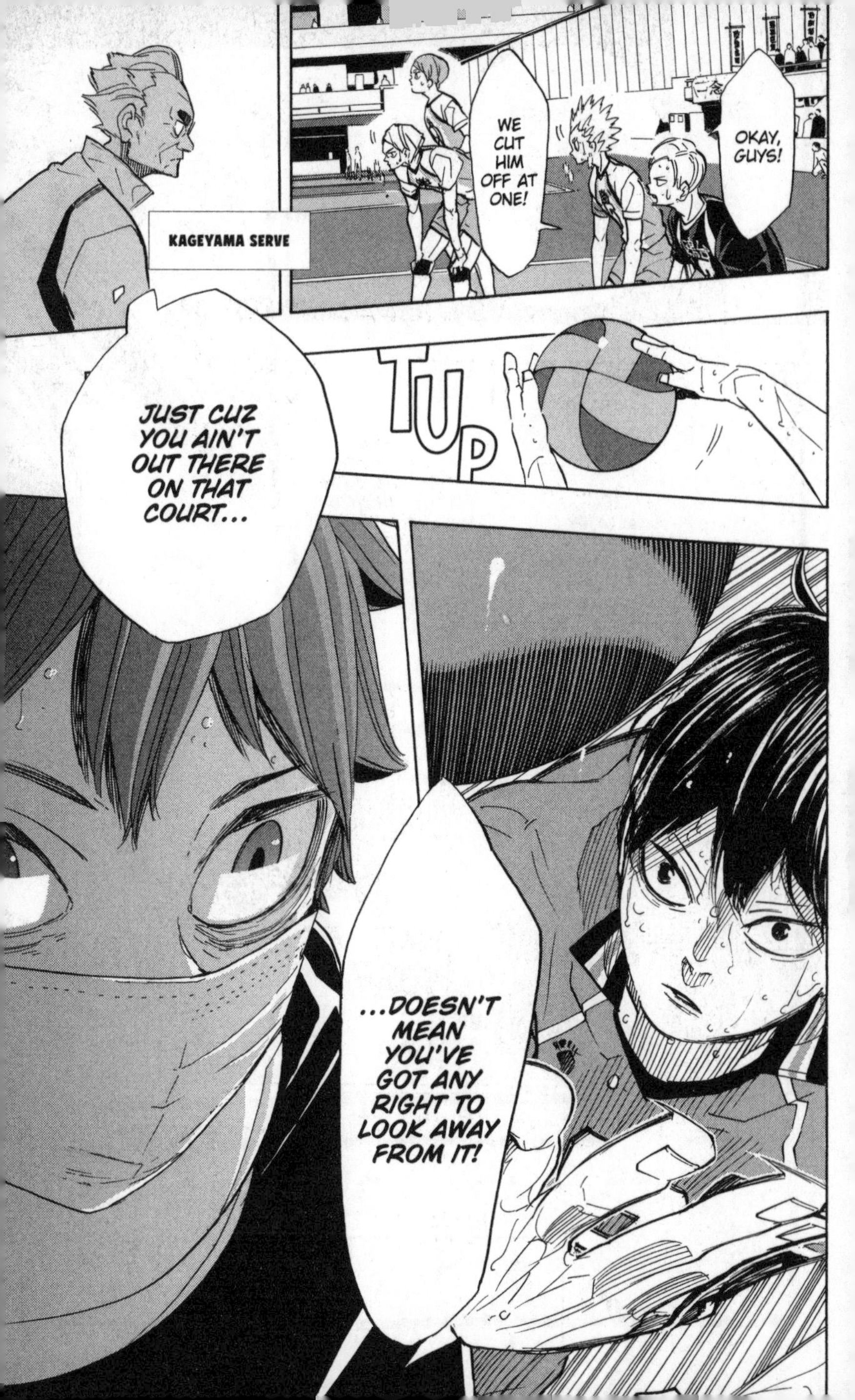
OKAY, GUYS!
WE CUT HIM OFF AT ONE!
KAGEYAMA SERVE
TUP
JUST CUZ YOU AIN'T OUT THERE ON THAT COURT...
...DOESN'T MEAN YOU'VE GOT ANY RIGHT TO LOOK AWAY FROM IT!

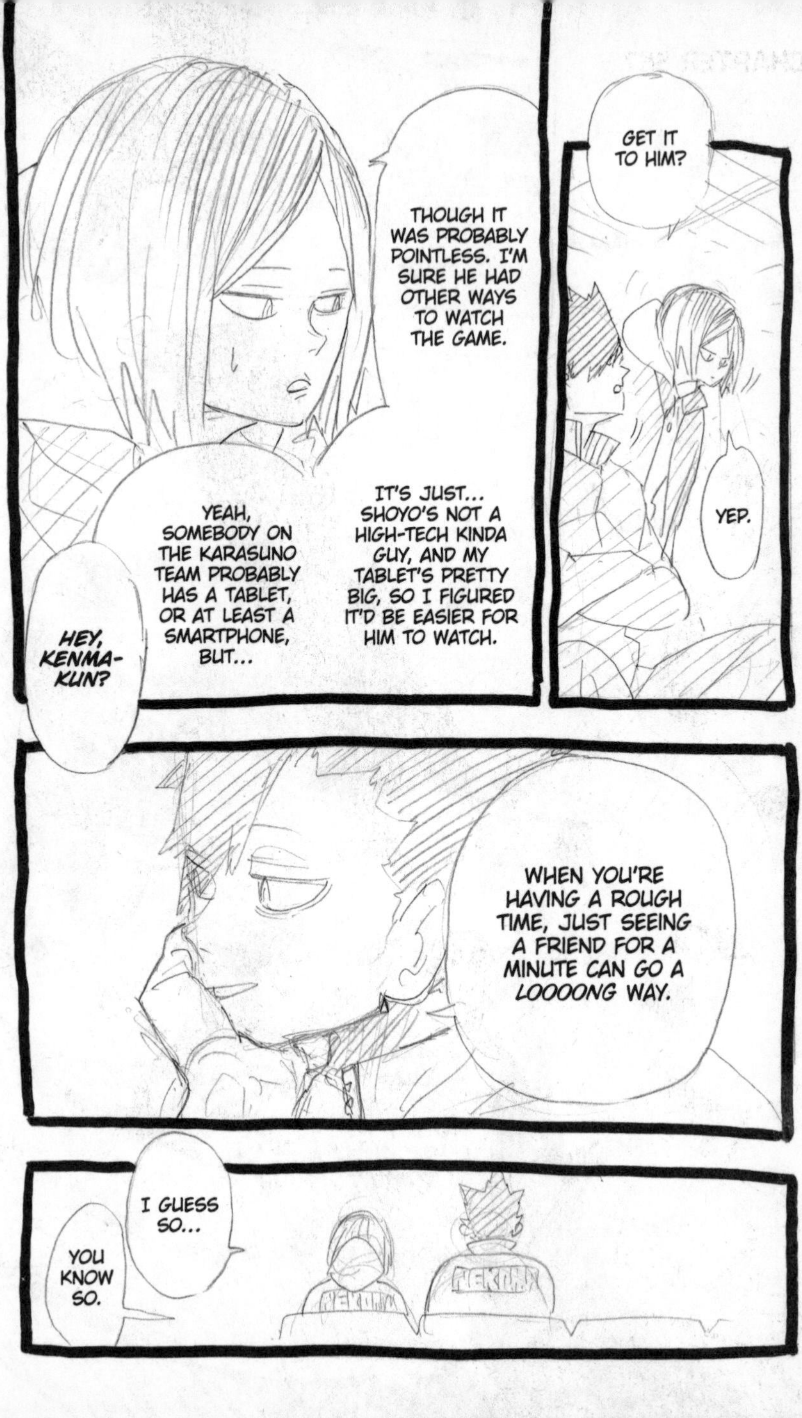
GET IT TO HIM?
YEP.
THOUGH IT WAS PROBABLY POINTLESS. I'M SURE HE HAD OTHER WAYS TO WATCH THE GAME.
IT'S JUST... SHOYO'S NOT A HIGH-TECH KINDA GUY, AND MY TABLET'S PRETTY BIG, SO I FIGURED IT'D BE EASIER FOR HIM TO WATCH.
YEAH, SOMEBODY ON THE KARASUNO TEAM PROBABLY HAS A TABLET, OR AT LEAST A SMARTPHONE, BUT...
HEY, KENMA-KUN?
WHEN YOU'RE HAVING A ROUGH TIME, JUST SEEING A FRIEND FOR A MINUTE CAN GO A LOOOONG WAY.
I GUESS SO...
YOU KNOW SO.

CHAPTER 367

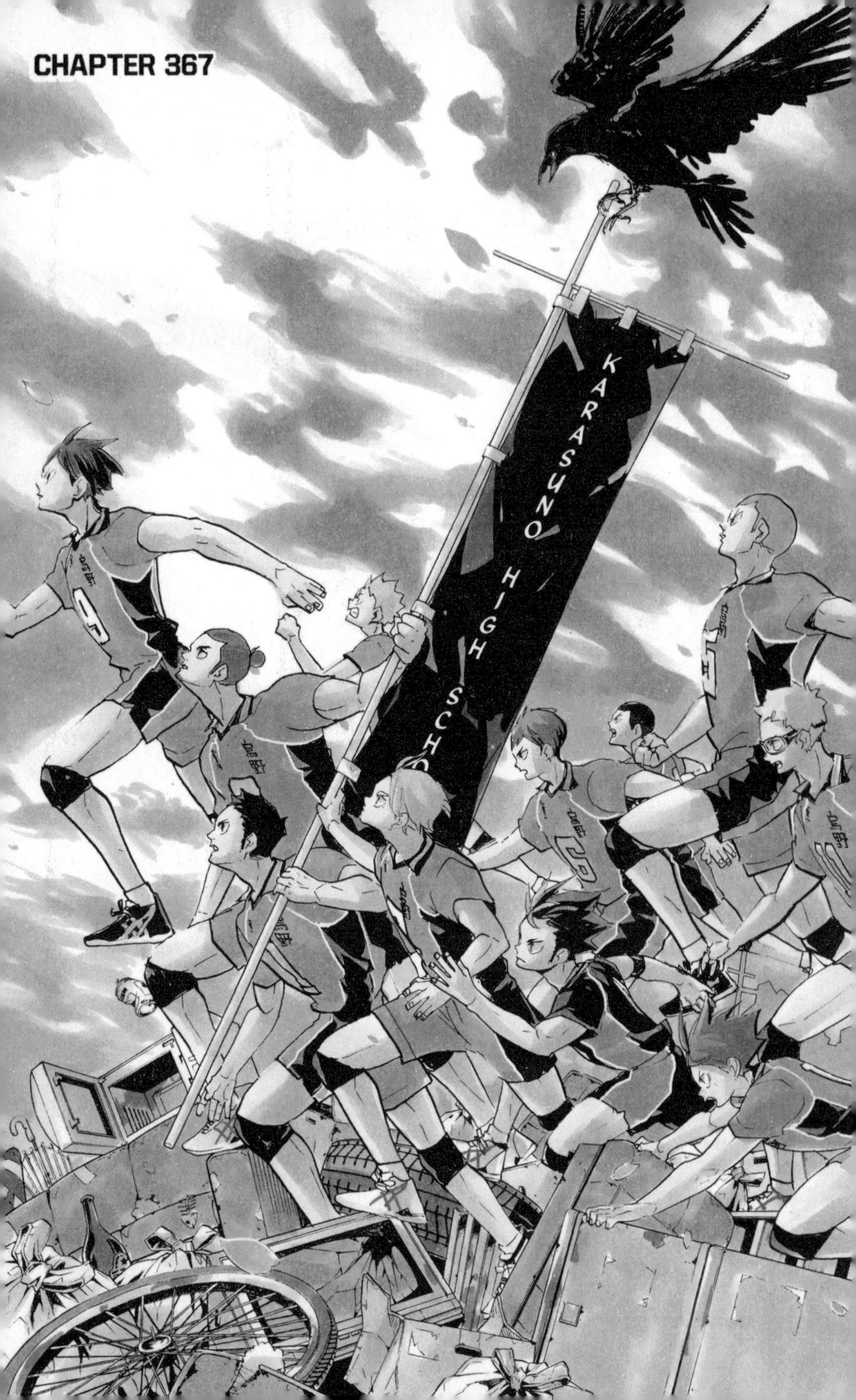
KARASUNO HIGH SCHO

HAIKYU!!

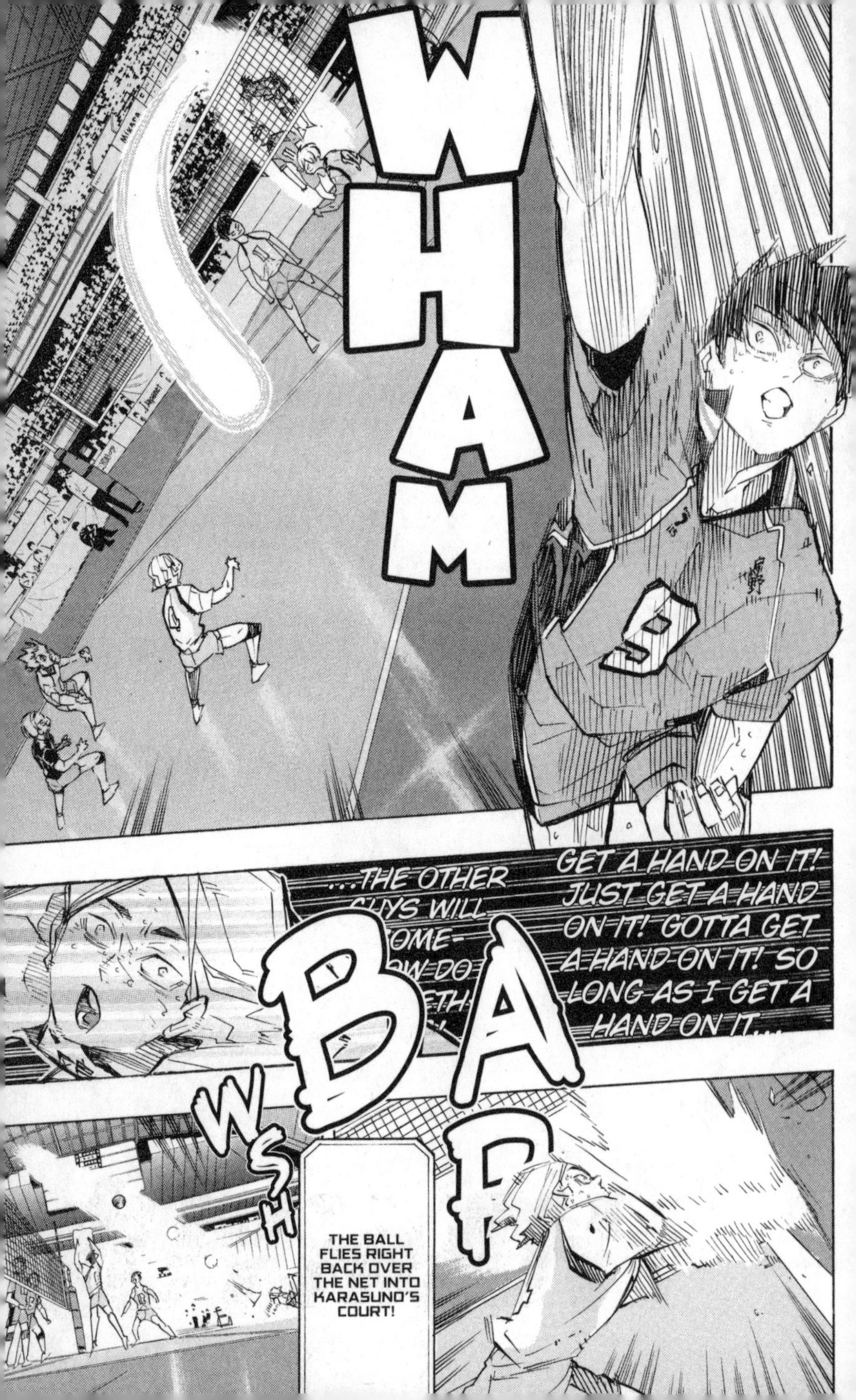
WHAM
GET A HAND ON IT! JUST GET A HAND ON IT! GOTTA GET A HAND ON IT! SO LONG AS I GET A HAND ON IT...
...THE OTHER GUYS WILL
BAM
WSH
THE BALL FLIES RIGHT BACK OVER THE NET INTO KARASUNO'S COURT!

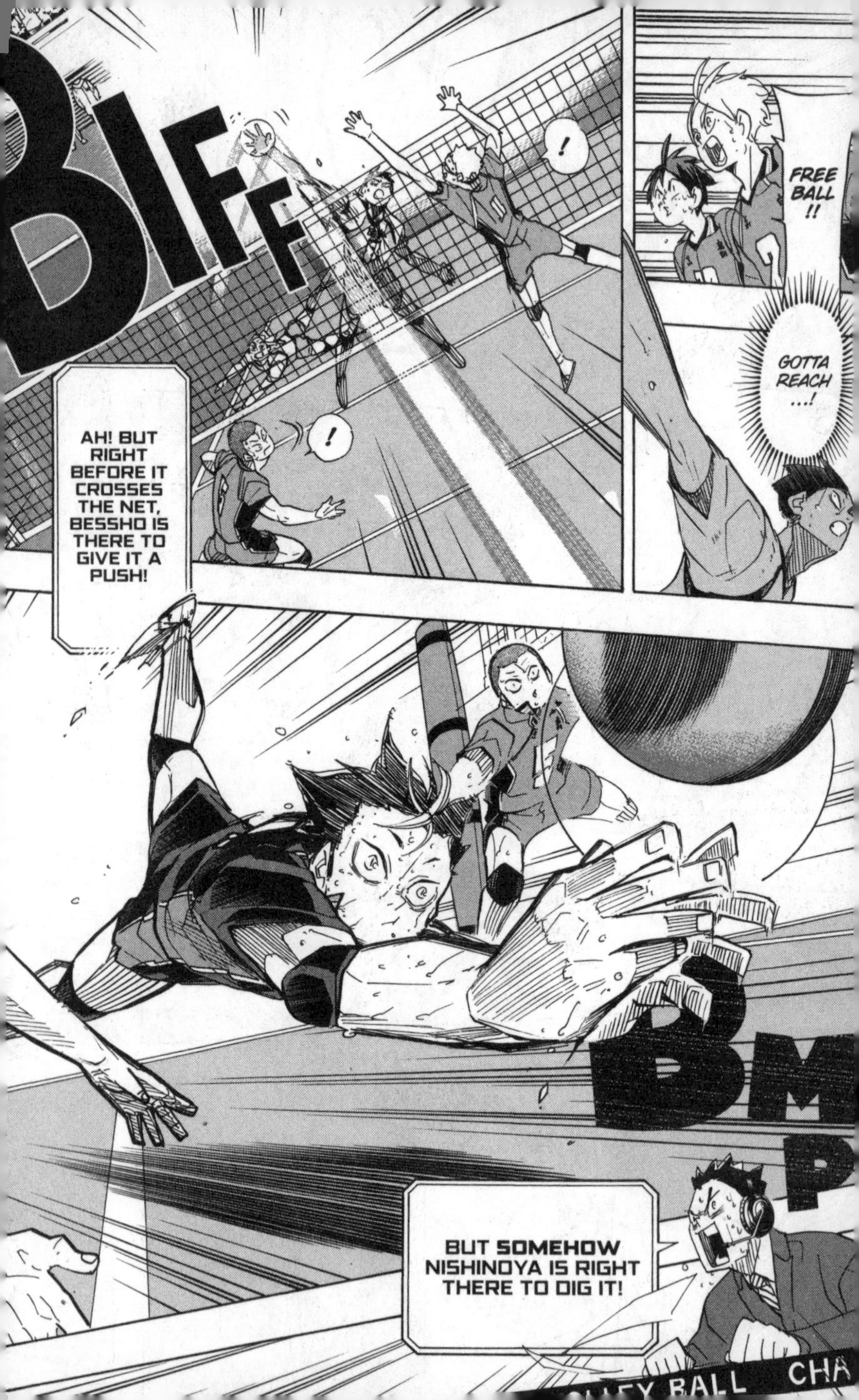
FREE BALL !!
GOTTA REACH ...!
!
BIFF
!
AH! BUT RIGHT BEFORE IT CROSSES THE NET, BESSHO IS THERE TO GIVE IT A PUSH!
BMP
BUT SOMEHOW NISHINOYA IS RIGHT THERE TO DIG IT!

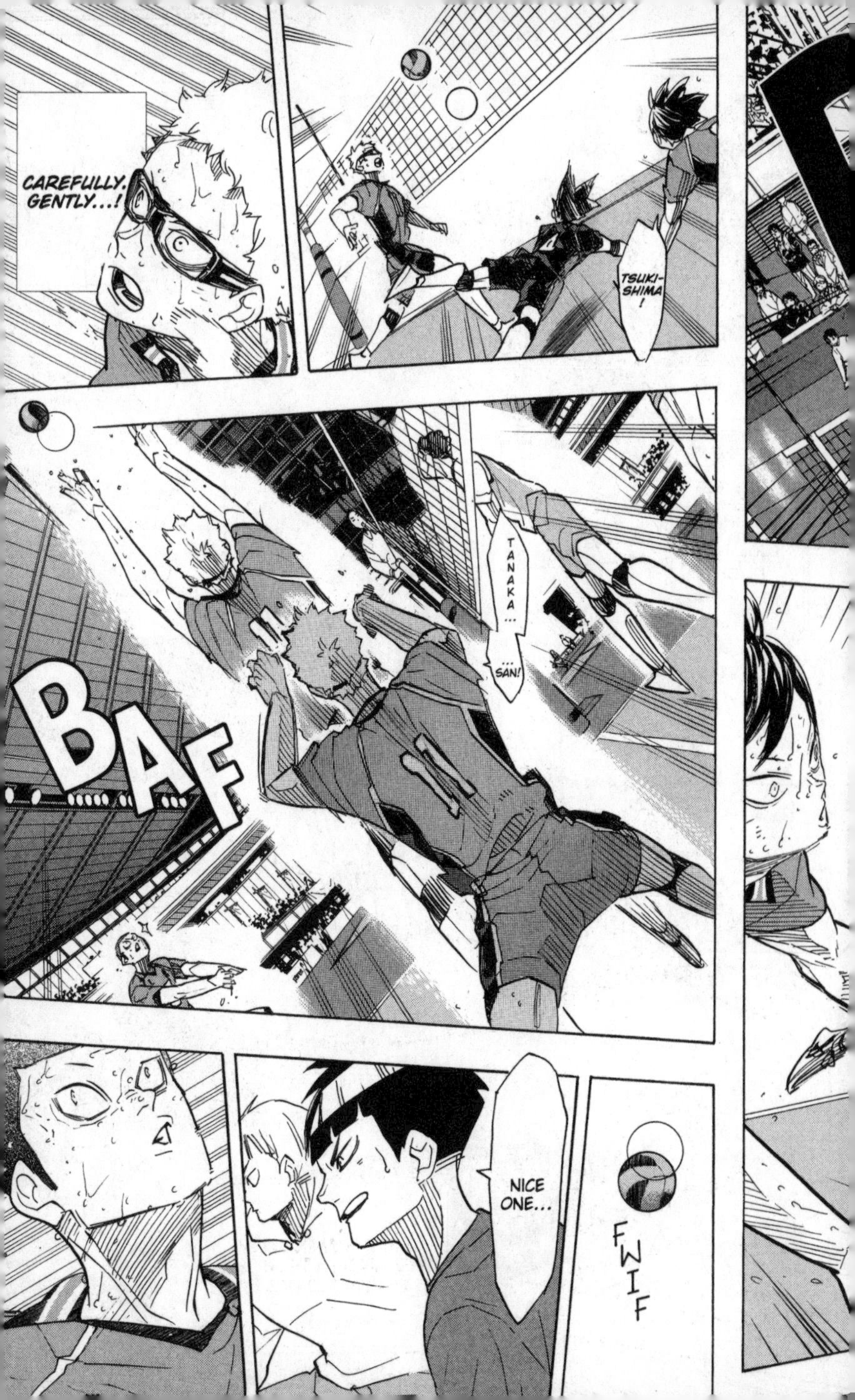

TSUKISHIMA!
CAREFULLY. GENTLY...!
TANAKA... ...SAN!
BAF
FWIF
NICE ONE...

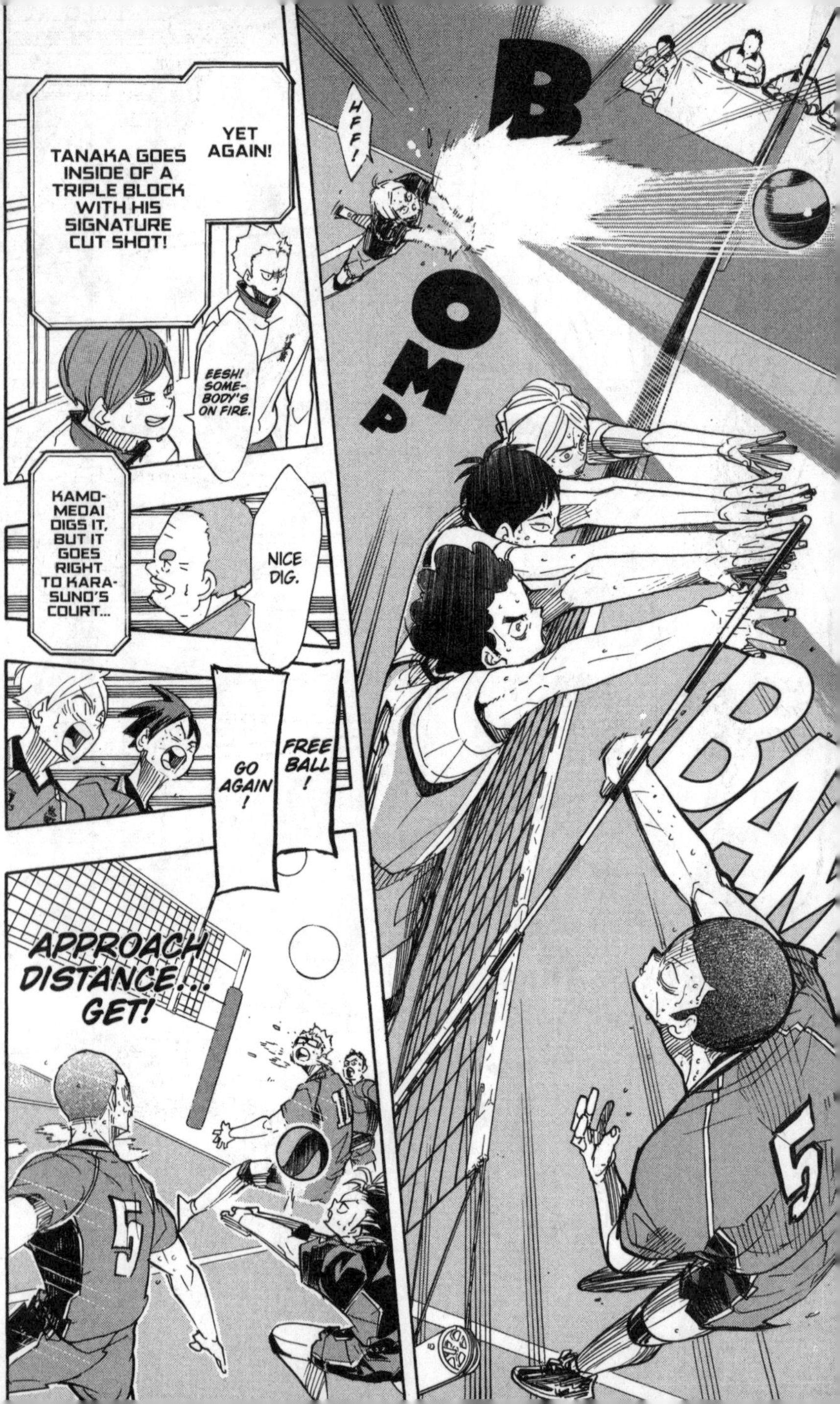
HFF!
BOOMP
BAM
TANAKA GOES INSIDE OF A TRIPLE BLOCK WITH HIS SIGNATURE CUT SHOT!
YET AGAIN!
EESH! SOMEBODY'S ON FIRE.
KAMOMEDAI DIGS IT, BUT IT GOES RIGHT TO KARASUNO'S COURT...
NICE DIG.
FREE BALL!
GO AGAIN!
APPROACH DISTANCE... GET!

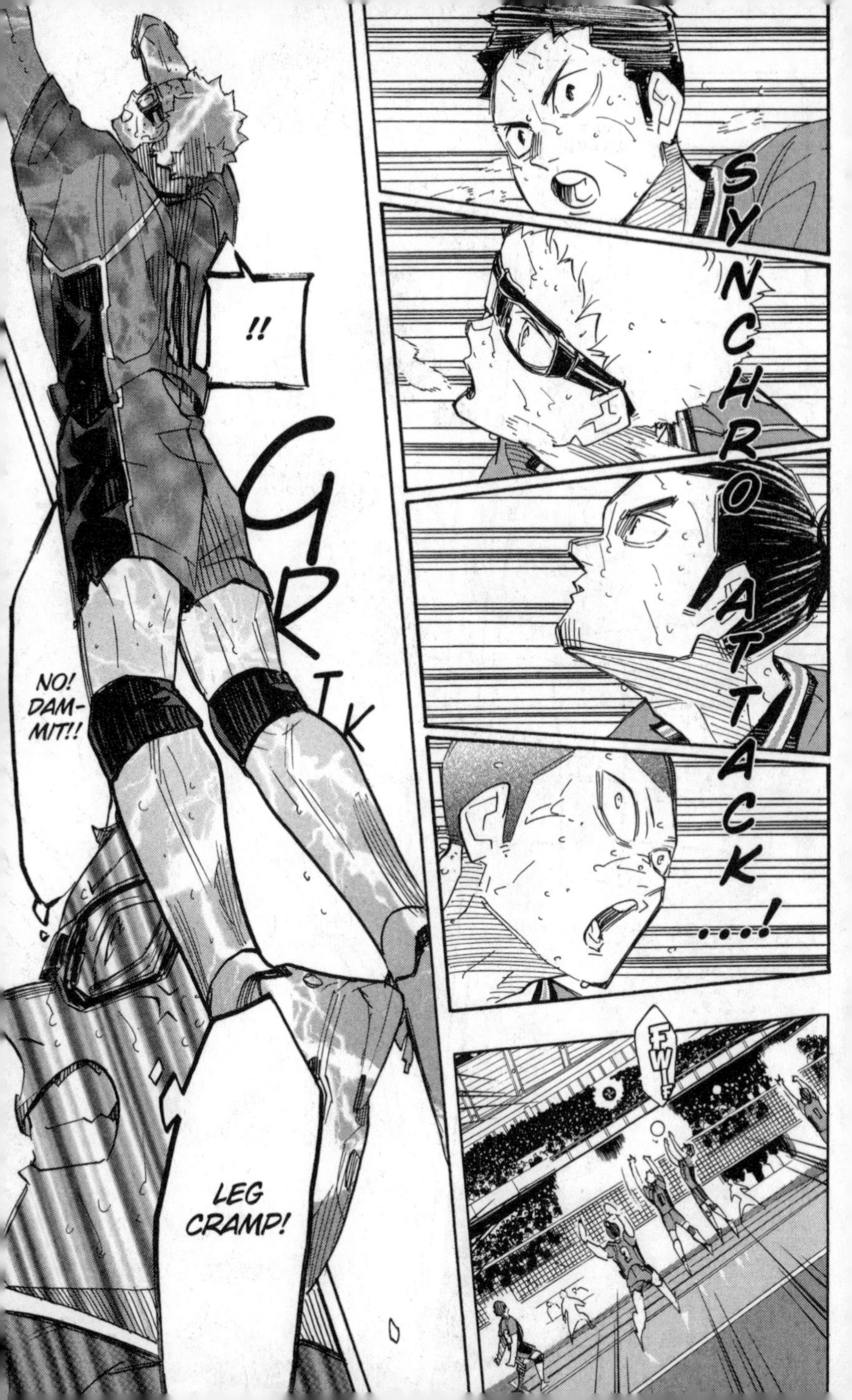

SYNCHRO ATTACK...!
FWIP
!!
GRIK
NO! DAM-MIT!!
LEG CRAMP!

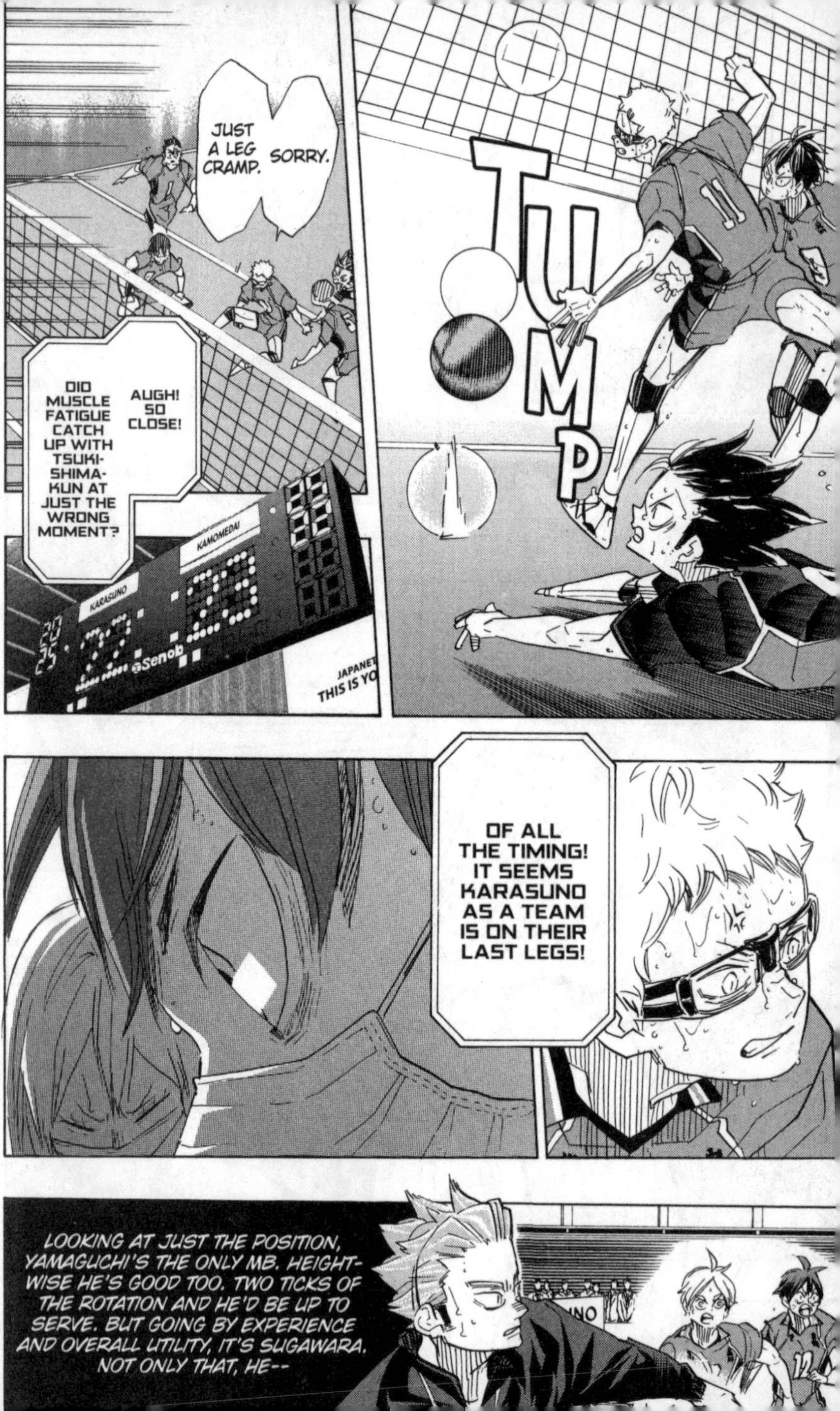
TUMP
SORRY.
JUST A LEG CRAMP.
AUGH! SO CLOSE!
DID MUSCLE FATIGUE CATCH UP WITH TSUKISHIMA-KUN AT JUST THE WRONG MOMENT?
KAMOMEDAI
KARASUNO
OF ALL THE TIMING! IT SEEMS KARASUNO AS A TEAM IS ON THEIR LAST LEGS!
LOOKING AT JUST THE POSITION, YAMAGUCHI'S THE ONLY MB. HEIGHT-WISE HE'S GOOD TOO. TWO TICKS OF THE ROTATION AND HE'D BE UP TO SERVE. BUT GOING BY EXPERIENCE AND OVERALL UTILITY, IT'S SUGAWARA. NOT ONLY THAT, HE--

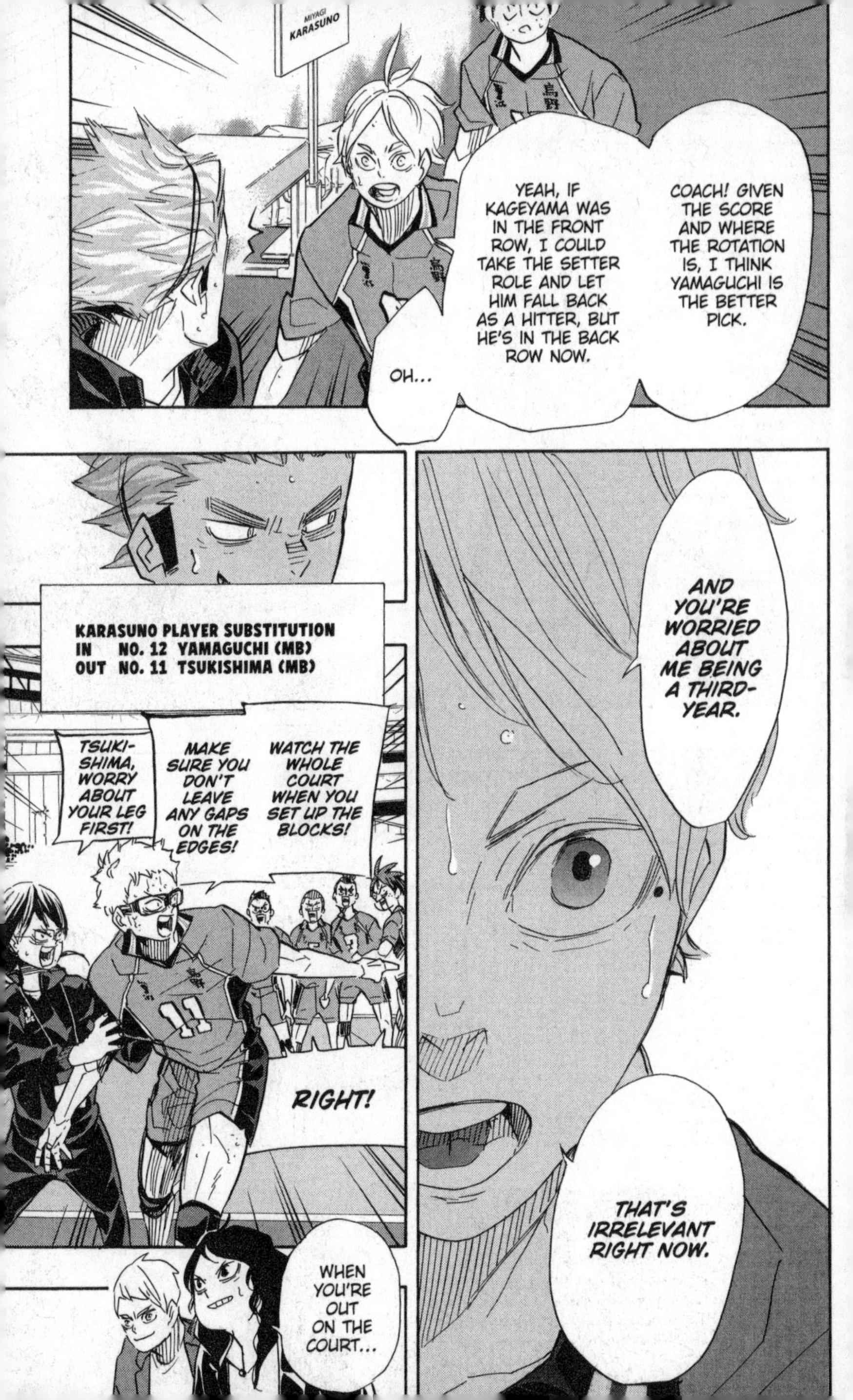
MIYAGI KARASUNO
COACH! GIVEN THE SCORE AND WHERE THE ROTATION IS, I THINK YAMAGUCHI IS THE BETTER PICK.
YEAH, IF KAGEYAMA WAS IN THE FRONT ROW, I COULD TAKE THE SETTER ROLE AND LET HIM FALL BACK AS A HITTER, BUT HE'S IN THE BACK ROW NOW.
OH...
AND YOU'RE WORRIED ABOUT ME BEING A THIRD-YEAR.
THAT'S IRRELEVANT RIGHT NOW.
KARASUNO PLAYER SUBSTITUTION
IN NO. 12 YAMAGUCHI (MB)
OUT NO. 11 TSUKISHIMA (MB)
WATCH THE WHOLE COURT WHEN YOU SET UP THE BLOCKS!
MAKE SURE YOU DON'T LEAVE ANY GAPS ON THE EDGES!
TSUKISHIMA, WORRY ABOUT YOUR LEG FIRST!
RIGHT!
WHEN YOU'RE OUT ON THE COURT...

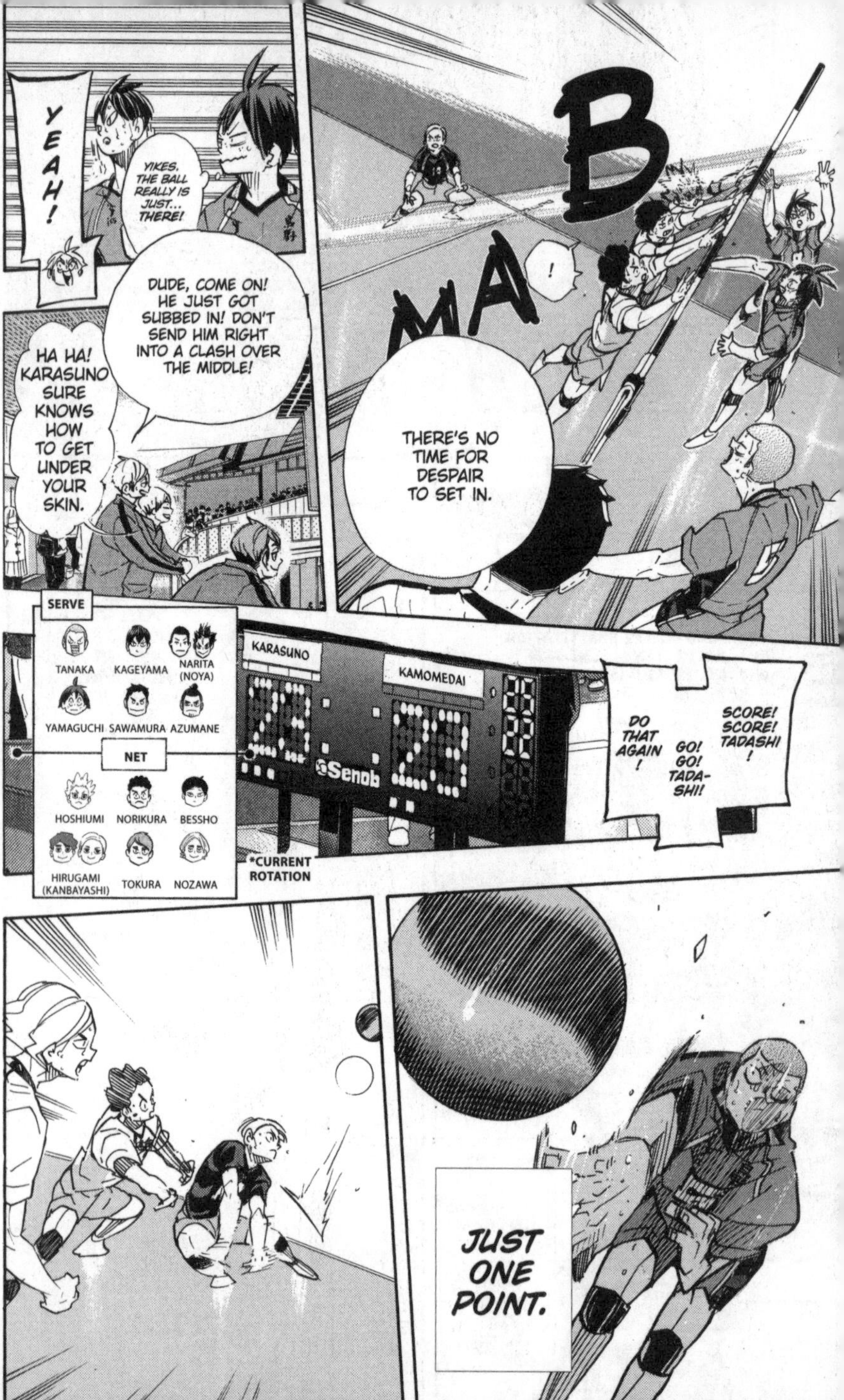
B
MA
!
THERE'S NO TIME FOR DESPAIR TO SET IN.
YEAH!
YIKES. THE BALL REALLY IS JUST... THERE!
DUDE, COME ON! HE JUST GOT SUBBED IN! DON'T SEND HIM RIGHT INTO A CLASH OVER THE MIDDLE!
HA HA! KARASUNO SURE KNOWS HOW TO GET UNDER YOUR SKIN.
SCORE! SCORE! TADASHI!
GO! GO! TADA-SHI!
DO THAT AGAIN!
KARASUNO
KAMOMEDAI
Senob
SERVE
TANAKA
KAGEYAMA
NARITA (NOYA)
YAMAGUCHI
SAWAMURA
AZUMANE
NET
HOSHIUMI
NORIKURA
BESSHO
HIRUGAMI (KANBAYASHI)
TOKURA
NOZAWA
*CURRENT ROTATION
JUST ONE POINT.

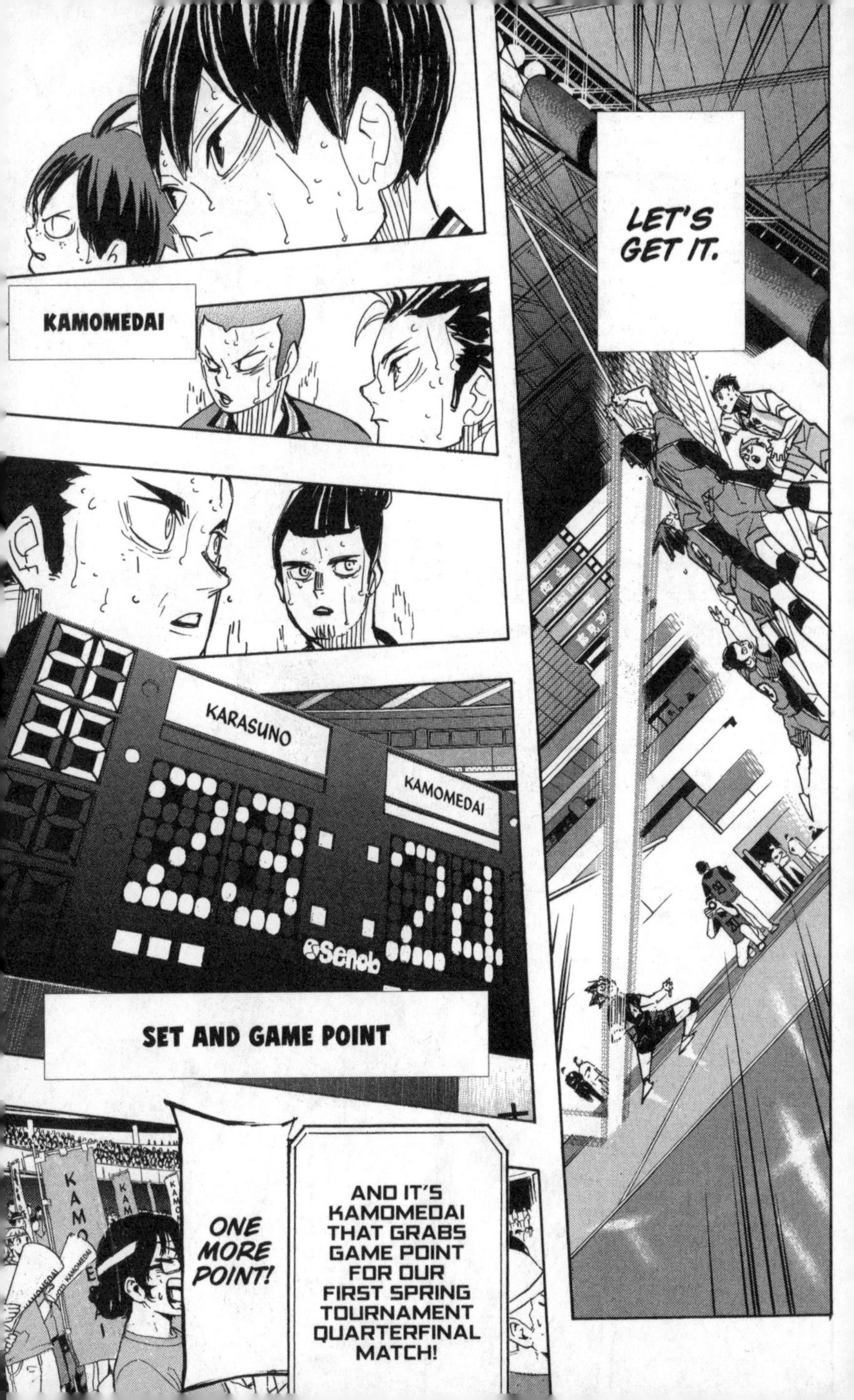
LET'S GET IT.
KAMOMEDAI
KARASUNO
KAMOMEDAI
SET AND GAME POINT
AND IT'S KAMOMEDAI THAT GRABS GAME POINT FOR OUR FIRST SPRING TOURNAMENT QUARTERFINAL MATCH!
ONE MORE POINT!

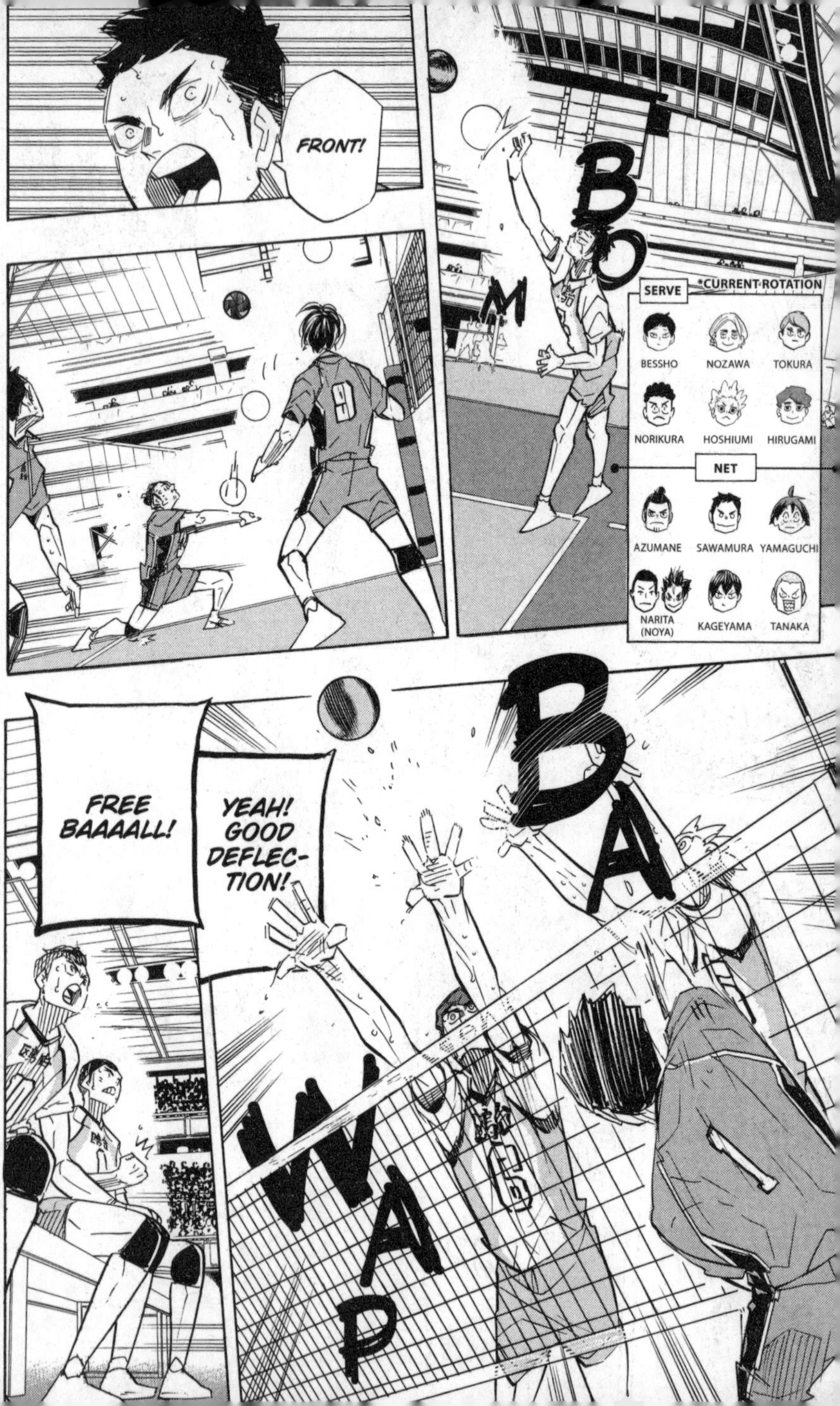
BOOM
*CURRENT ROTATION
SERVE
BESSHO
NOZAWA
TOKURA
NORIKURA
HOSHIUMI
HIRUGAMI
NET
AZUMANE
SAWAMURA
YAMAGUCHI
NARITA (NOYA)
KAGEYAMA
TANAKA
FRONT!
BA
YEAH! GOOD DEFLECTION!
FREE BAAAAALL!
WAP

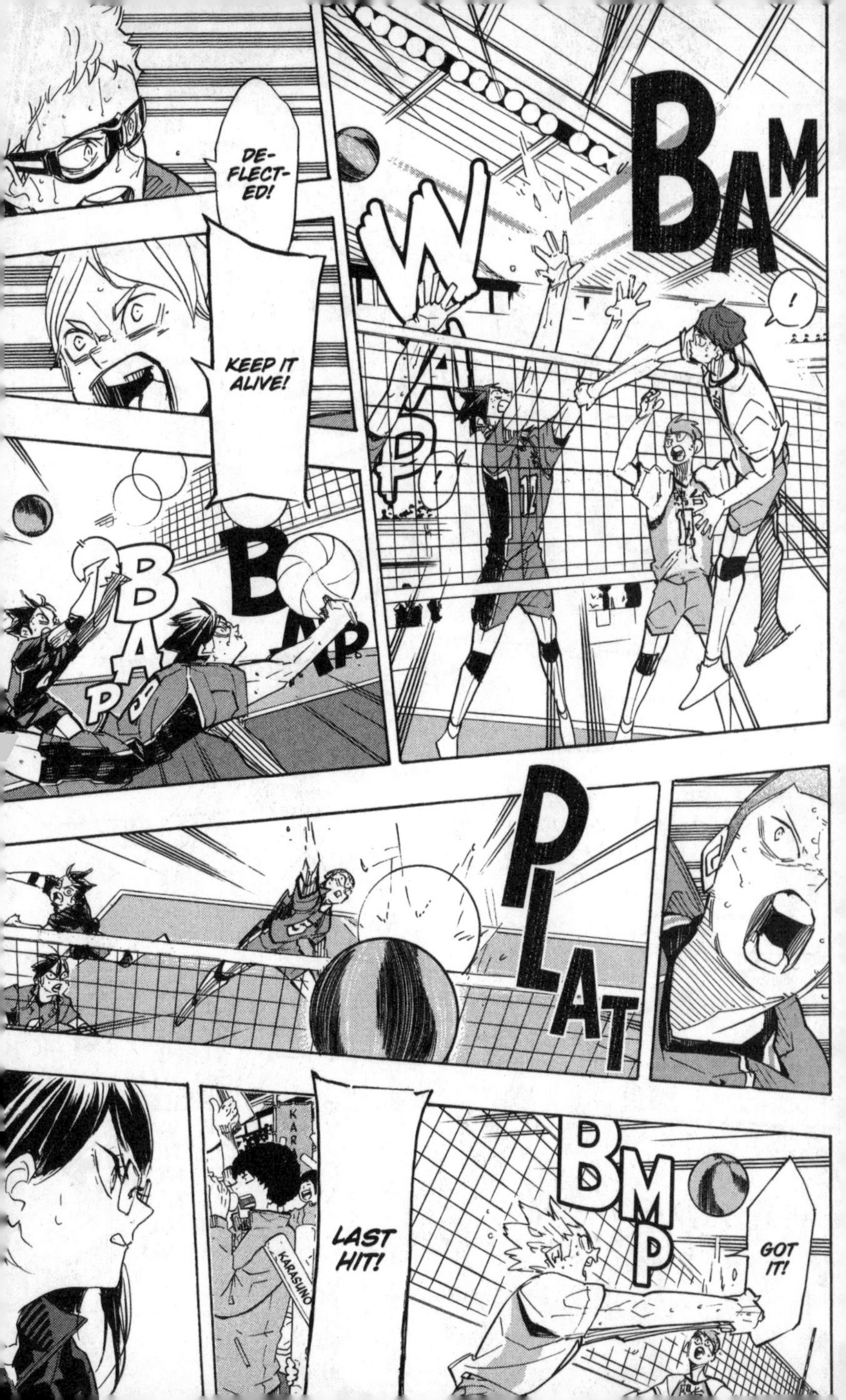
BAM
!
WAP
DE-FLECTED!
KEEP IT ALIVE!
BAP
BAP
PLAT
BMP
GOT IT!
LAST HIT!

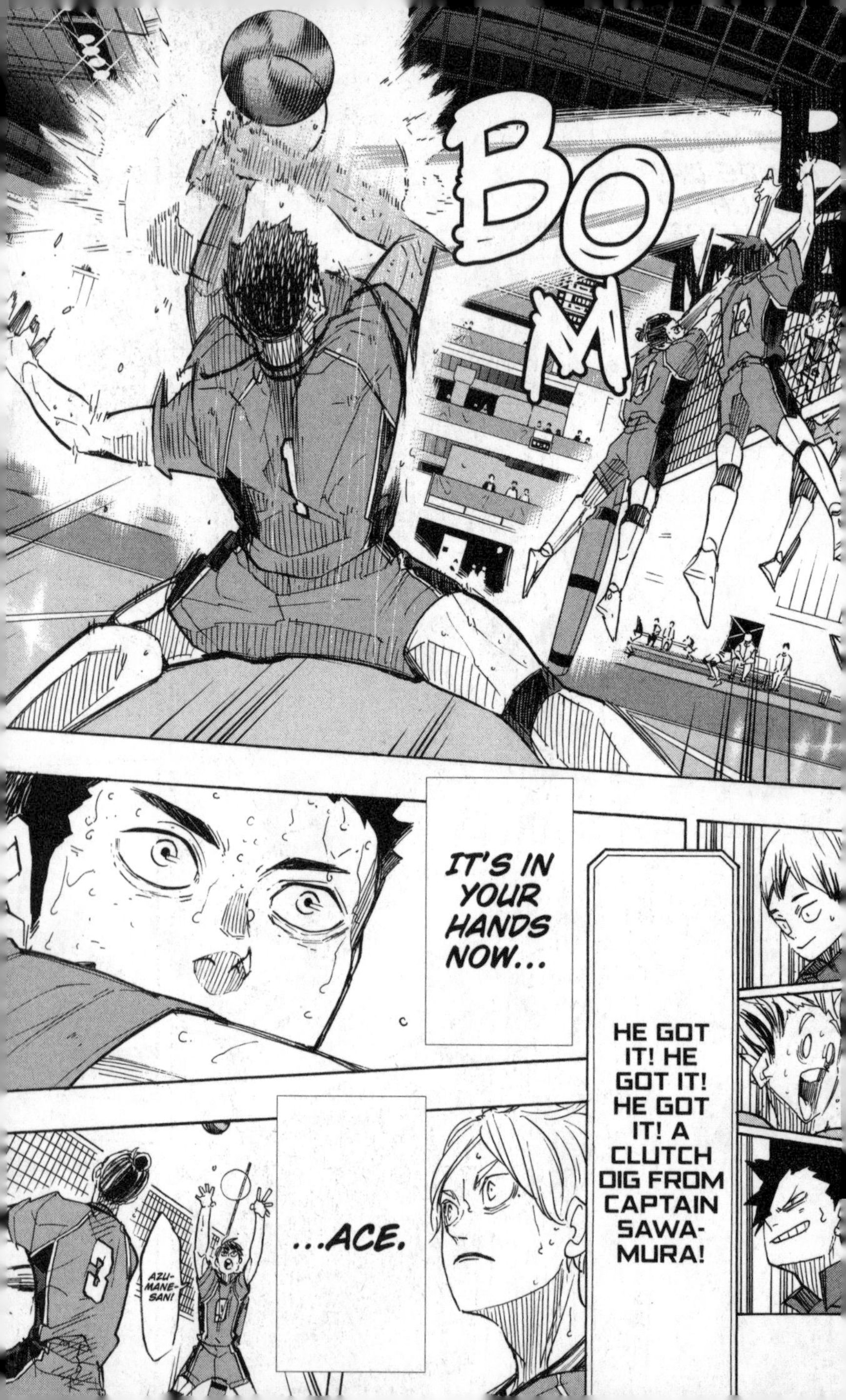
BOOM
HE GOT IT! HE GOT IT! HE GOT IT! A CLUTCH DIG FROM CAPTAIN SAWAMURA!
IT'S IN YOUR HANDS NOW...
...ACE.
AZUMANE-SAN!

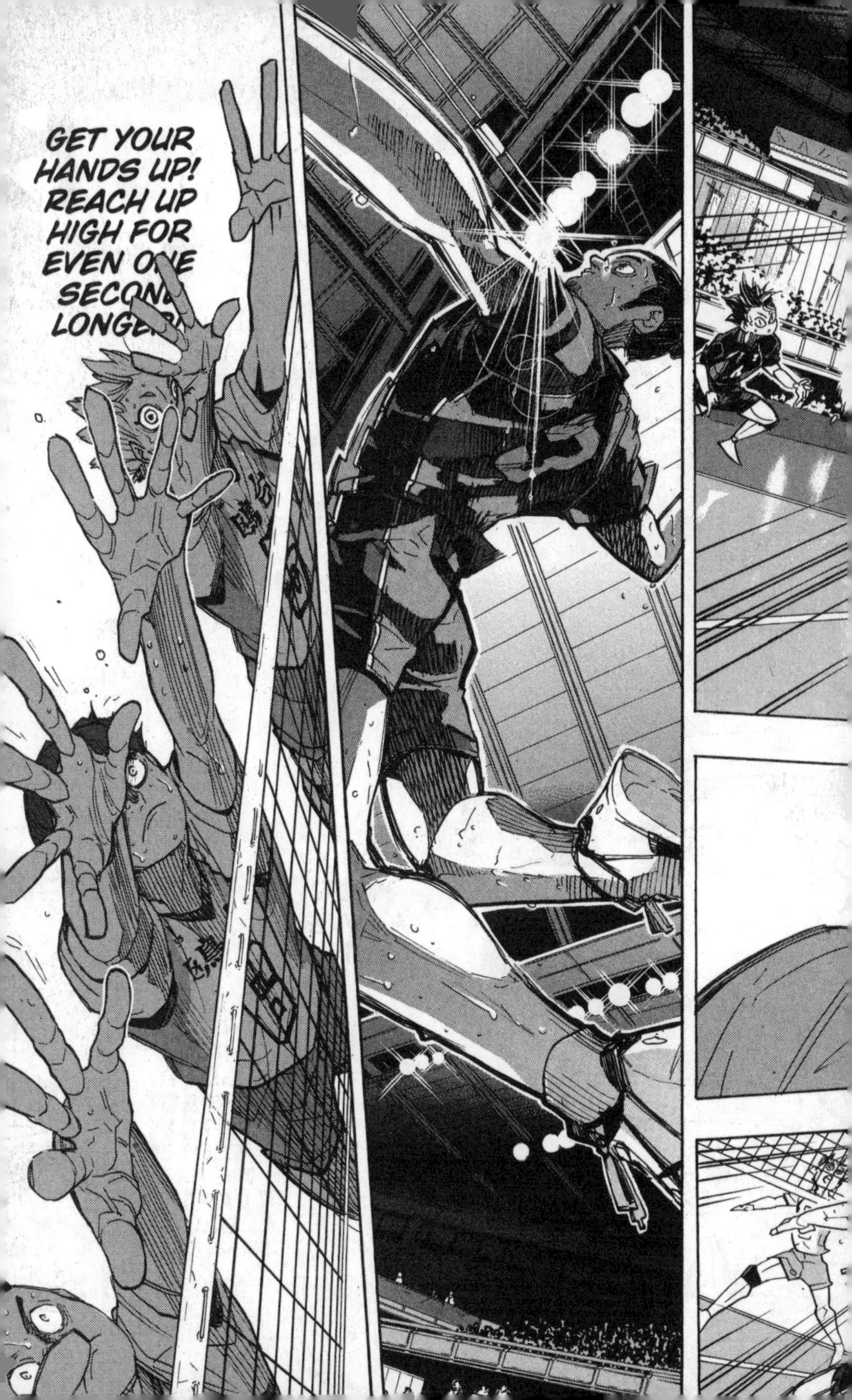
GET YOUR HANDS UP! REACH UP HIGH FOR EVEN ONE SECOND LONGER!

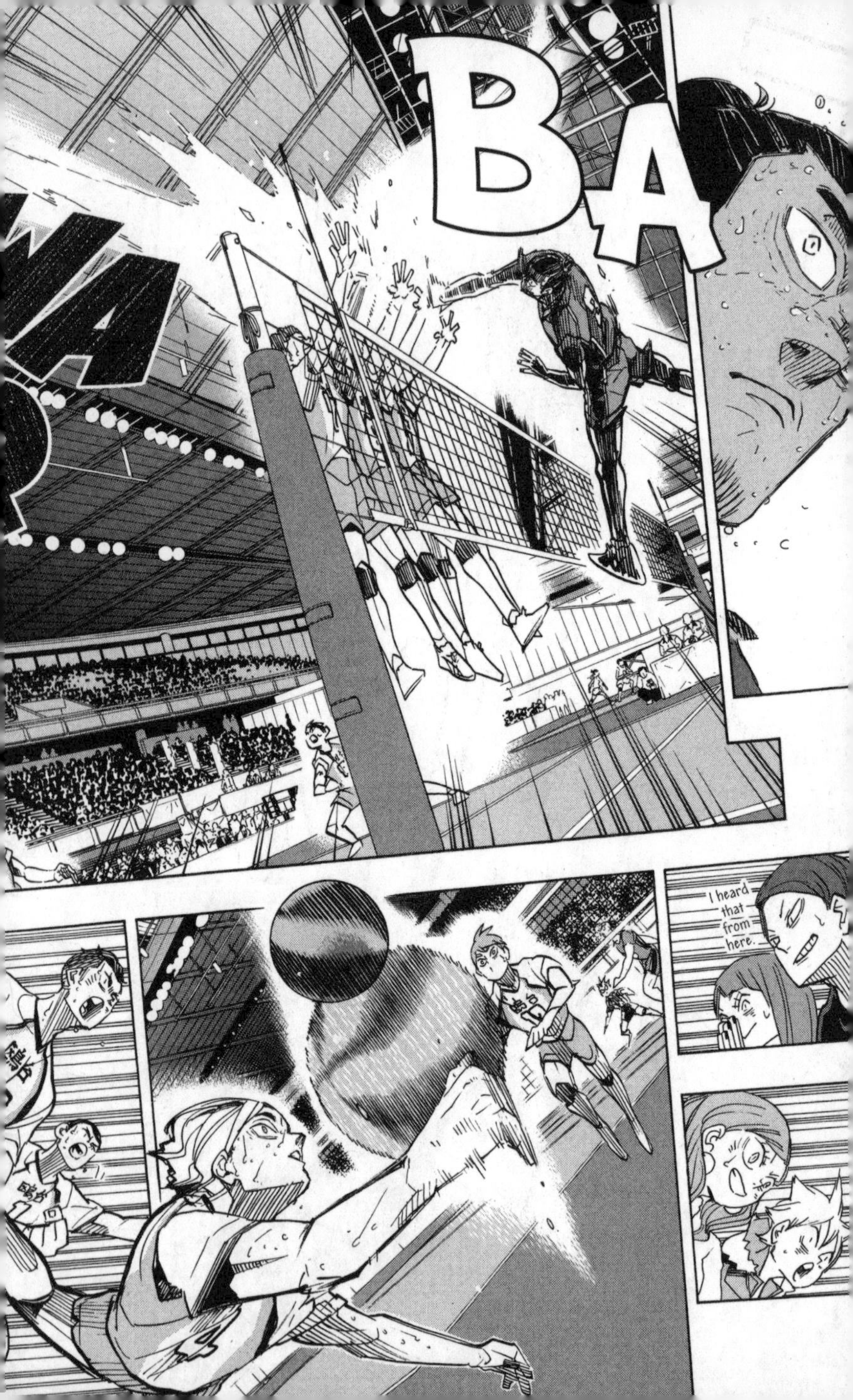
BA
WA
I heard that from here.

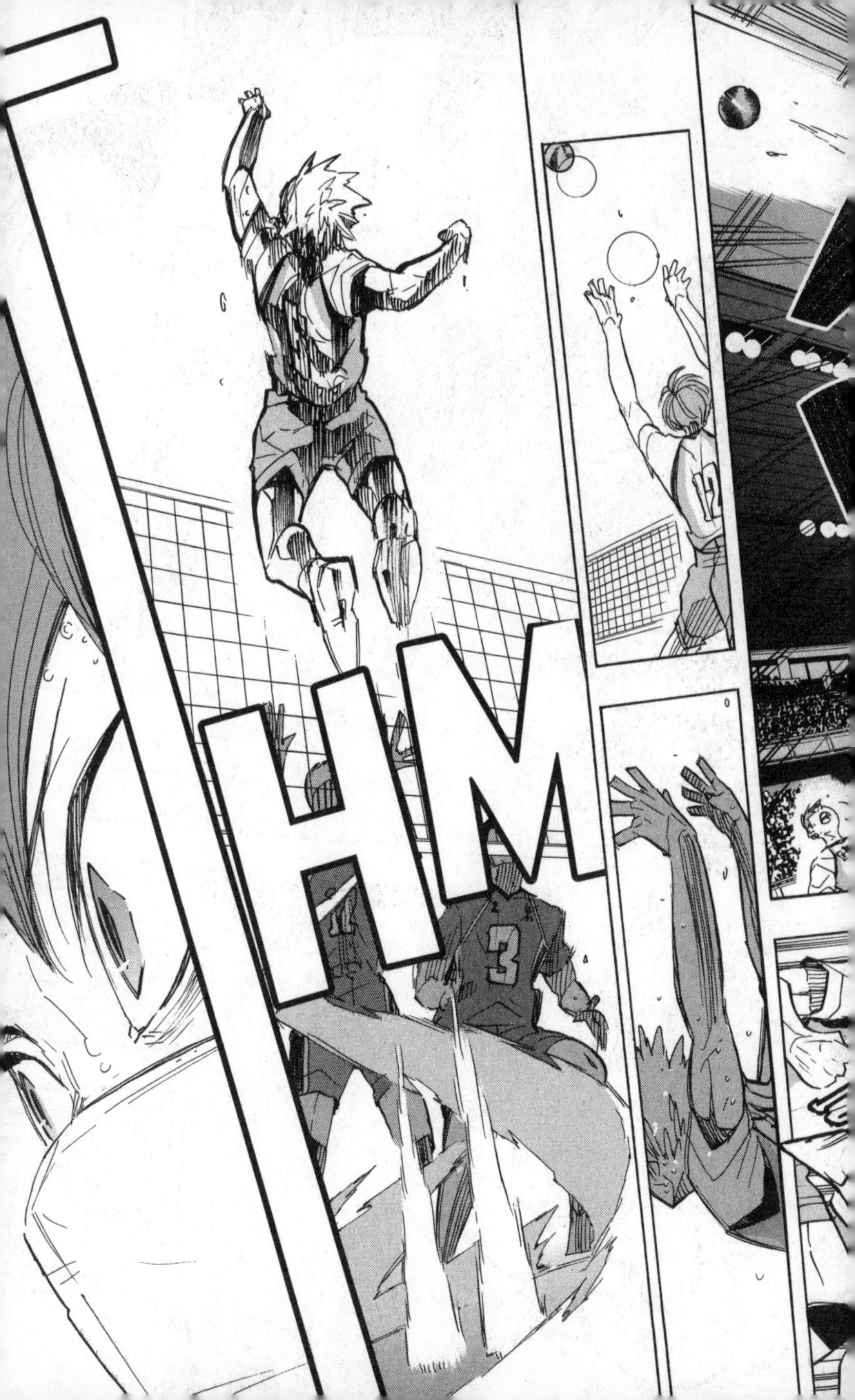
HM

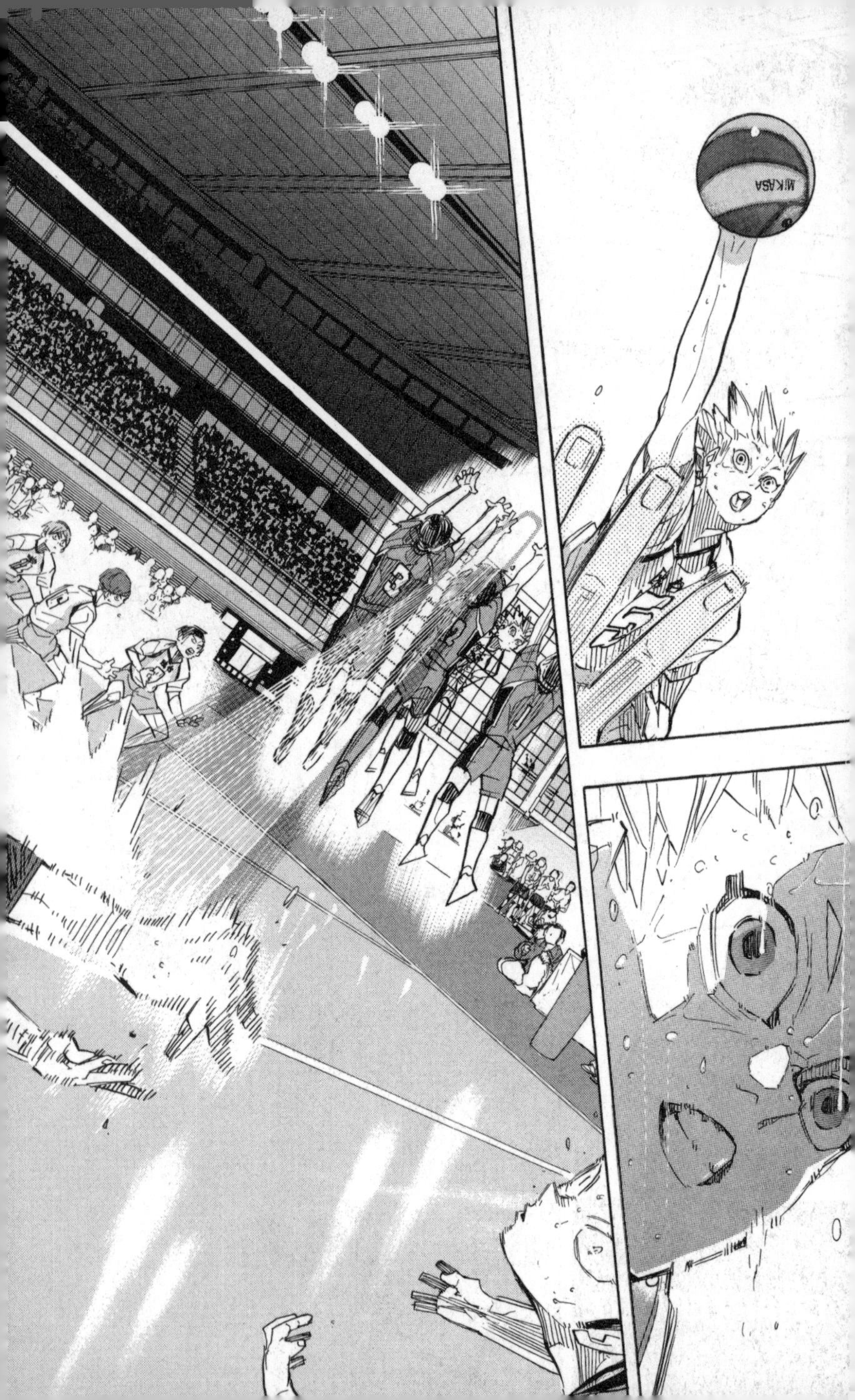
MIKASA

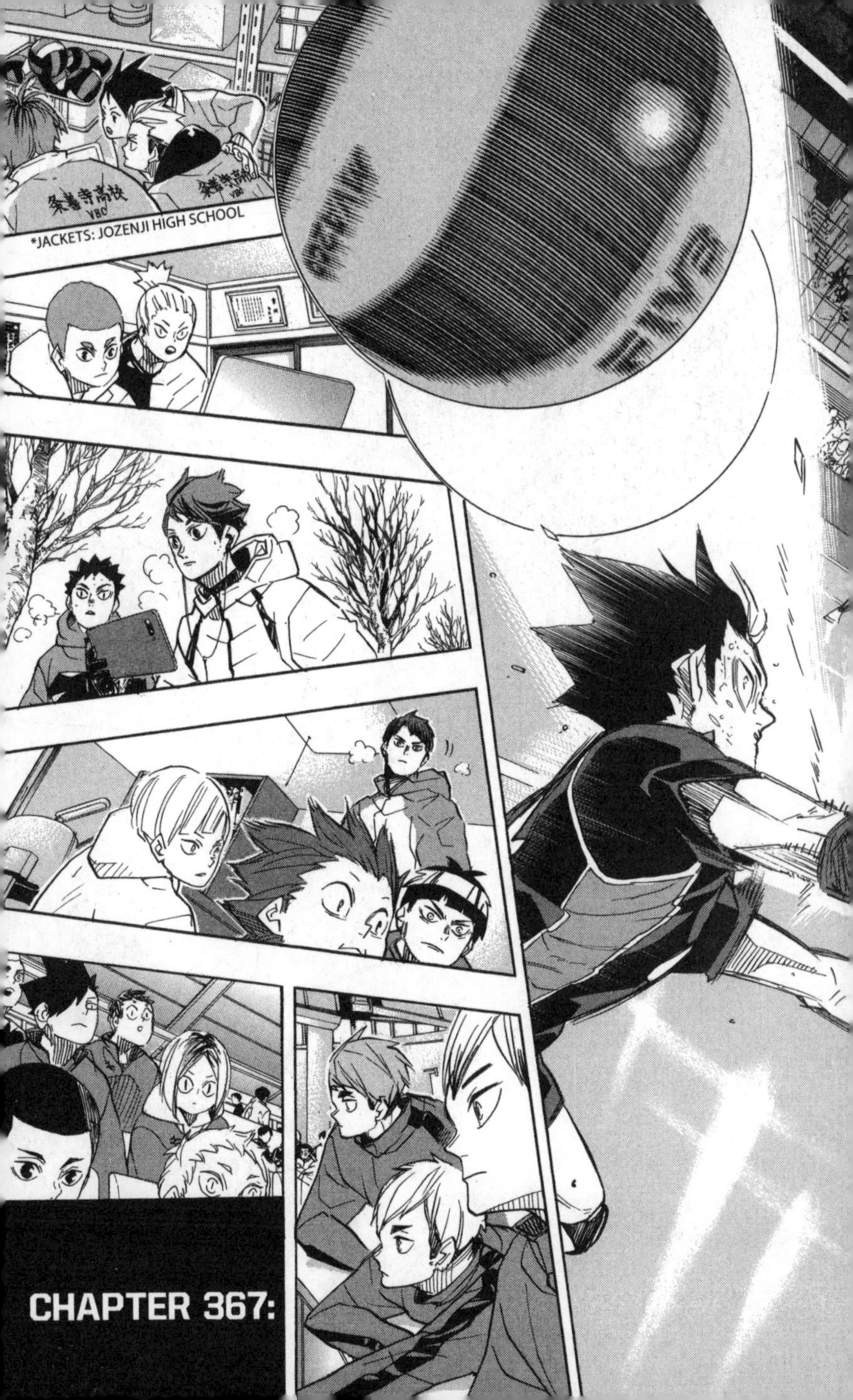
*JACKETS: JOZENJI HIGH SCHOOL
CHAPTER 367:

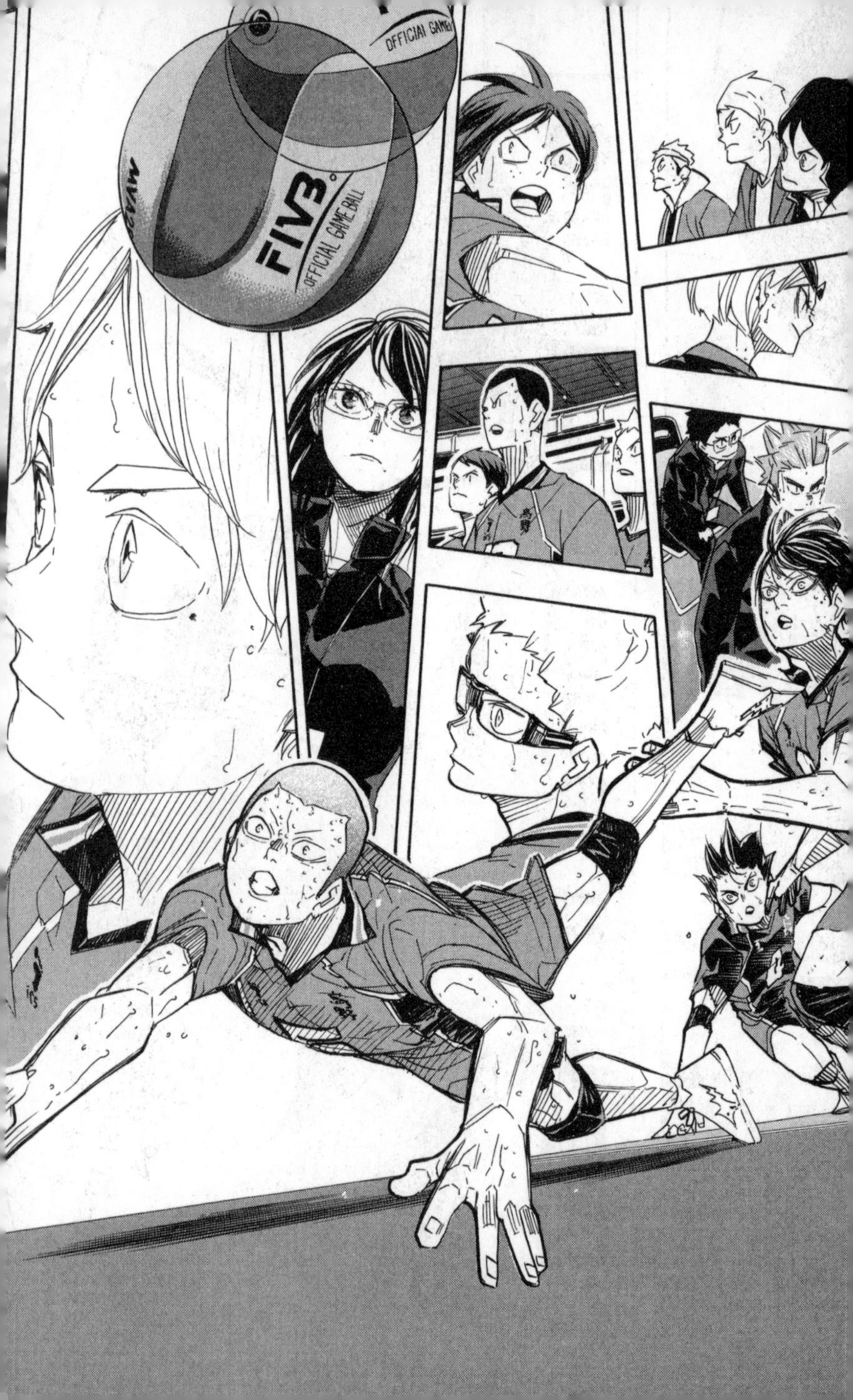
OFFICIAL GAME BALL

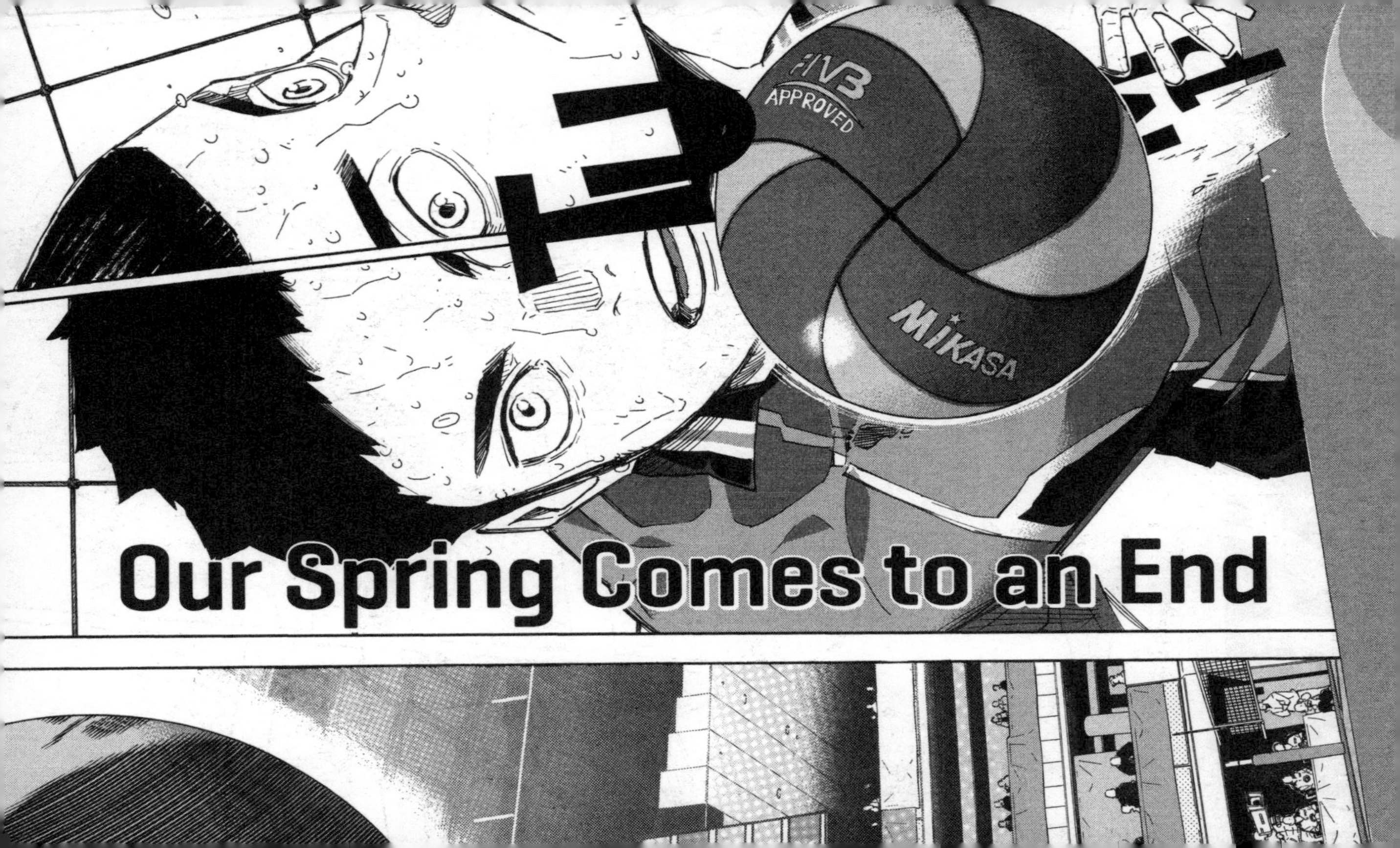
Our Spring Comes to an End
APPROVED
MIKASA

HAIKYU!!

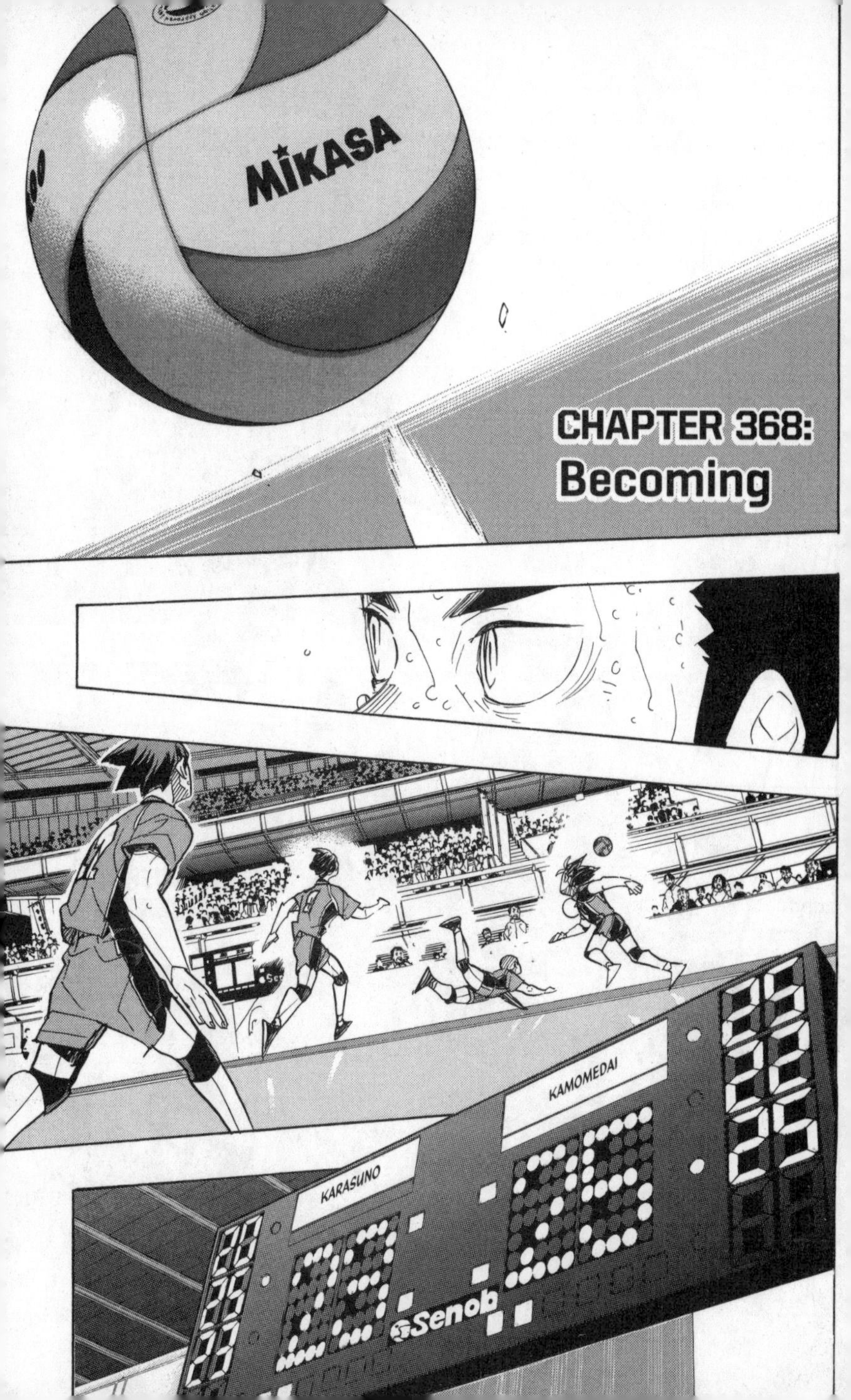
CHAPTER 368:
Becoming
MIKASA
KAMOMEDAI
KARASUNO
Senob

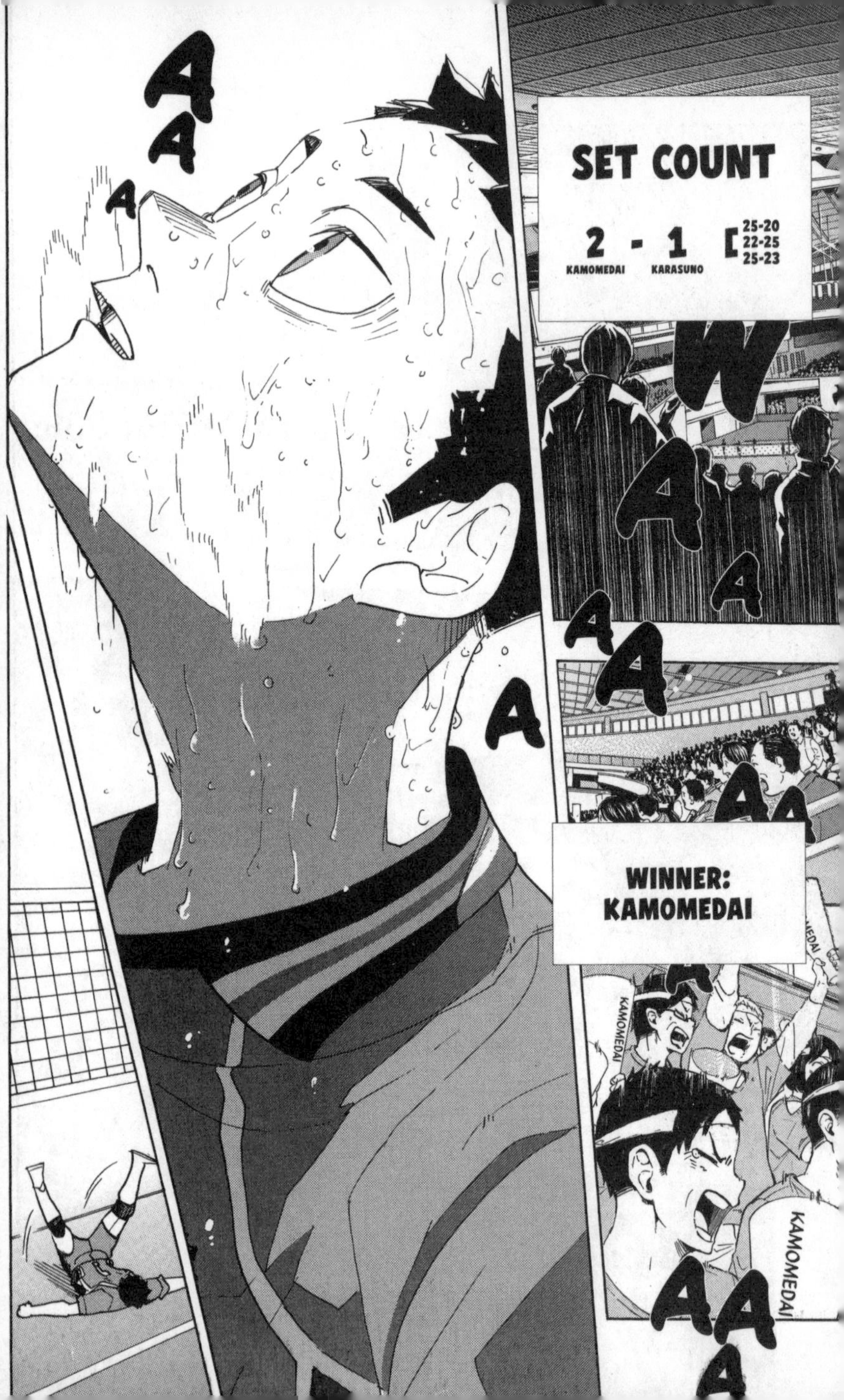
SET COUNT
2 - 1 [25-20 22-25 25-23
KAMOMEDAI KARASUNO
WAAAAAA
WINNER: KAMOMEDAI
KAMOMEDAI
KAMOMEDAI
AAAA
AAA
A

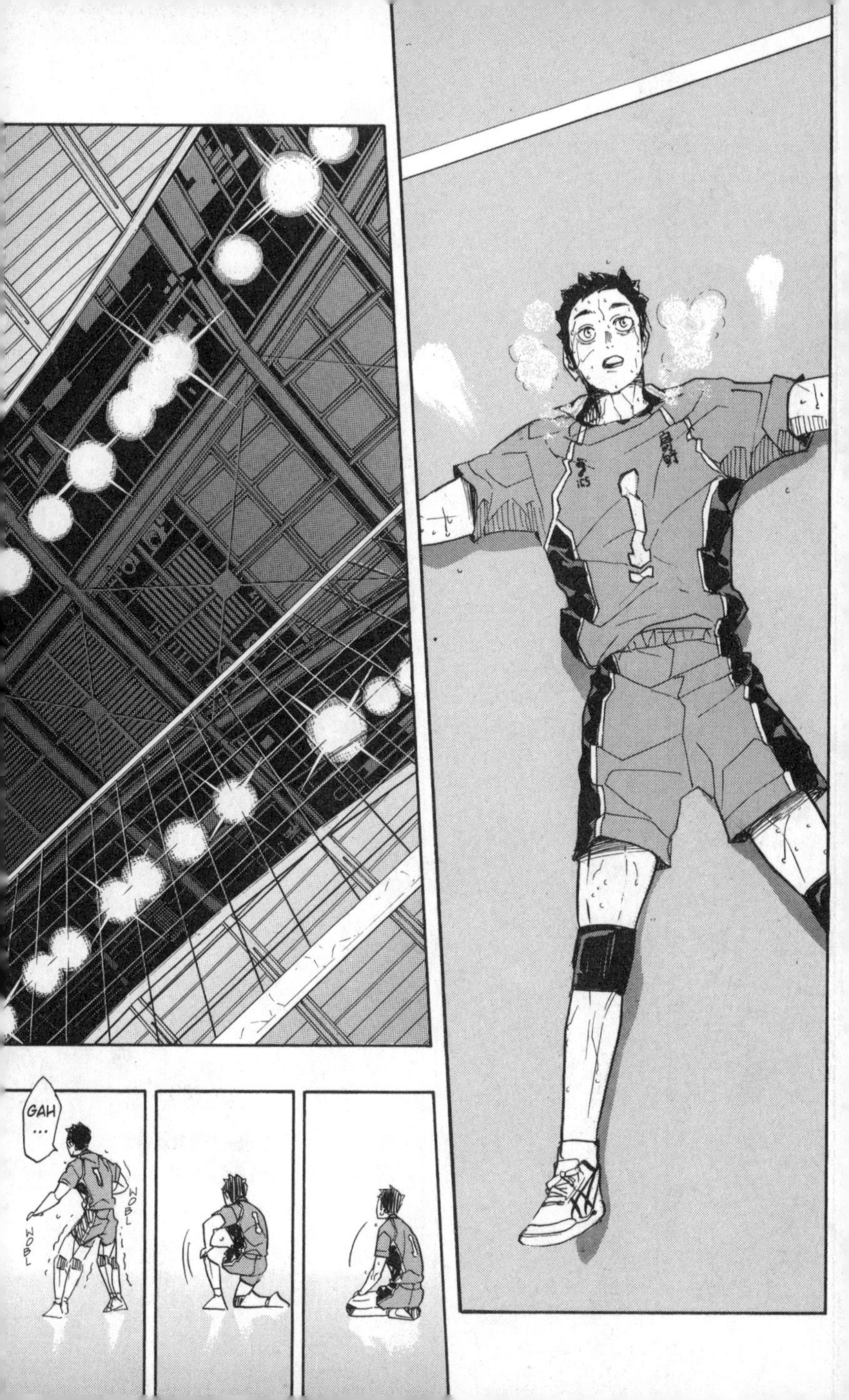
GAH …
WOBL
WOBL

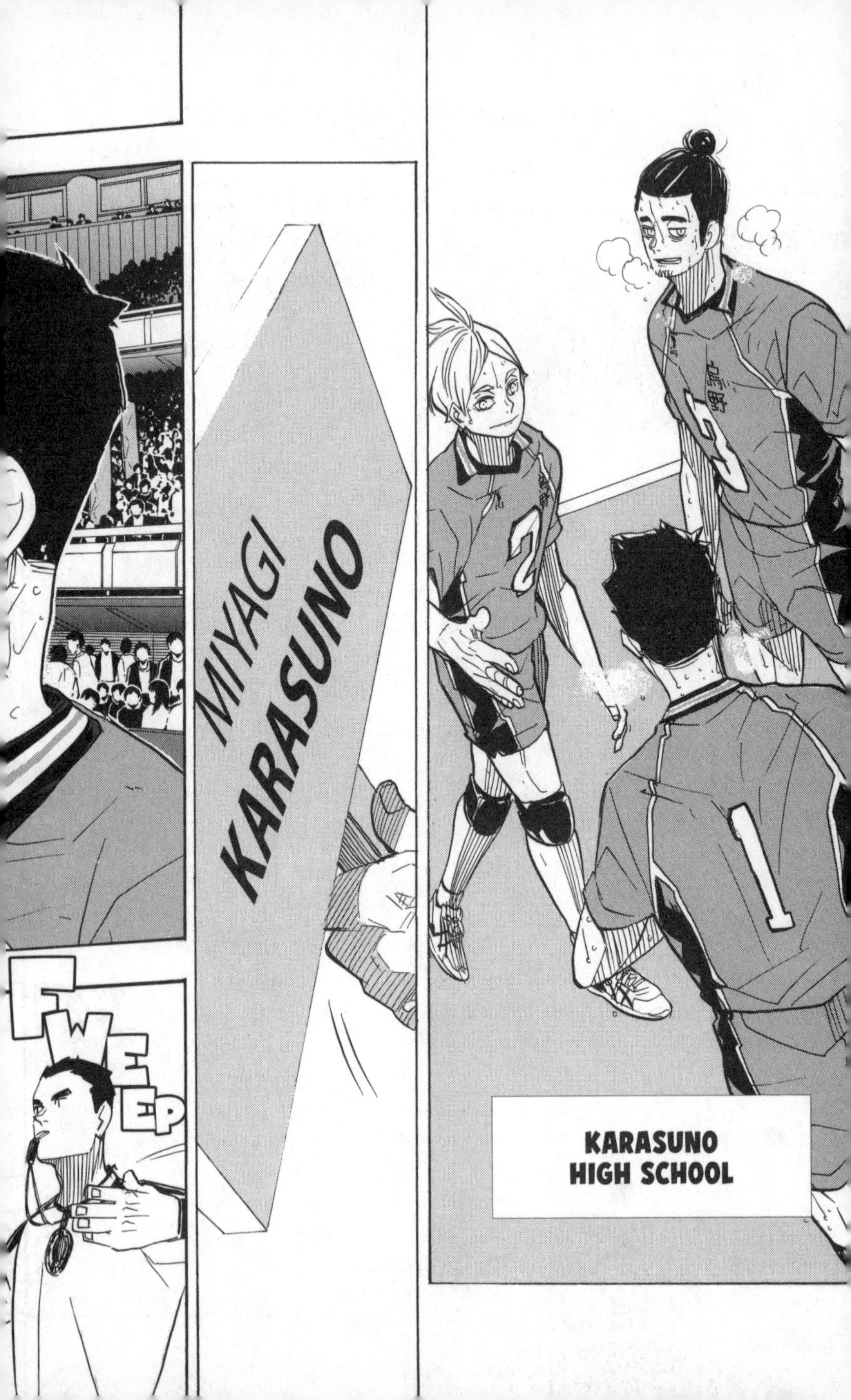
KARASUNO
HIGH SCHOOL
MIYAGI
KARASUNO
FWEEP

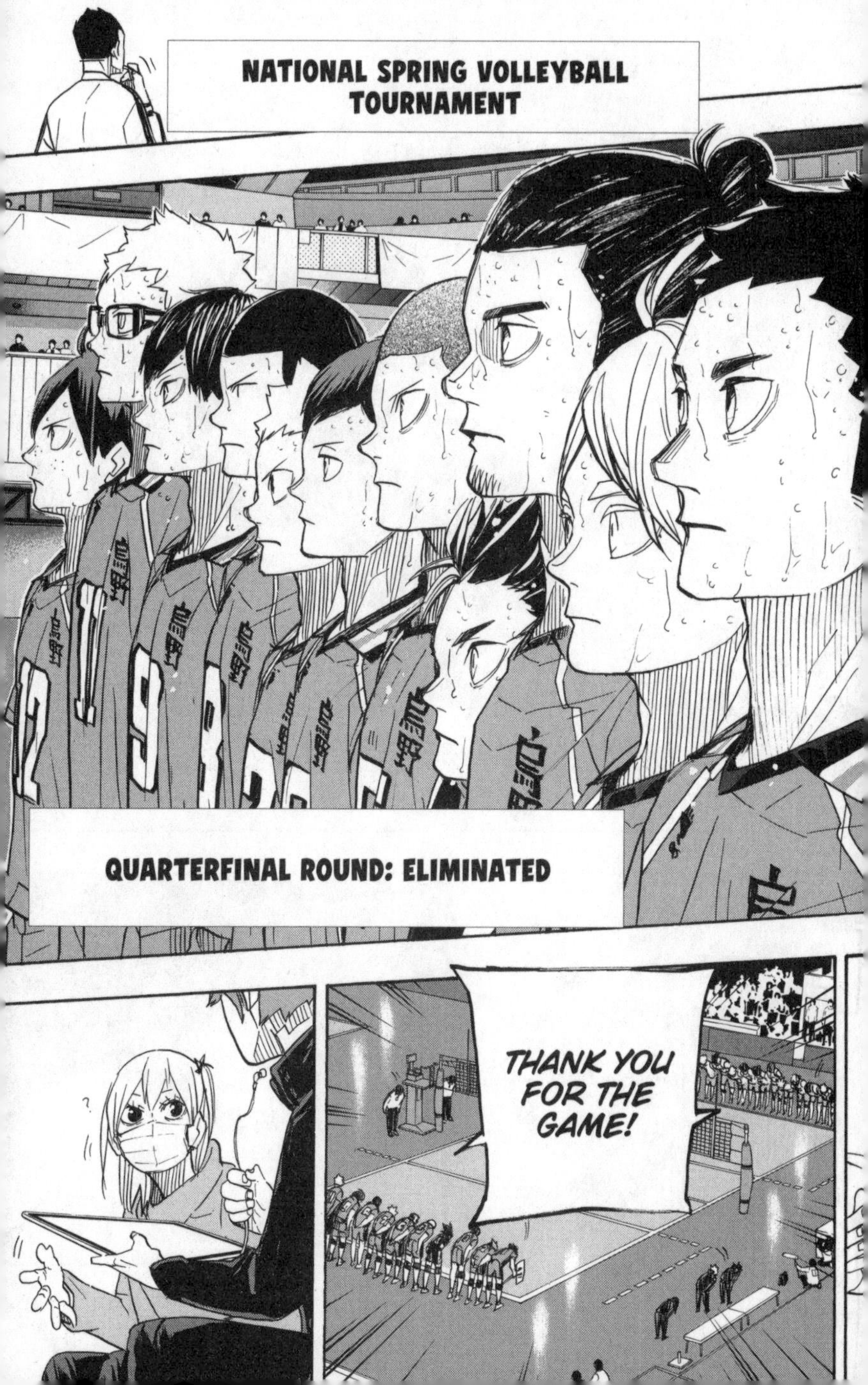
NATIONAL SPRING VOLLEYBALL TOURNAMENT
QUARTERFINAL ROUND: ELIMINATED
THANK YOU FOR THE GAME!

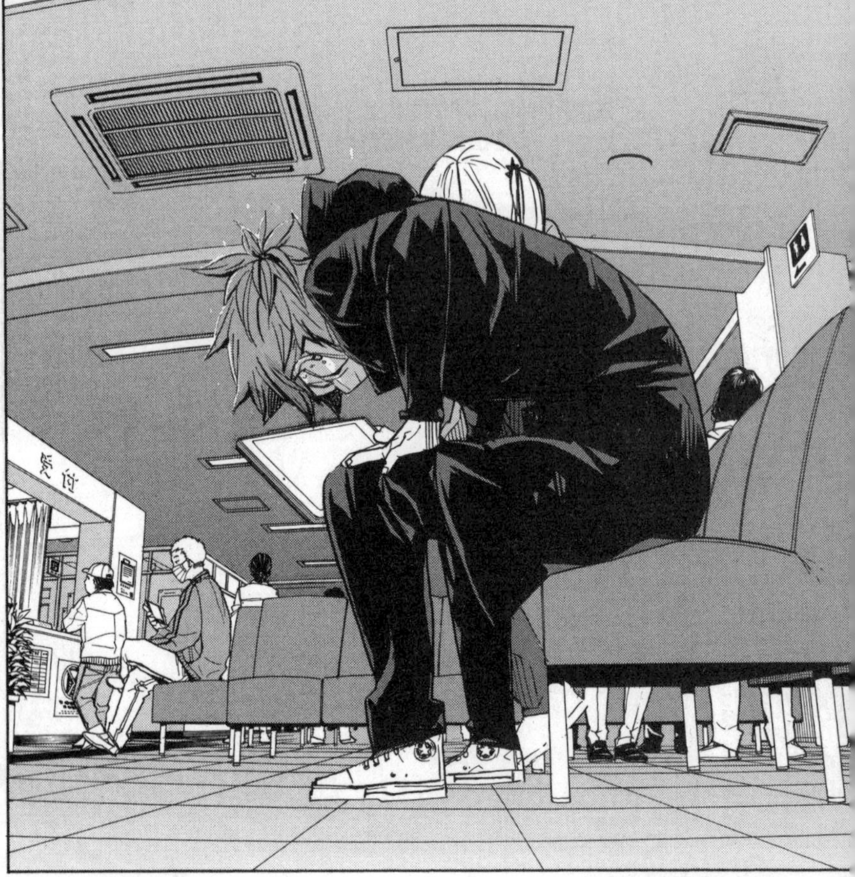
受付
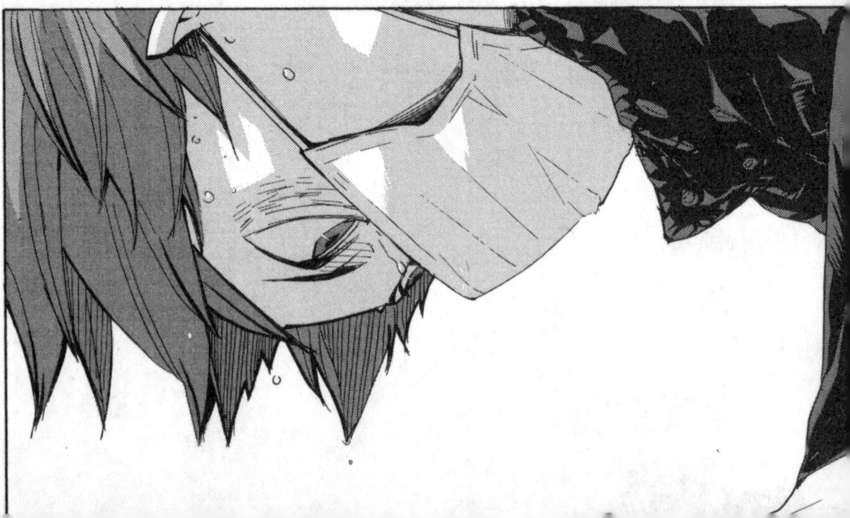

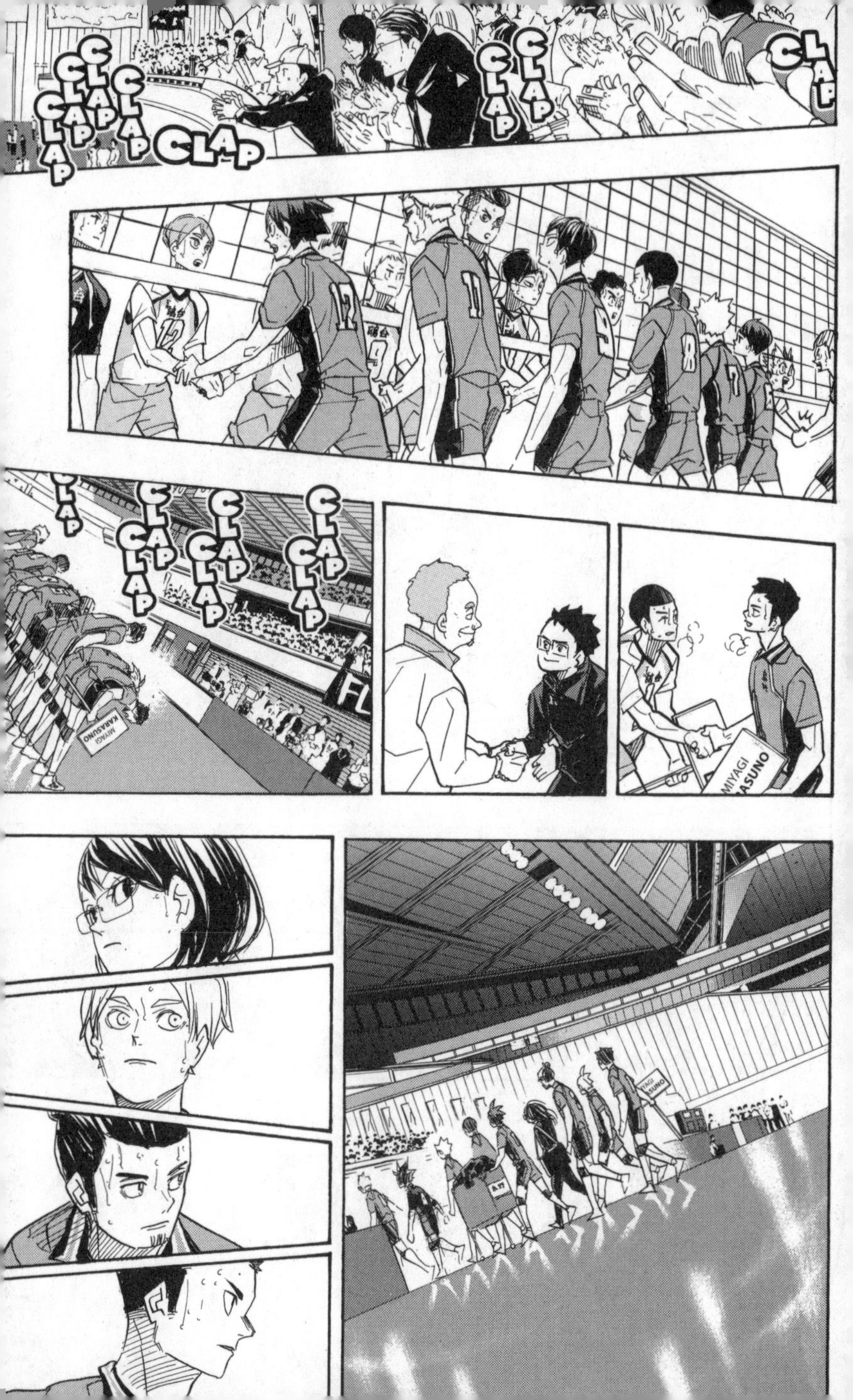
CLAP
CLAP
CLAP
CLAP
CLAP
CLAP
CLAP
CLAP
CLAP
CLAP
CLAP
CLAP
CLAP
CLAP
MIYAGI KARASUNO

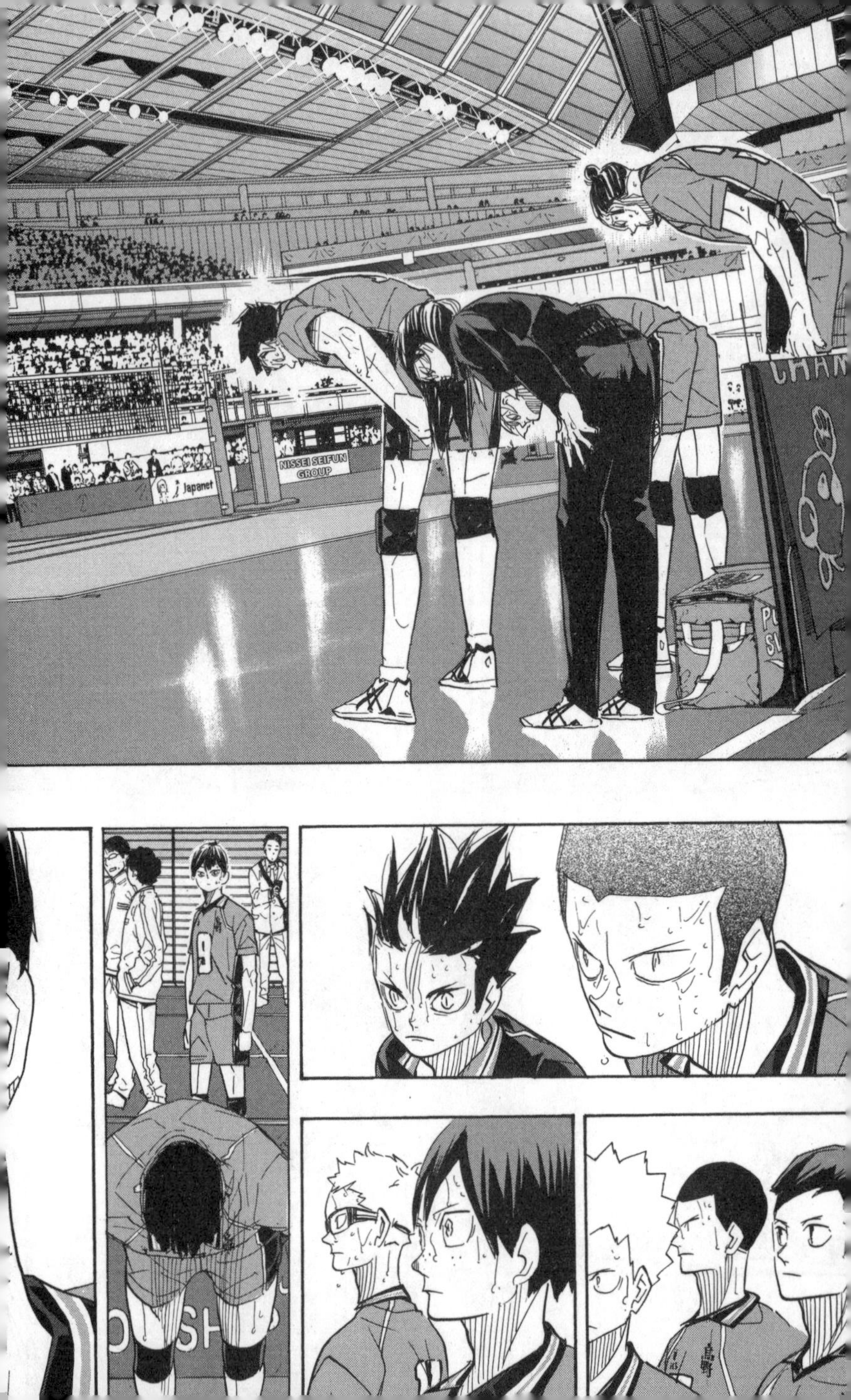
NISSEI SEIFUN
GROUP
Japanet

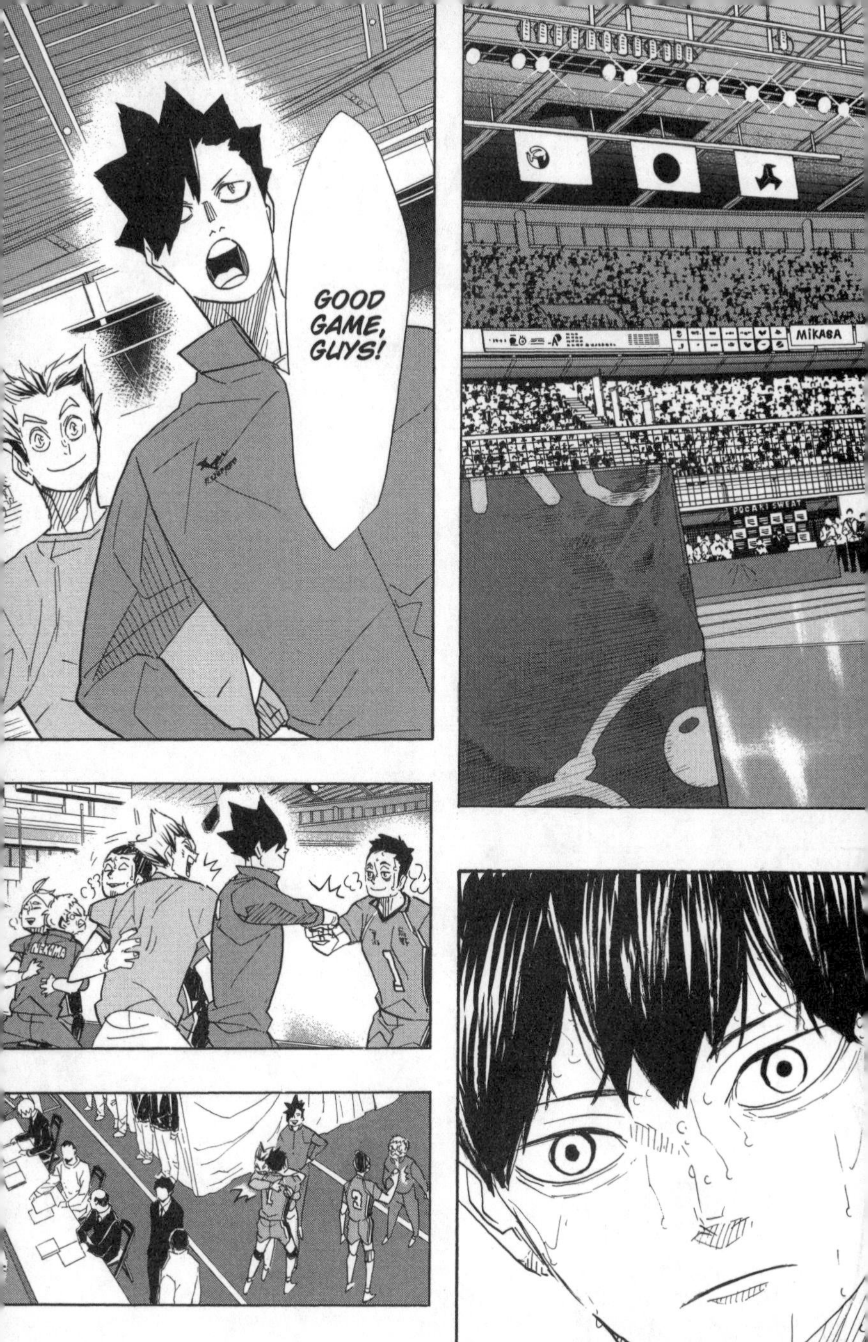
MIKASA
POCARI SWEAT
GOOD GAME, GUYS!
NEKOMA

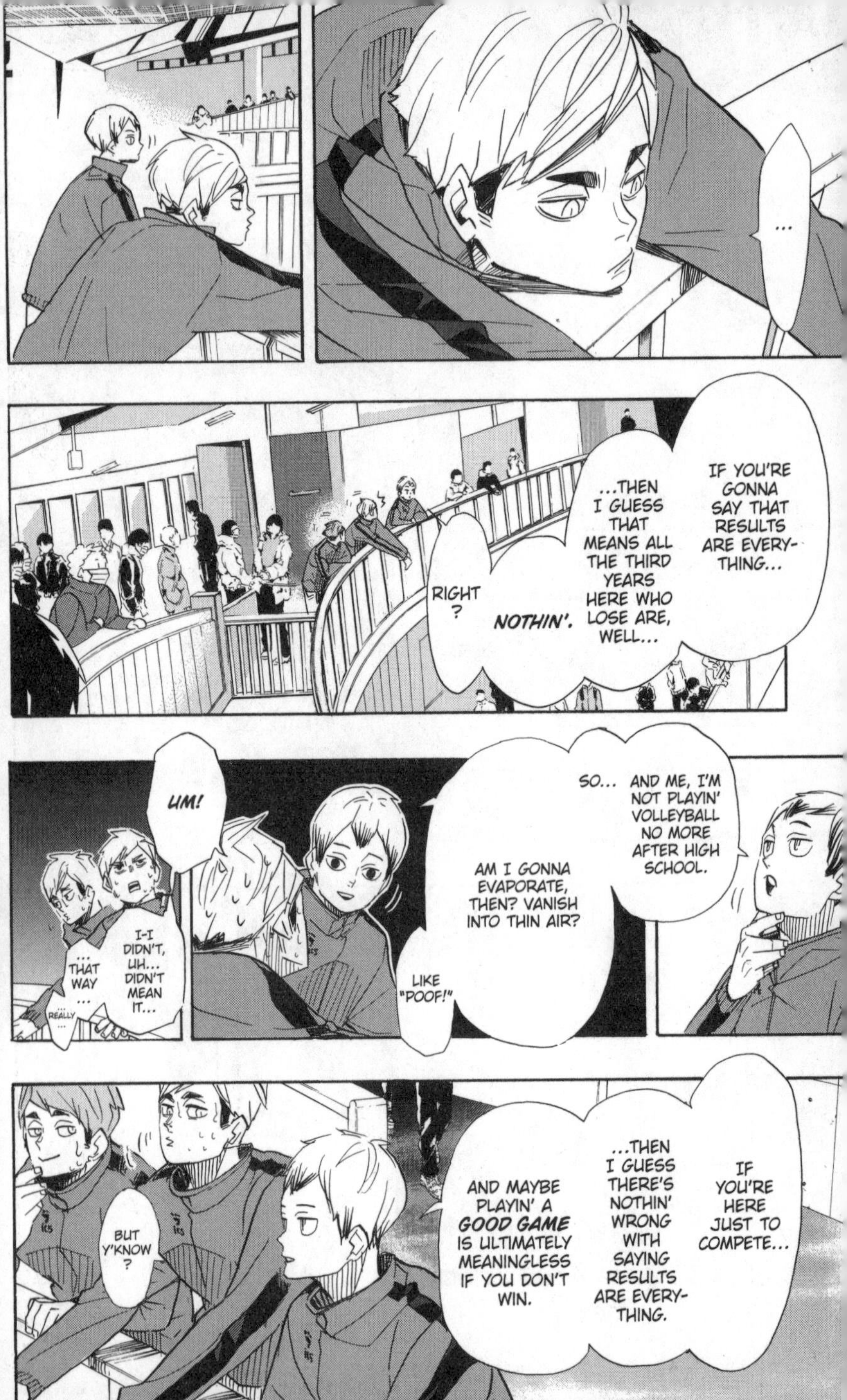
...
IF YOU'RE GONNA SAY THAT RESULTS ARE EVERY-THING...
...THEN I GUESS THAT MEANS ALL THE THIRD YEARS HERE WHO LOSE ARE, WELL...
NOTHIN'.
RIGHT?
SO... AND ME, I'M NOT PLAYIN' VOLLEYBALL NO MORE AFTER HIGH SCHOOL.
AM I GONNA EVAPORATE, THEN? VANISH INTO THIN AIR?
LIKE "POOF!"
UM!
I-I DIDN'T, UH... DIDN'T MEAN IT...
...THAT WAY...
...REALLY...
IF YOU'RE HERE JUST TO COMPETE...
...THEN I GUESS THERE'S NOTHIN' WRONG WITH SAYING RESULTS ARE EVERY-THING.
AND MAYBE PLAYIN' A GOOD GAME IS ULTIMATELY MEANINGLESS IF YOU DON'T WIN.
BUT Y'KNOW?

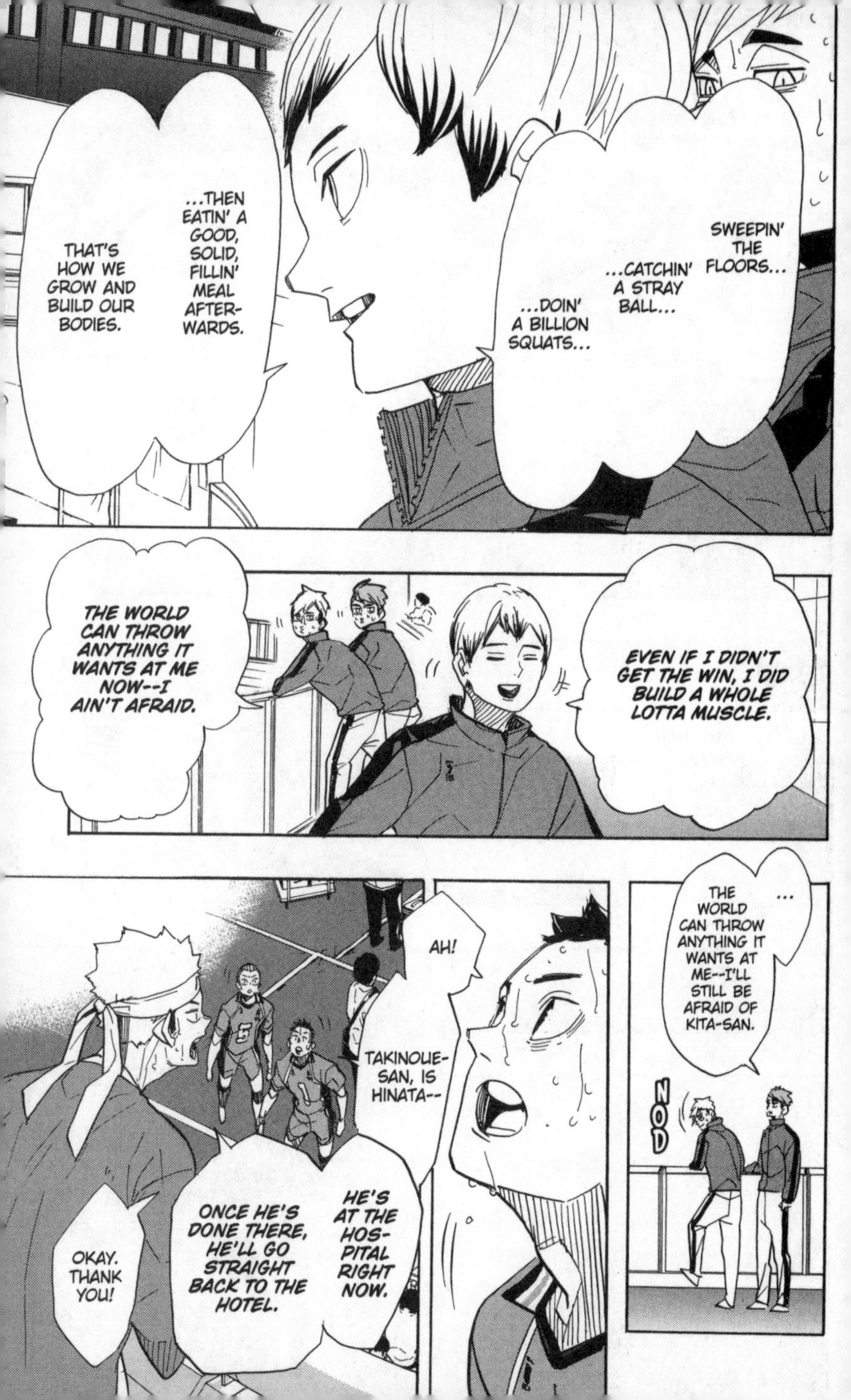
SWEEPIN' THE FLOORS...
...CATCHIN' A STRAY BALL...
...DOIN' A BILLION SQUATS...
...THEN EATIN' A GOOD, SOLID, FILLIN' MEAL AFTER-WARDS.
THAT'S HOW WE GROW AND BUILD OUR BODIES.
EVEN IF I DIDN'T GET THE WIN, I DID BUILD A WHOLE LOTTA MUSCLE.
THE WORLD CAN THROW ANYTHING IT WANTS AT ME NOW--I AIN'T AFRAID.
...
THE WORLD CAN THROW ANYTHING IT WANTS AT ME--I'LL STILL BE AFRAID OF KITA-SAN.
NOD
AH!
TAKINOUE-SAN, IS HINATA--
HE'S AT THE HOS-PITAL RIGHT NOW.
ONCE HE'S DONE THERE, HE'LL GO STRAIGHT BACK TO THE HOTEL.
OKAY. THANK YOU!

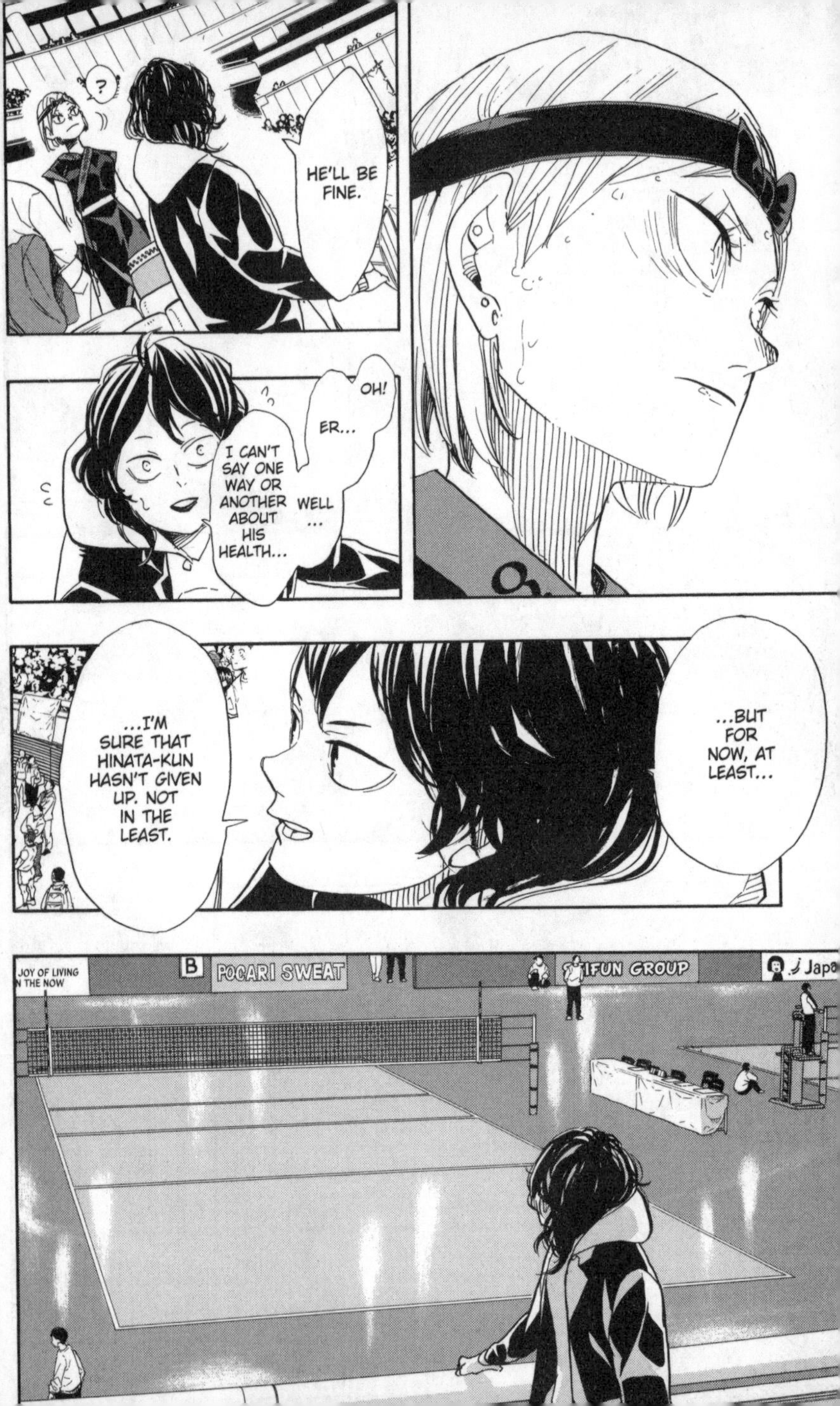

?
HE'LL BE FINE.
OH!
ER...
WELL...
I CAN'T SAY ONE WAY OR ANOTHER ABOUT HIS HEALTH...
...BUT FOR NOW, AT LEAST...
...I'M SURE THAT HINATA-KUN HASN'T GIVEN UP. NOT IN THE LEAST.
POCARI SWEAT
B
JOY OF LIVING

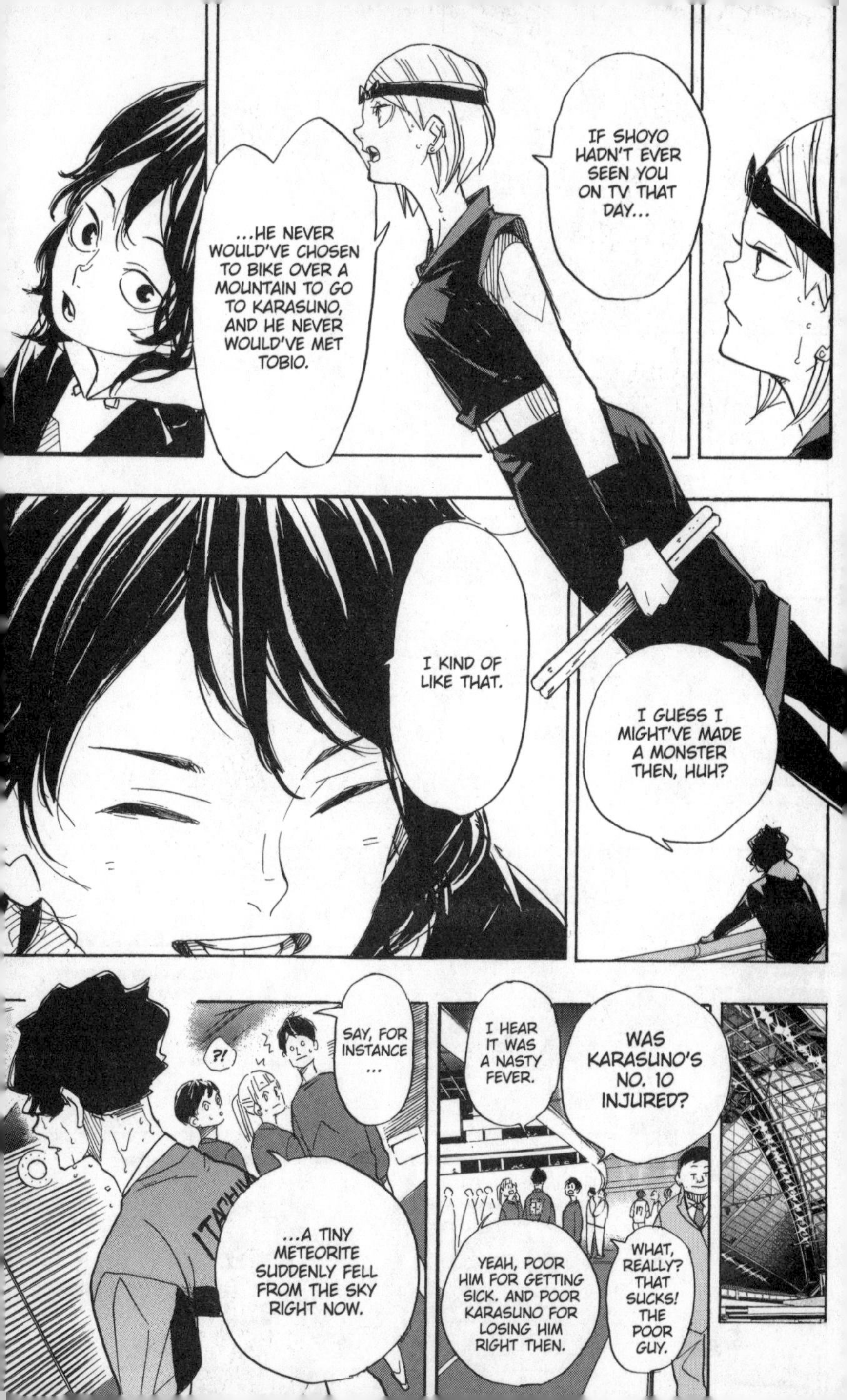
IF SHOYO HADN'T EVER SEEN YOU ON TV THAT DAY...
...HE NEVER WOULD'VE CHOSEN TO BIKE OVER A MOUNTAIN TO GO TO KARASUNO, AND HE NEVER WOULD'VE MET TOBIO.
I GUESS I MIGHT'VE MADE A MONSTER THEN, HUH?
I KIND OF LIKE THAT.
WAS KARASUNO'S NO. 10 INJURED?
I HEAR IT WAS A NASTY FEVER.
WHAT, REALLY? THAT SUCKS! THE POOR GUY.
YEAH, POOR HIM FOR GETTING SICK. AND POOR KARASUNO FOR LOSING HIM RIGHT THEN.
?!
SAY, FOR INSTANCE ...
...A TINY METEORITE SUDDENLY FELL FROM THE SKY RIGHT NOW.

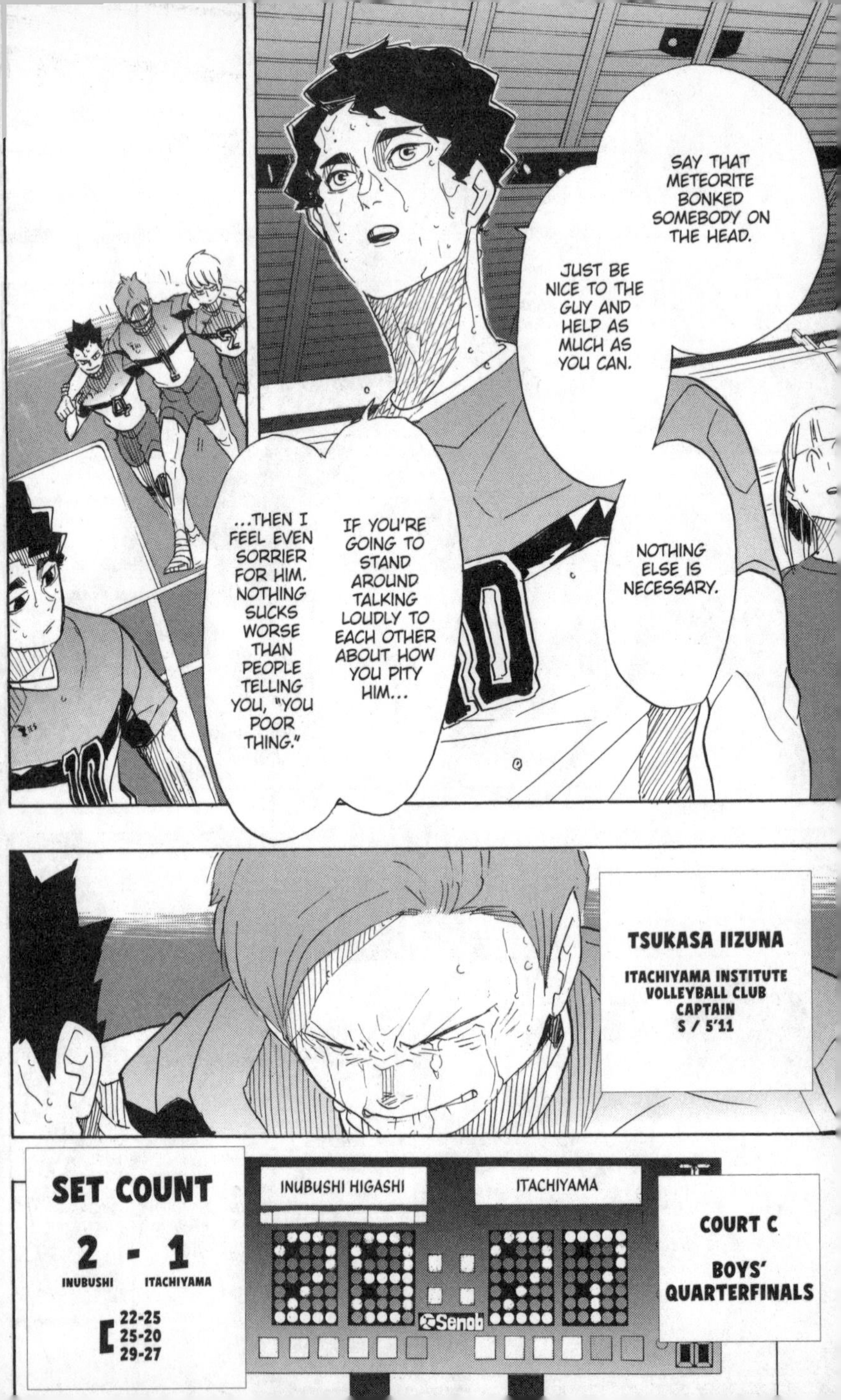
SAY THAT METEORITE BONKED SOMEBODY ON THE HEAD.
JUST BE NICE TO THE GUY AND HELP AS MUCH AS YOU CAN.
NOTHING ELSE IS NECESSARY.
IF YOU'RE GOING TO STAND AROUND TALKING LOUDLY TO EACH OTHER ABOUT HOW YOU PITY HIM...
...THEN I FEEL EVEN SORRIER FOR HIM. NOTHING SUCKS WORSE THAN PEOPLE TELLING YOU, "YOU POOR THING."
TSUKASA IIZUNA
ITACHIYAMA INSTITUTE VOLLEYBALL CLUB CAPTAIN
S / 5'11
COURT C
BOYS' QUARTERFINALS
INUBUSHI HIGASHI
ITACHIYAMA
SET COUNT
2 - 1
INUBUSHI
ITACHIYAMA
22-25
25-20
29-27

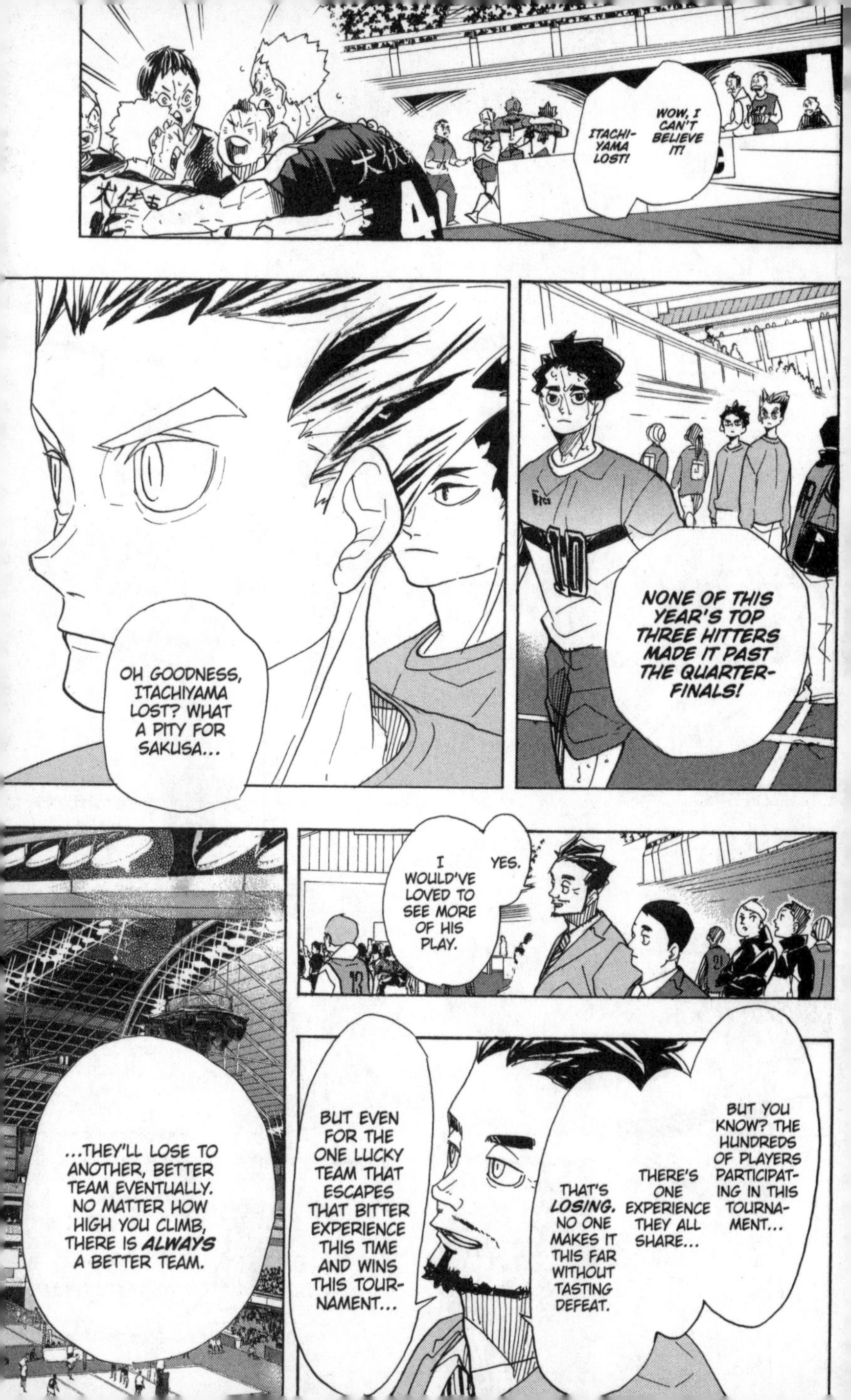
WOW, I CAN'T BELIEVE IT!
ITACHIYAMA LOST!
NONE OF THIS YEAR'S TOP THREE HITTERS MADE IT PAST THE QUARTER-FINALS!
OH GOODNESS, ITACHIYAMA LOST? WHAT A PITY FOR SAKUSA...
YES.
I WOULD'VE LOVED TO SEE MORE OF HIS PLAY.
BUT YOU KNOW? THE HUNDREDS OF PLAYERS PARTICIPATING IN THIS TOURNAMENT...
THERE'S ONE EXPERIENCE THEY ALL SHARE...
THAT'S **LOSING.** NO ONE MAKES IT THIS FAR WITHOUT TASTING DEFEAT.
BUT EVEN FOR THE ONE LUCKY TEAM THAT ESCAPES THAT BITTER EXPERIENCE THIS TIME AND WINS THIS TOURNAMENT...
...THEY'LL LOSE TO ANOTHER, BETTER TEAM EVENTUALLY. NO MATTER HOW HIGH YOU CLIMB, THERE IS ***ALWAYS*** A BETTER TEAM.

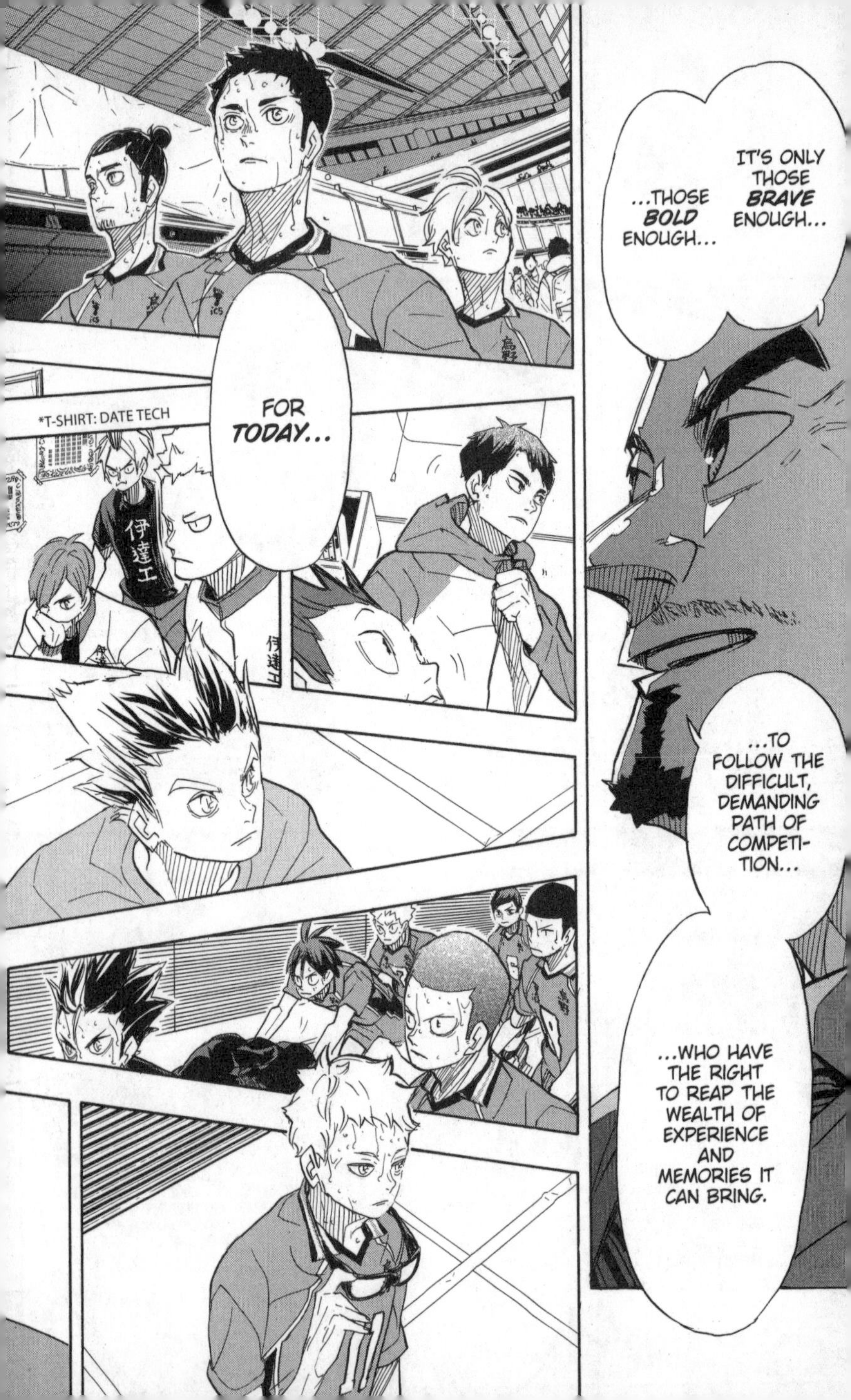
IT'S ONLY THOSE BRAVE ENOUGH...
...THOSE BOLD ENOUGH...
...TO FOLLOW THE DIFFICULT, DEMANDING PATH OF COMPETITION...
...WHO HAVE THE RIGHT TO REAP THE WEALTH OF EXPERIENCE AND MEMORIES IT CAN BRING.
FOR TODAY...
*T-SHIRT: DATE TECH
伊達工

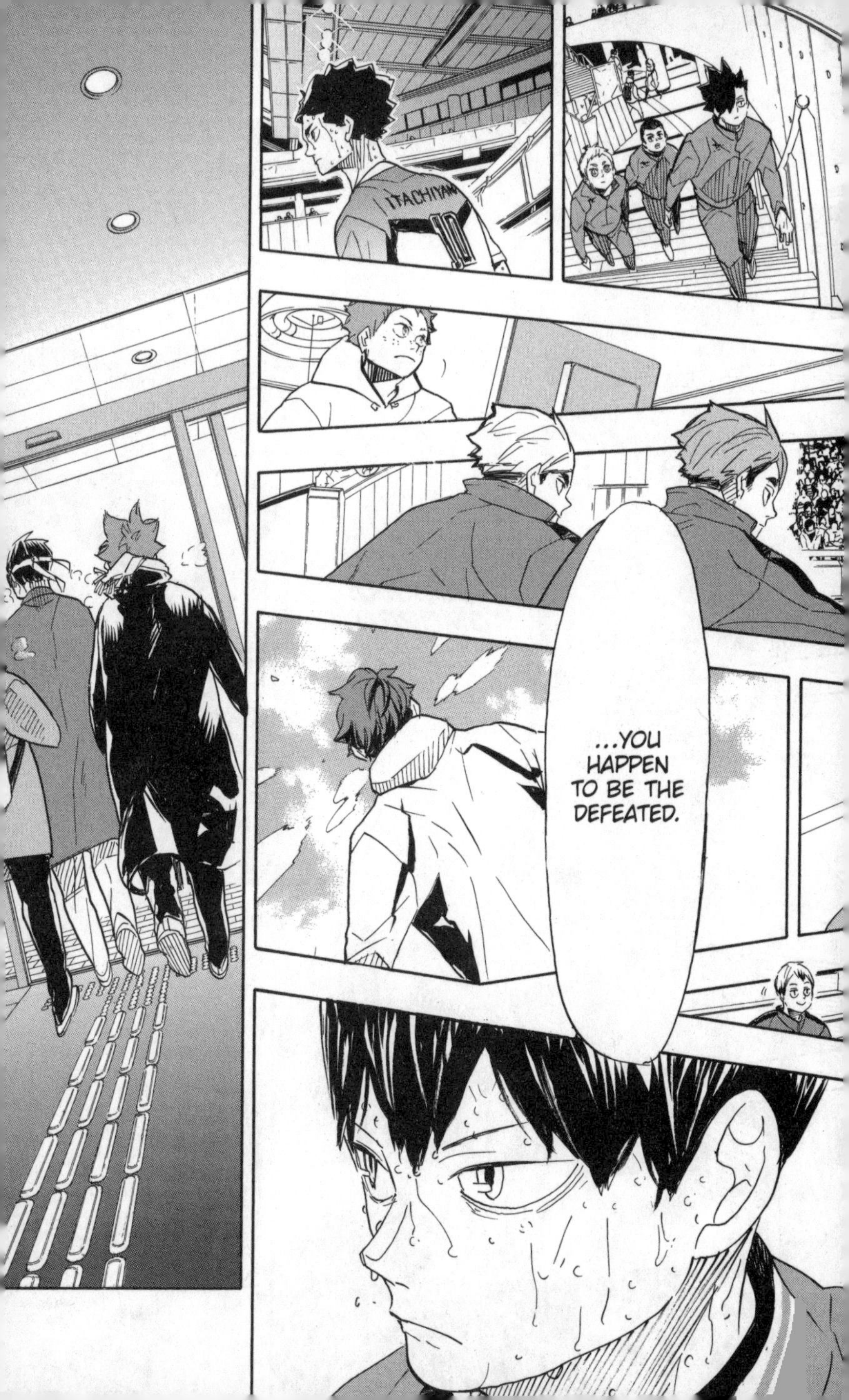
ITACHIYAMA
...YOU HAPPEN TO BE THE DEFEATED.

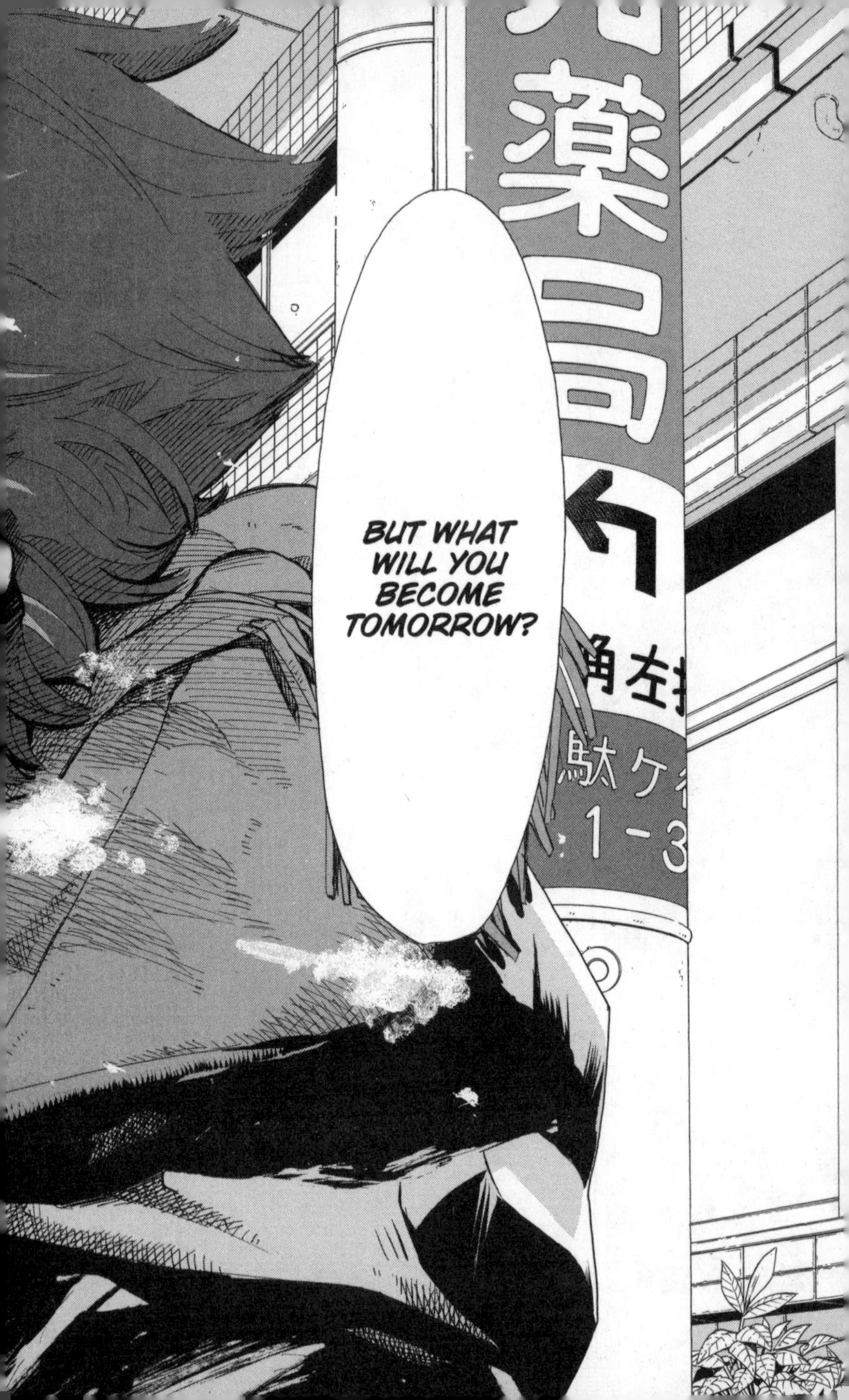
BUT WHAT WILL YOU BECOME TOMORROW?
薬局

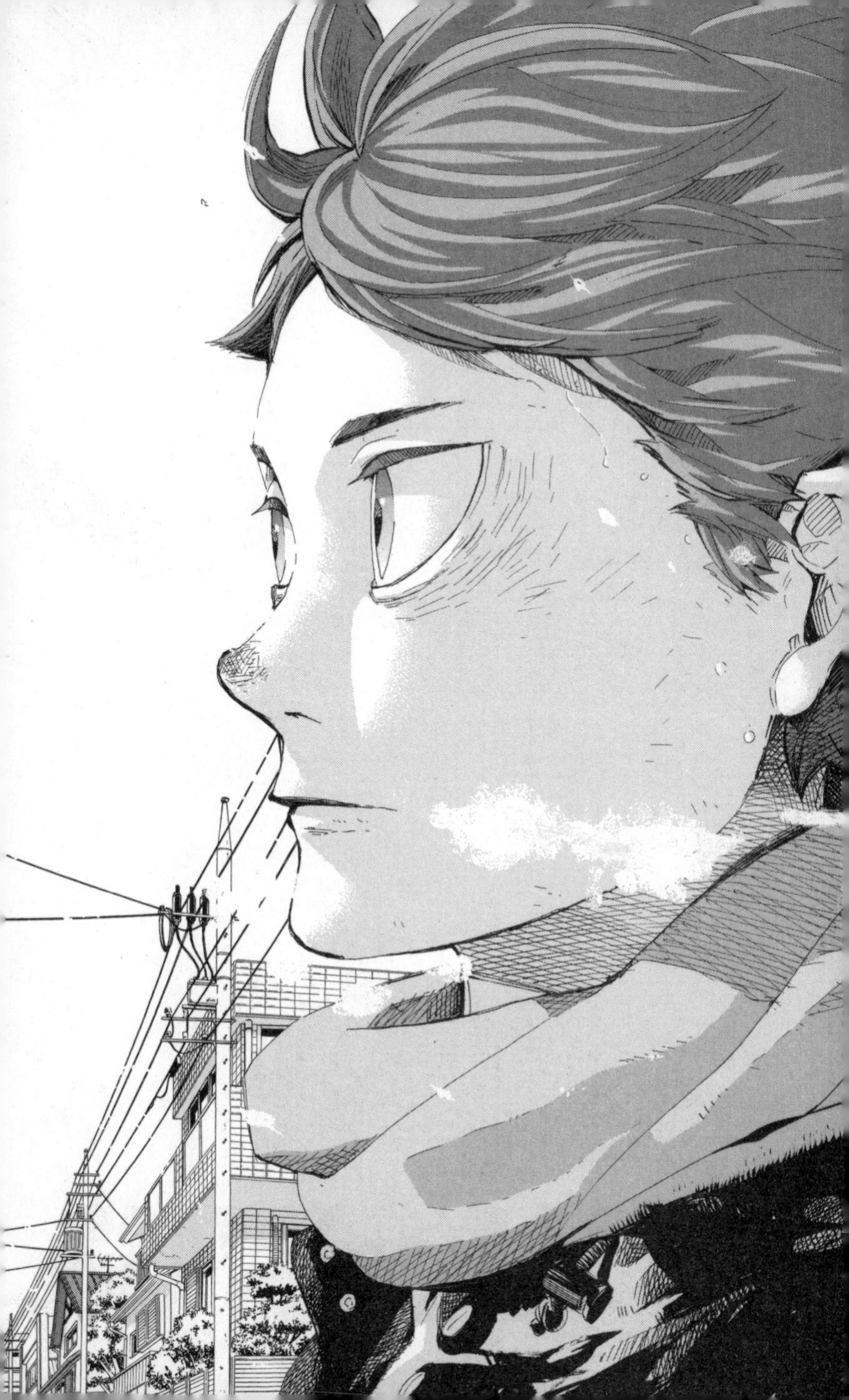

HAIKYU!!

CHAPTER 369: Food Becomes Muscle

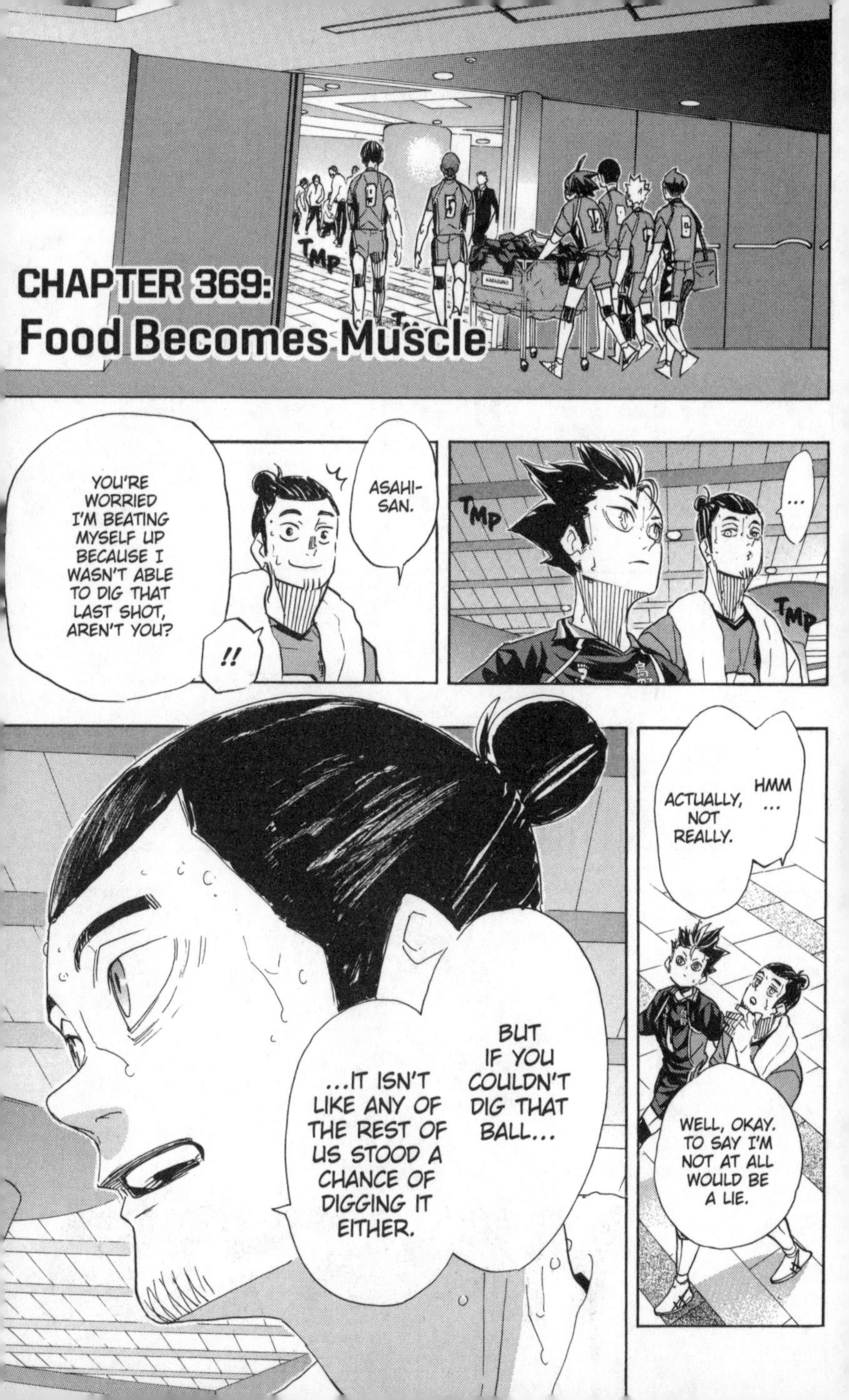
TMP
T...
...
TMP
TMP
ASAHI-SAN.
YOU'RE WORRIED I'M BEATING MYSELF UP BECAUSE I WASN'T ABLE TO DIG THAT LAST SHOT, AREN'T YOU?
!!
HMM...
ACTUALLY, NOT REALLY.
WELL, OKAY. TO SAY I'M NOT AT ALL WOULD BE A LIE.
BUT IF YOU COULDN'T DIG THAT BALL...
...IT ISN'T LIKE ANY OF THE REST OF US STOOD A CHANCE OF DIGGING IT EITHER.

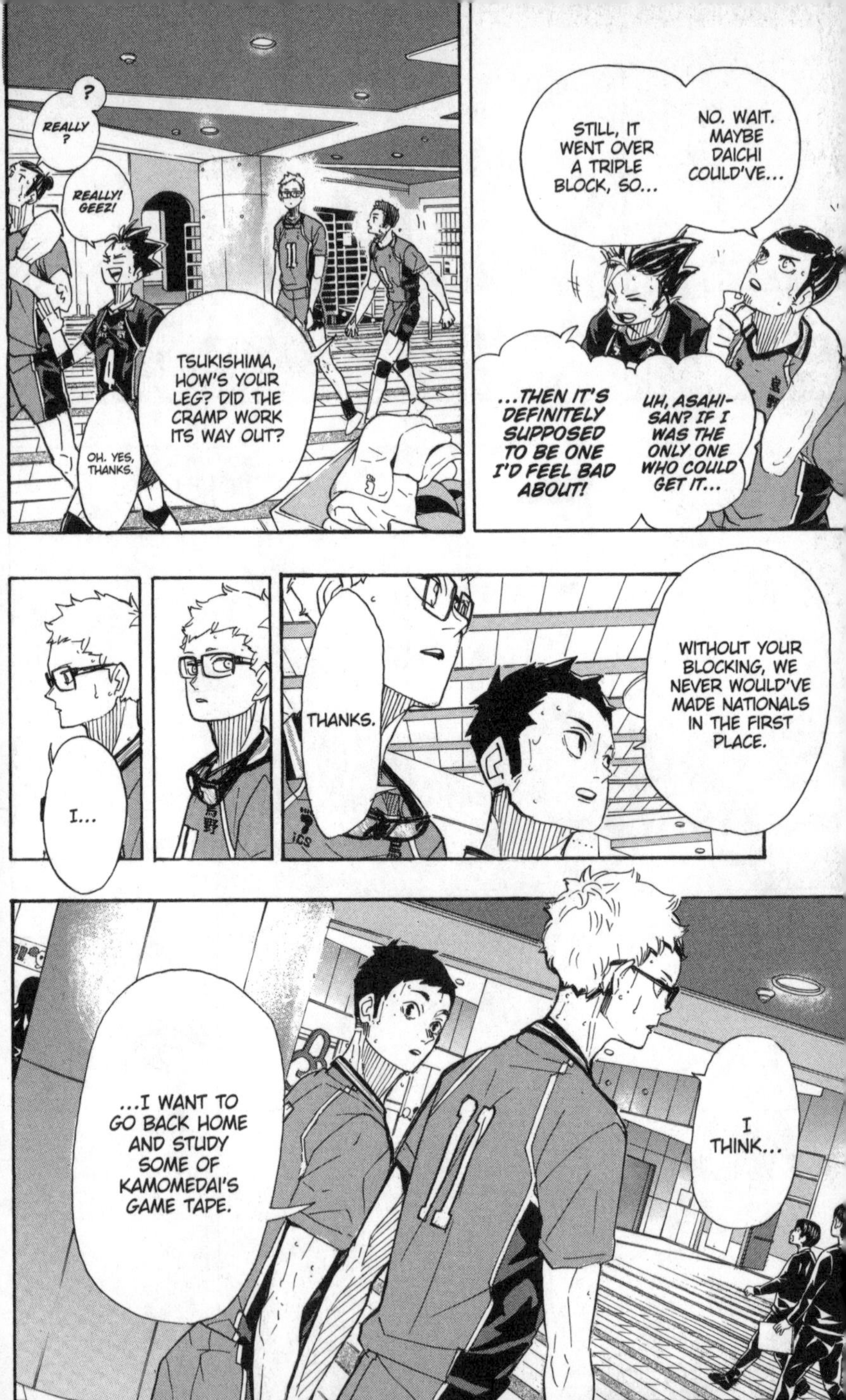
NO. WAIT. MAYBE DAICHI COULD'VE...
STILL, IT WENT OVER A TRIPLE BLOCK, SO...
UH, ASAHI-SAN? IF I WAS THE ONLY ONE WHO COULD GET IT...
...THEN IT'S DEFINITELY SUPPOSED TO BE ONE I'D FEEL BAD ABOUT!
?
REALLY?
REALLY! GEEZ!
TSUKISHIMA, HOW'S YOUR LEG? DID THE CRAMP WORK ITS WAY OUT?
OH. YES, THANKS.
WITHOUT YOUR BLOCKING, WE NEVER WOULD'VE MADE NATIONALS IN THE FIRST PLACE.
....
THANKS.
I...
I THINK...
...I WANT TO GO BACK HOME AND STUDY SOME OF KAMOMEDAI'S GAME TAPE.

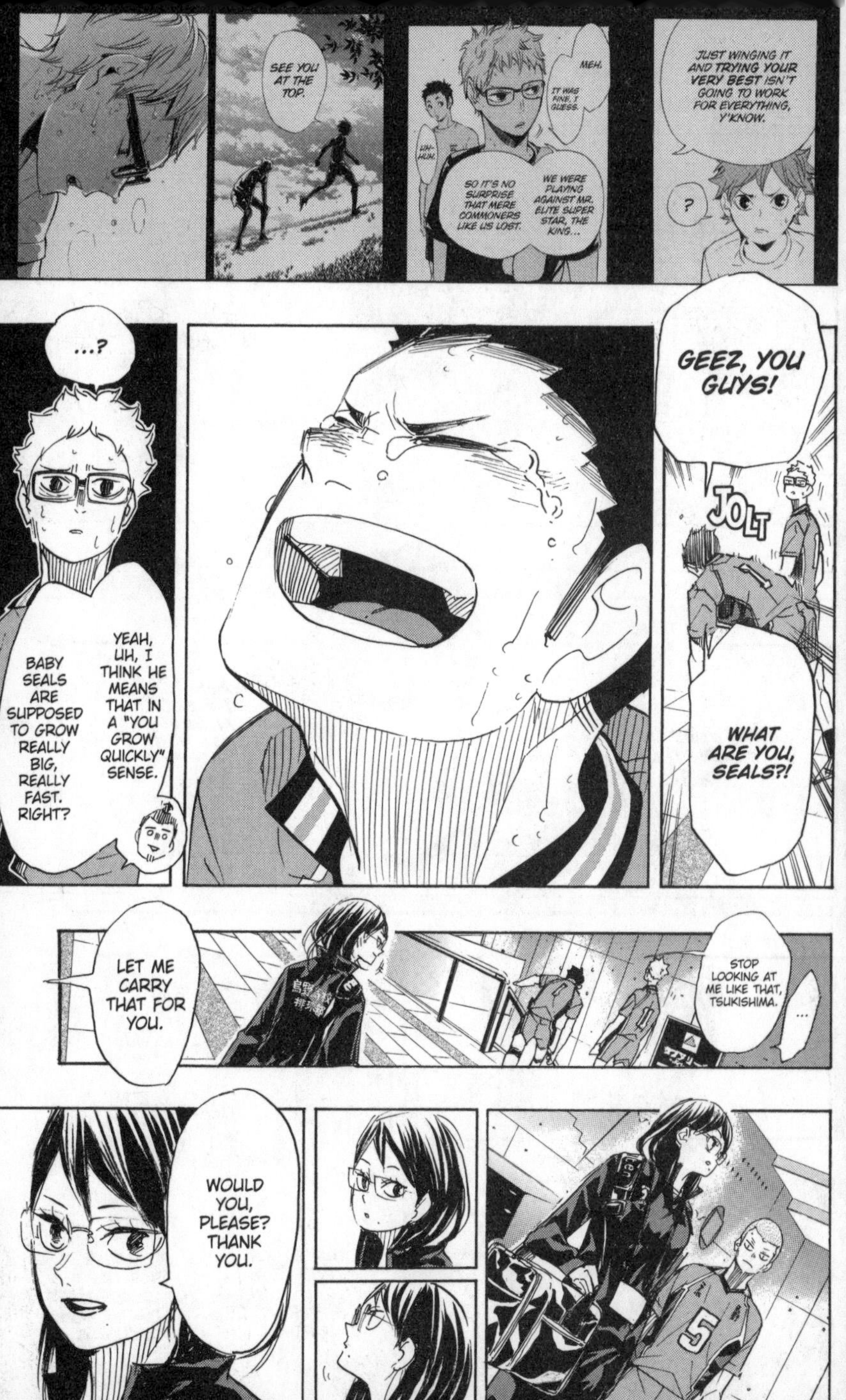
JUST WINGING IT AND TRYING YOUR VERY BEST ISN'T GOING TO WORK FOR EVERYTHING, Y'KNOW.
?
MEH.
IT WAS FINE, I GUESS.
UH-HUH.
WE WERE PLAYING AGAINST MR. ELITE SUPER STAR, THE KING...
SO IT'S NO SURPRISE THAT MERE COMMONERS LIKE US LOST.
SEE YOU AT THE TOP.
GEEZ, YOU GUYS!
JOLT
WHAT ARE YOU, SEALS?!
...?
YEAH, UH, I THINK HE MEANS THAT IN A "YOU GROW QUICKLY" SENSE.
BABY SEALS ARE SUPPOSED TO GROW REALLY BIG, REALLY FAST. RIGHT?
STOP LOOKING AT ME LIKE THAT, TSUKISHIMA.
...
LET ME CARRY THAT FOR YOU.
WOULD YOU, PLEASE? THANK YOU.

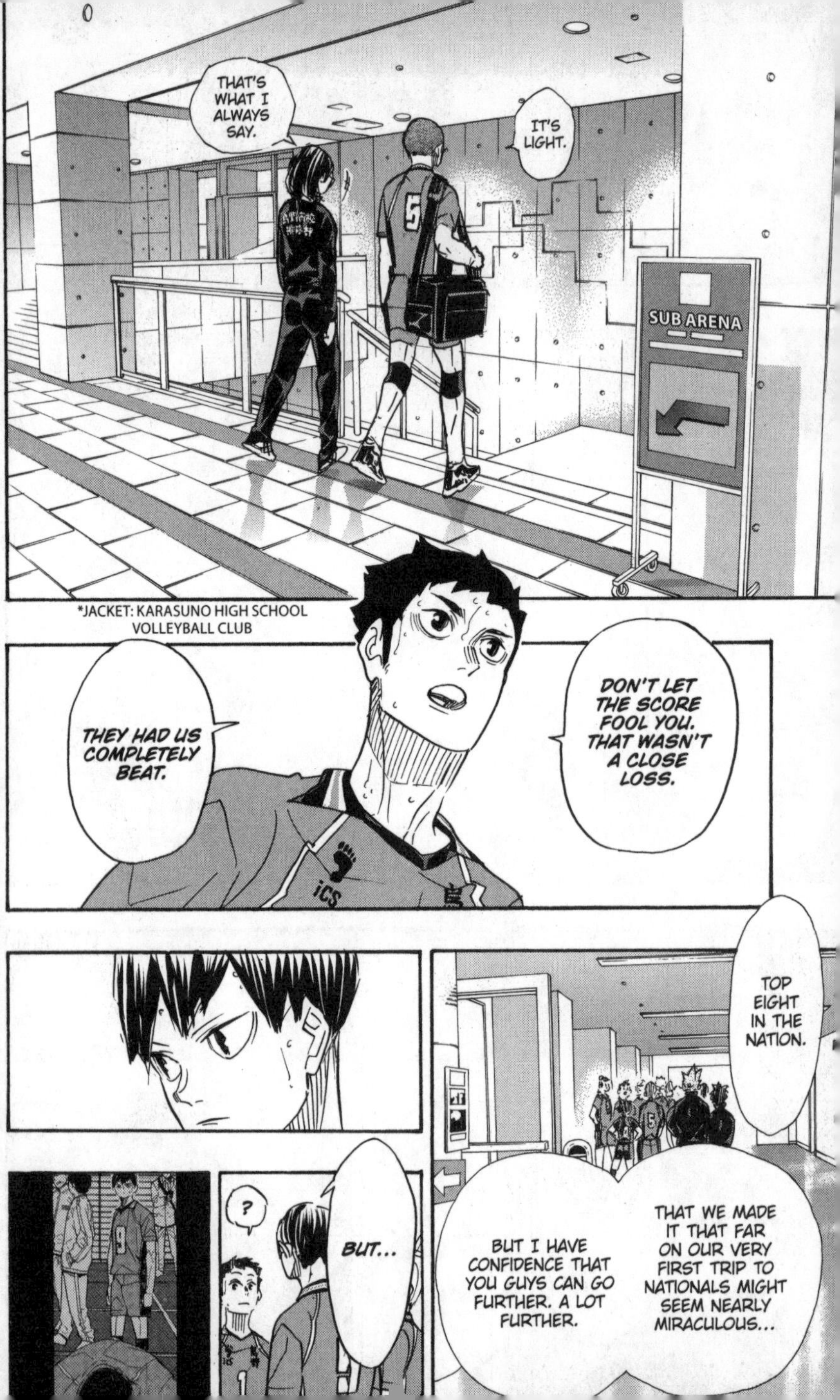
IT'S LIGHT.
THAT'S WHAT I ALWAYS SAY.
SUB ARENA
*JACKET: KARASUNO HIGH SCHOOL VOLLEYBALL CLUB
DON'T LET THE SCORE FOOL YOU. THAT WASN'T A CLOSE LOSS.
THEY HAD US COMPLETELY BEAT.
TOP EIGHT IN THE NATION.
THAT WE MADE IT THAT FAR ON OUR VERY FIRST TRIP TO NATIONALS MIGHT SEEM NEARLY MIRACULOUS...
BUT I HAVE CONFIDENCE THAT YOU GUYS CAN GO FURTHER. A LOT FURTHER.
BUT...
?

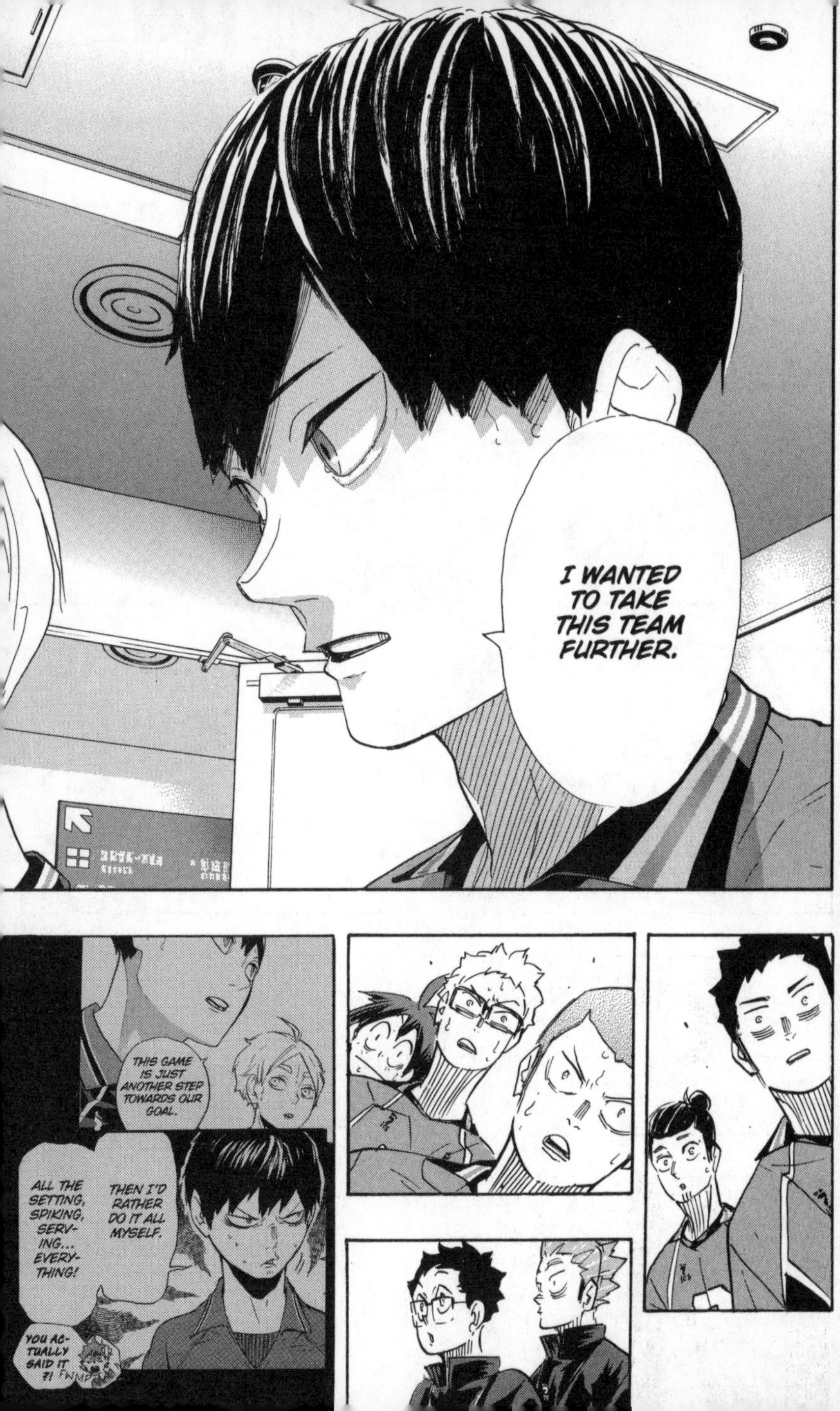
I WANTED TO TAKE THIS TEAM FURTHER.
THIS GAME IS JUST ANOTHER STEP TOWARDS OUR GOAL.
THEN I'D RATHER DO IT ALL MYSELF.
ALL THE SETTING, SPIKING, SERV-ING... EVERY-THING!
YOU AC-TUALLY SAID IT ?!
FWMP

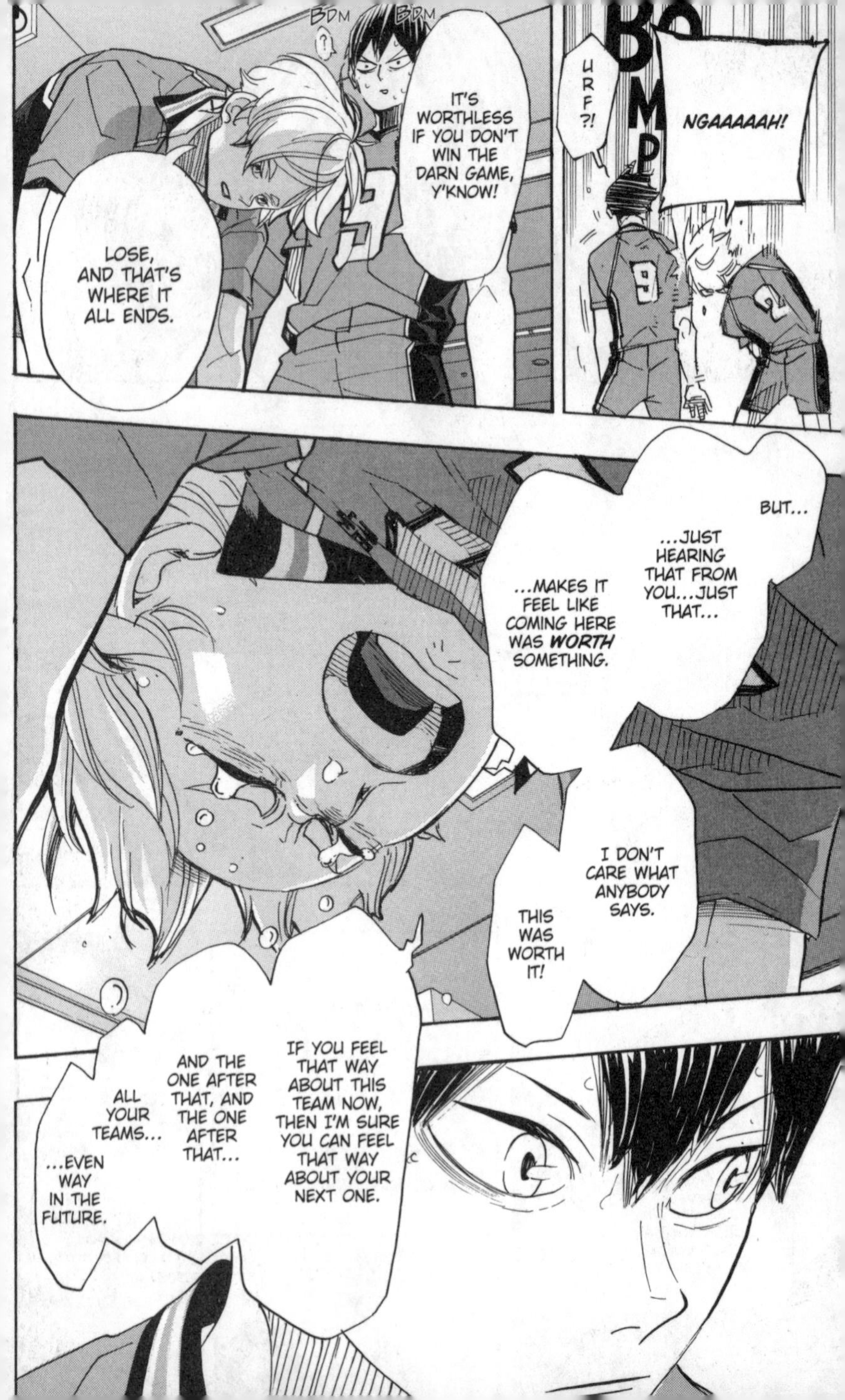
NGAAAAH!
BOMP
URF?!
BDM BDM
?
IT'S WORTHLESS IF YOU DON'T WIN THE DARN GAME, Y'KNOW!
LOSE, AND THAT'S WHERE IT ALL ENDS.
BUT...
...JUST HEARING THAT FROM YOU...JUST THAT...
...MAKES IT FEEL LIKE COMING HERE WAS **WORTH** SOMETHING.
I DON'T CARE WHAT ANYBODY SAYS.
THIS WAS WORTH IT!
IF YOU FEEL THAT WAY ABOUT THIS TEAM NOW, THEN I'M SURE YOU CAN FEEL THAT WAY ABOUT YOUR NEXT ONE.
AND THE ONE AFTER THAT, AND THE ONE AFTER THAT...
ALL YOUR TEAMS...
...EVEN WAY IN THE FUTURE.

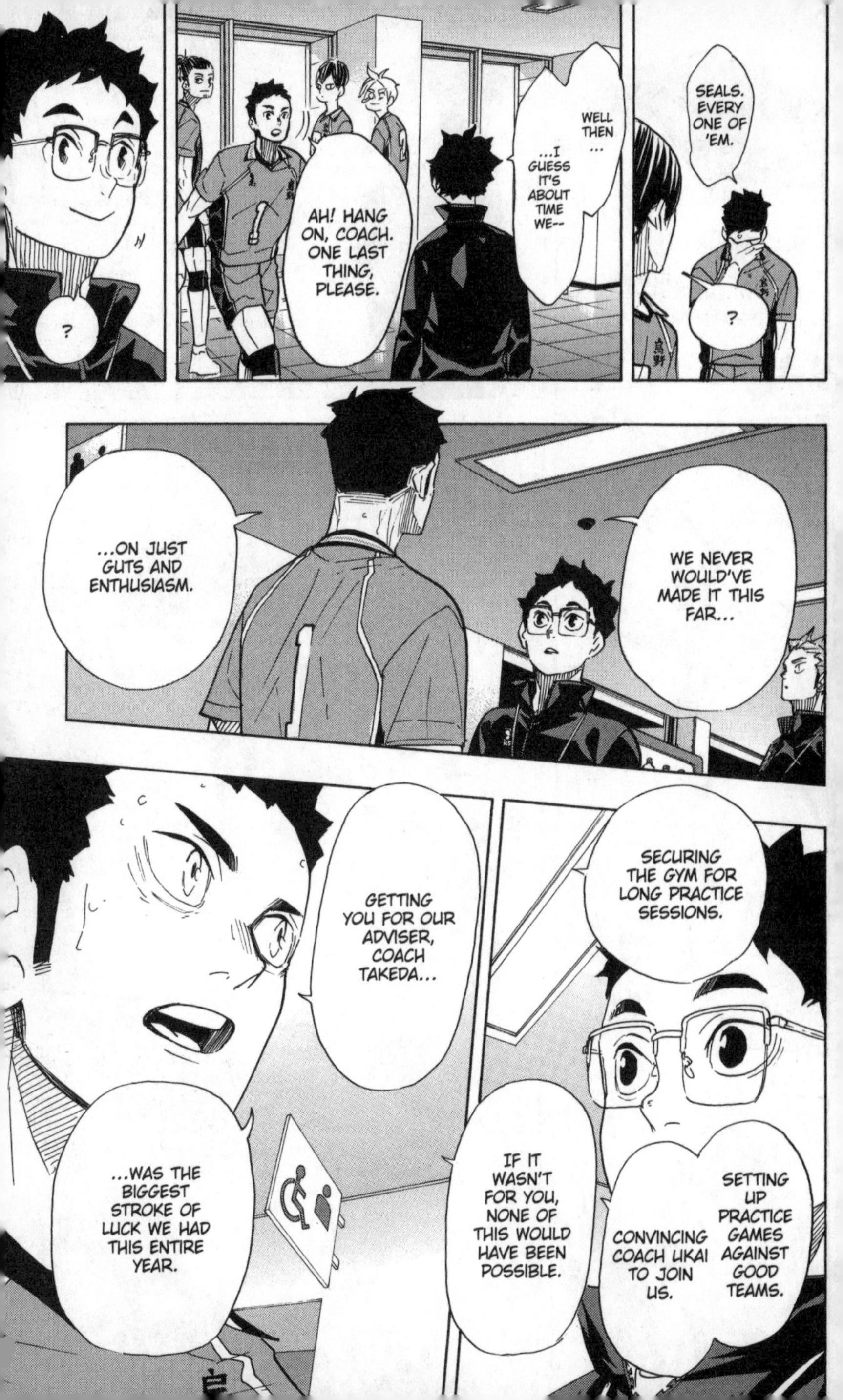
SEALS. EVERY ONE OF 'EM.
?
WELL THEN ...
...I GUESS IT'S ABOUT TIME WE--
AH! HANG ON, COACH. ONE LAST THING, PLEASE.
?
WE NEVER WOULD'VE MADE IT THIS FAR...
...ON JUST GUTS AND ENTHUSIASM.
SECURING THE GYM FOR LONG PRACTICE SESSIONS.
SETTING UP PRACTICE GAMES AGAINST GOOD TEAMS.
CONVINCING COACH UKAI TO JOIN US.
IF IT WASN'T FOR YOU, NONE OF THIS WOULD HAVE BEEN POSSIBLE.
GETTING YOU FOR OUR ADVISER, COACH TAKEDA...
...WAS THE BIGGEST STROKE OF LUCK WE HAD THIS ENTIRE YEAR.

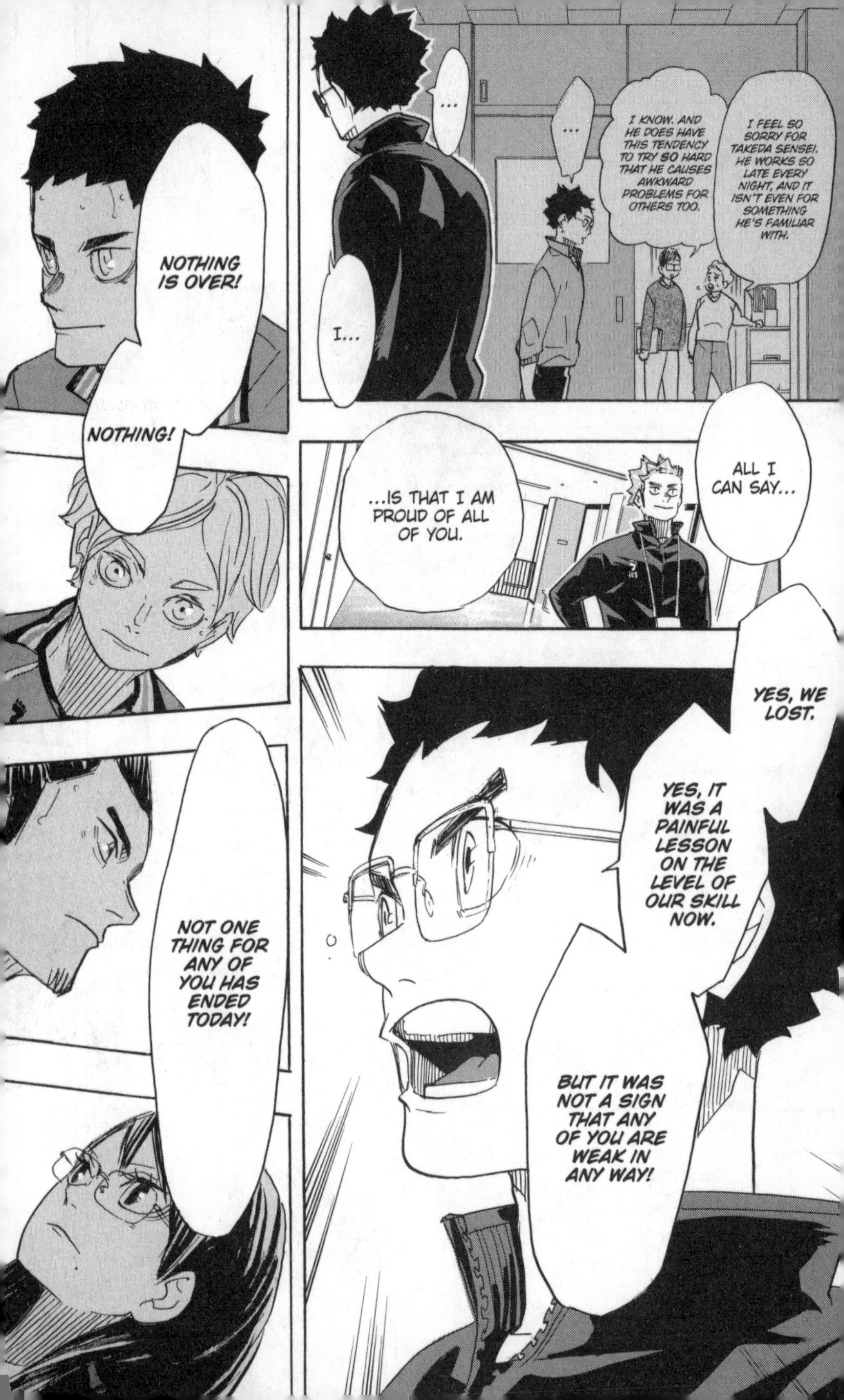
I FEEL SO SORRY FOR TAKEDA SENSEI. HE WORKS SO LATE EVERY NIGHT, AND IT ISN'T EVEN FOR SOMETHING HE'S FAMILIAR WITH.
I KNOW. AND HE DOES HAVE THIS TENDENCY TO TRY SO HARD THAT HE CAUSES AWKWARD PROBLEMS FOR OTHERS TOO.
...
...
I...
ALL I CAN SAY...
...IS THAT I AM PROUD OF ALL OF YOU.
YES, WE LOST.
YES, IT WAS A PAINFUL LESSON ON THE LEVEL OF OUR SKILL NOW.
BUT IT WAS NOT A SIGN THAT ANY OF YOU ARE WEAK IN ANY WAY!
NOT ONE THING FOR ANY OF YOU HAS ENDED TODAY!
NOTHING IS OVER!
NOTHING!

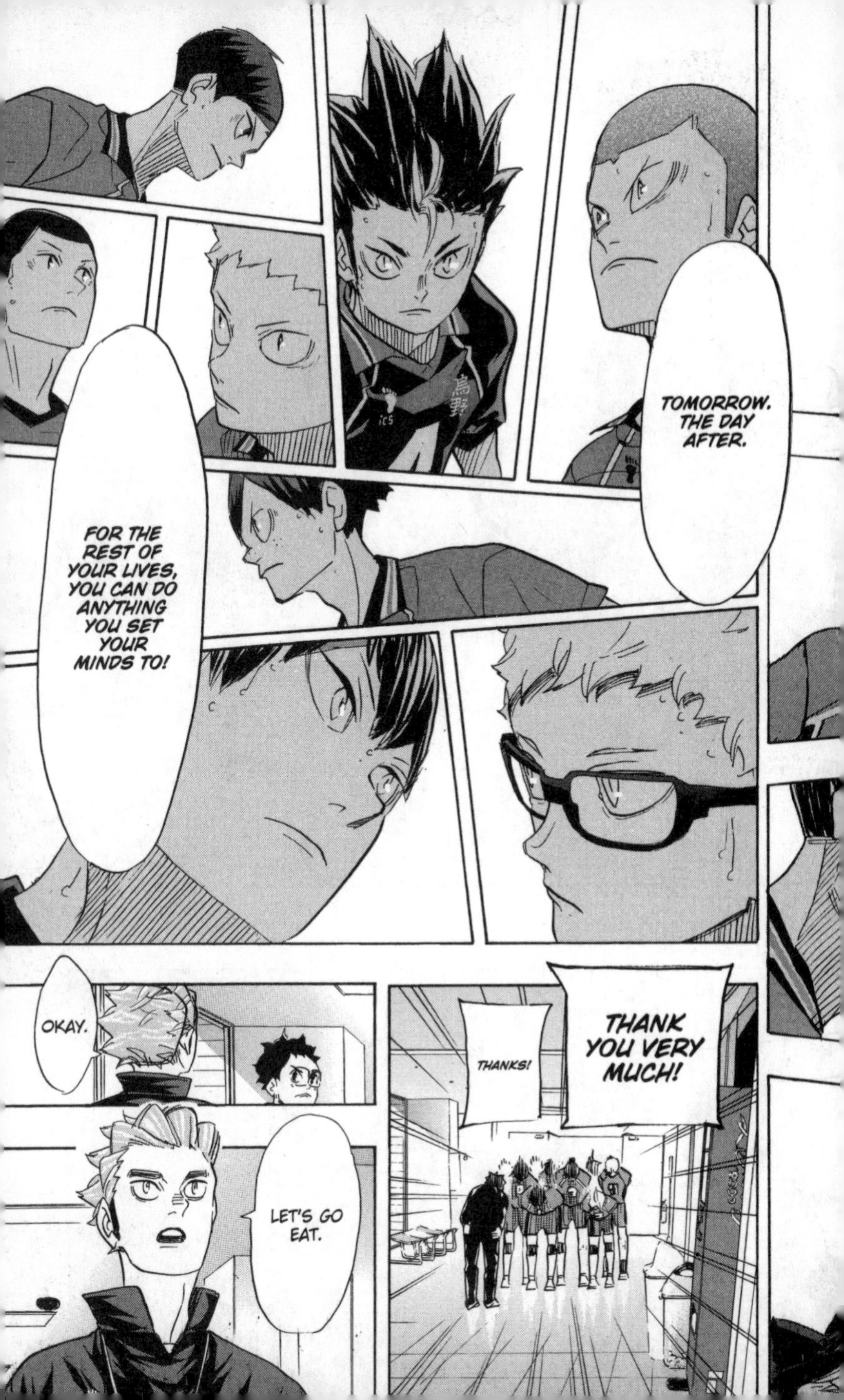
TOMORROW. THE DAY AFTER.
FOR THE REST OF YOUR LIVES, YOU CAN DO ANYTHING YOU SET YOUR MINDS TO!
THANK YOU VERY MUCH!
THANKS!
OKAY.
LET'S GO EAT.

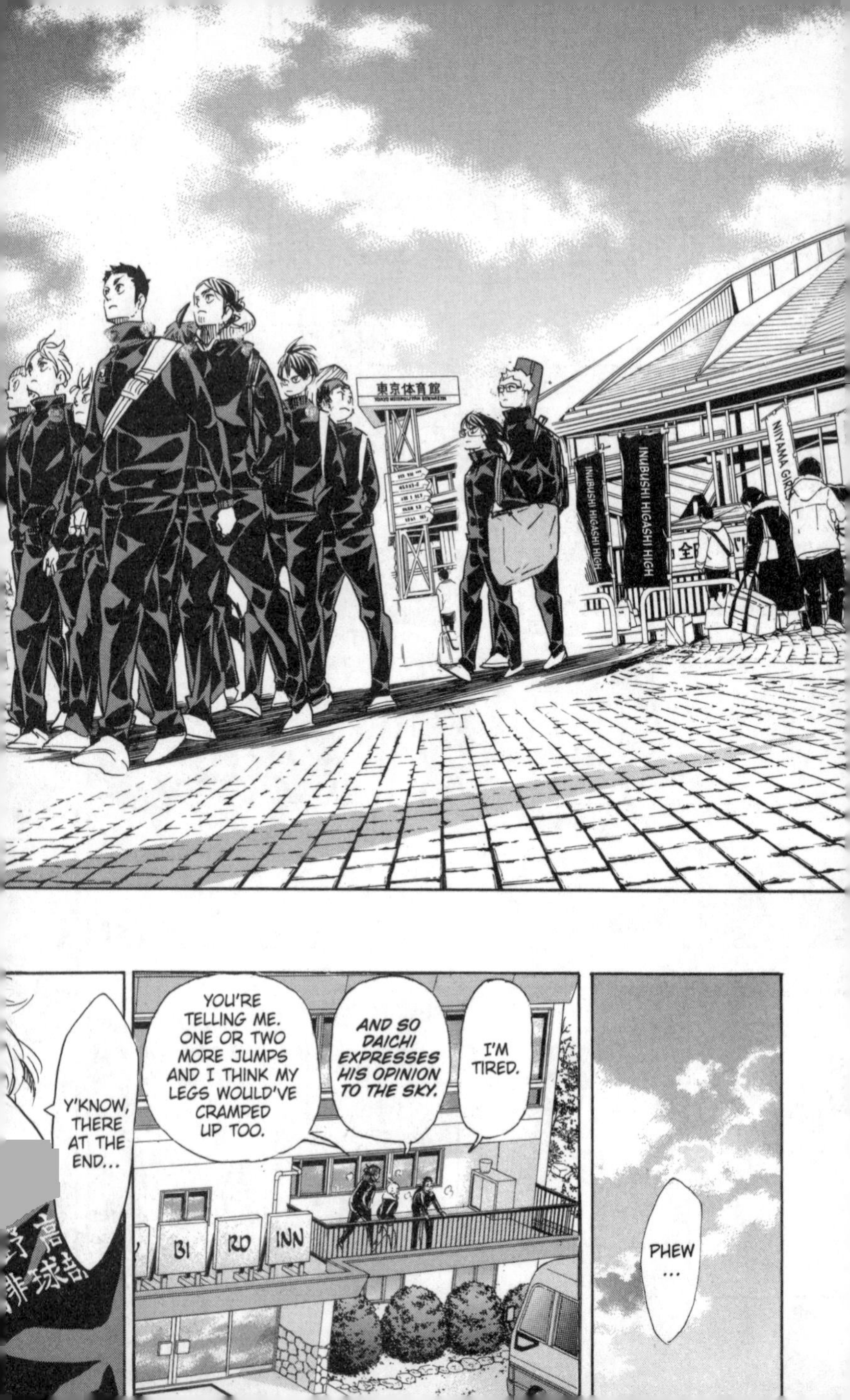
東京体育館
NIIYAMA GIRL
INUBUSHI HIGASHI HIGH
INUBUSHI HIGASHI HIGH
PHEW...
I'M TIRED.
AND SO DAICHI EXPRESSES HIS OPINION TO THE SKY.
YOU'RE TELLING ME. ONE OR TWO MORE JUMPS AND I THINK MY LEGS WOULD'VE CRAMPED UP TOO.
BI RO INN
Y'KNOW, THERE AT THE END...

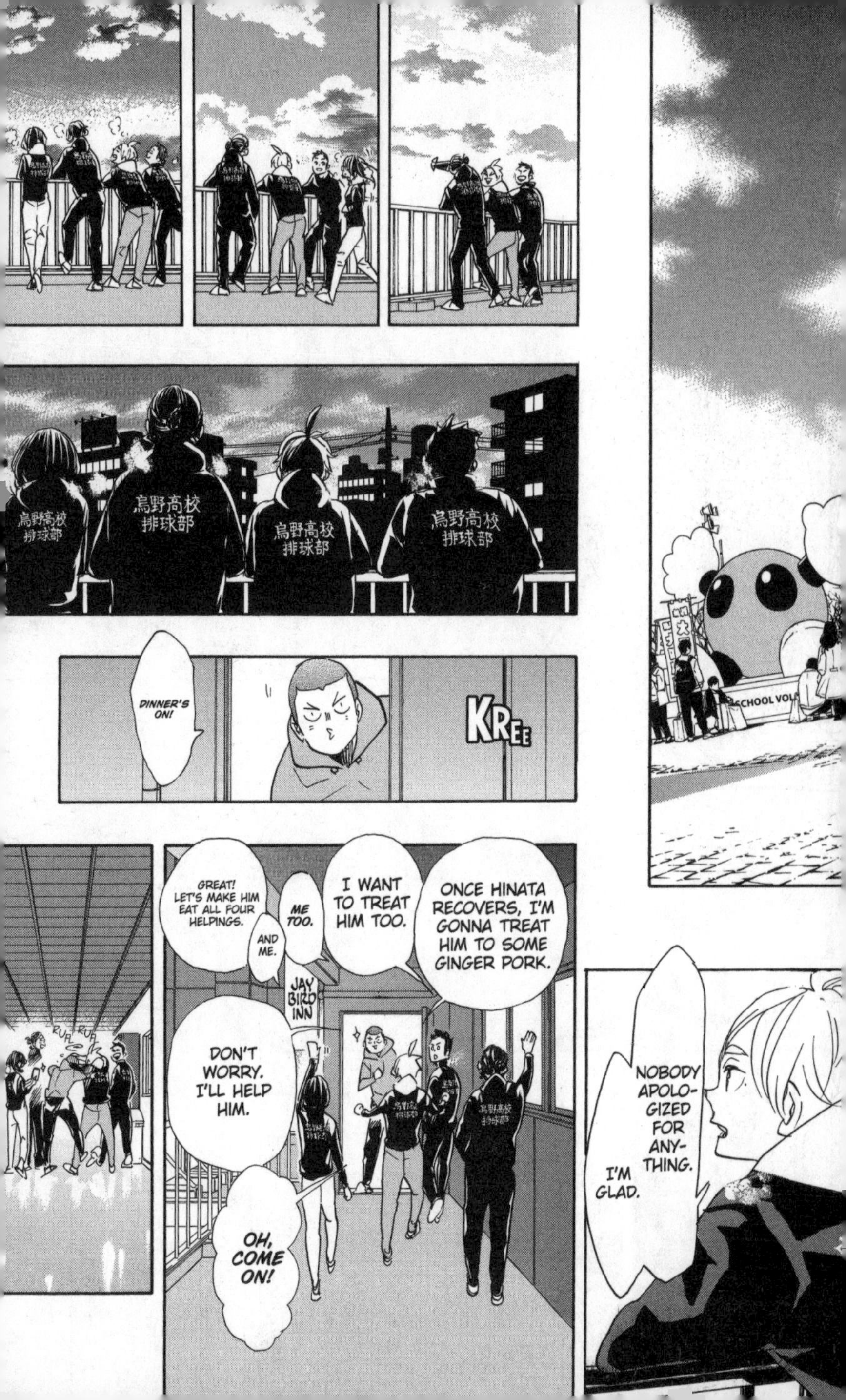
SCHOOL VOL
NOBODY APOLOGIZED FOR ANYTHING.
I'M GLAD.
烏野高校
排球部
烏野高校
排球部
烏野高校
排球部
烏野高校
排球部
KREE
DINNER'S ON!
ONCE HINATA RECOVERS, I'M GONNA TREAT HIM TO SOME GINGER PORK.
I WANT TO TREAT HIM TOO.
ME TOO.
AND ME.
GREAT! LET'S MAKE HIM EAT ALL FOUR HELPINGS.
JAY BIRD INN
DON'T WORRY. I'LL HELP HIM.
OH, COME ON!
RUF RUF

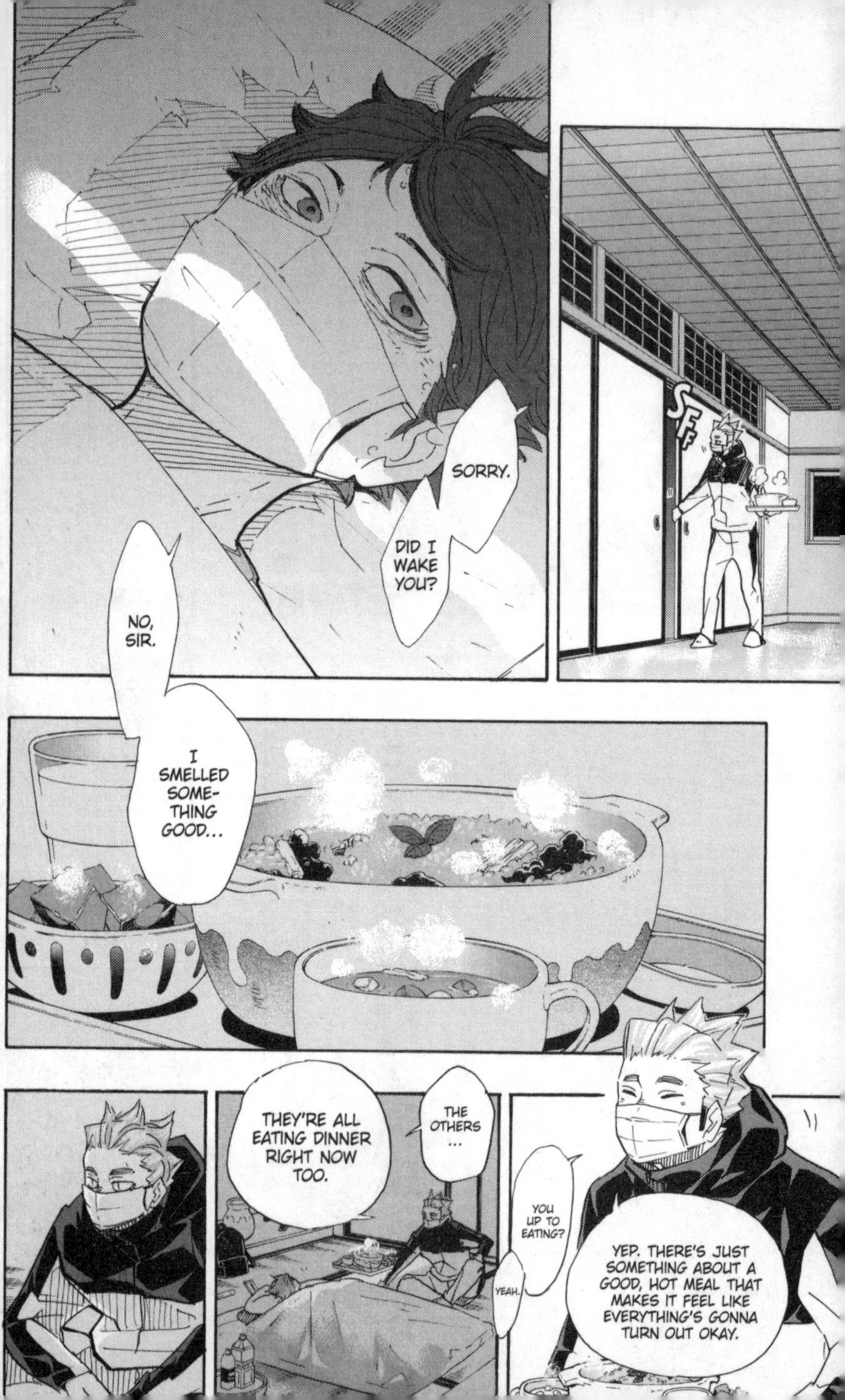
SFF
SORRY.
DID I WAKE YOU?
NO, SIR.
I SMELLED SOMETHING-THING GOOD...
YOU UP TO EATING?
YEAH.
YEP. THERE'S JUST SOMETHING ABOUT A GOOD, HOT MEAL THAT MAKES IT FEEL LIKE EVERYTHING'S GONNA TURN OUT OKAY.
THE OTHERS...
THEY'RE ALL EATING DINNER RIGHT NOW TOO.

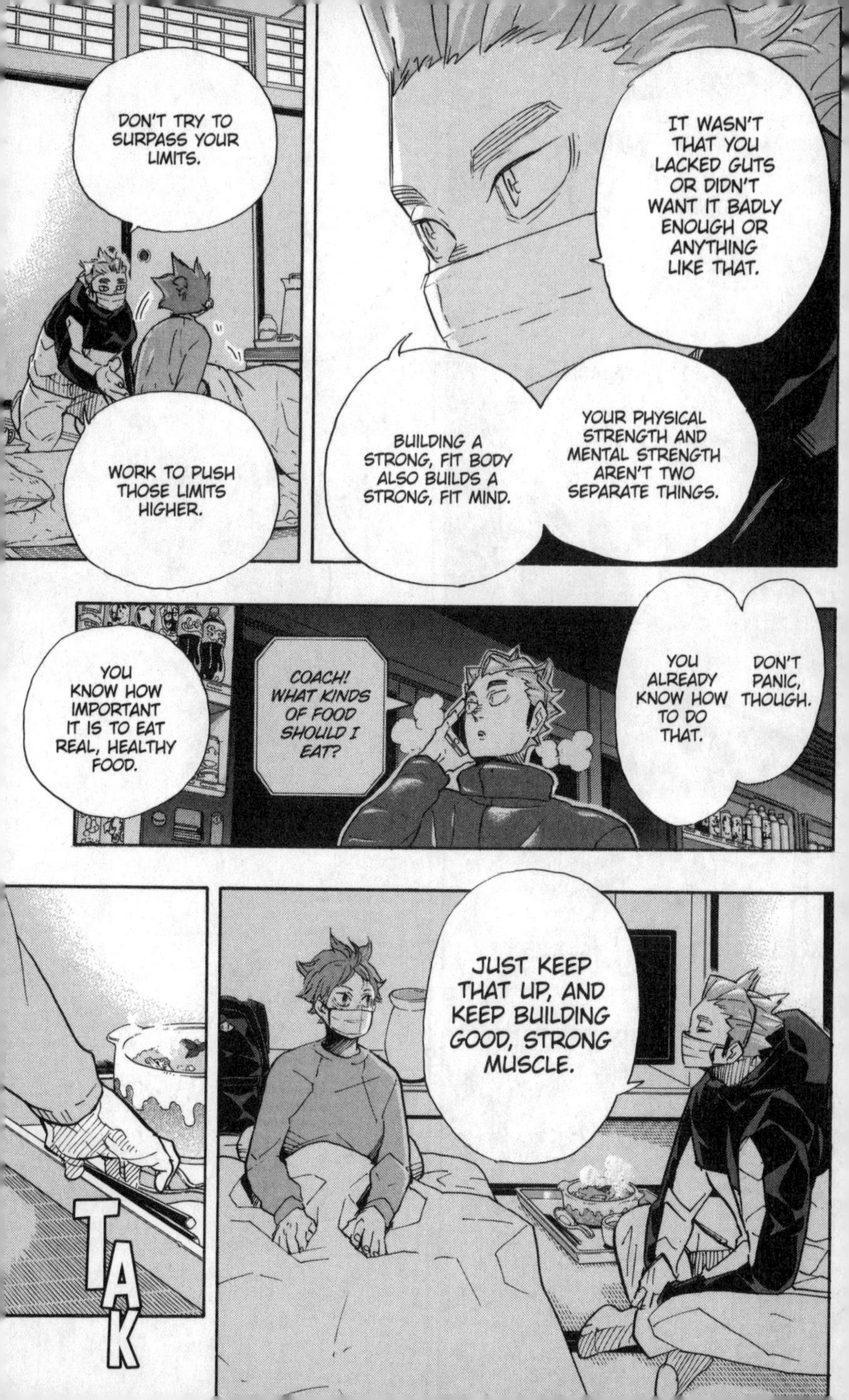
IT WASN'T THAT YOU LACKED GUTS OR DIDN'T WANT IT BADLY ENOUGH OR ANYTHING LIKE THAT.
YOUR PHYSICAL STRENGTH AND MENTAL STRENGTH AREN'T TWO SEPARATE THINGS.
BUILDING A STRONG, FIT BODY ALSO BUILDS A STRONG, FIT MIND.
DON'T TRY TO SURPASS YOUR LIMITS.
WORK TO PUSH THOSE LIMITS HIGHER.
DON'T PANIC, THOUGH.
YOU ALREADY KNOW HOW TO DO THAT.
COACH! WHAT KINDS OF FOOD SHOULD I EAT?
YOU KNOW HOW IMPORTANT IT IS TO EAT REAL, HEALTHY FOOD.
JUST KEEP THAT UP, AND KEEP BUILDING GOOD, STRONG MUSCLE.
TAK

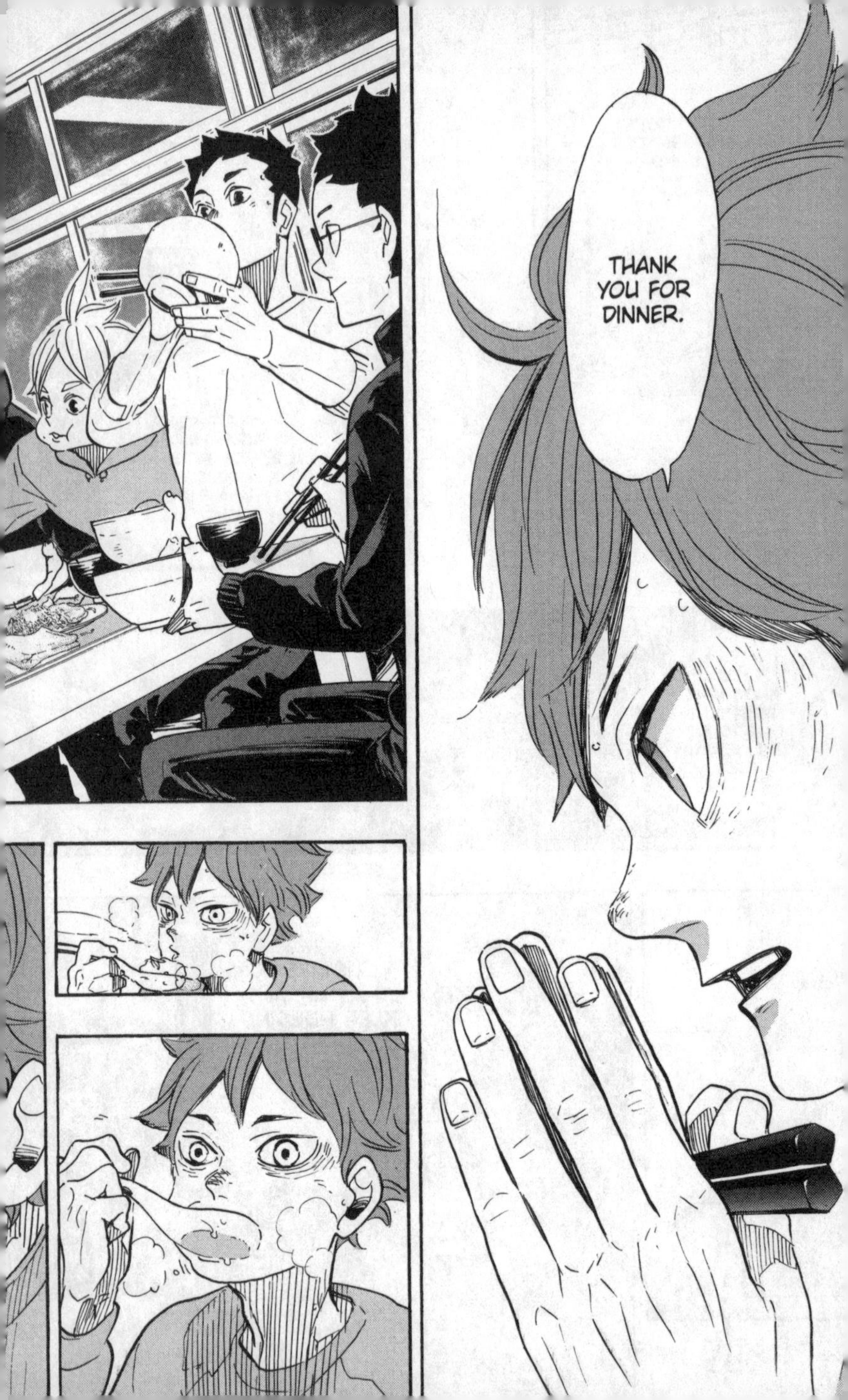
THANK YOU FOR DINNER.

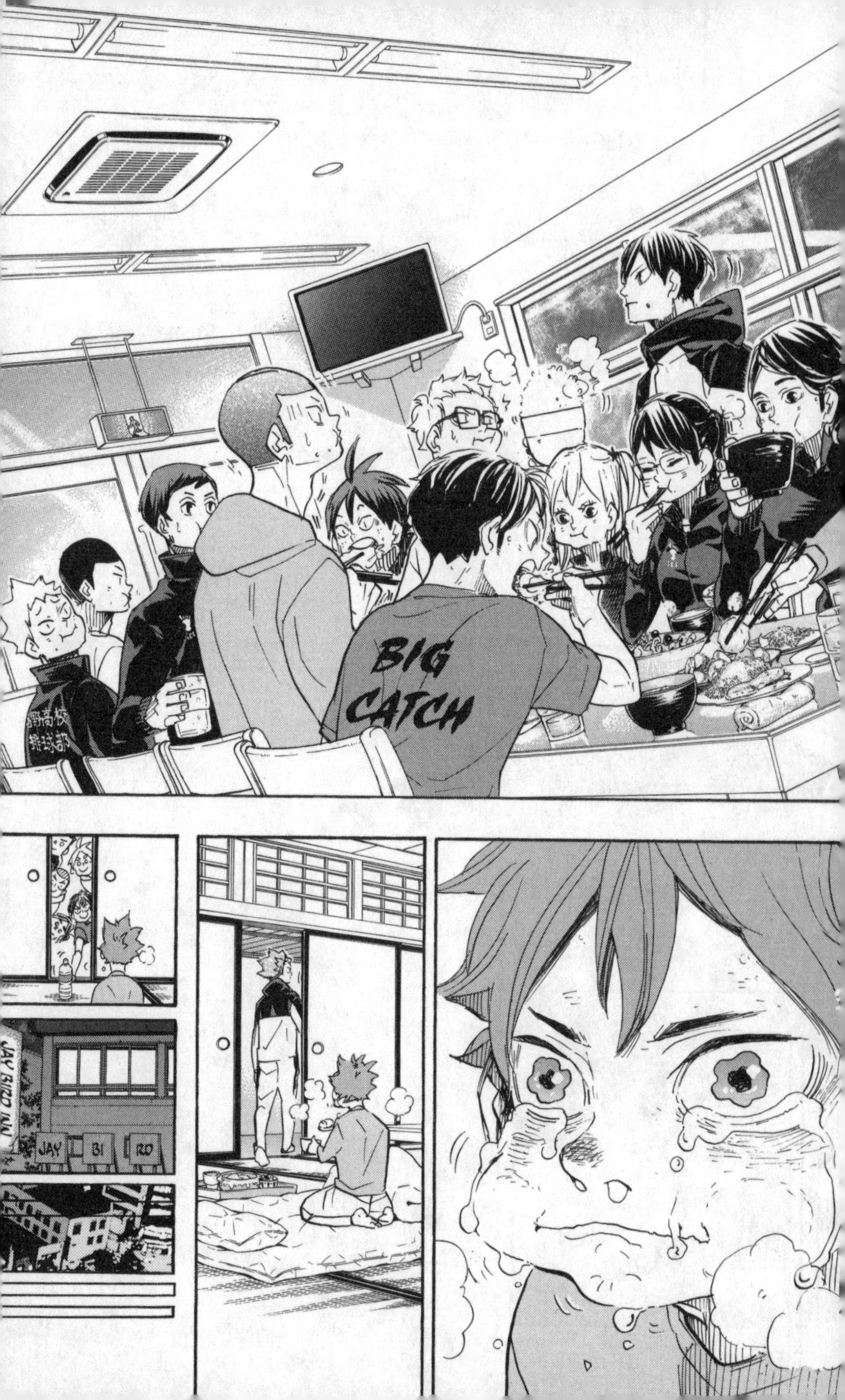
BIG CATCH
野高校
排球部
JAY BIRD INN
JAY
BI
RD

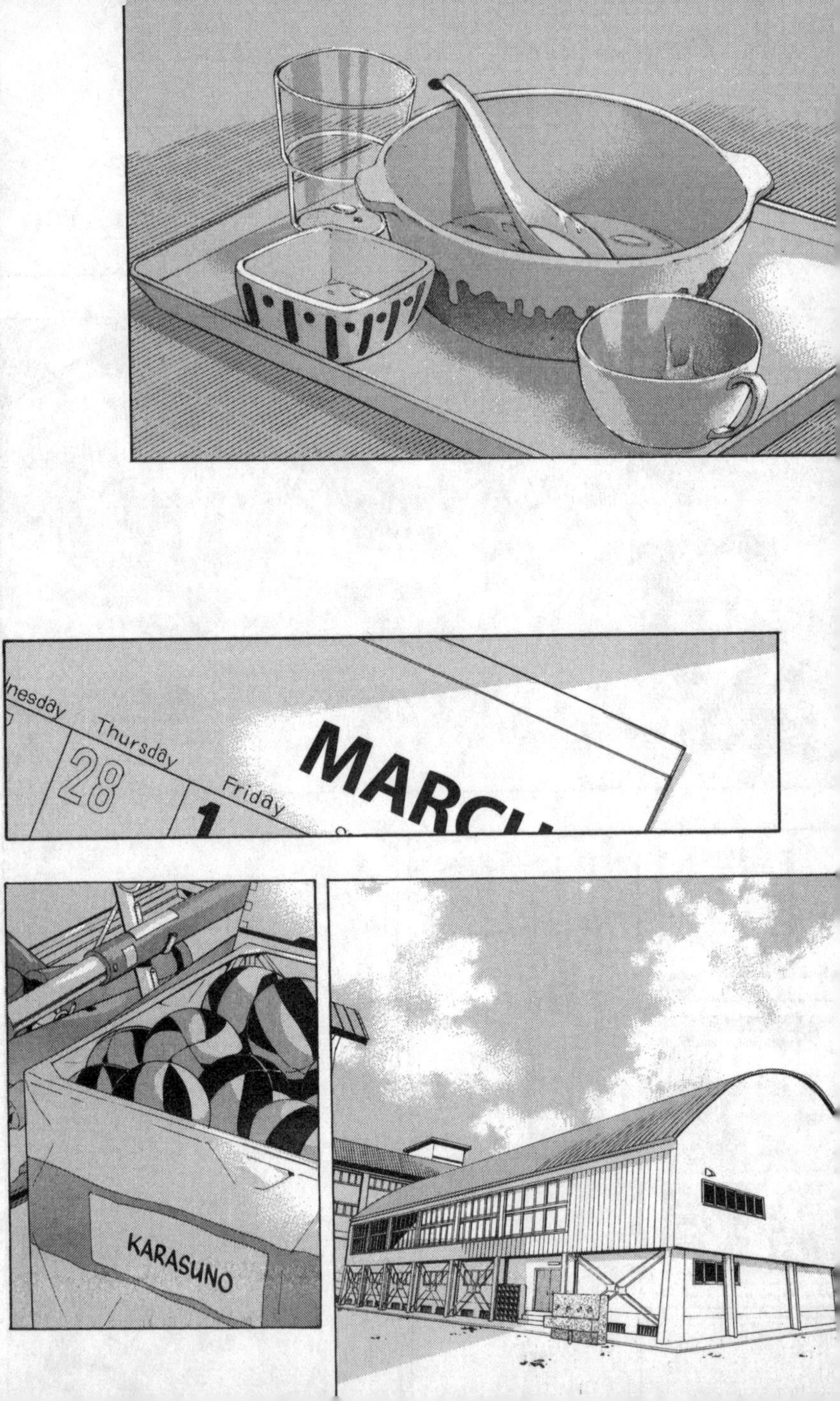
Thursday
28
Friday
1
MARCH
KARASUNO

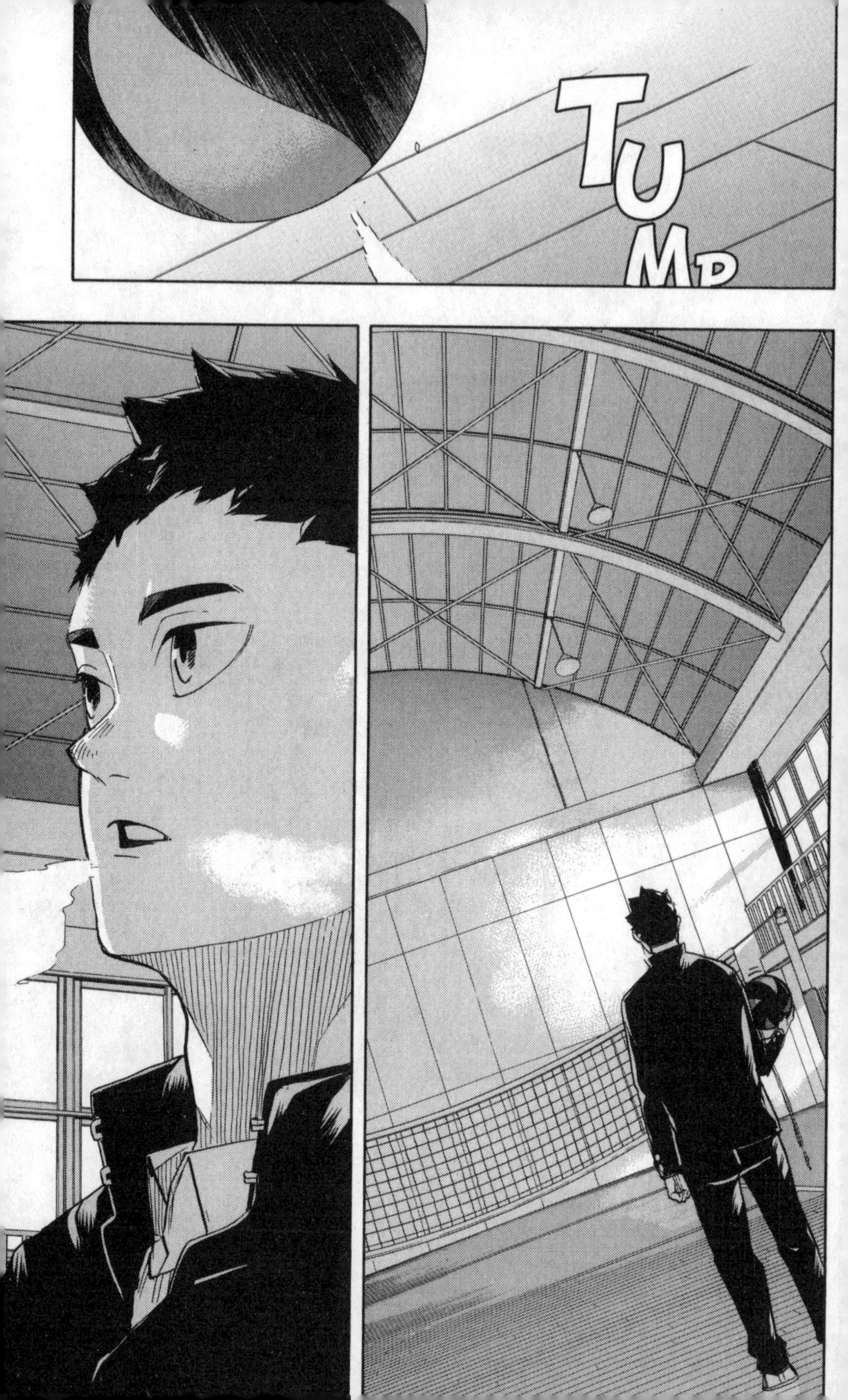
TUMP

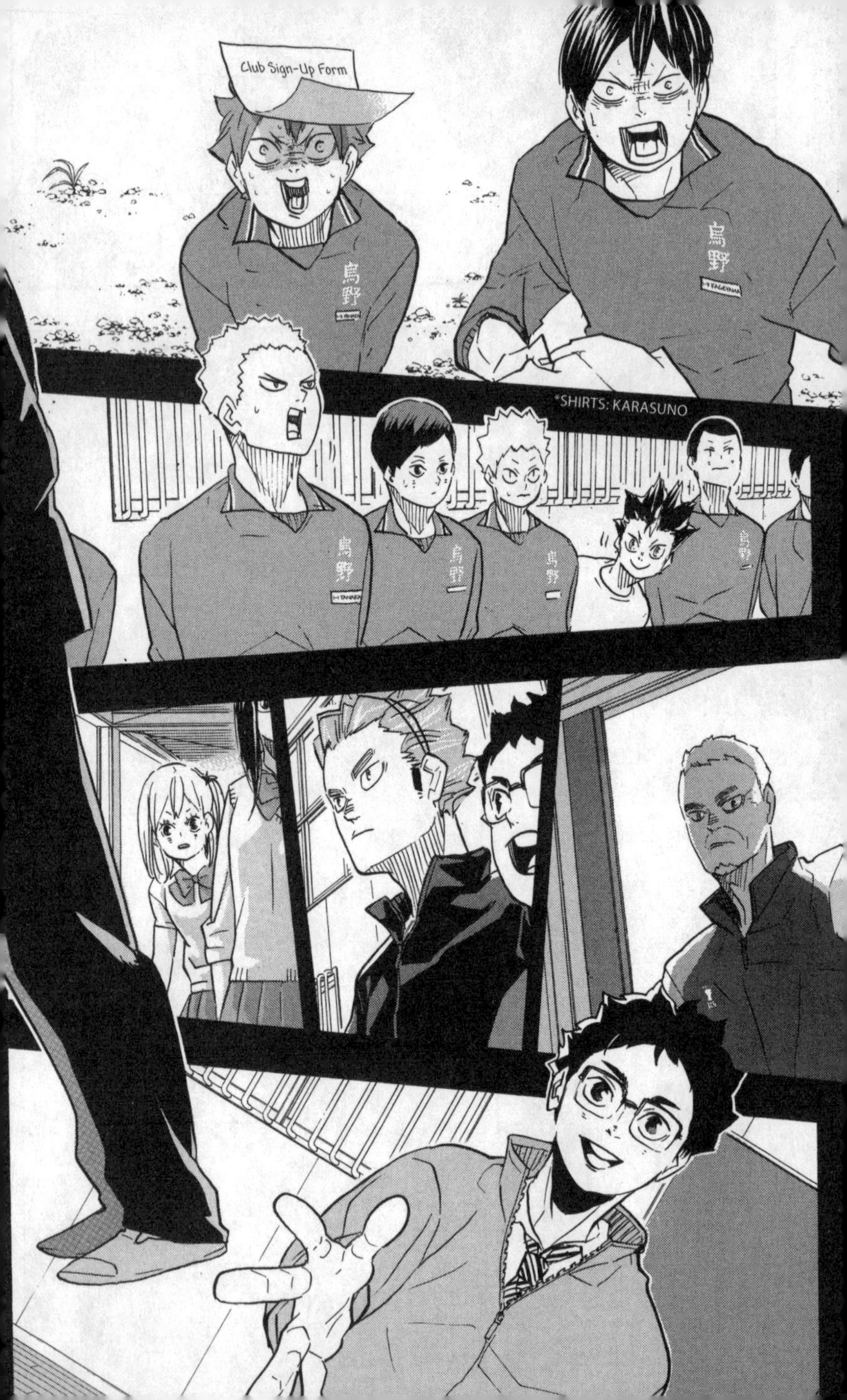
Club Sign-Up Form
*SHIRTS: KARASUNO

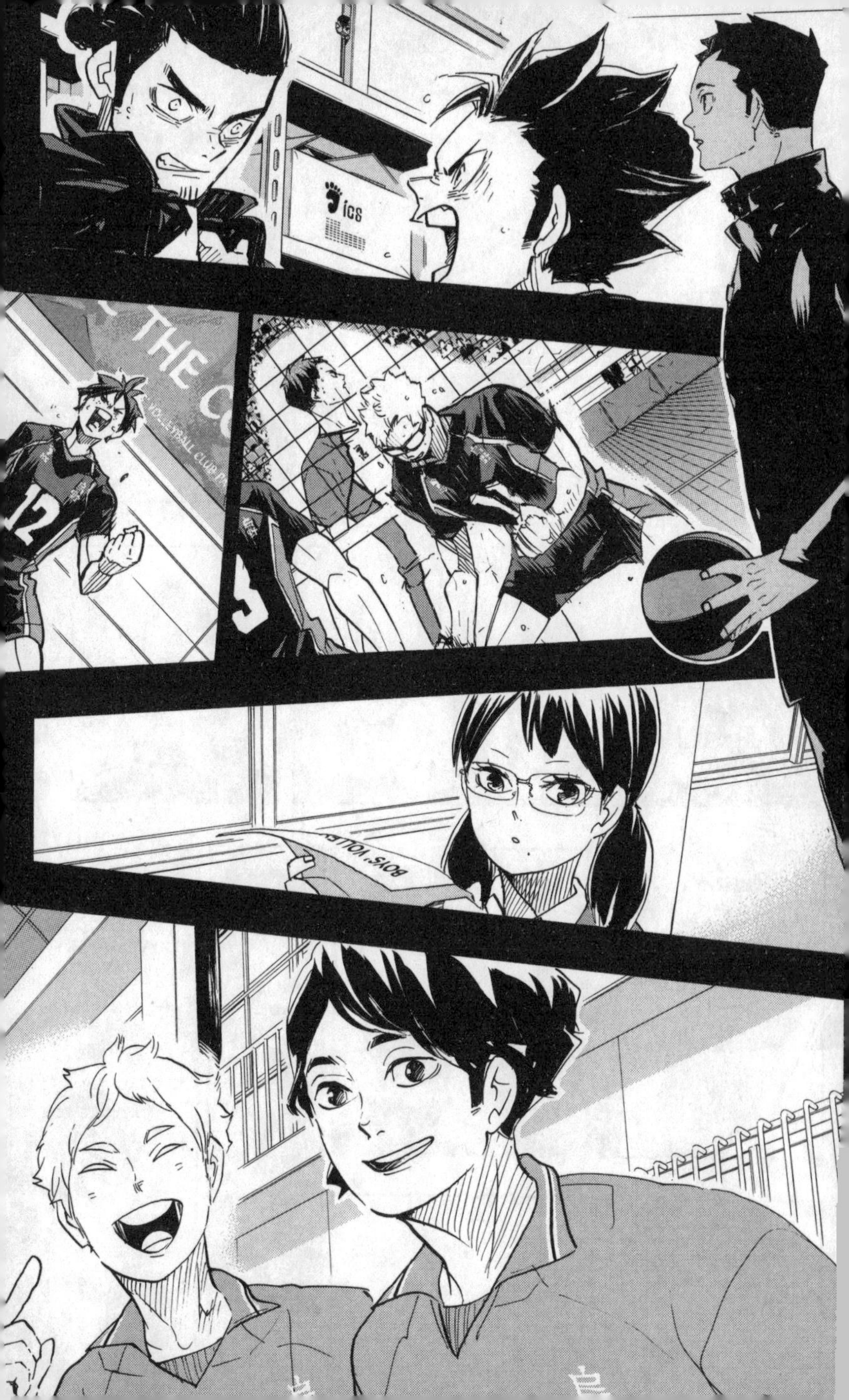
ics
THE

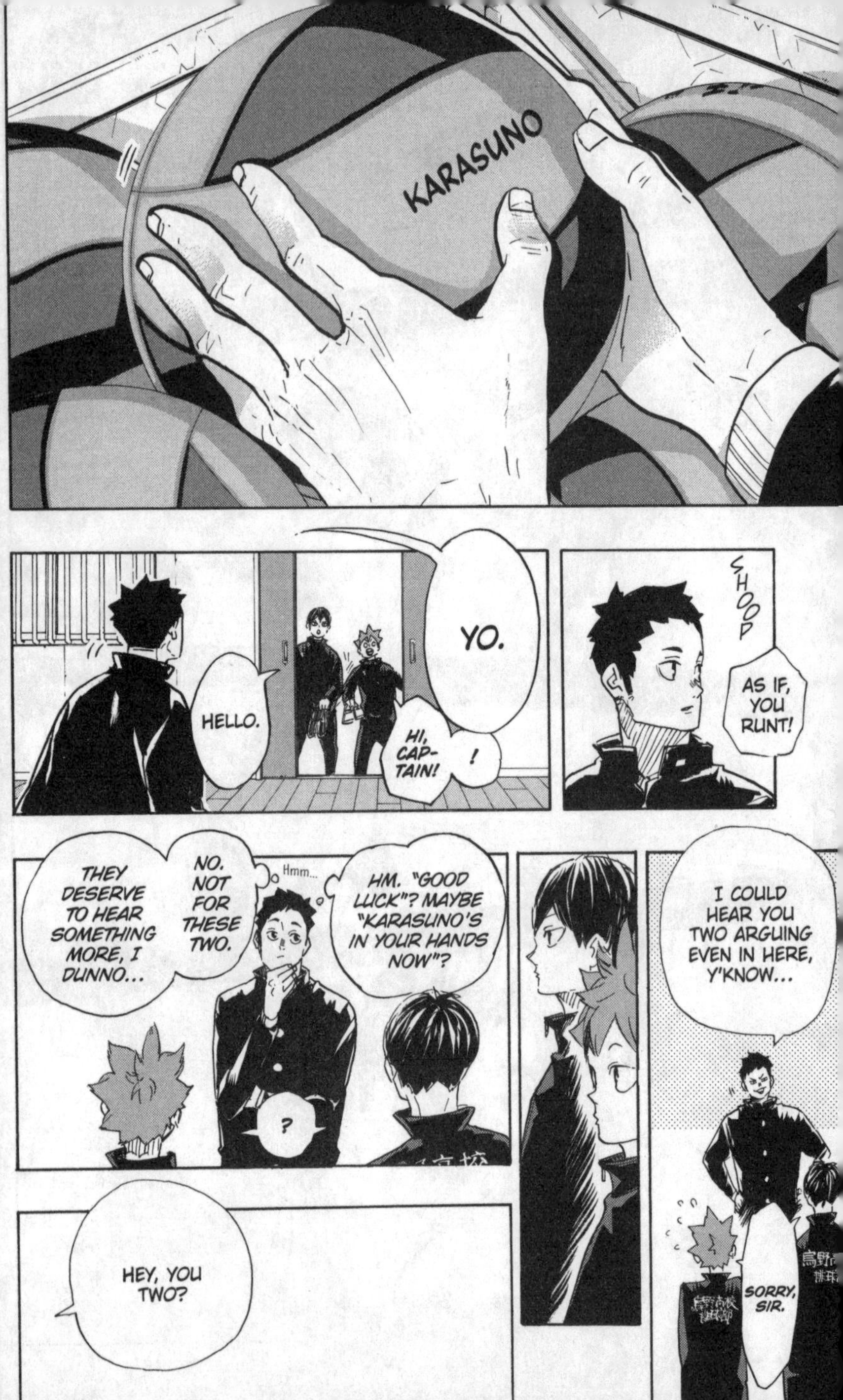
KARASUNO
SHOOP
AS IF, YOU RUNT!
YO.
!
HI, CAPTAIN!
HELLO.
I COULD HEAR YOU TWO ARGUING EVEN IN HERE, Y'KNOW...
SORRY, SIR.
HM. "GOOD LUCK"? MAYBE "KARASUNO'S IN YOUR HANDS NOW"?
Hmm...
NO. NOT FOR THESE TWO.
THEY DESERVE TO HEAR SOMETHING MORE, I DUNNO...
?
HEY, YOU TWO?

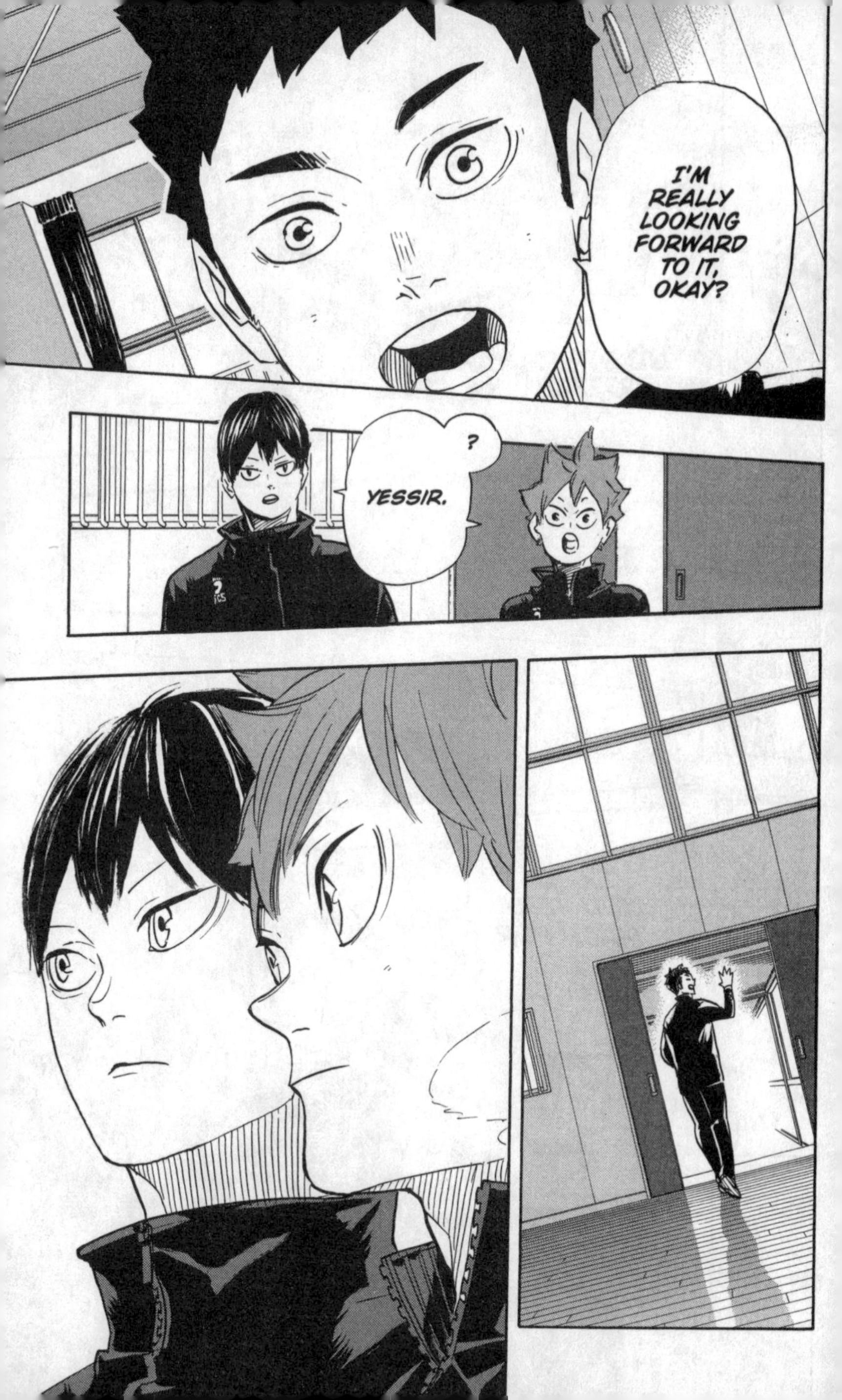
I'M REALLY LOOKING FORWARD TO IT, OKAY?
YESSIR.
?

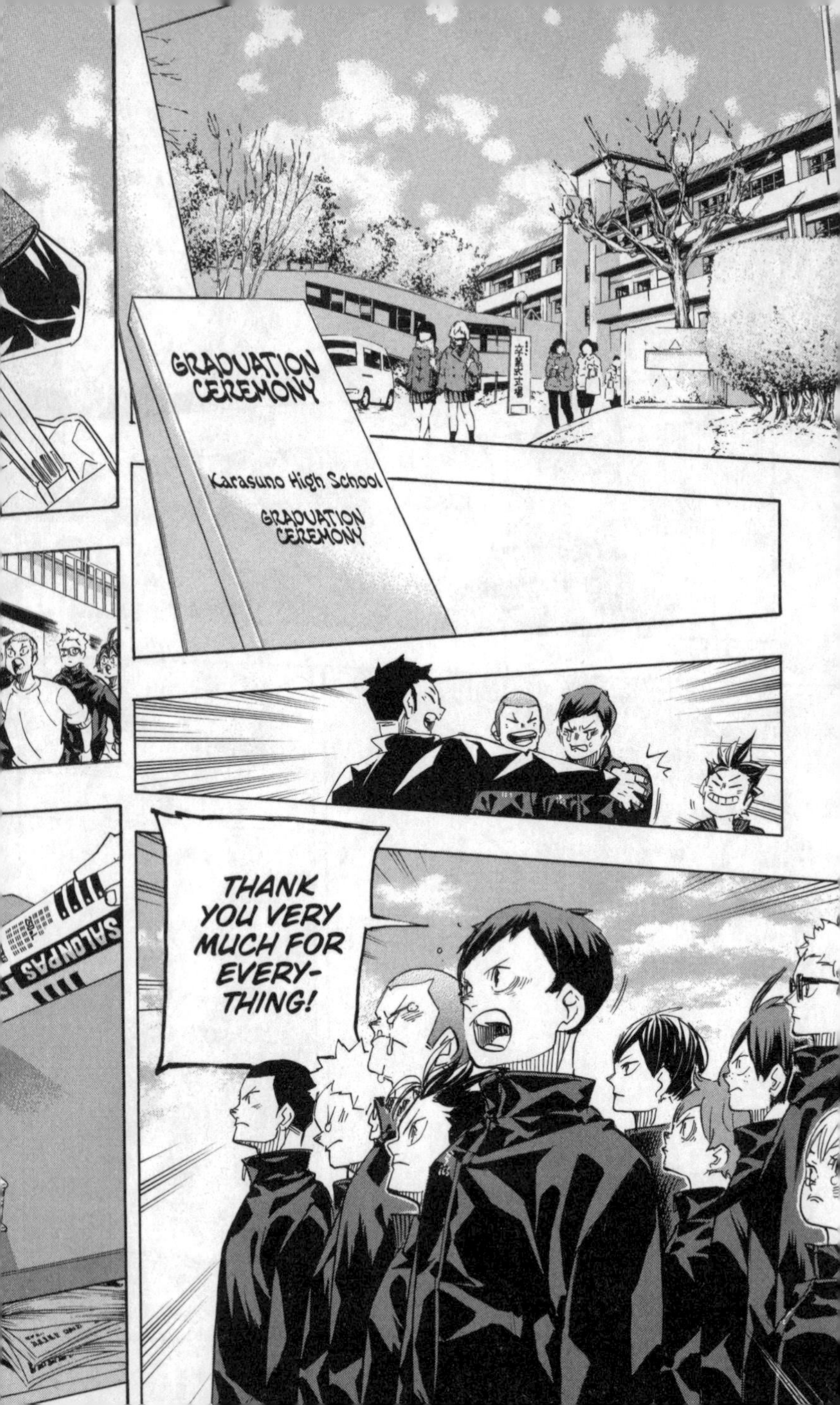
GRADUATION CEREMONY
Karasuno High School
GRADUATION CEREMONY
THANK YOU VERY MUCH FOR EVERY-THING!
SALONPAS

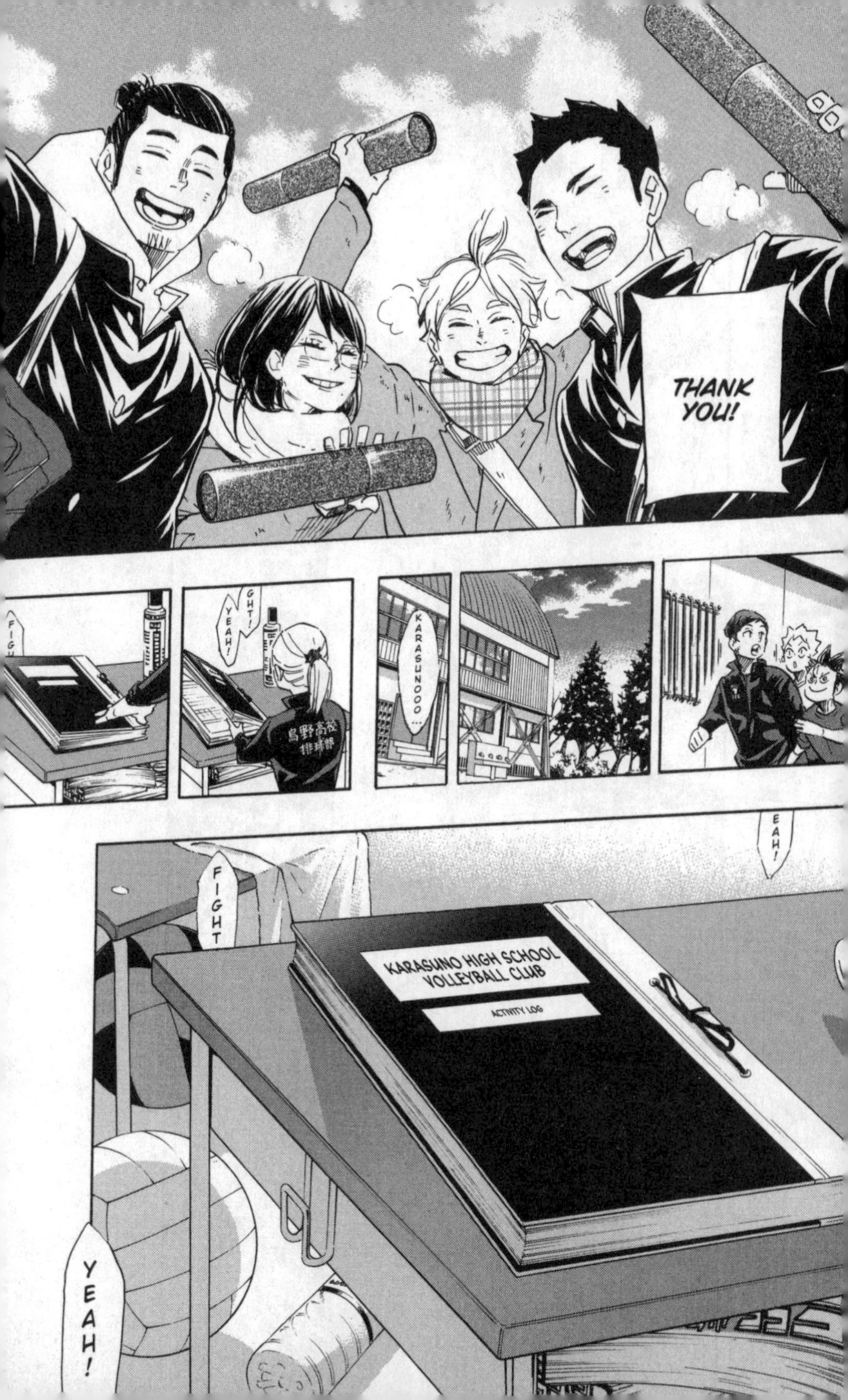

THANK YOU!
KARASUNOOO...
GHT!
YEAH!
烏野高校
排球部
FIGH
EAH!
FIGHT
KARASUNO HIGH SCHOOL VOLLEYBALL CLUB
ACTIVITY LOG
YEAH!

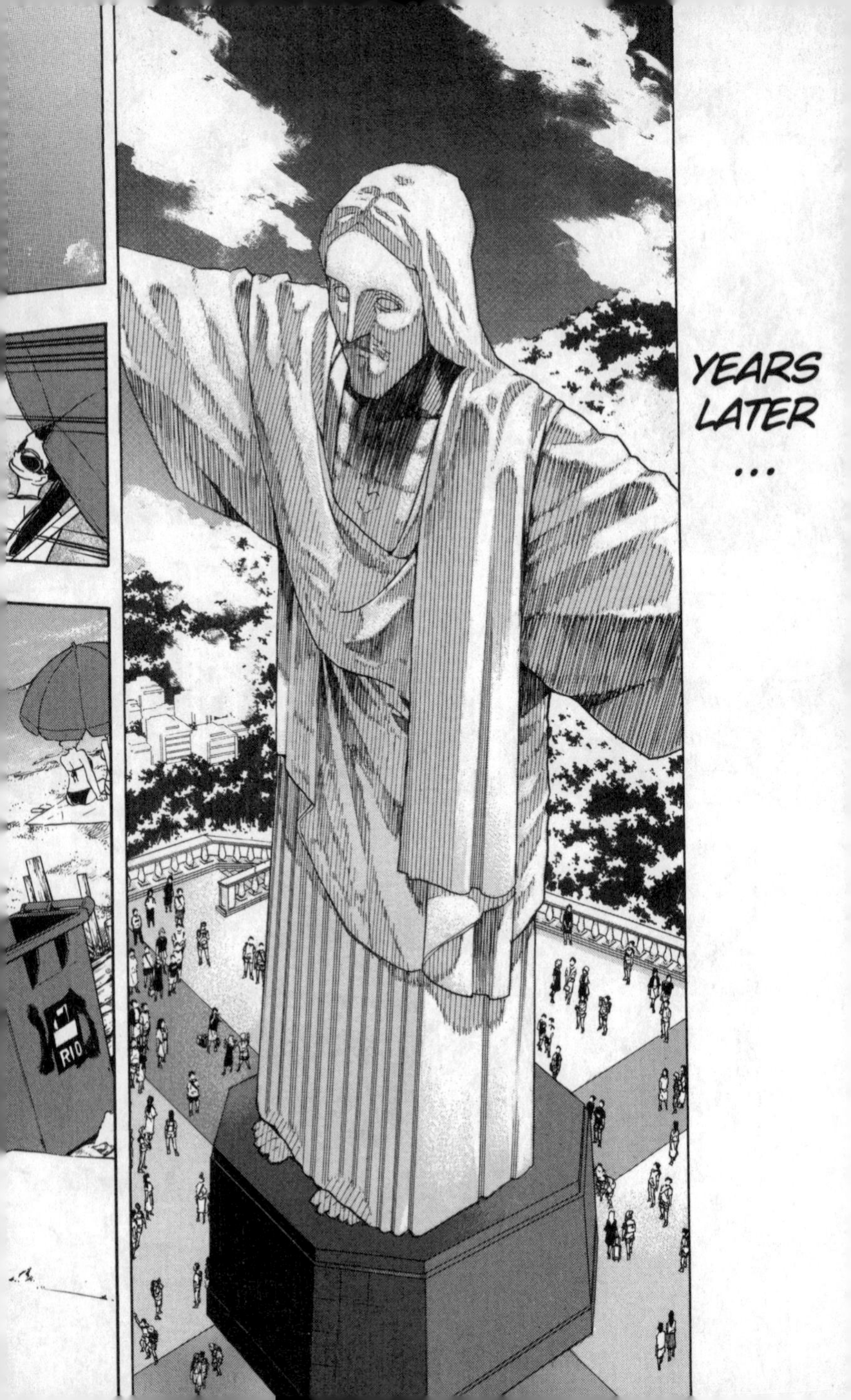
YEARS LATER ...
RIO

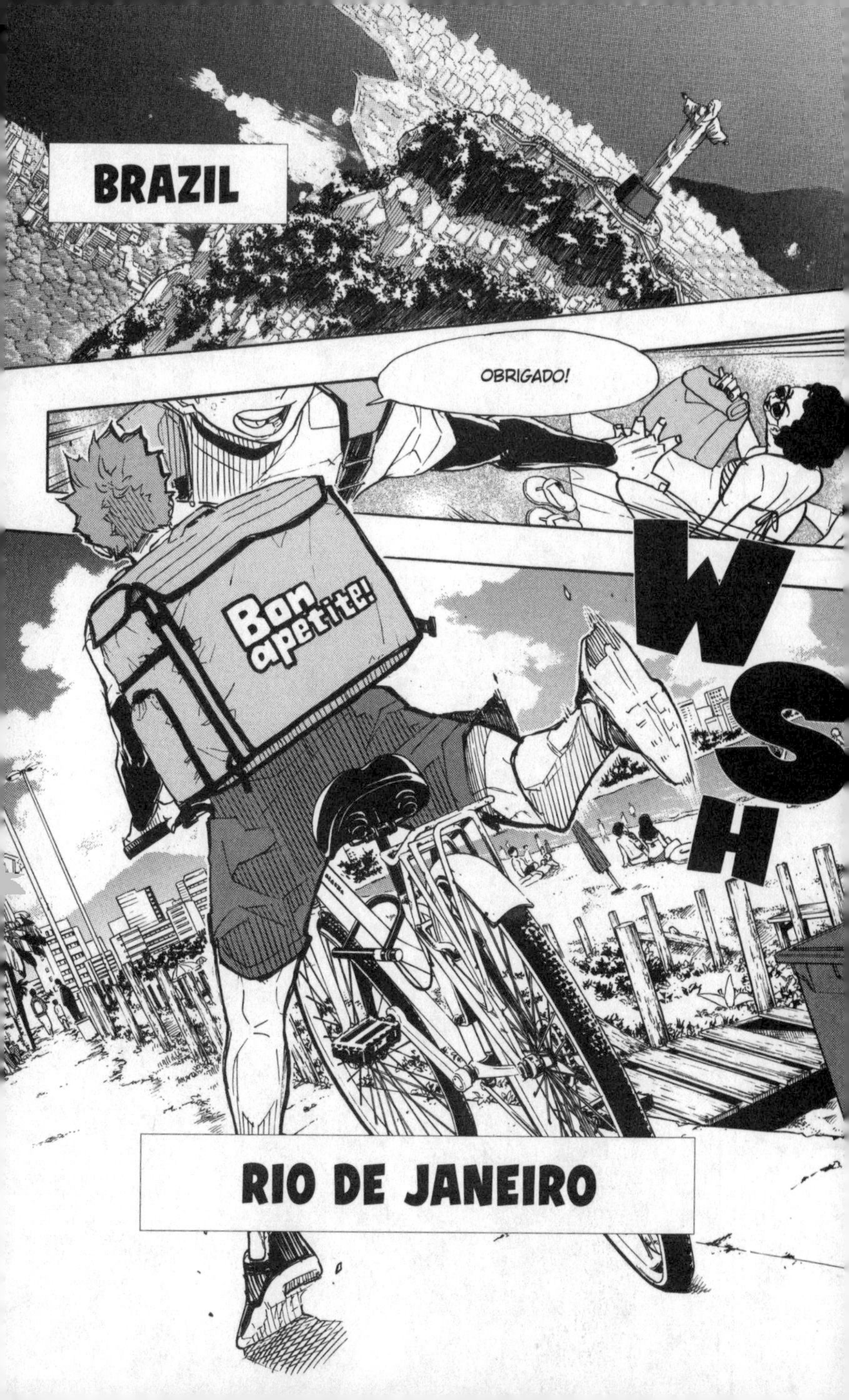
BRAZIL
OBRIGADO!
WSH
Bon apetite!
RIO DE JANEIRO

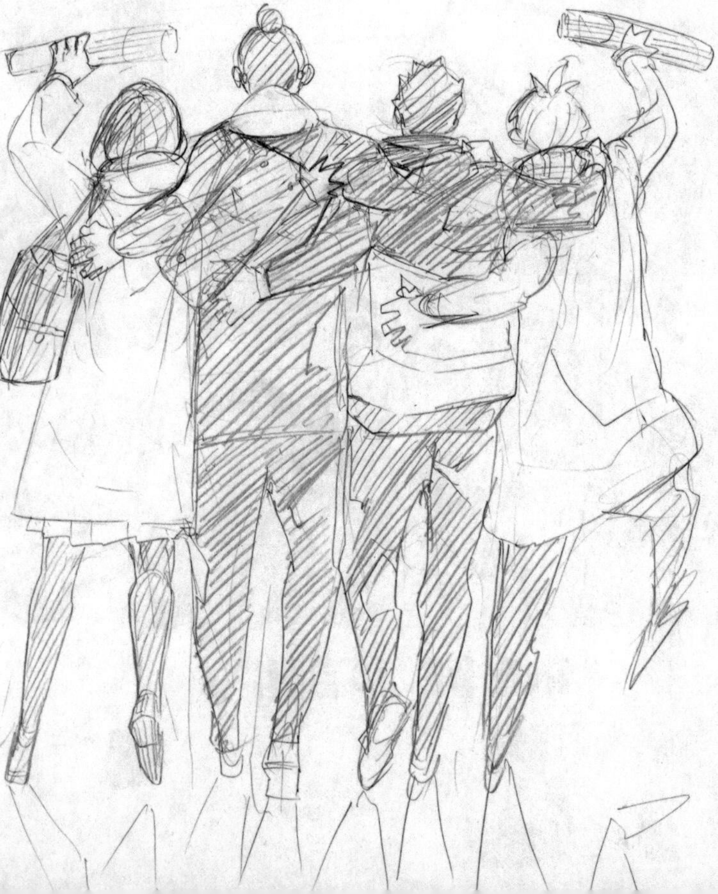

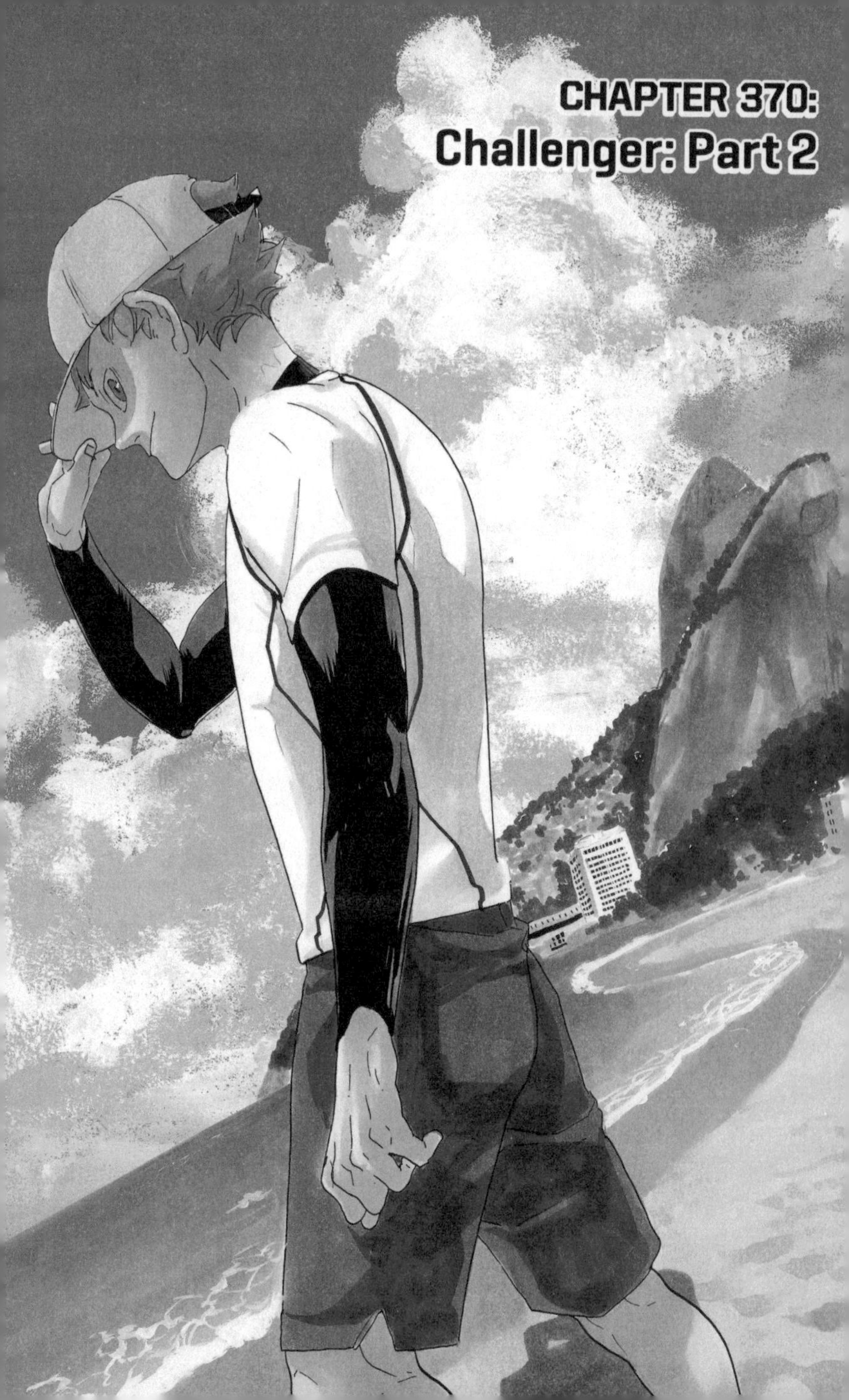
CHAPTER 370:
Challenger: Part 2

HAIKYU!!

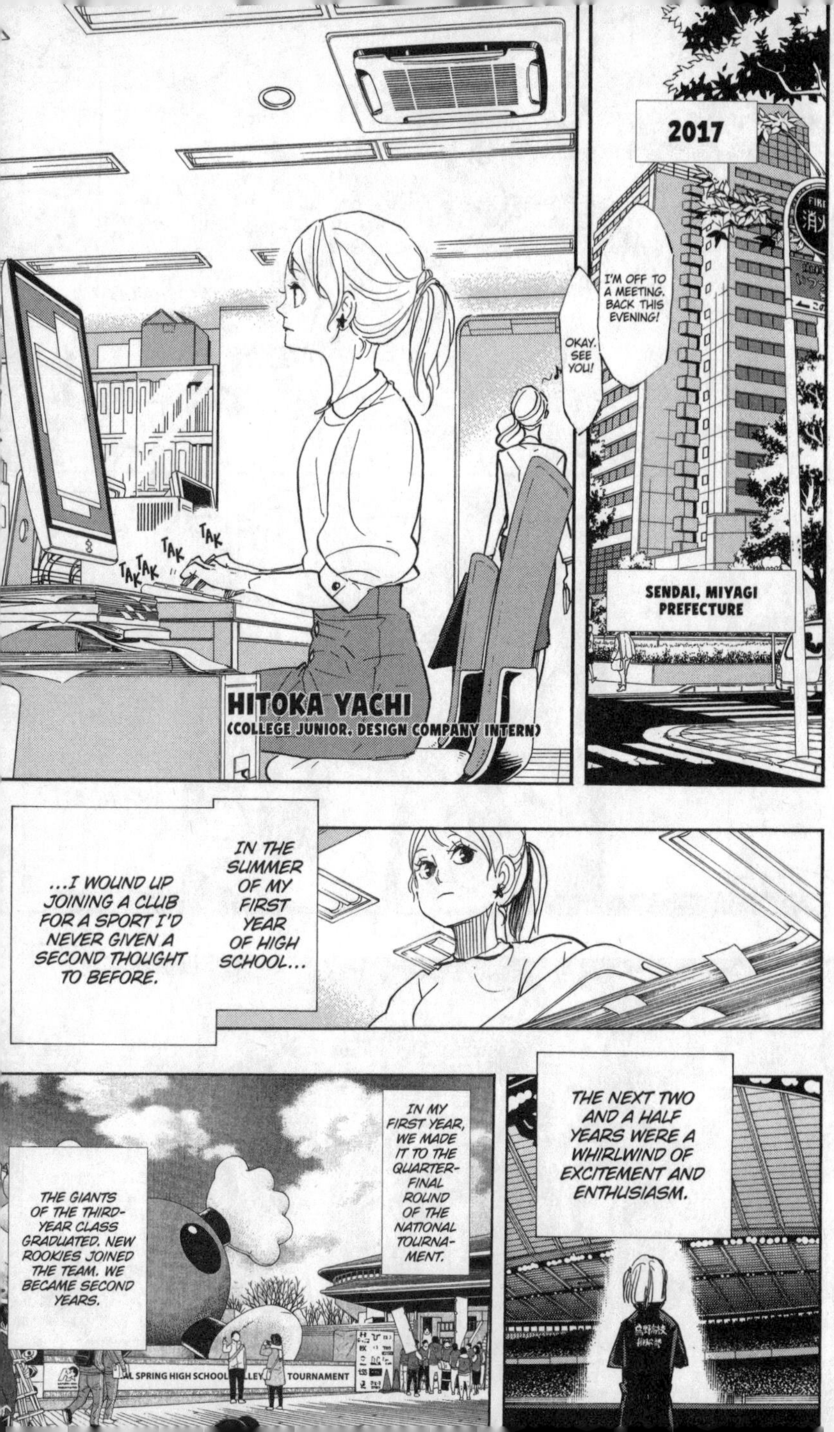

2017
I'M OFF TO A MEETING. BACK THIS EVENING!
OKAY. SEE YOU!
SENDAI, MIYAGI PREFECTURE
TAK TAK TAK TAK
HITOKA YACHI
(COLLEGE JUNIOR, DESIGN COMPANY INTERN)
IN THE SUMMER OF MY FIRST YEAR OF HIGH SCHOOL...
...I WOUND UP JOINING A CLUB FOR A SPORT I'D NEVER GIVEN A SECOND THOUGHT TO BEFORE.
THE NEXT TWO AND A HALF YEARS WERE A WHIRLWIND OF EXCITEMENT AND ENTHUSIASM.
IN MY FIRST YEAR, WE MADE IT TO THE QUARTER-FINAL ROUND OF THE NATIONAL TOURNA-MENT.
THE GIANTS OF THE THIRD-YEAR CLASS GRADUATED. NEW ROOKIES JOINED THE TEAM. WE BECAME SECOND YEARS.
AL SPRING HIGH SCHOOL LLEY TOURNAMENT

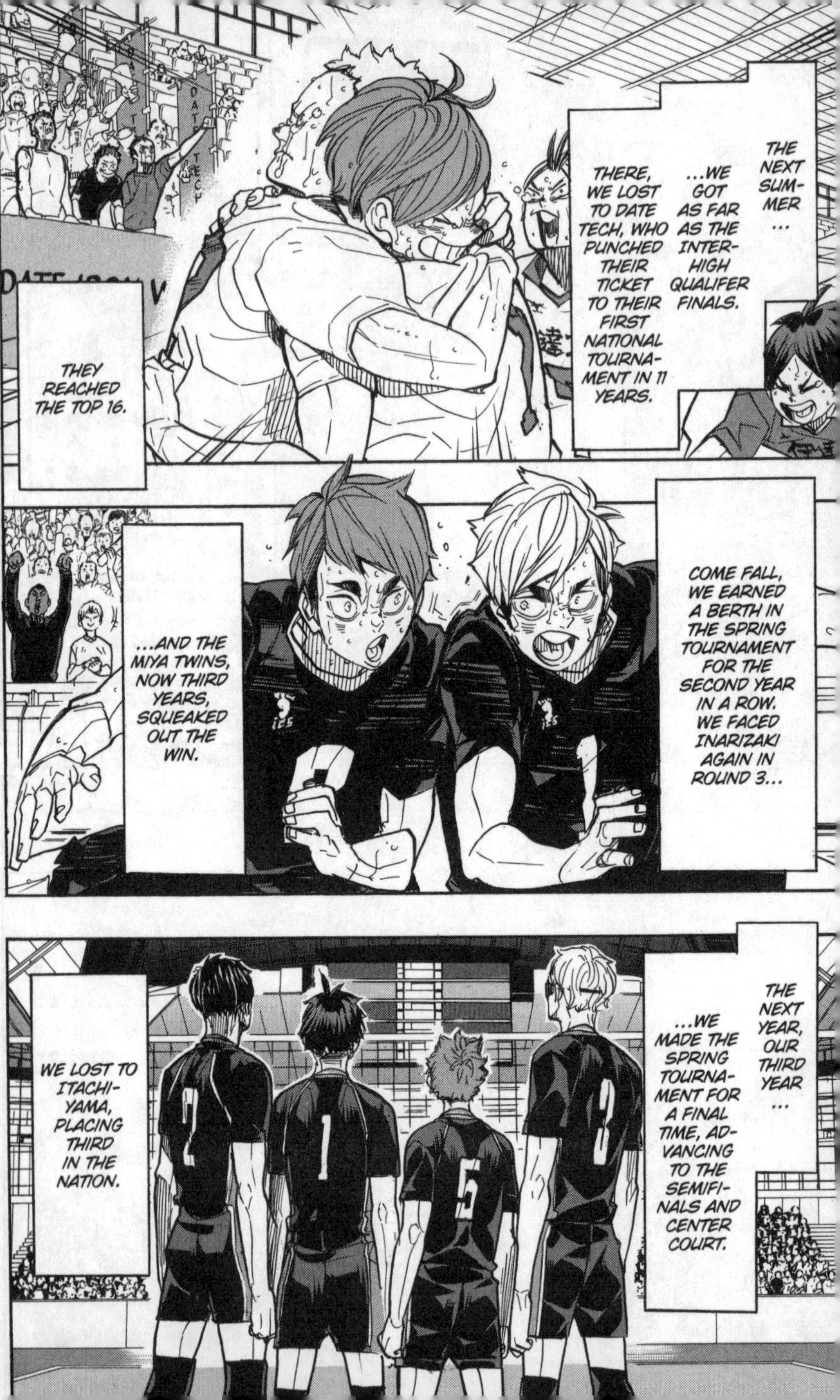

THE NEXT SUMMER...
...WE GOT AS FAR AS THE INTER-HIGH QUALIFER FINALS.
THERE, WE LOST TO DATE TECH, WHO PUNCHED THEIR TICKET TO THEIR FIRST NATIONAL TOURNAMENT IN 11 YEARS.
THEY REACHED THE TOP 16.
COME FALL, WE EARNED A BERTH IN THE SPRING TOURNAMENT FOR THE SECOND YEAR IN A ROW. WE FACED INARIZAKI AGAIN IN ROUND 3...
...AND THE MIYA TWINS, NOW THIRD YEARS, SQUEAKED OUT THE WIN.
THE NEXT YEAR, OUR THIRD YEAR...
...WE MADE THE SPRING TOURNAMENT FOR A FINAL TIME, ADVANCING TO THE SEMIFINALS AND CENTER COURT.
WE LOST TO ITACHIYAMA, PLACING THIRD IN THE NATION.

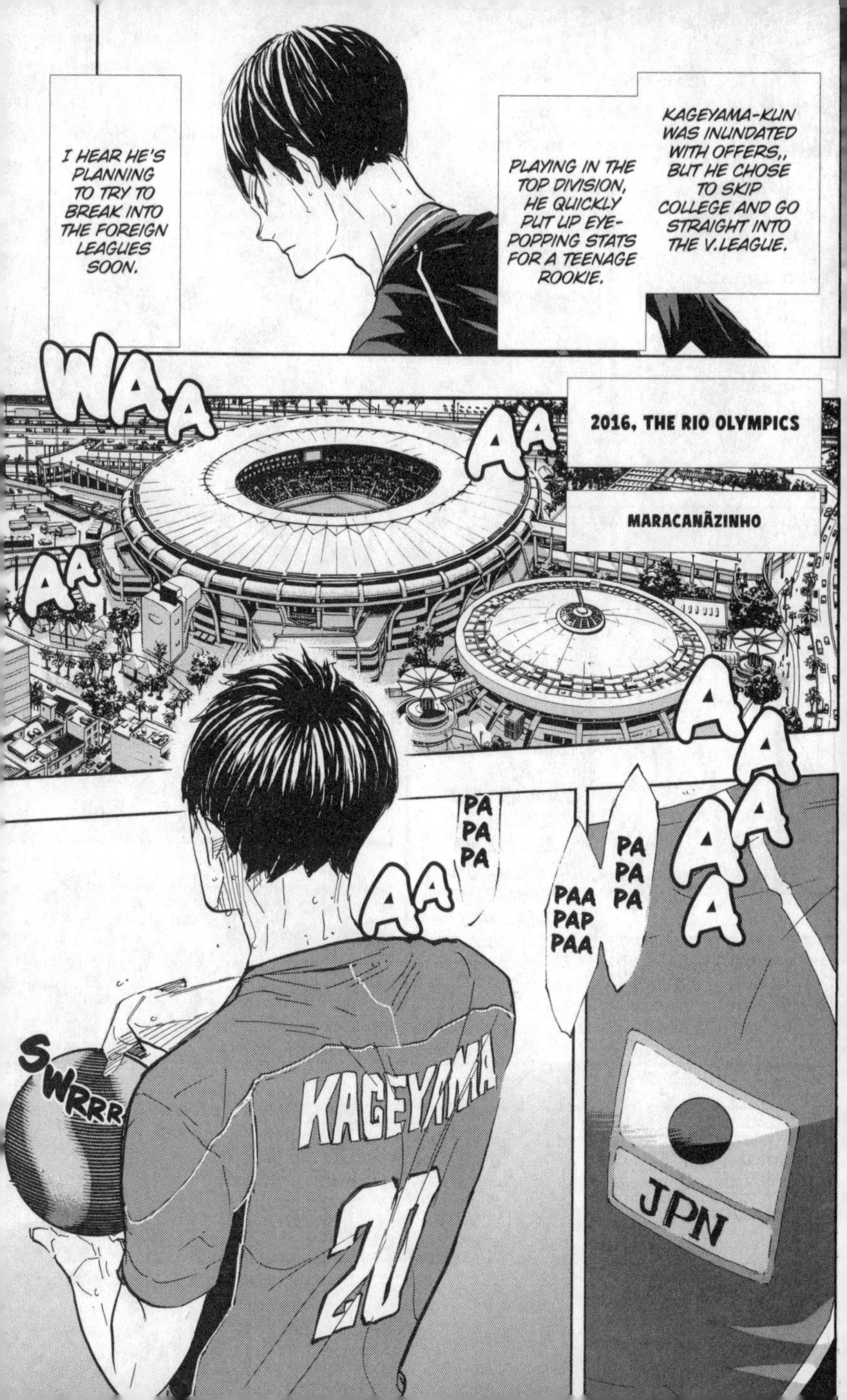
KAGEYAMA-KUN WAS INUNDATED WITH OFFERS,, BUT HE CHOSE TO SKIP COLLEGE AND GO STRAIGHT INTO THE V.LEAGUE.
PLAYING IN THE TOP DIVISION, HE QUICKLY PUT UP EYE-POPPING STATS FOR A TEENAGE ROOKIE.
I HEAR HE'S PLANNING TO TRY TO BREAK INTO THE FOREIGN LEAGUES SOON.
2016, THE RIO OLYMPICS
MARACANÃZINHO
WAA
AA
AA
AAAA
AAAA
PA PA PA
PAA PAP PAA
PA PA PA
AA
SWRRR
KAGEYAMA
20
JPN

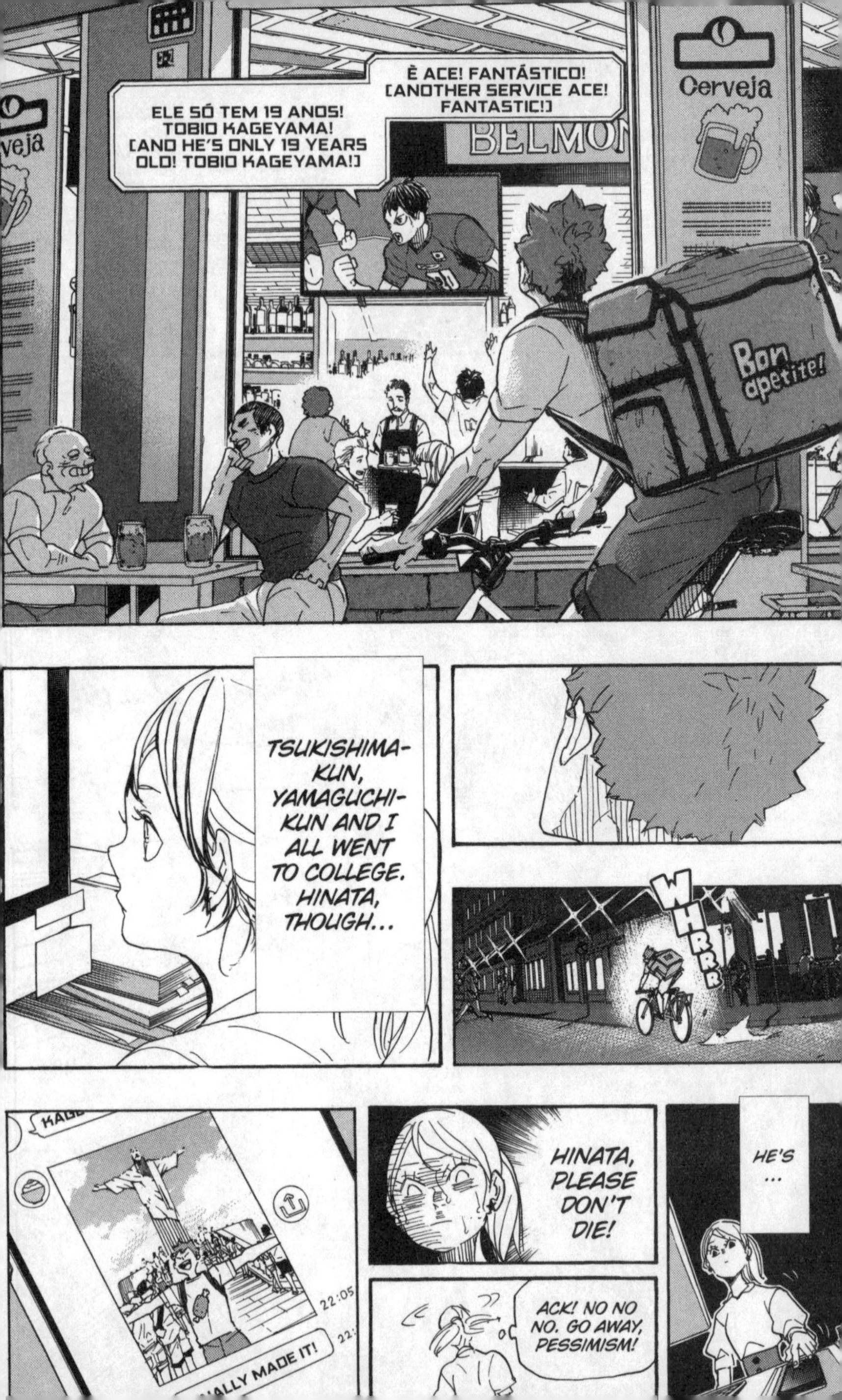
Cerveja
È ACE! FANTÁSTICO! [ANOTHER SERVICE ACE! FANTASTIC!]
ELE SÓ TEM 19 ANOS! TOBIO KAGEYAMA! [AND HE'S ONLY 19 YEARS OLD! TOBIO KAGEYAMA!]
Bon apetite!
WHRRR
TSUKISHIMA-KUN, YAMAGUCHI-KUN AND I ALL WENT TO COLLEGE. HINATA, THOUGH...
HE'S ...
HINATA, PLEASE DON'T DIE!
ACK! NO NO NO. GO AWAY, PESSIMISM!
22:05

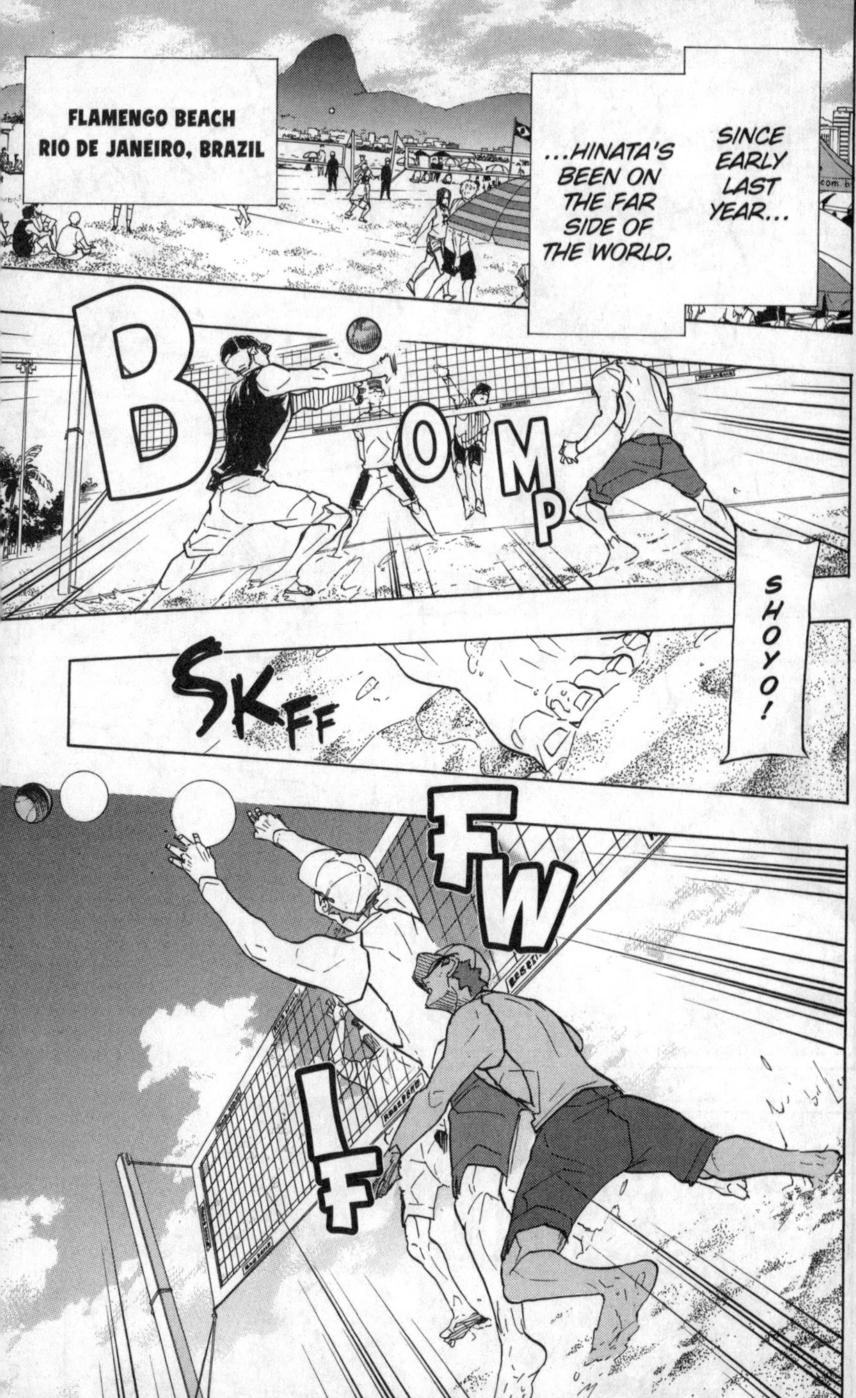
SINCE EARLY LAST YEAR...
...HINATA'S BEEN ON THE FAR SIDE OF THE WORLD.
FLAMENGO BEACH
RIO DE JANEIRO, BRAZIL
BOMP
SHOYO!
SKFF
FW
IF

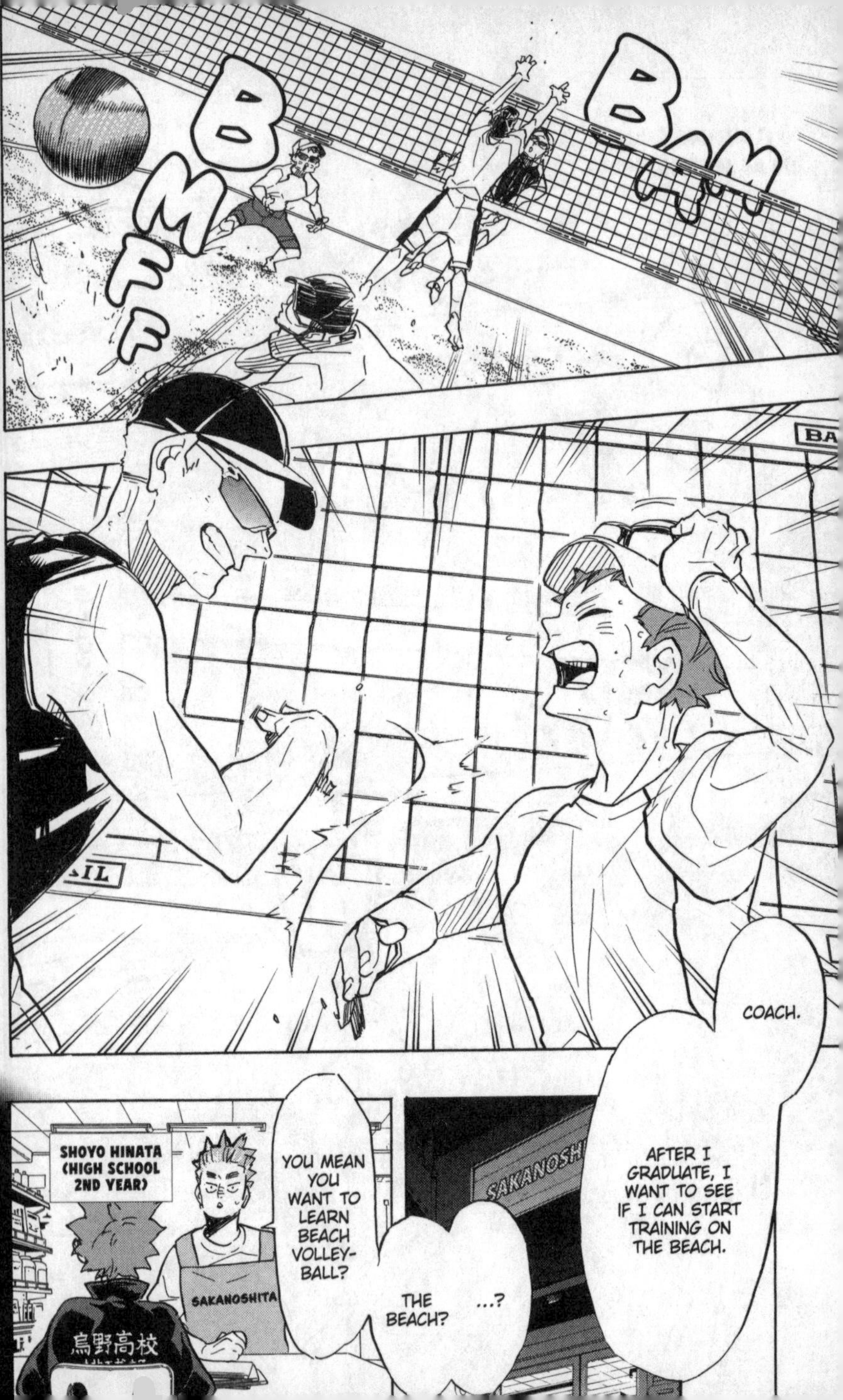
BAM
BMFF
COACH.
AFTER I GRADUATE, I WANT TO SEE IF I CAN START TRAINING ON THE BEACH.
SAKANOSHITA
...?
THE BEACH?
YOU MEAN YOU WANT TO LEARN BEACH VOLLEY-BALL?
SAKANOSHITA
SHOYO HINATA (HIGH SCHOOL 2ND YEAR)
烏野高校

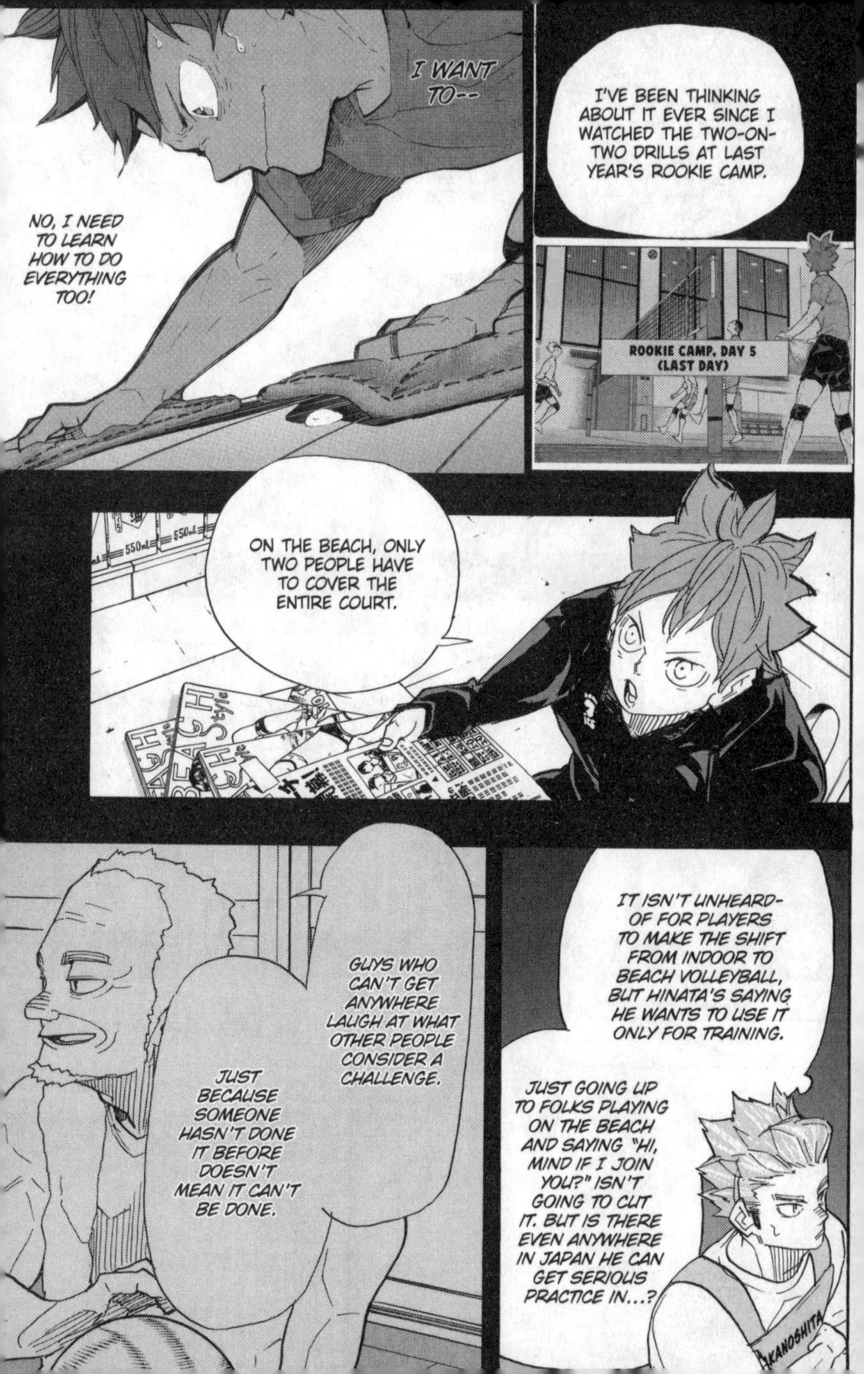
I'VE BEEN THINKING ABOUT IT EVER SINCE I WATCHED THE TWO-ON-TWO DRILLS AT LAST YEAR'S ROOKIE CAMP.
ROOKIE CAMP, DAY 5 (LAST DAY)
I WANT TO--
NO, I NEED TO LEARN HOW TO DO EVERYTHING TOO!
ON THE BEACH, ONLY TWO PEOPLE HAVE TO COVER THE ENTIRE COURT.
550ml
BEACH
IT ISN'T UNHEARD-OF FOR PLAYERS TO MAKE THE SHIFT FROM INDOOR TO BEACH VOLLEYBALL, BUT HINATA'S SAYING HE WANTS TO USE IT ONLY FOR TRAINING.
JUST GOING UP TO FOLKS PLAYING ON THE BEACH AND SAYING "HI, MIND IF I JOIN YOU?" ISN'T GOING TO CUT IT. BUT IS THERE EVEN ANYWHERE IN JAPAN HE CAN GET SERIOUS PRACTICE IN...?
KANOSHITA
GUYS WHO CAN'T GET ANYWHERE LAUGH AT WHAT OTHER PEOPLE CONSIDER A CHALLENGE.
JUST BECAUSE SOMEONE HASN'T DONE IT BEFORE DOESN'T MEAN IT CAN'T BE DONE.

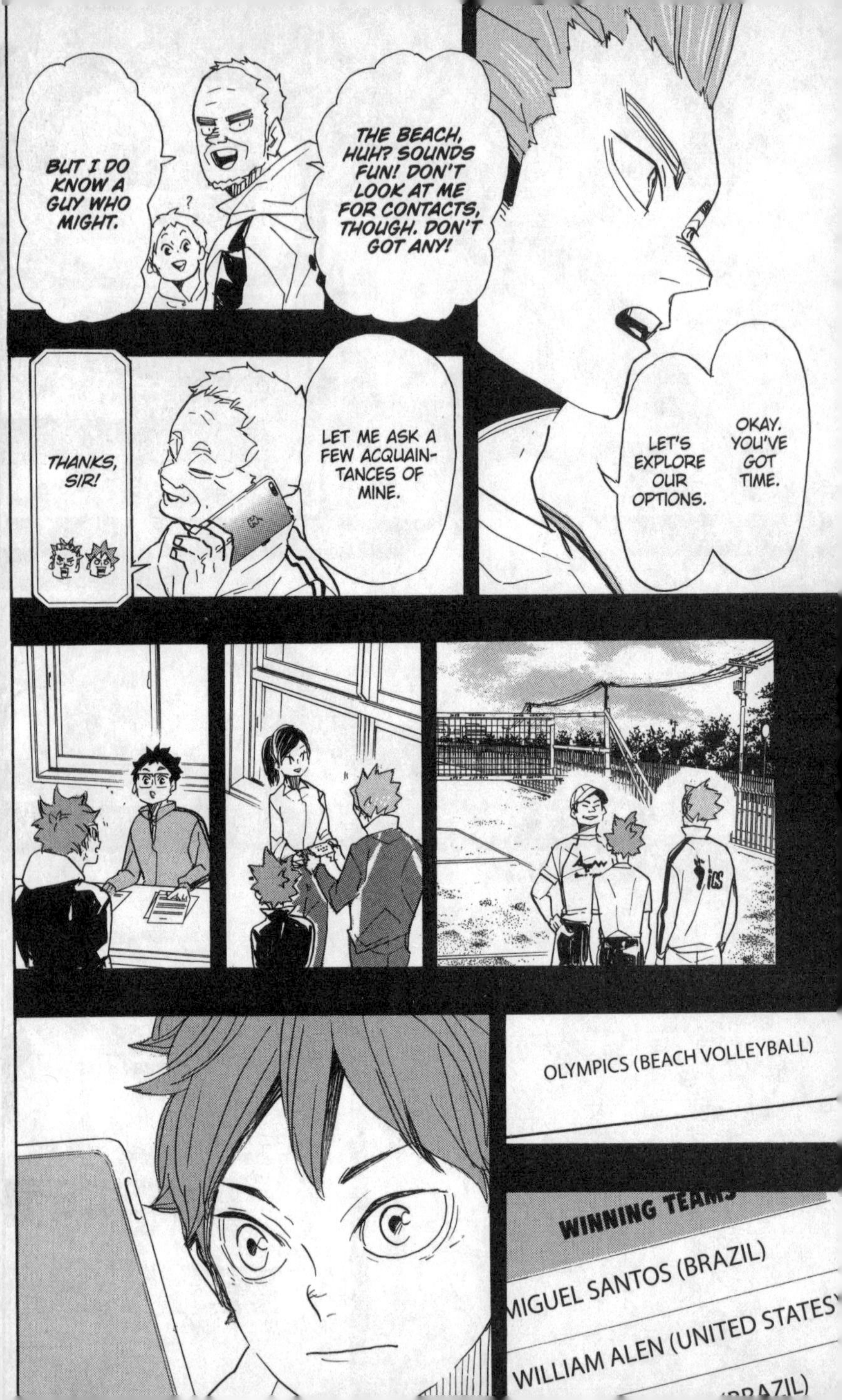
OKAY. YOU'VE GOT TIME.
LET'S EXPLORE OUR OPTIONS.
THE BEACH, HUH? SOUNDS FUN! DON'T LOOK AT ME FOR CONTACTS, THOUGH. DON'T GOT ANY!
BUT I DO KNOW A GUY WHO MIGHT.
LET ME ASK A FEW ACQUAINTANCES OF MINE.
THANKS, SIR!
OLYMPICS (BEACH VOLLEYBALL)
WINNING TEAMS
MIGUEL SANTOS (BRAZIL)
WILLIAM ALEN (UNITED STATES

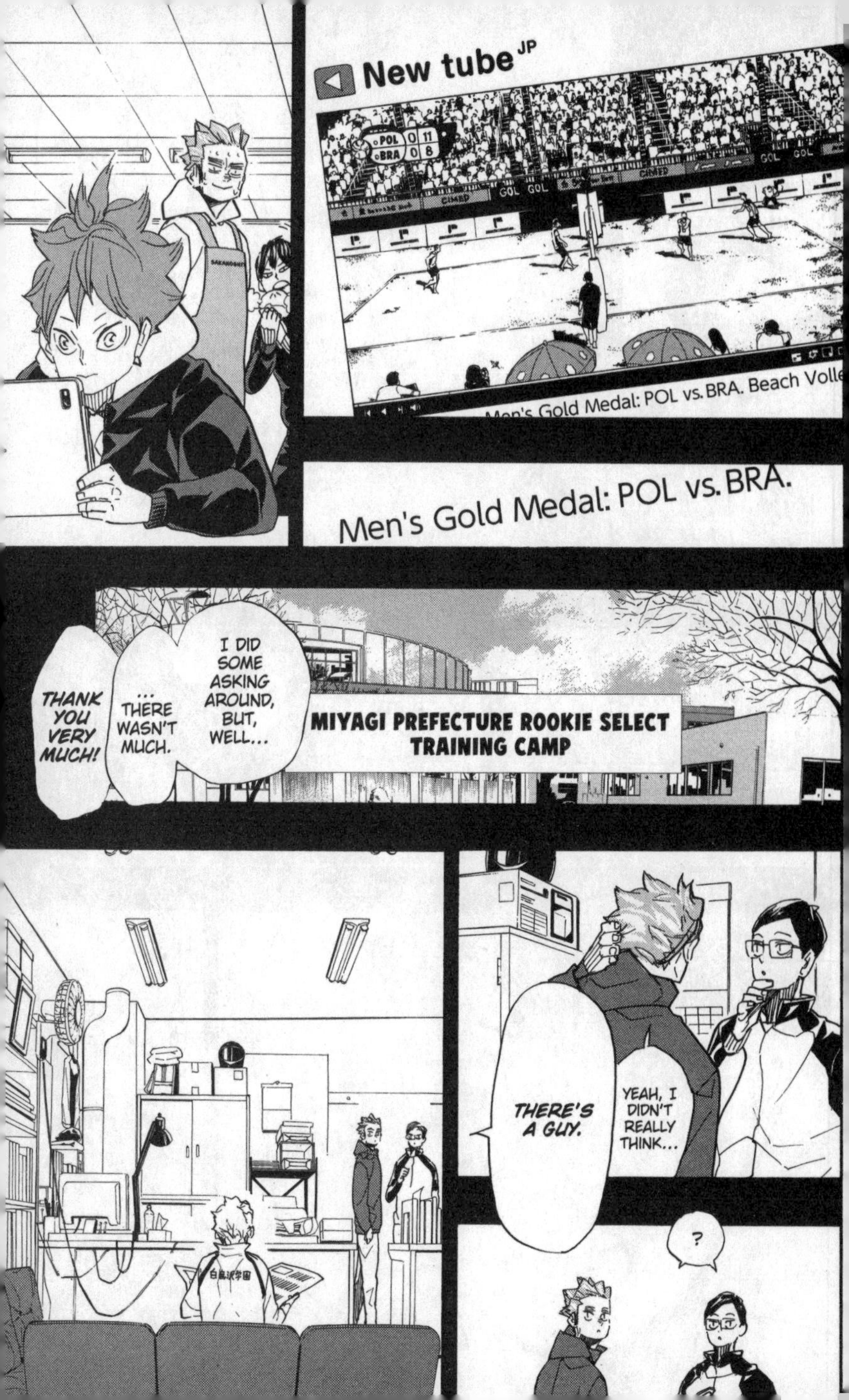

New tube JP
POL 0 11
BRA 0 8
Men's Gold Medal: POL vs. BRA. Beach Volle
Men's Gold Medal: POL vs. BRA.
MIYAGI PREFECTURE ROOKIE SELECT TRAINING CAMP
I DID SOME ASKING AROUND, BUT, WELL...
... THERE WASN'T MUCH.
THANK YOU VERY MUCH!
YEAH, I DIDN'T REALLY THINK...
THERE'S A GUY.
?

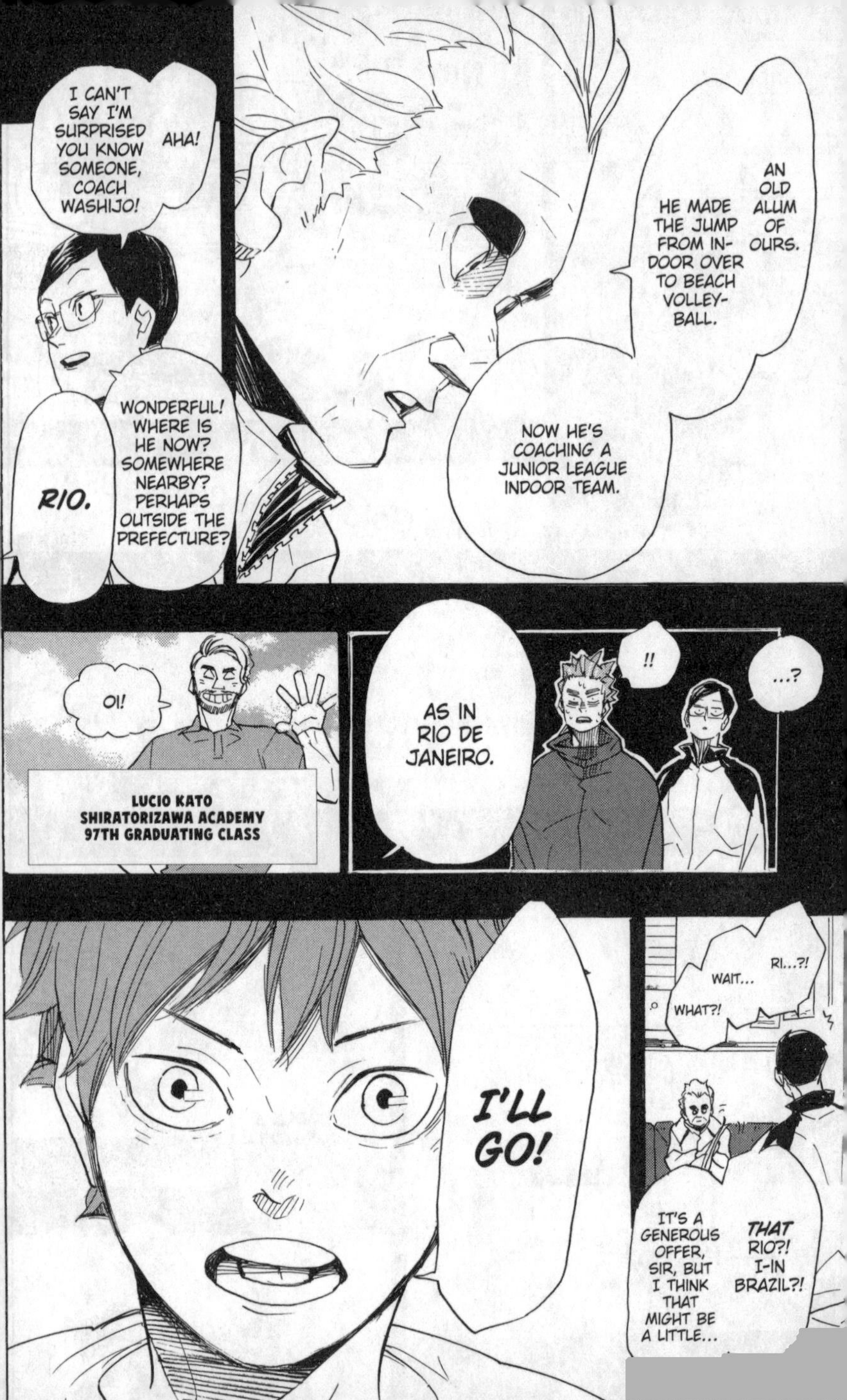

AN OLD ALUM OF OURS.
HE MADE THE JUMP FROM IN-DOOR OVER TO BEACH VOLLEY-BALL.
NOW HE'S COACHING A JUNIOR LEAGUE INDOOR TEAM.
AHA!
I CAN'T SAY I'M SURPRISED YOU KNOW SOMEONE, COACH WASHIJO!
WONDERFUL! WHERE IS HE NOW? SOMEWHERE NEARBY? PERHAPS OUTSIDE THE PREFECTURE?
RIO.
AS IN RIO DE JANEIRO.
!!
...?
OI!
LUCIO KATO
SHIRATORIZAWA ACADEMY
97TH GRADUATING CLASS
RI...?!
WAIT... WHAT?!
THAT RIO?! I-IN BRAZIL?!
IT'S A GENEROUS OFFER, SIR, BUT I THINK THAT MIGHT BE A LITTLE...
I'LL GO!

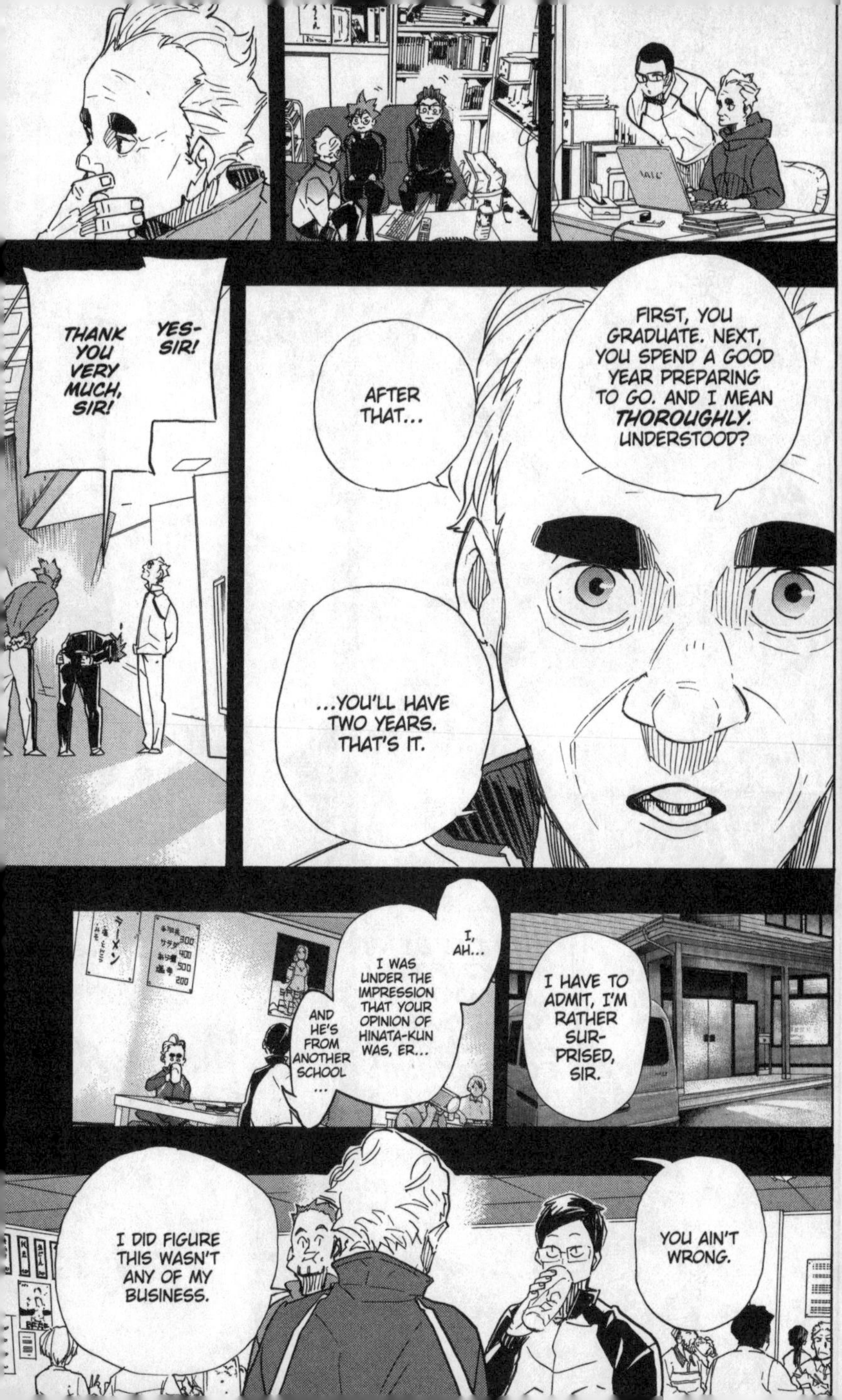
FIRST, YOU GRADUATE. NEXT, YOU SPEND A GOOD YEAR PREPARING TO GO. AND I MEAN *THOROUGHLY.* UNDERSTOOD?
AFTER THAT...
...YOU'LL HAVE TWO YEARS. THAT'S IT.
YES-SIR!
THANK YOU VERY MUCH, SIR!
I HAVE TO ADMIT, I'M RATHER SURPRISED, SIR.
I, AH...
I WAS UNDER THE IMPRESSION THAT YOUR OPINION OF HINATA-KUN WAS, ER...
AND HE'S FROM ANOTHER SCHOOL...
YOU AIN'T WRONG.
I DID FIGURE THIS WASN'T ANY OF MY BUSINESS.

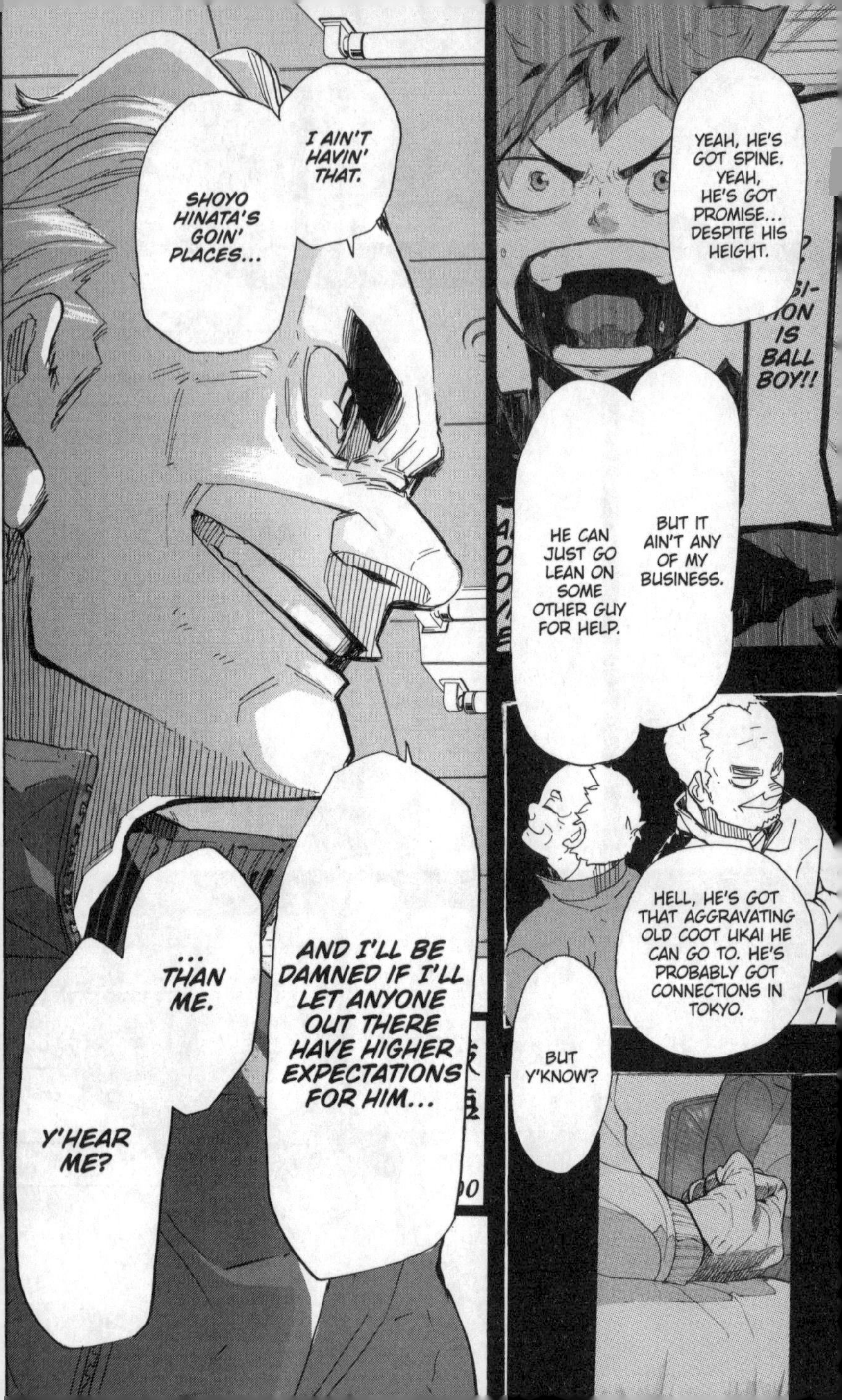
YEAH, HE'S GOT SPINE. YEAH, HE'S GOT PROMISE... DESPITE HIS HEIGHT.
SI-TION IS BALL BOY!!
BUT IT AIN'T ANY OF MY BUSINESS.
HE CAN JUST GO LEAN ON SOME OTHER GUY FOR HELP.
HELL, HE'S GOT THAT AGGRAVATING OLD COOT UKAI HE CAN GO TO. HE'S PROBABLY GOT CONNECTIONS IN TOKYO.
BUT Y'KNOW?
I AIN'T HAVIN' THAT.
SHOYO HINATA'S GOIN' PLACES...
AND I'LL BE DAMNED IF I'LL LET ANYONE OUT THERE HAVE HIGHER EXPECTATIONS FOR HIM...
... THAN ME.
Y'HEAR ME?

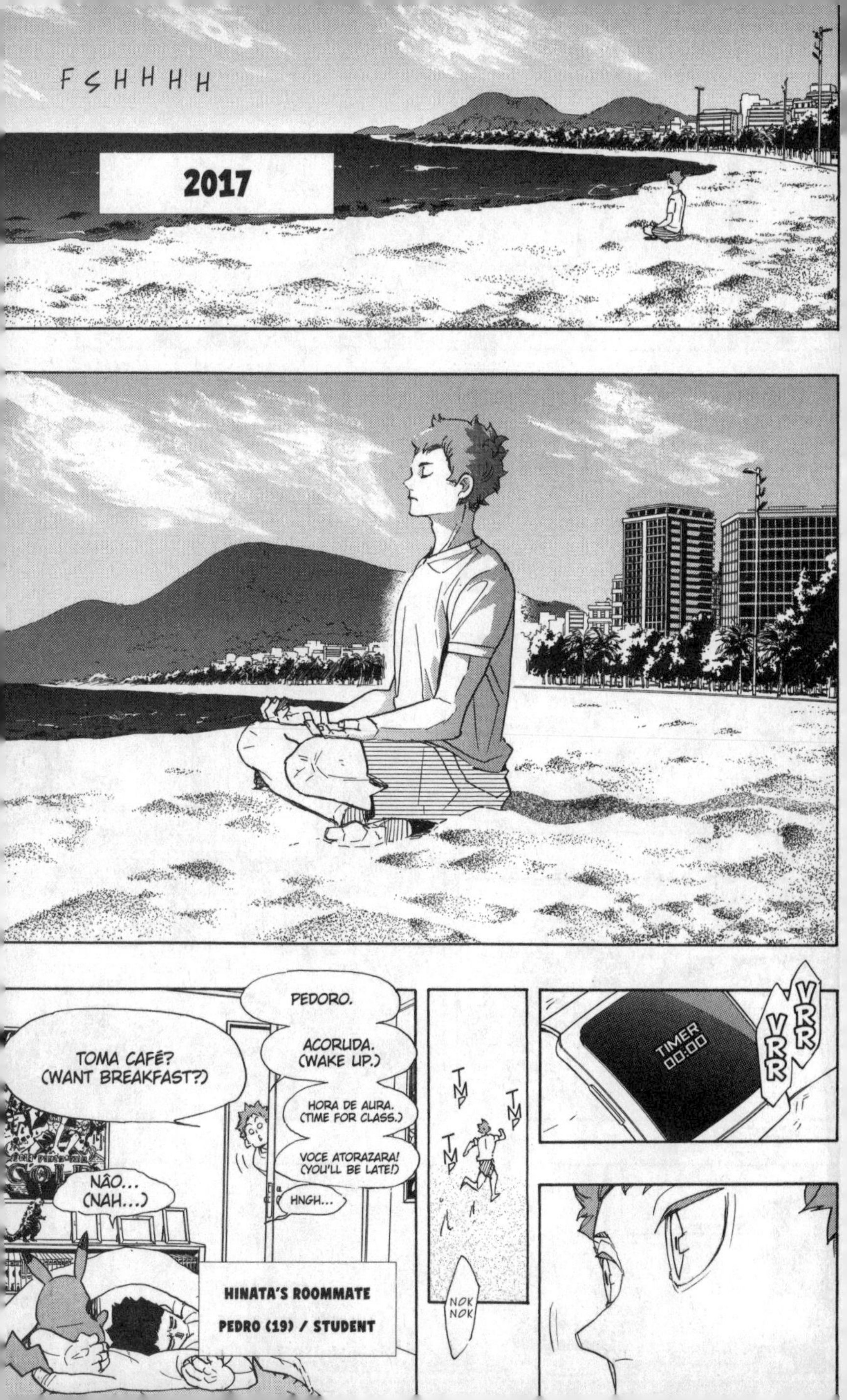
FSHHHH
2017
VRR VRR
TIMER 00:00
TMP TMP TMP
NOK NOK
PEDORO.
ACORUDA. (WAKE UP.)
HORA DE AURA. (TIME FOR CLASS.)
VOCE ATORAZARA! (YOU'LL BE LATE!)
HNGH...
TOMA CAFÉ? (WANT BREAKFAST?)
NÃO... (NAH...)
HINATA'S ROOMMATE
PEDRO (19) / STUDENT

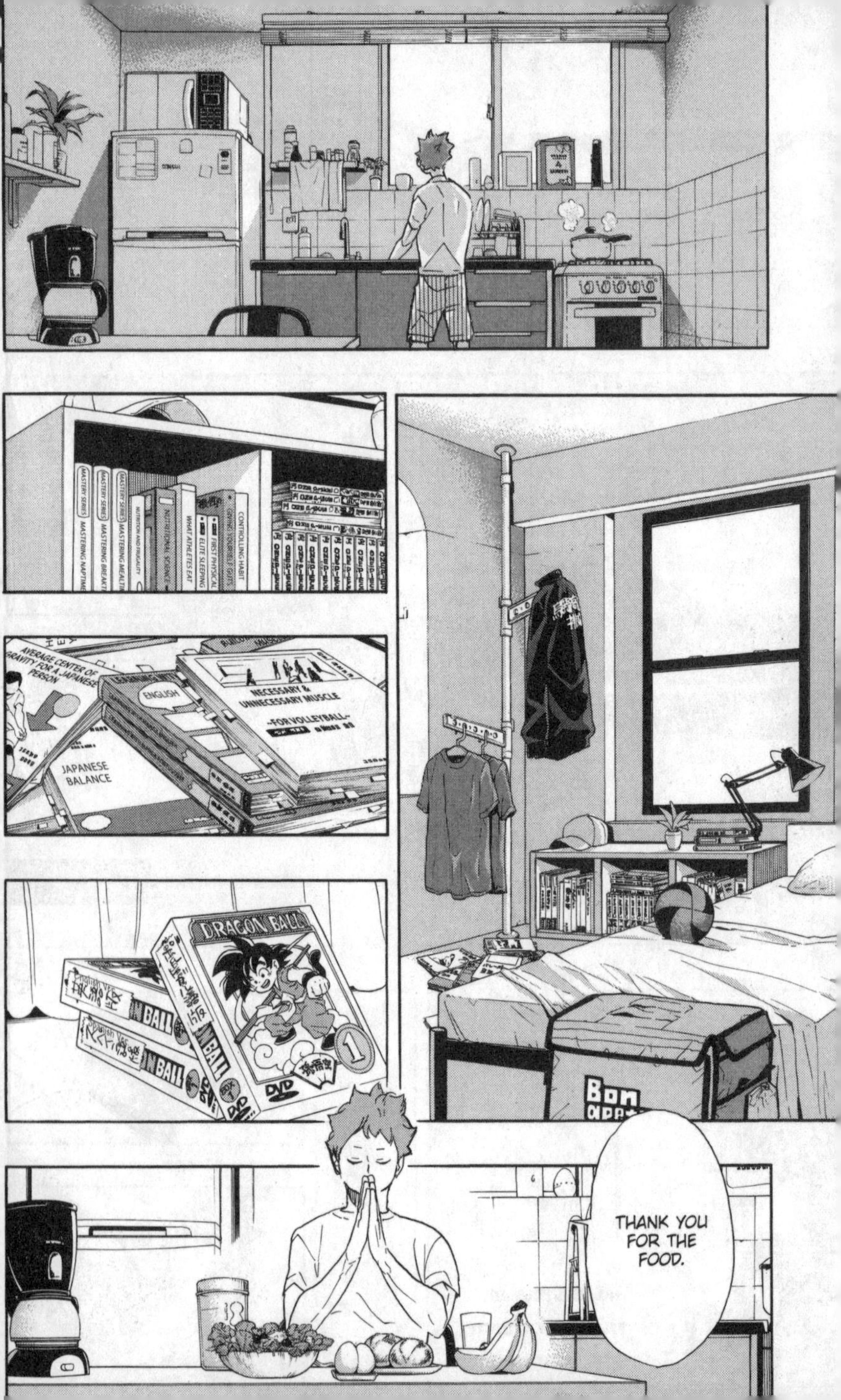
MASTERY SERIES
NUTRITION AND FRUGALITY
NUTRITIONAL SCIENCE
WHAT ATHLETES EAT
ELITE SLEEPING
FIRST PHYSICAL
GIVING YOURSELF GIFTS
CONTROLLING HABIT
AVERAGE CENTER OF GRAVITY FOR A JAPANESE PERSON
ENGLISH
NECESSARY & UNNECESSARY MUSCLE
-FOR VOLLEYBALL-
JAPANESE BALANCE
DRAGON BALL
DVD
THANK YOU FOR THE FOOD.

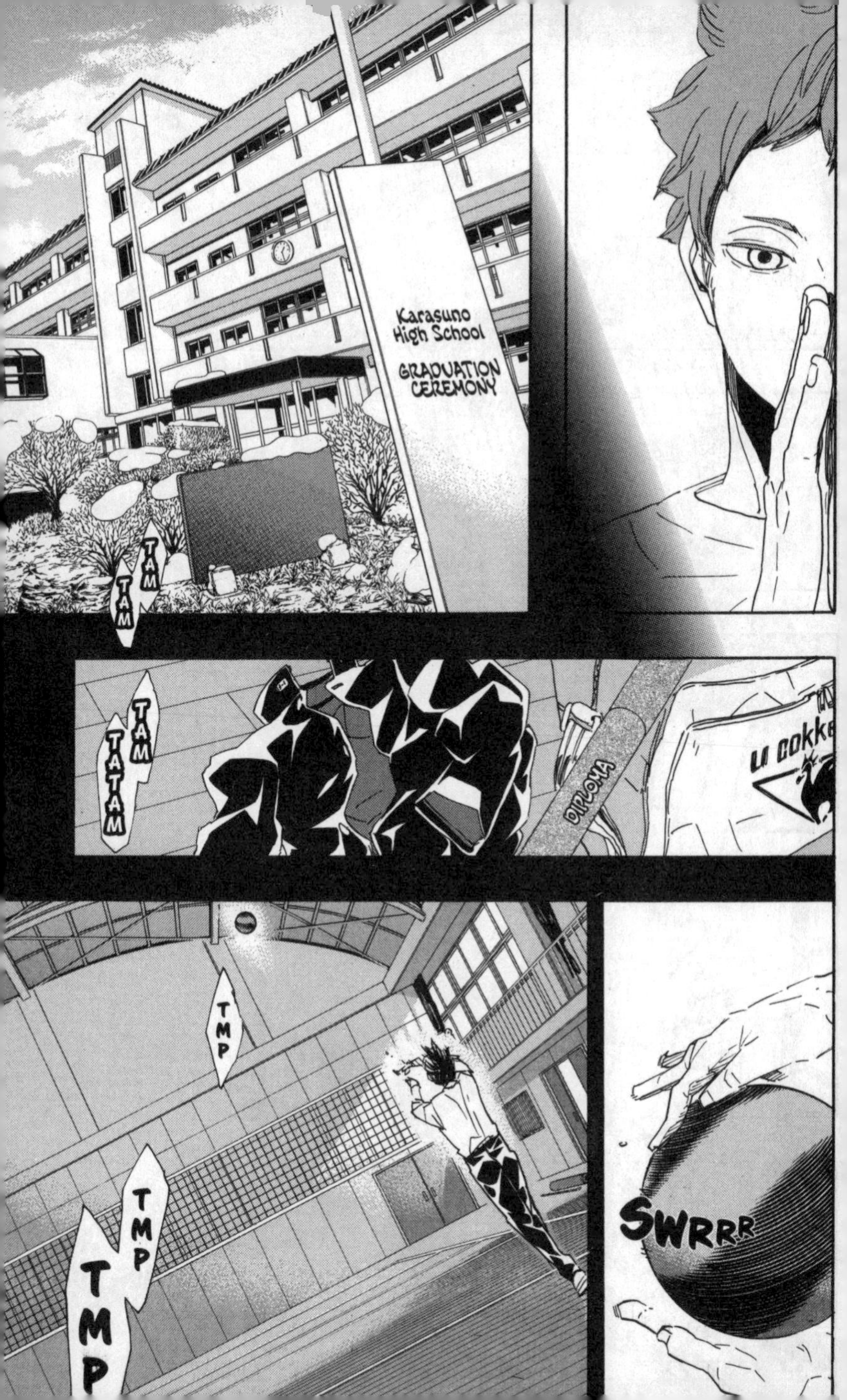
Karasuno High School
GRADUATION CEREMONY
TAM TAM
DIPLOMA
TATAM TAM
SWRRR
TMP
TMP
TMP

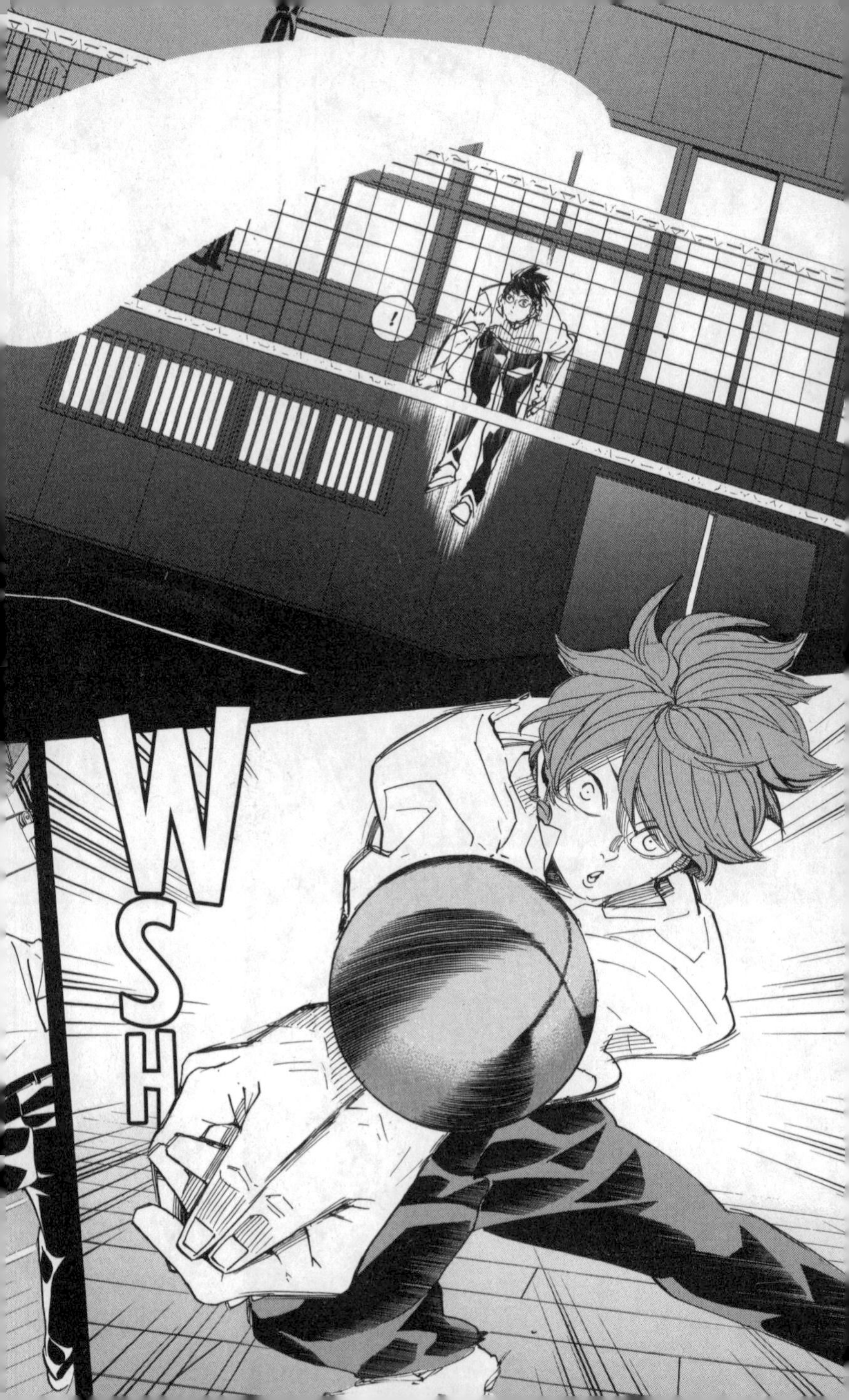
!
WSSH

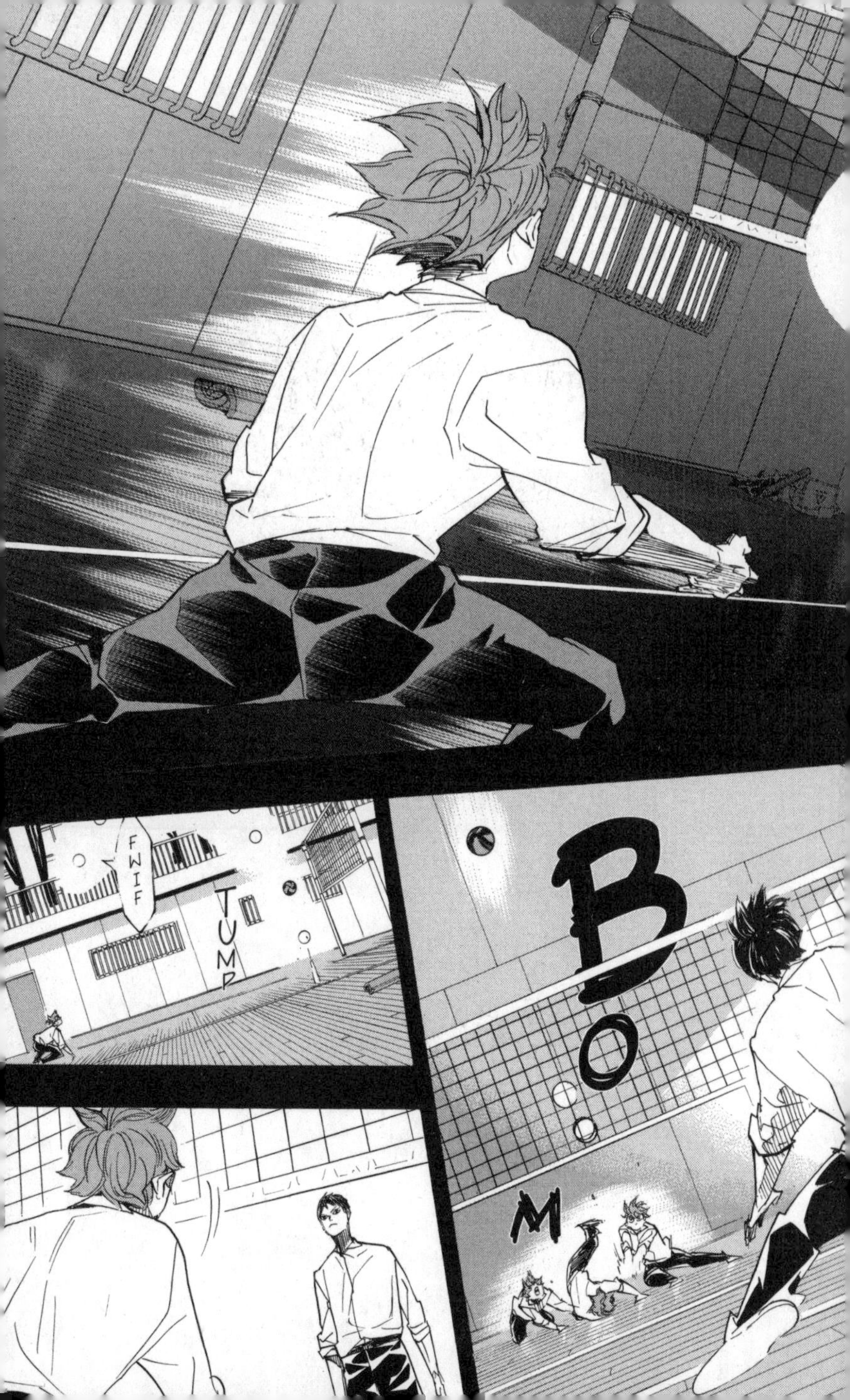
BOM
FWIF
TUMP

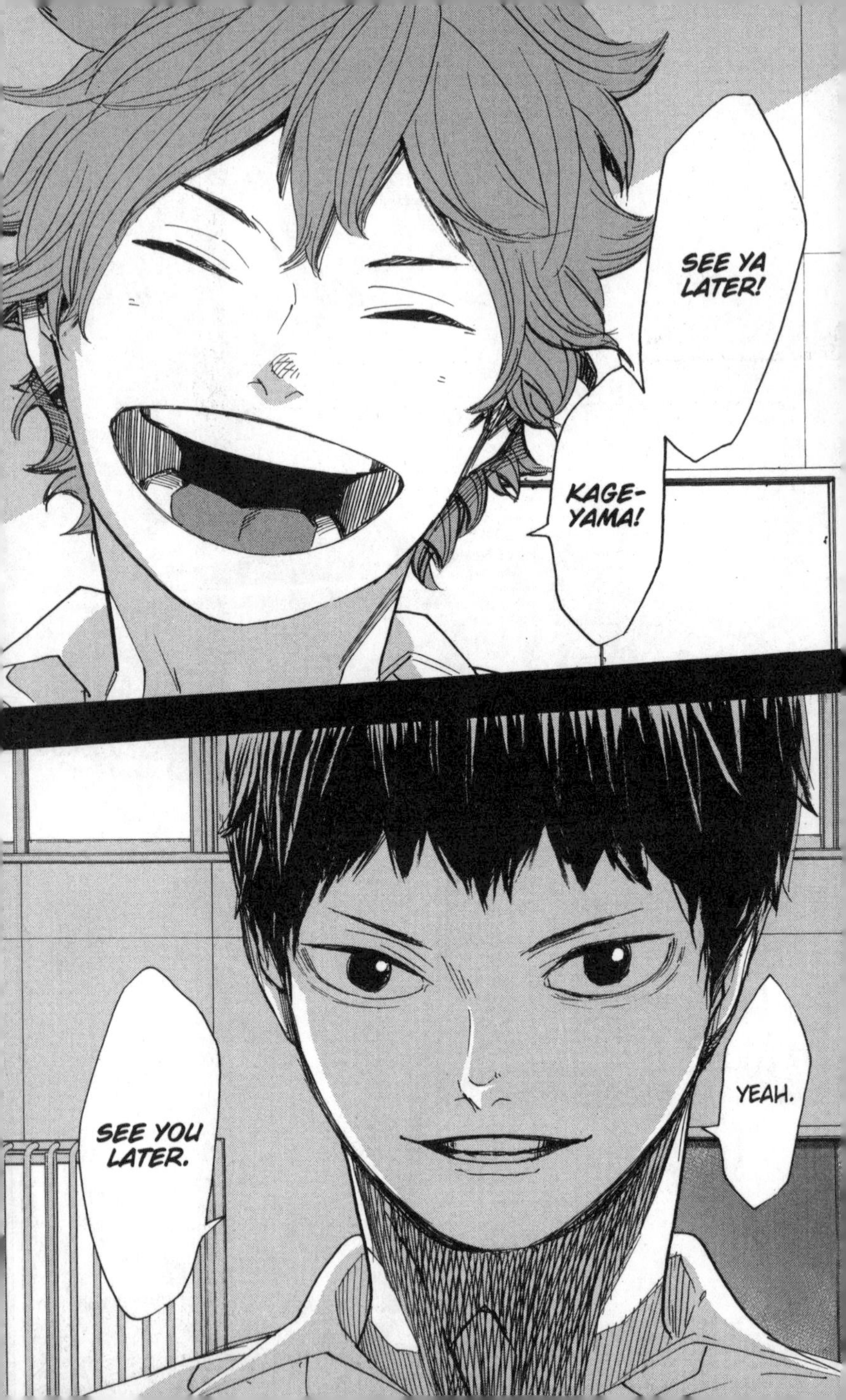
SEE YA LATER!
KAGE-YAMA!
YEAH.
SEE YOU LATER.

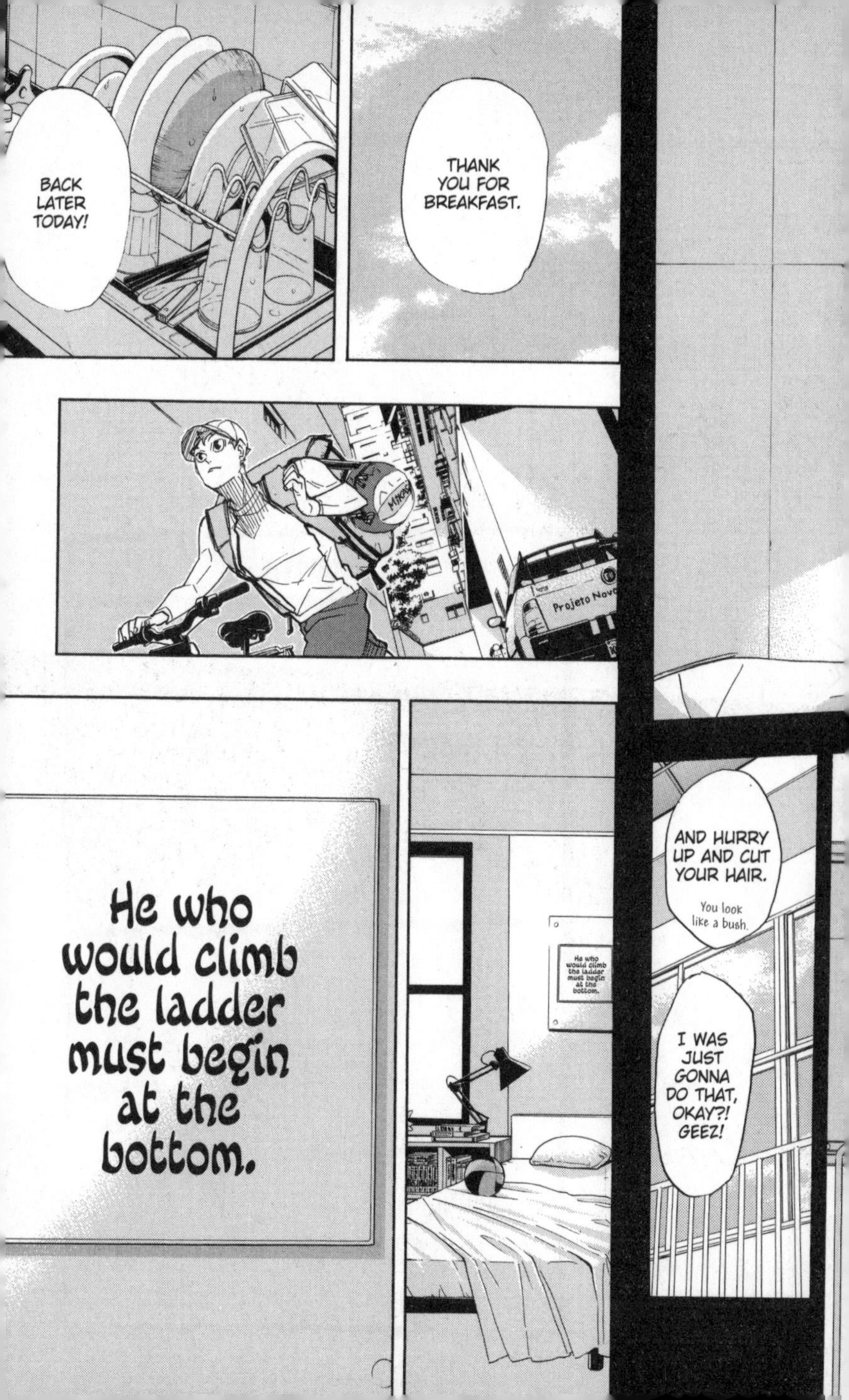
THANK YOU FOR BREAKFAST.
BACK LATER TODAY!
Projeto Nova
AND HURRY UP AND CUT YOUR HAIR.
You look like a bush.
I WAS JUST GONNA DO THAT, OKAY?! GEEZ!
He who would climb the ladder must begin at the bottom.
He who would climb the ladder must begin at the bottom.

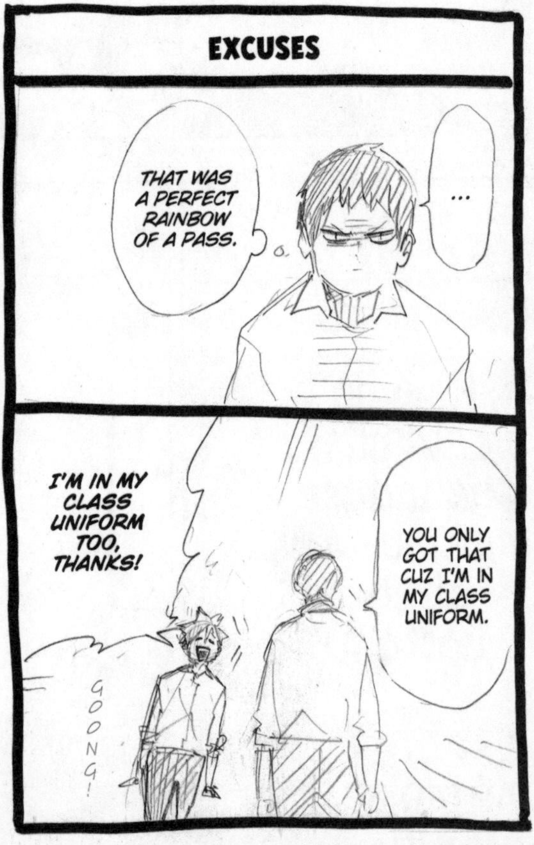
EXCUSES
...
THAT WAS A PERFECT RAINBOW OF A PASS.
YOU ONLY GOT THAT CUZ I'M IN MY CLASS UNIFORM.
I'M IN MY CLASS UNIFORM TOO, THANKS!
GOOONG!

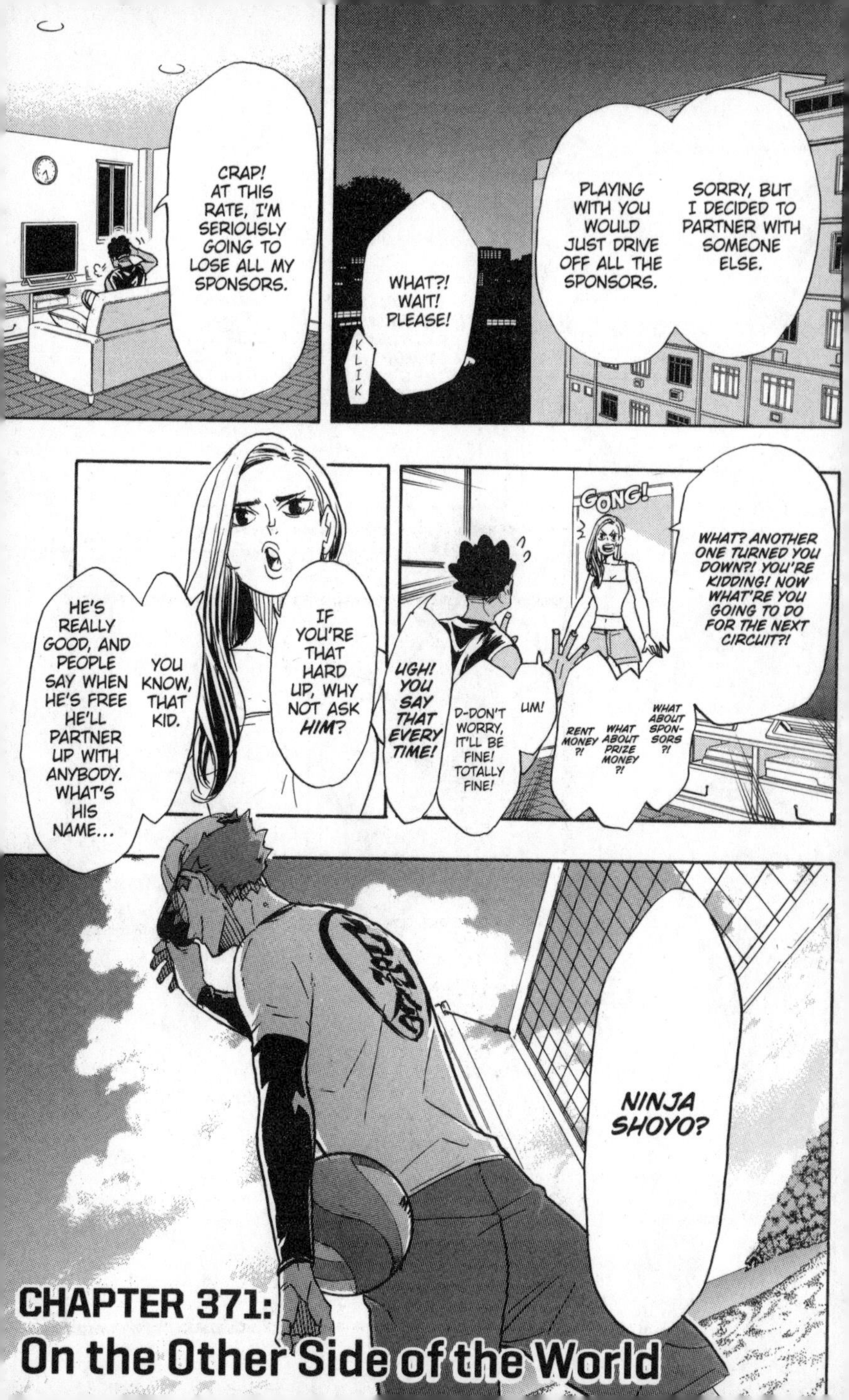
SORRY, BUT I DECIDED TO PARTNER WITH SOMEONE ELSE.
PLAYING WITH YOU WOULD JUST DRIVE OFF ALL THE SPONSORS.
WHAT?! WAIT! PLEASE!
KLIK
CRAP! AT THIS RATE, I'M SERIOUSLY GOING TO LOSE ALL MY SPONSORS.
GONG!
WHAT? ANOTHER ONE TURNED YOU DOWN?! YOU'RE KIDDING! NOW WHAT'RE YOU GOING TO DO FOR THE NEXT CIRCUIT?!
WHAT ABOUT SPON-SORS?!
WHAT ABOUT PRIZE MONEY?!
RENT MONEY?!
UM!
D-DON'T WORRY, IT'LL BE FINE! TOTALLY FINE!
UGH! YOU SAY THAT EVERY TIME!
IF YOU'RE THAT HARD UP, WHY NOT ASK HIM?
YOU KNOW, THAT KID.
HE'S REALLY GOOD, AND PEOPLE SAY WHEN HE'S FREE HE'LL PARTNER UP WITH ANYBODY. WHAT'S HIS NAME...
NINJA SHOYO?

CHAPTER 371:
On the Other Side of the World

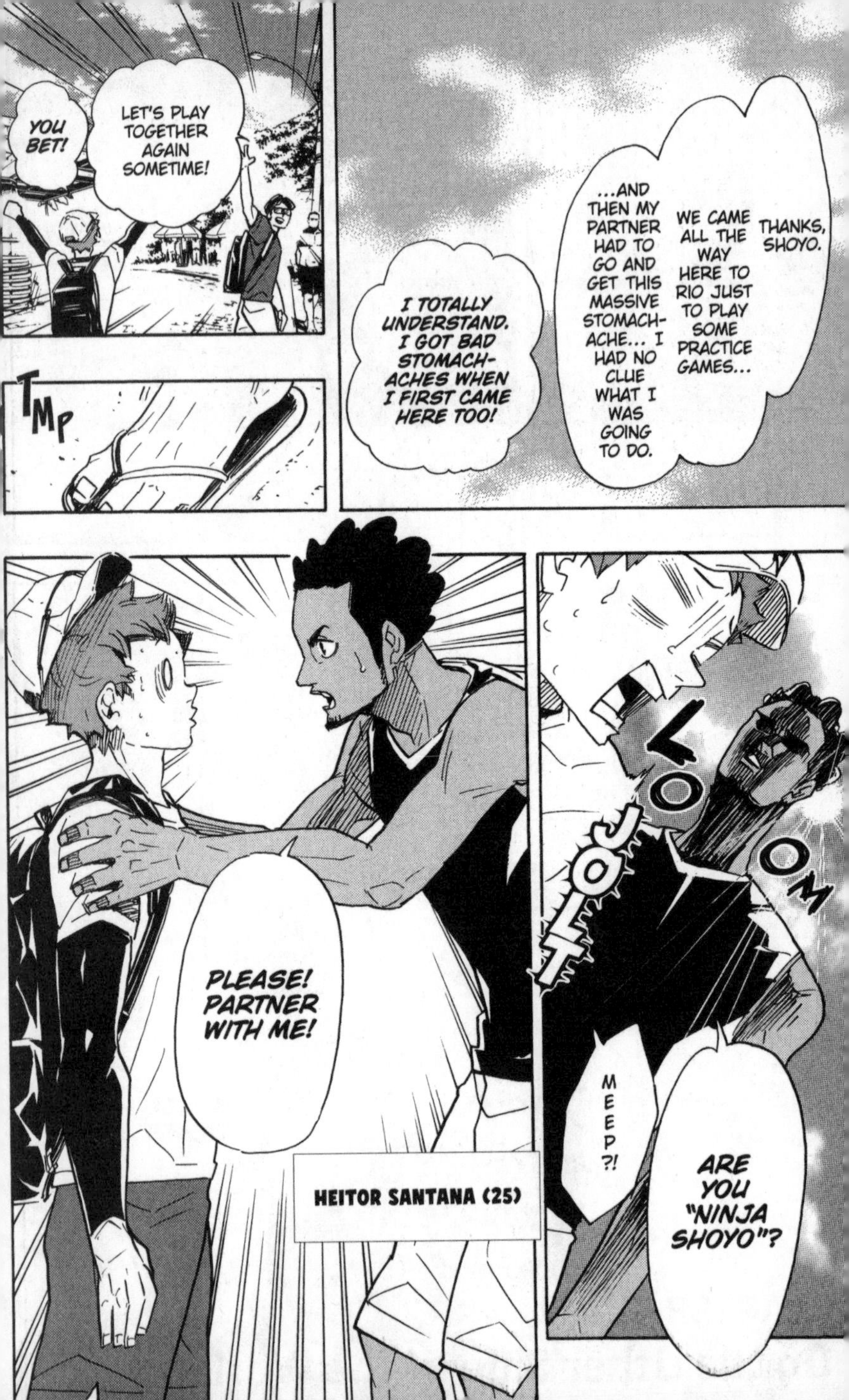
THANKS, SHOYO.
WE CAME ALL THE WAY HERE TO RIO JUST TO PLAY SOME PRACTICE GAMES...
...AND THEN MY PARTNER HAD TO GO AND GET THIS MASSIVE STOMACH-ACHE... I HAD NO CLUE WHAT I WAS GOING TO DO.
I TOTALLY UNDERSTAND. I GOT BAD STOMACH-ACHES WHEN I FIRST CAME HERE TOO!
LET'S PLAY TOGETHER AGAIN SOMETIME!
YOU BET!
TMP
LOOM
JOLT
ARE YOU "NINJA SHOYO"?
MEEP?!
PLEASE! PARTNER WITH ME!
HEITOR SANTANA (25)

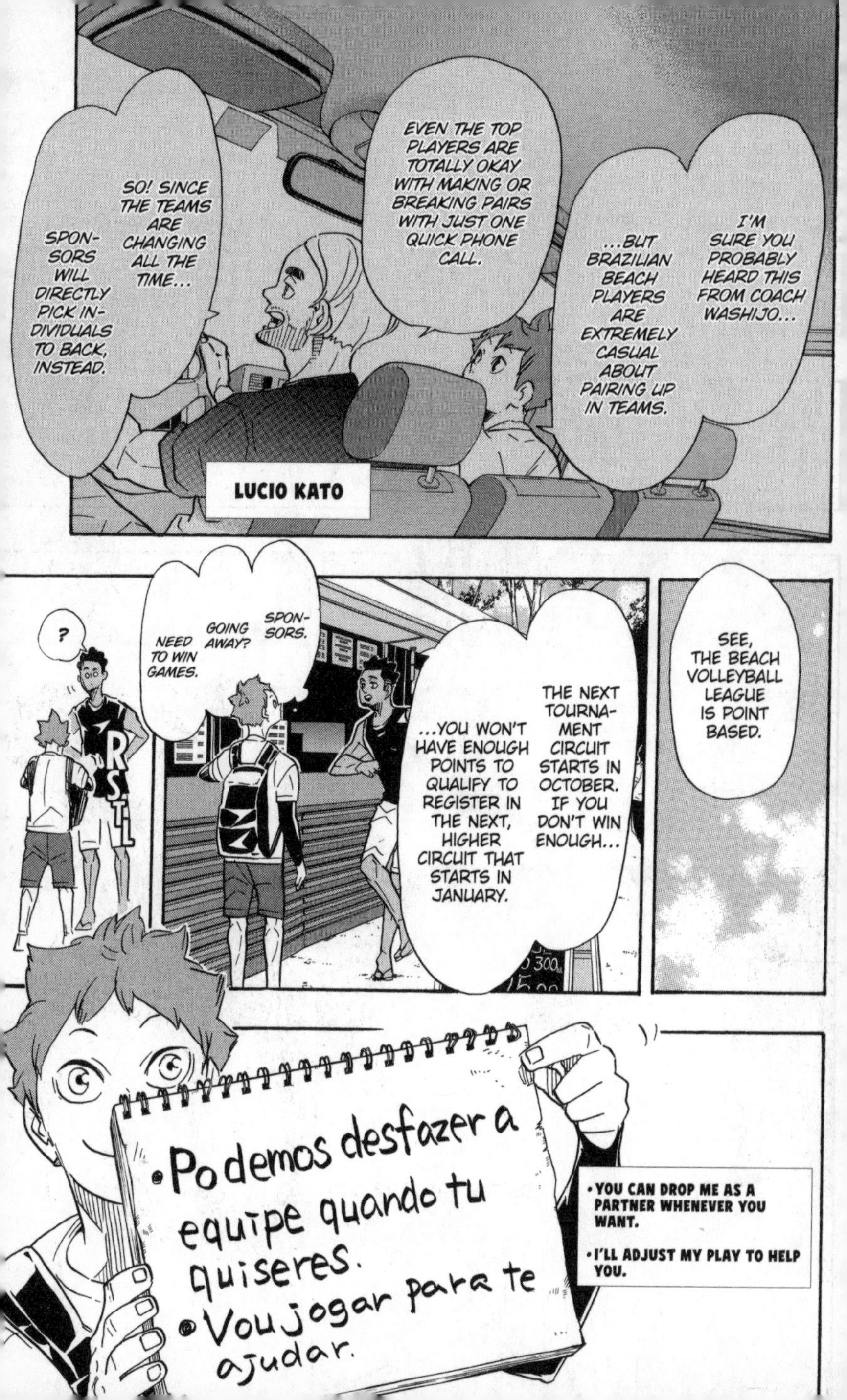
I'M SURE YOU PROBABLY HEARD THIS FROM COACH WASHIJO...
...BUT BRAZILIAN BEACH PLAYERS ARE EXTREMELY CASUAL ABOUT PAIRING UP IN TEAMS.
EVEN THE TOP PLAYERS ARE TOTALLY OKAY WITH MAKING OR BREAKING PAIRS WITH JUST ONE QUICK PHONE CALL.
SO! SINCE THE TEAMS ARE CHANGING ALL THE TIME...
SPON-SORS WILL DIRECTLY PICK IN-DIVIDUALS TO BACK, INSTEAD.
LUCIO KATO
SEE, THE BEACH VOLLEYBALL LEAGUE IS POINT BASED.
THE NEXT TOURNA-MENT CIRCUIT STARTS IN OCTOBER. IF YOU DON'T WIN ENOUGH...
...YOU WON'T HAVE ENOUGH POINTS TO QUALIFY TO REGISTER IN THE NEXT, HIGHER CIRCUIT THAT STARTS IN JANUARY.
SPON-SORS.
GOING AWAY?
NEED TO WIN GAMES.
?
• YOU CAN DROP ME AS A PARTNER WHENEVER YOU WANT.
• I'LL ADJUST MY PLAY TO HELP YOU.
• Podemos desfazer a equipe quando tu quiseres.
• Vou jogar para te ajudar.

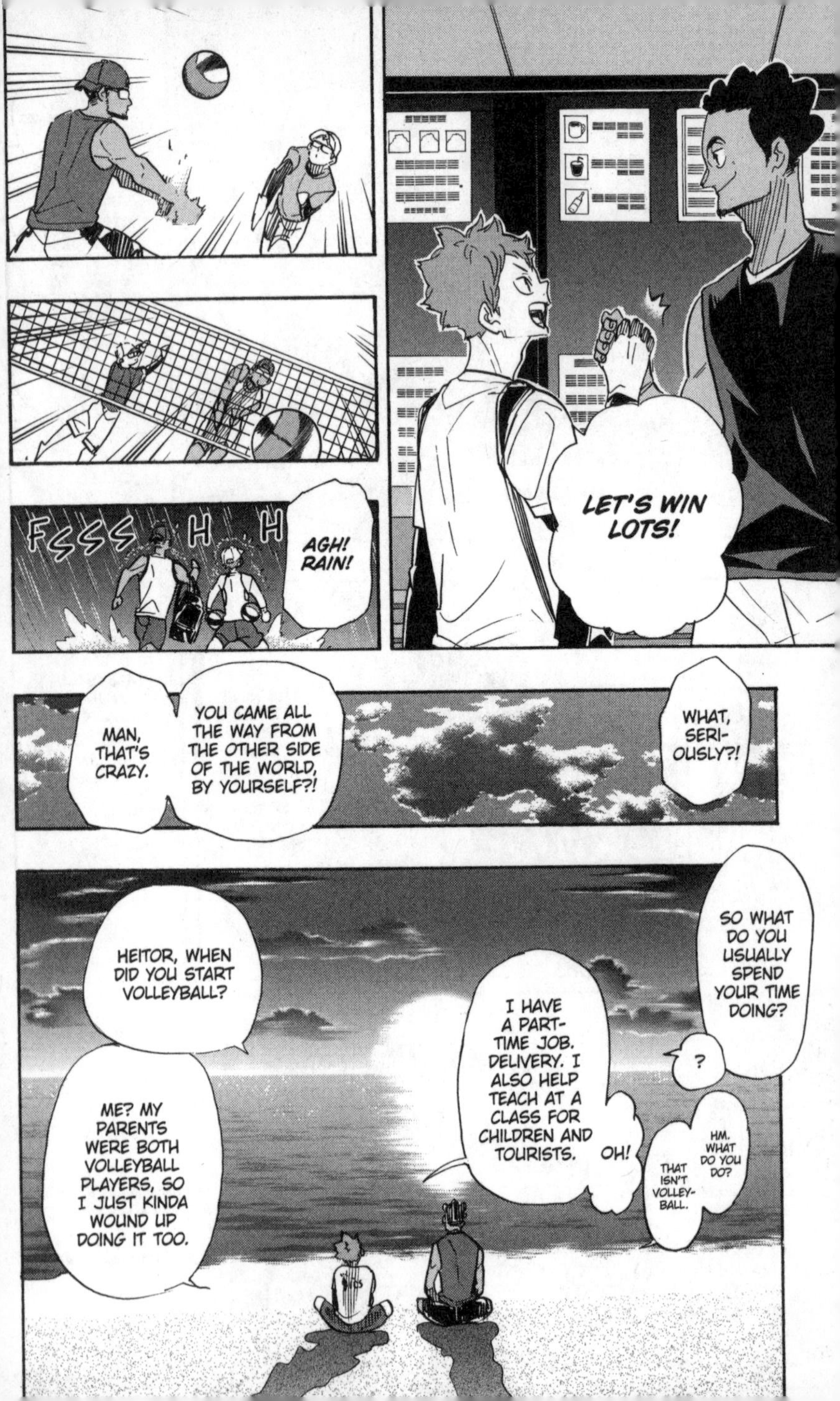

LET'S WIN LOTS!
FSSS H H
AGH! RAIN!
WHAT, SERI-OUSLY?!
YOU CAME ALL THE WAY FROM THE OTHER SIDE OF THE WORLD, BY YOURSELF?!
MAN, THAT'S CRAZY.
SO WHAT DO YOU USUALLY SPEND YOUR TIME DOING?
?
I HAVE A PART-TIME JOB. DELIVERY. I ALSO HELP TEACH AT A CLASS FOR CHILDREN AND TOURISTS.
OH!
HM. WHAT DO YOU DO?
THAT ISN'T VOLLEY-BALL.
HEITOR, WHEN DID YOU START VOLLEYBALL?
ME? MY PARENTS WERE BOTH VOLLEYBALL PLAYERS, SO I JUST KINDA WOUND UP DOING IT TOO.

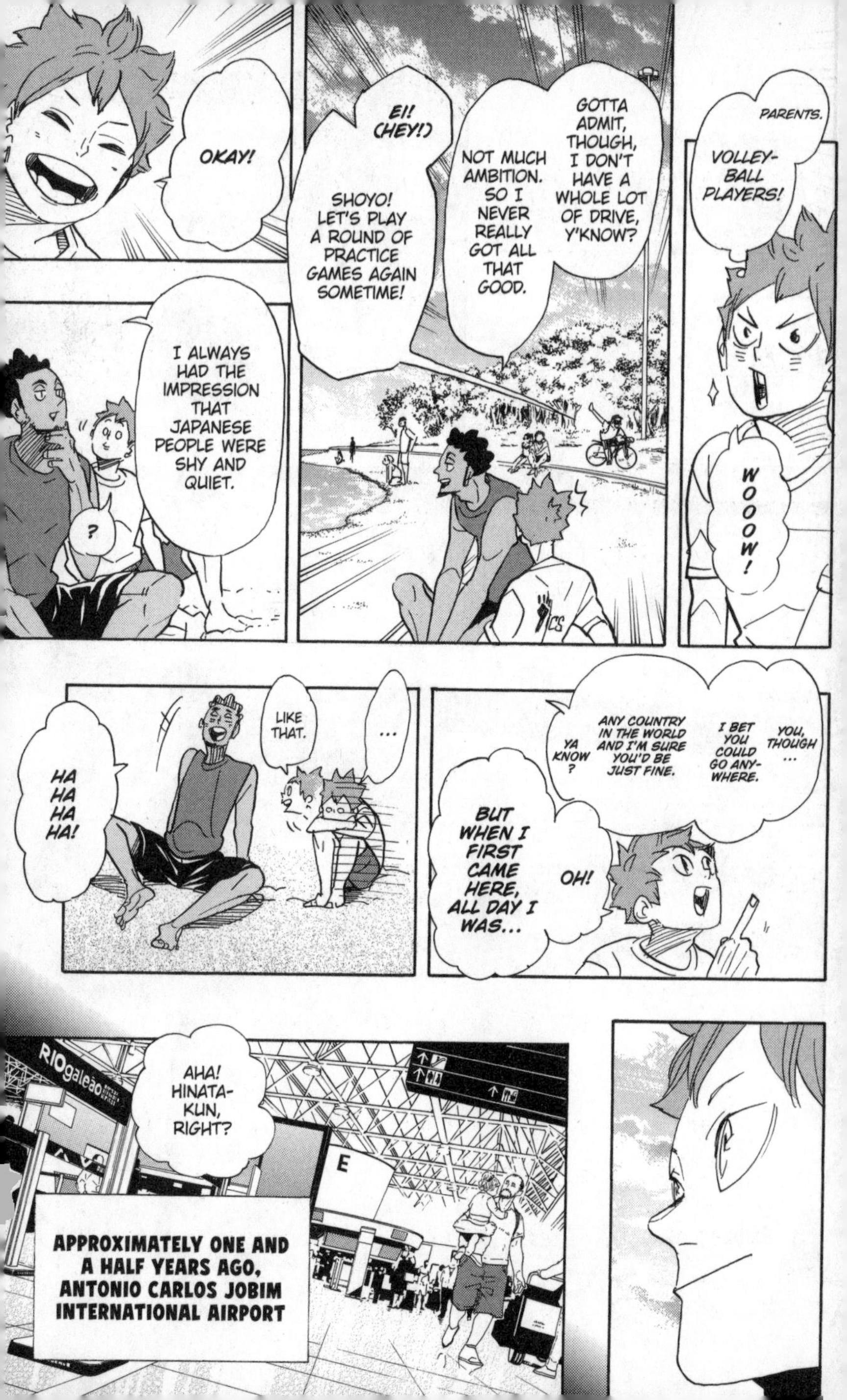

PARENTS.
VOLLEY-BALL PLAYERS!
WOOOOW!
GOTTA ADMIT, THOUGH, I DON'T HAVE A WHOLE LOT OF DRIVE, Y'KNOW?
NOT MUCH AMBITION. SO I NEVER REALLY GOT ALL THAT GOOD.
EI! (HEY!)
SHOYO! LET'S PLAY A ROUND OF PRACTICE GAMES AGAIN SOMETIME!
OKAY!
I ALWAYS HAD THE IMPRESSION THAT JAPANESE PEOPLE WERE SHY AND QUIET.
?
YOU, THOUGH...
I BET YOU COULD GO ANYWHERE.
ANY COUNTRY IN THE WORLD AND I'M SURE YOU'D BE JUST FINE.
YA KNOW?
OH!
BUT WHEN I FIRST CAME HERE, ALL DAY I WAS...
...
LIKE THAT.
HA HA HA HA!
RIOgaleão
E
AHA! HINATA-KUN, RIGHT?
APPROXIMATELY ONE AND A HALF YEARS AGO, ANTONIO CARLOS JOBIM INTERNATIONAL AIRPORT

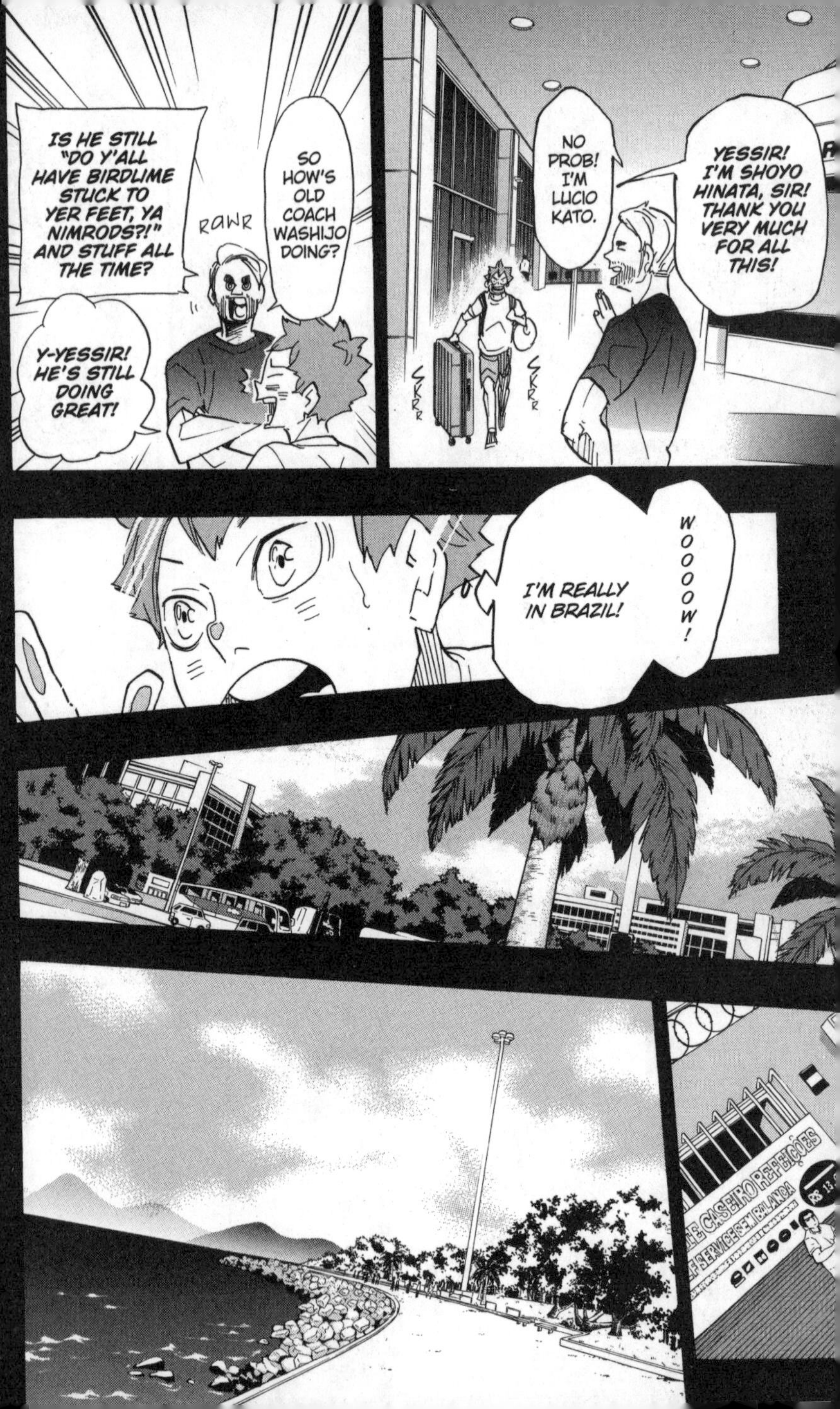
YESSIR! I'M SHOYO HINATA, SIR! THANK YOU VERY MUCH FOR ALL THIS!
NO PROB! I'M LUCIO KATO.
SKRR
SKRR
SO HOW'S OLD COACH WASHIJO DOING?
IS HE STILL "DO Y'ALL HAVE BIRDLIME STUCK TO YER FEET, YA NIMRODS?!" AND STUFF ALL THE TIME?
RAWR
Y-YESSIR! HE'S STILL DOING GREAT!
WOOOOOW!
I'M REALLY IN BRAZIL!
CASEIRO REFEIÇÕES

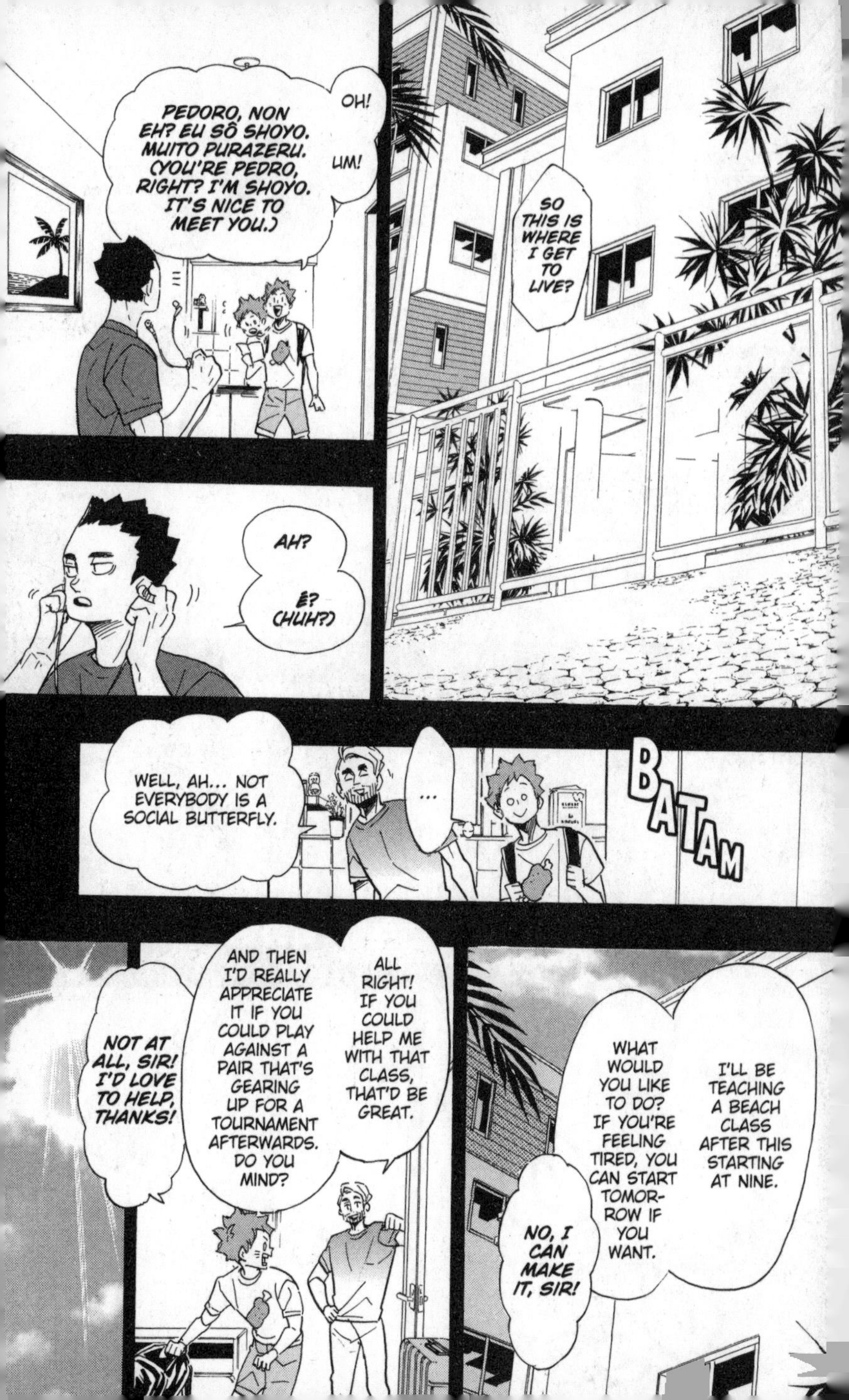
SO THIS IS WHERE I GET TO LIVE?
OH!
UM!
PEDORO, NON EH? EU SÔ SHOYO. MUITO PURAZERU. (YOU'RE PEDRO, RIGHT? I'M SHOYO. IT'S NICE TO MEET YOU.)
AH?
Ê? (HUH?)
BATAM
...
WELL, AH... NOT EVERYBODY IS A SOCIAL BUTTERFLY.
I'LL BE TEACHING A BEACH CLASS AFTER THIS STARTING AT NINE.
WHAT WOULD YOU LIKE TO DO? IF YOU'RE FEELING TIRED, YOU CAN START TOMOR-ROW IF YOU WANT.
NO, I CAN MAKE IT, SIR!
ALL RIGHT! IF YOU COULD HELP ME WITH THAT CLASS, THAT'D BE GREAT.
AND THEN I'D REALLY APPRECIATE IT IF YOU COULD PLAY AGAINST A PAIR THAT'S GEARING UP FOR A TOURNAMENT AFTERWARDS. DO YOU MIND?
NOT AT ALL, SIR! I'D LOVE TO HELP, THANKS!

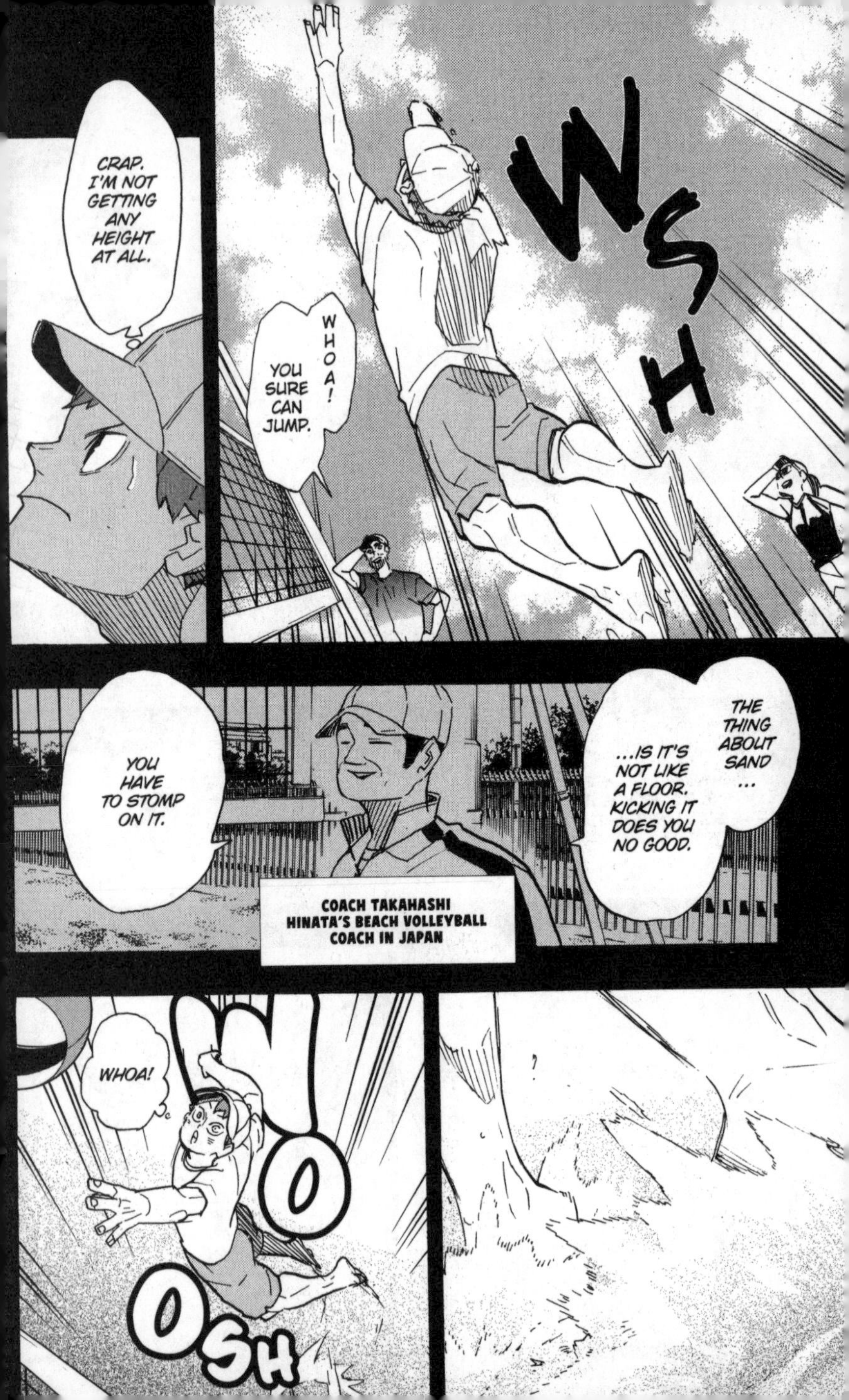
WSH
WHOA! YOU SURE CAN JUMP.
CRAP. I'M NOT GETTING ANY HEIGHT AT ALL.
THE THING ABOUT SAND...
...IS IT'S NOT LIKE A FLOOR. KICKING IT DOES YOU NO GOOD.
YOU HAVE TO STOMP ON IT.
COACH TAKAHASHI HINATA'S BEACH VOLLEYBALL COACH IN JAPAN
WHOA!
OOSH

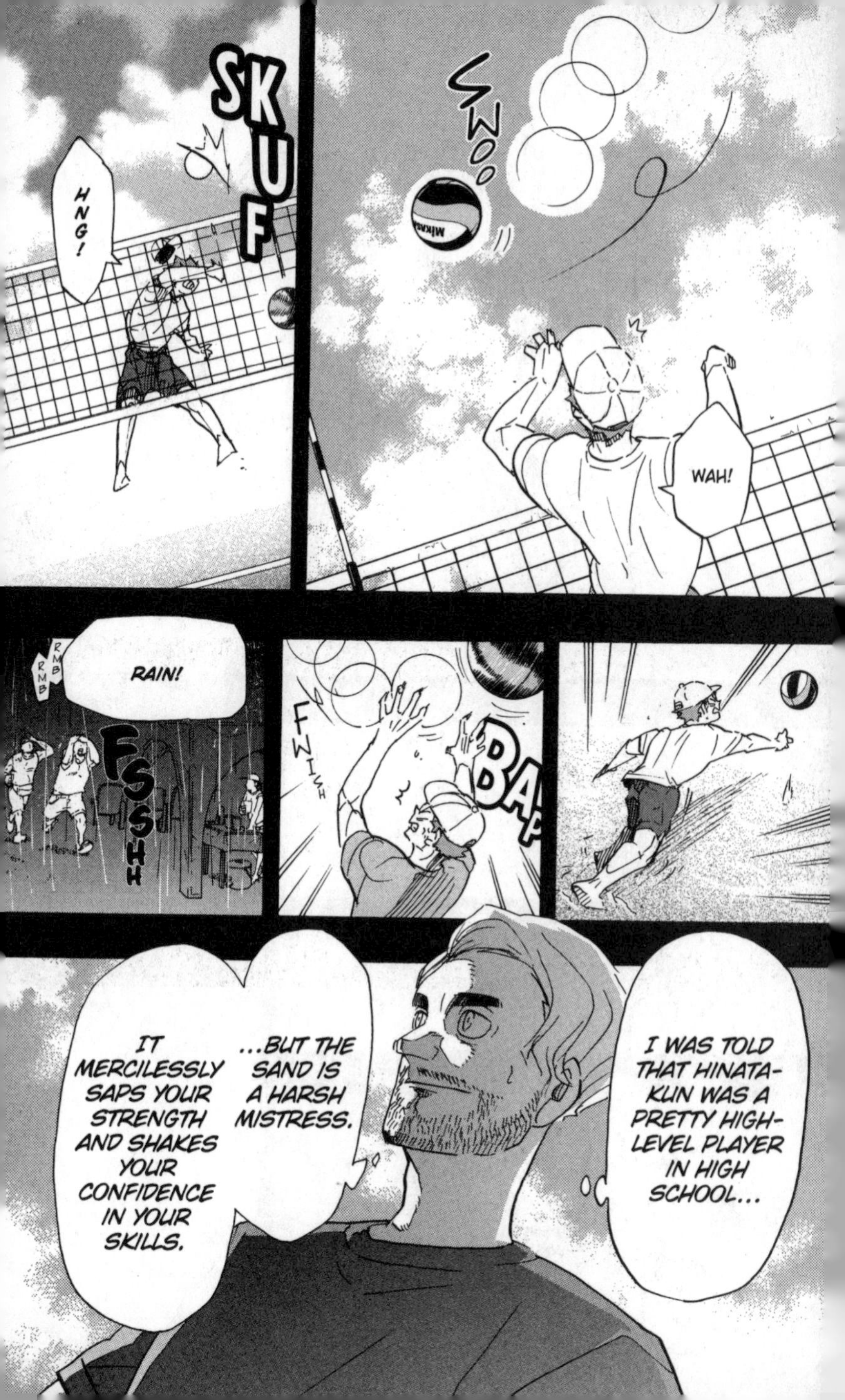
SWOOO
WAH!
SKUF
HNG!
FWISH
BAP
RAIN!
RMB RMB
FSSHH
I WAS TOLD THAT HINATA-KUN WAS A PRETTY HIGH-LEVEL PLAYER IN HIGH SCHOOL...
...BUT THE SAND IS A HARSH MISTRESS.
IT MERCILESSLY SAPS YOUR STRENGTH AND SHAKES YOUR CONFIDENCE IN YOUR SKILLS.

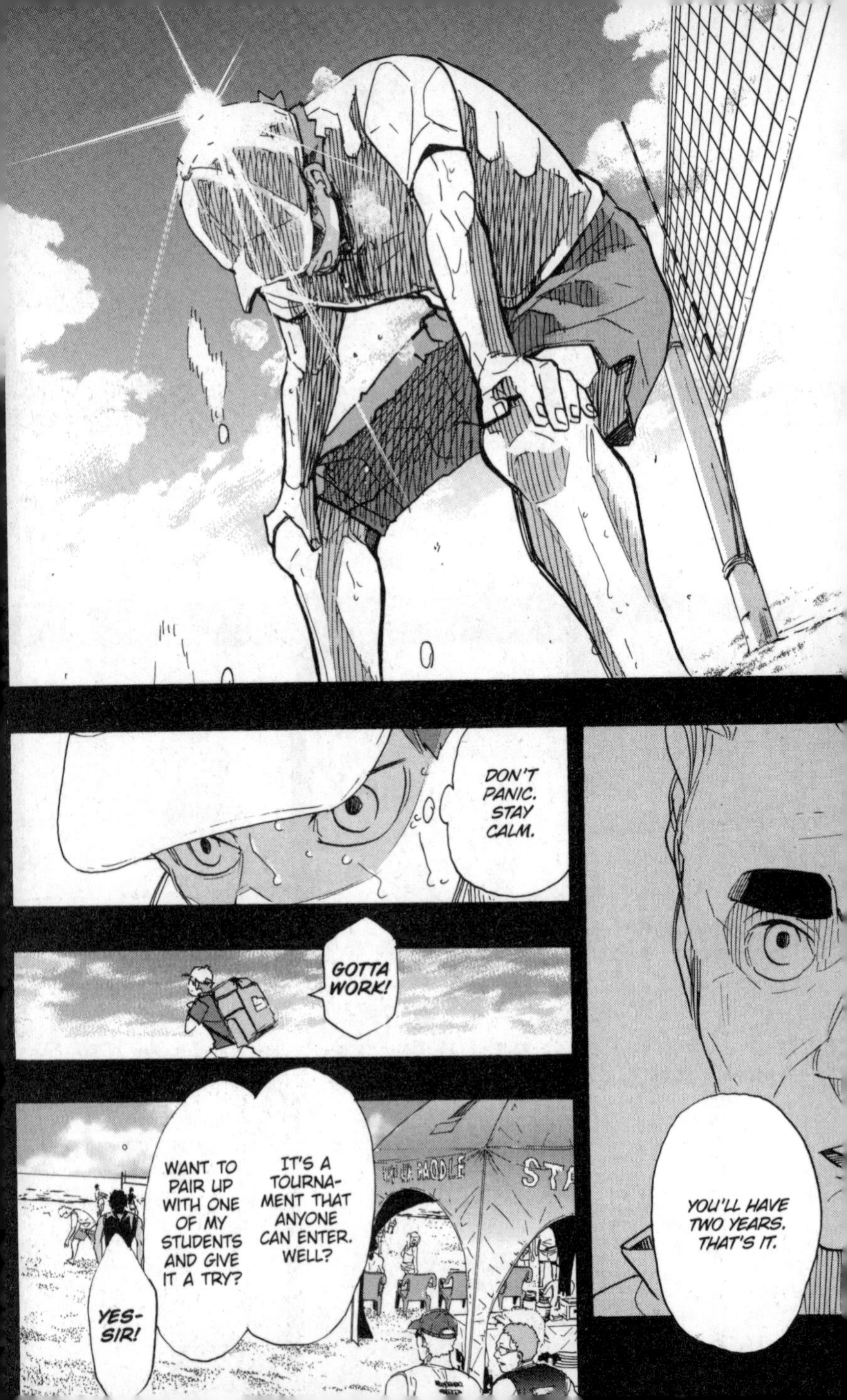
YOU'LL HAVE TWO YEARS. THAT'S IT.
DON'T PANIC. STAY CALM.
GOTTA WORK!
IT'S A TOURNA-MENT THAT ANYONE CAN ENTER. WELL?
WANT TO PAIR UP WITH ONE OF MY STUDENTS AND GIVE IT A TRY?
YES-SIR!

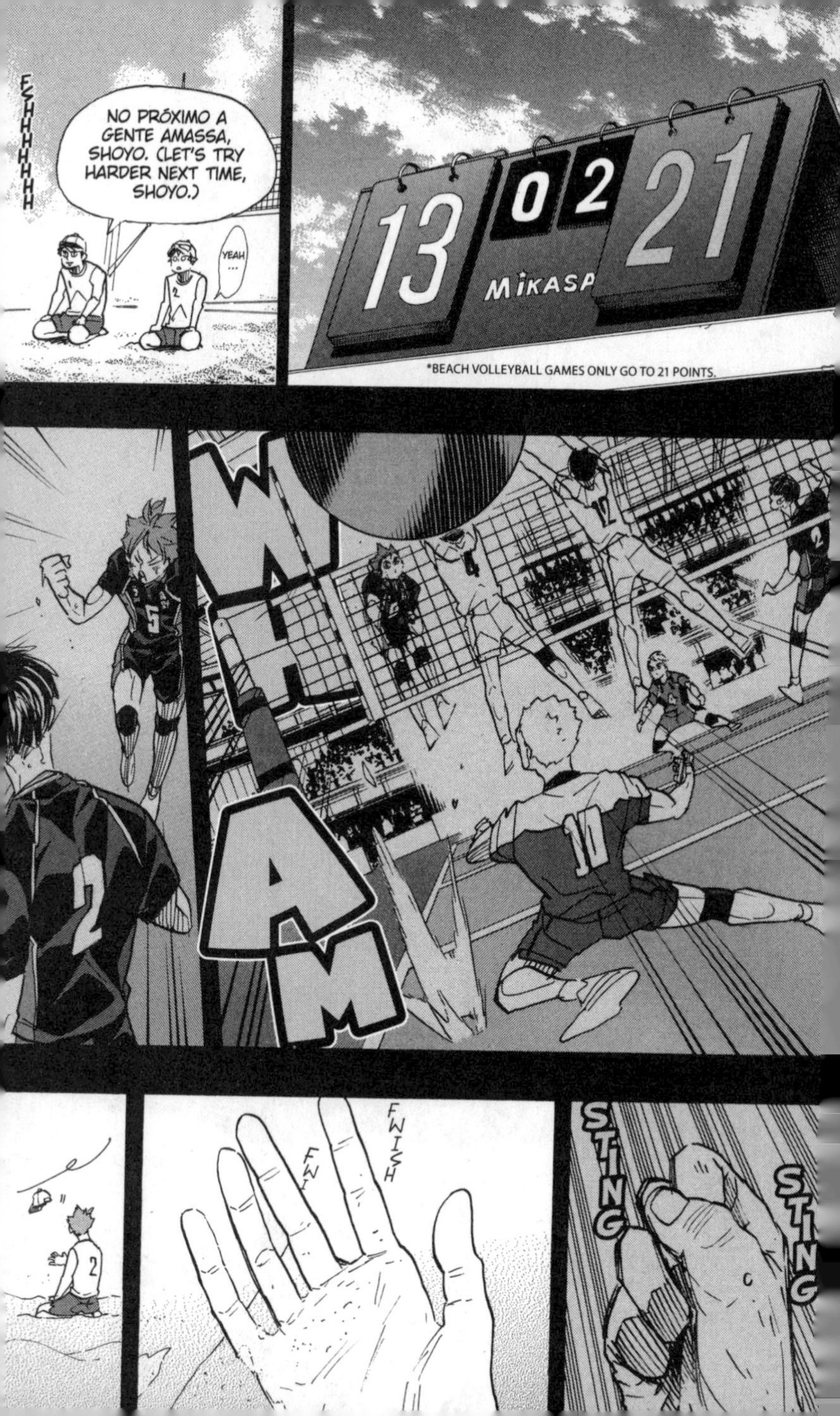
13 02 21
*BEACH VOLLEYBALL GAMES ONLY GO TO 21 POINTS.
FSHHHHHHH
NO PRÓXIMO A GENTE AMASSA, SHOYO. (LET'S TRY HARDER NEXT TIME, SHOYO.)
YEAH ...
WHAM
STING STING
FWISH
FWI

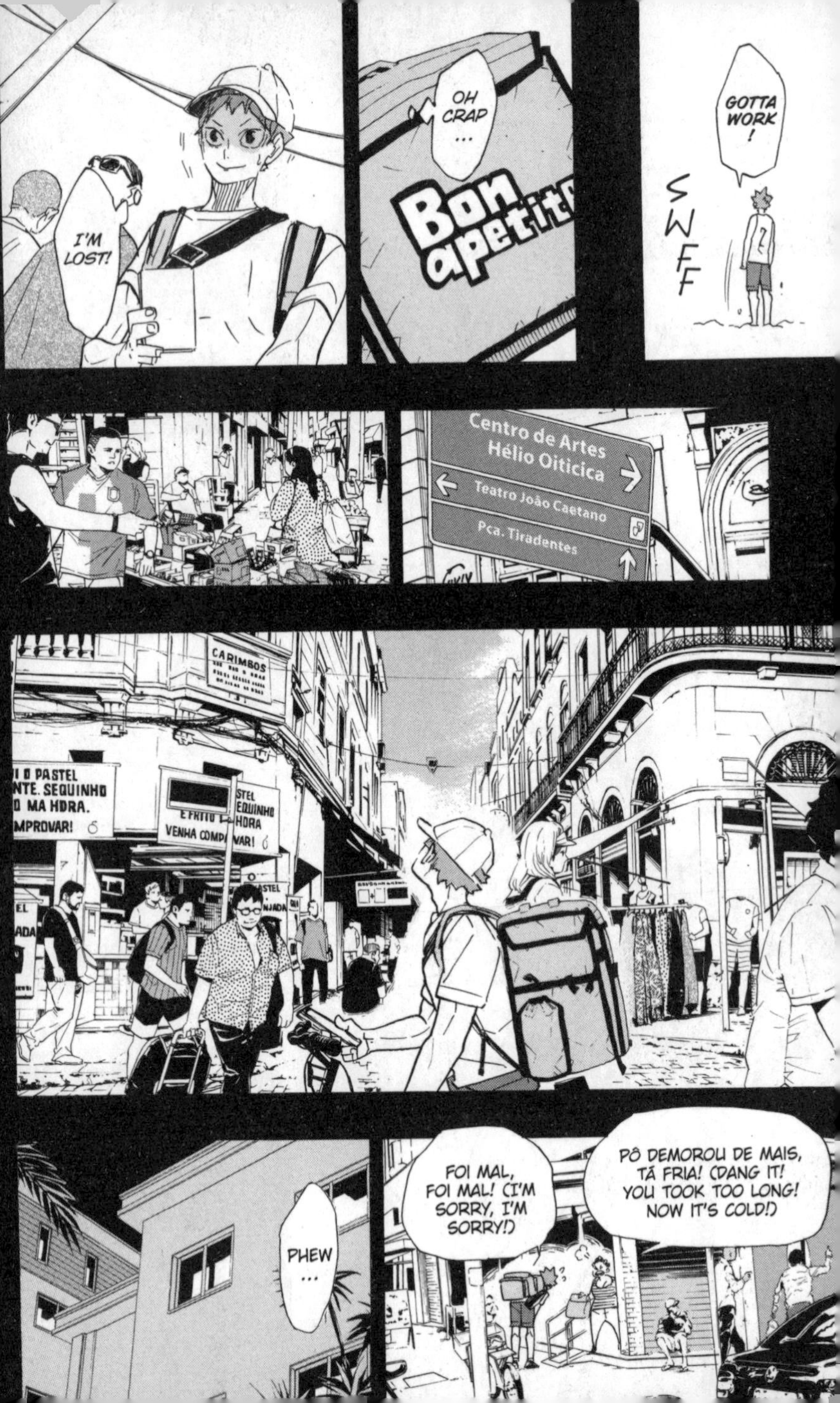
GOTTA WORK!
SWFF
OH CRAP ...
Bon apetit
I'M LOST!
Centro de Artes Hélio Oiticica
Teatro João Caetano
Pca. Tiradentes
CARIMBOS
PÔ DEMOROU DE MAIS, TÁ FRIA! (DANG IT! YOU TOOK TOO LONG! NOW IT'S COLD!)
FOI MAL, FOI MAL! (I'M SORRY, I'M SORRY!)
PHEW ...

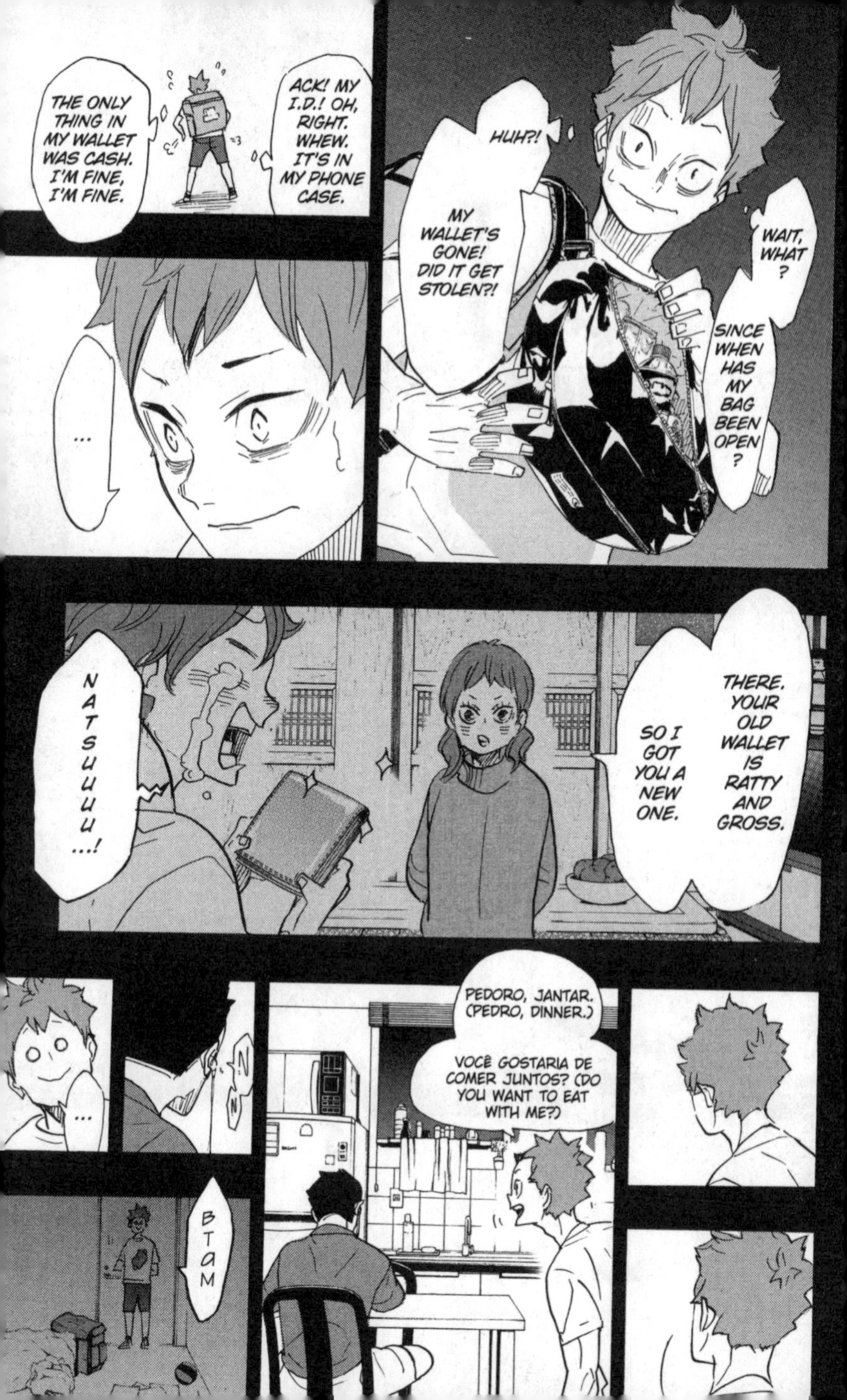
HUH?!
MY WALLET'S GONE! DID IT GET STOLEN?!
WAIT, WHAT?
SINCE WHEN HAS MY BAG BEEN OPEN?
ACK! MY I.D.! OH, RIGHT. WHEW. IT'S IN MY PHONE CASE.
THE ONLY THING IN MY WALLET WAS CASH. I'M FINE, I'M FINE.
...
THERE. YOUR OLD WALLET IS RATTY AND GROSS.
SO I GOT YOU A NEW ONE.
NATSUUUUU...!
PEDORO, JANTAR. (PEDRO, DINNER.)
VOCÊ GOSTARIA DE COMER JUNTOS? (DO YOU WANT TO EAT WITH ME?)
NNN
...
BTAM

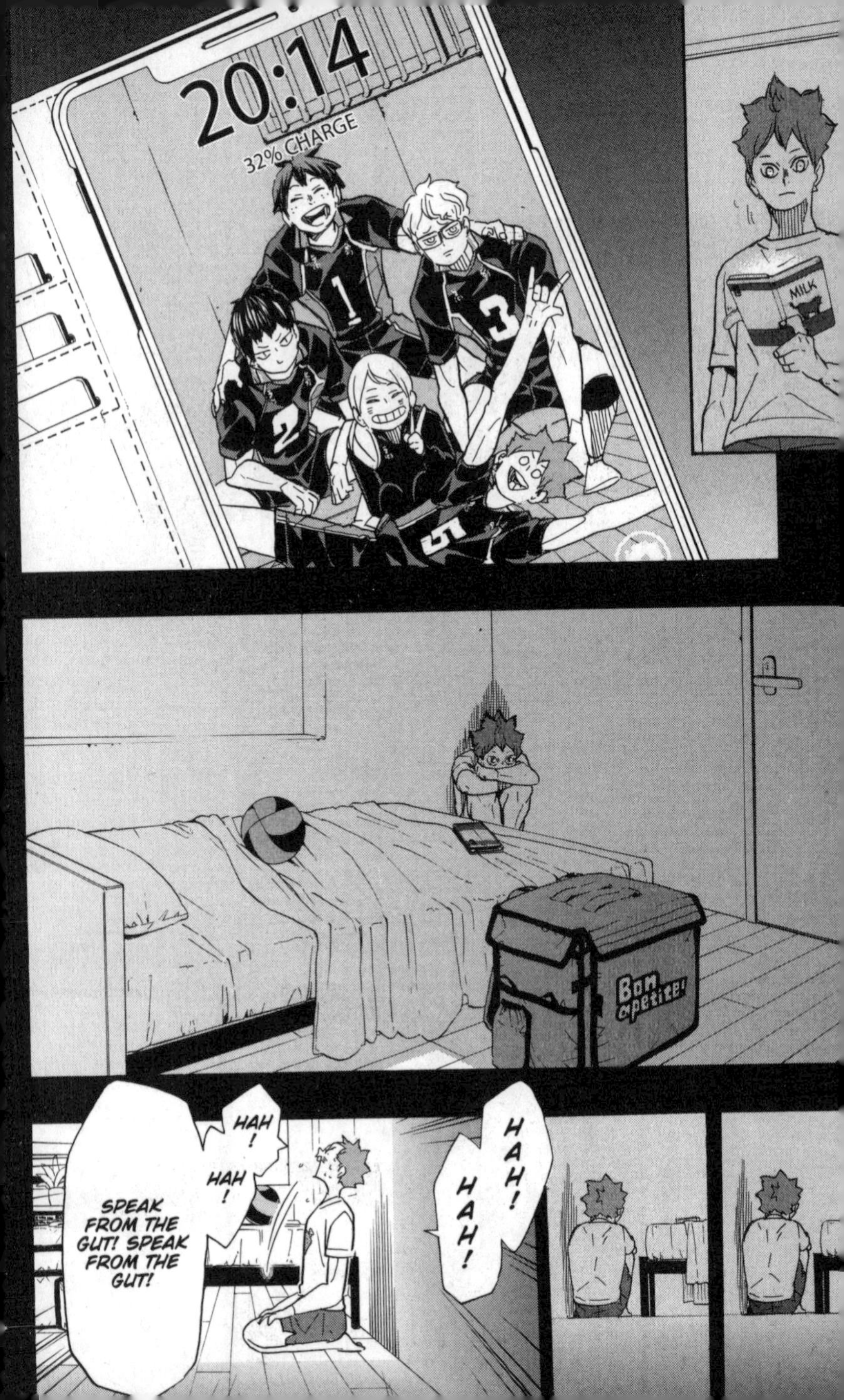
20:14
32% CHARGE
MILK
Bon appetite!
HAH! HAH!
HAH! HAH!
SPEAK FROM THE GUT! SPEAK FROM THE GUT!

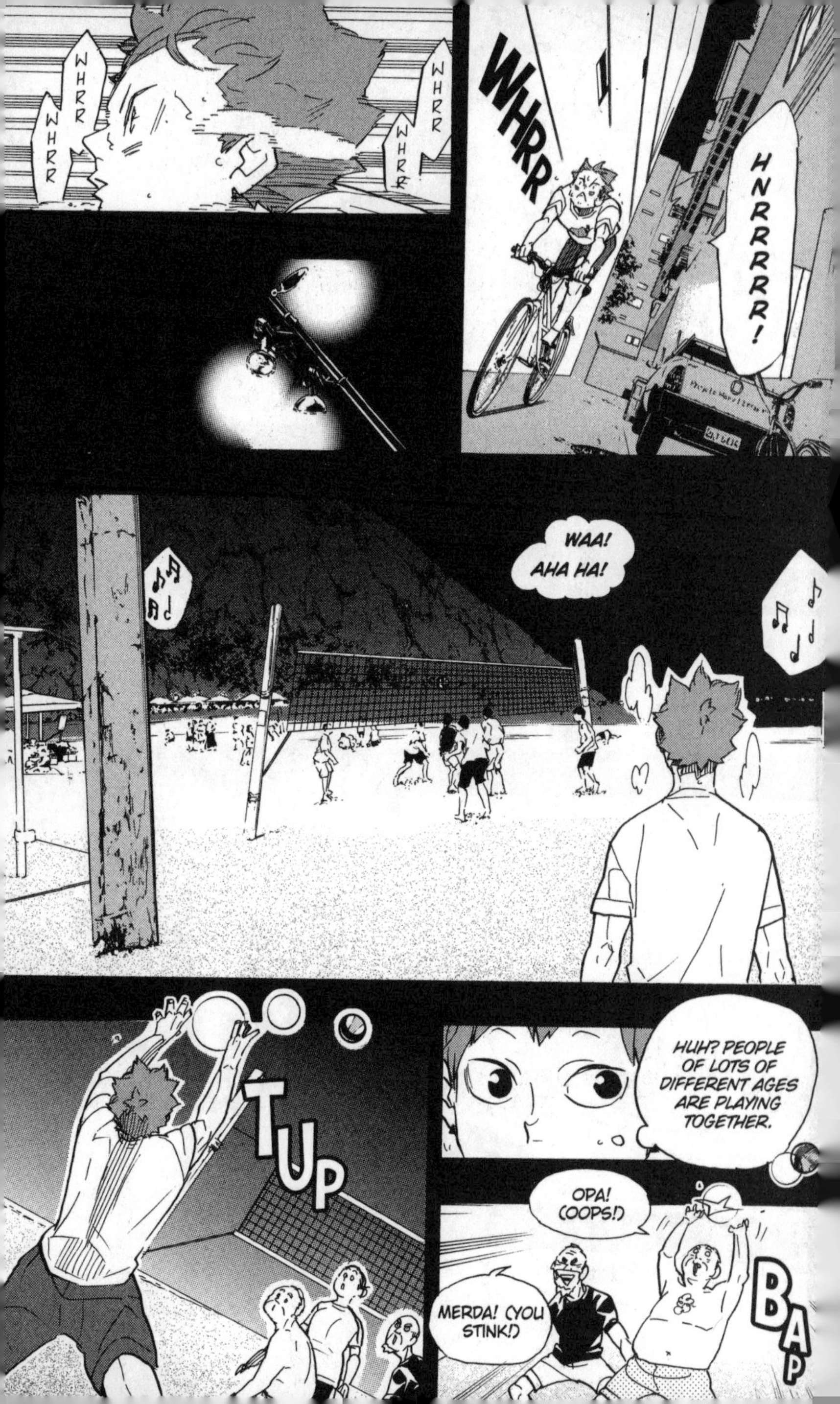
WHRR
HNRRRRRR!
WHRR
WHRR
WHRR
WHRR
WAA! AHA HA!
HUH? PEOPLE OF LOTS OF DIFFERENT AGES ARE PLAYING TOGETHER.
OPA! (OOPS!)
MERDA! (YOU STINK!)
BAP
TUP

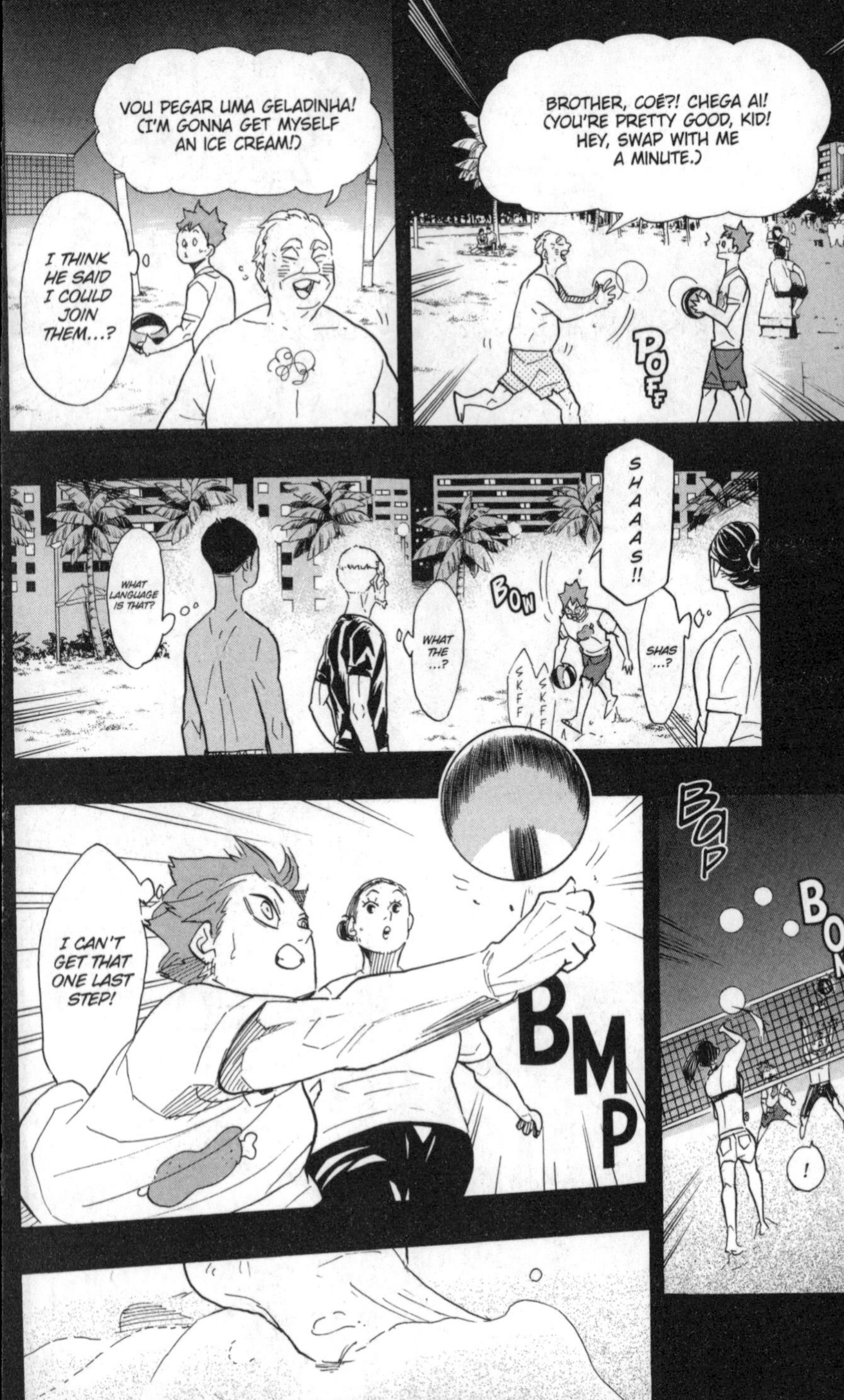

BROTHER, COÉ?! CHEGA AI! (YOU'RE PRETTY GOOD, KID! HEY, SWAP WITH ME A MINUTE.)
POFF
VOU PEGAR UMA GELADINHA! (I'M GONNA GET MYSELF AN ICE CREAM!)
I THINK HE SAID I COULD JOIN THEM...?
SHAAAAS!!
BOW
SKFF
SKFF
SHAS ...?
WHAT THE ...?
WHAT LANGUAGE IS THAT?
BOP
BOM
!
I CAN'T GET THAT ONE LAST STEP!
BMP

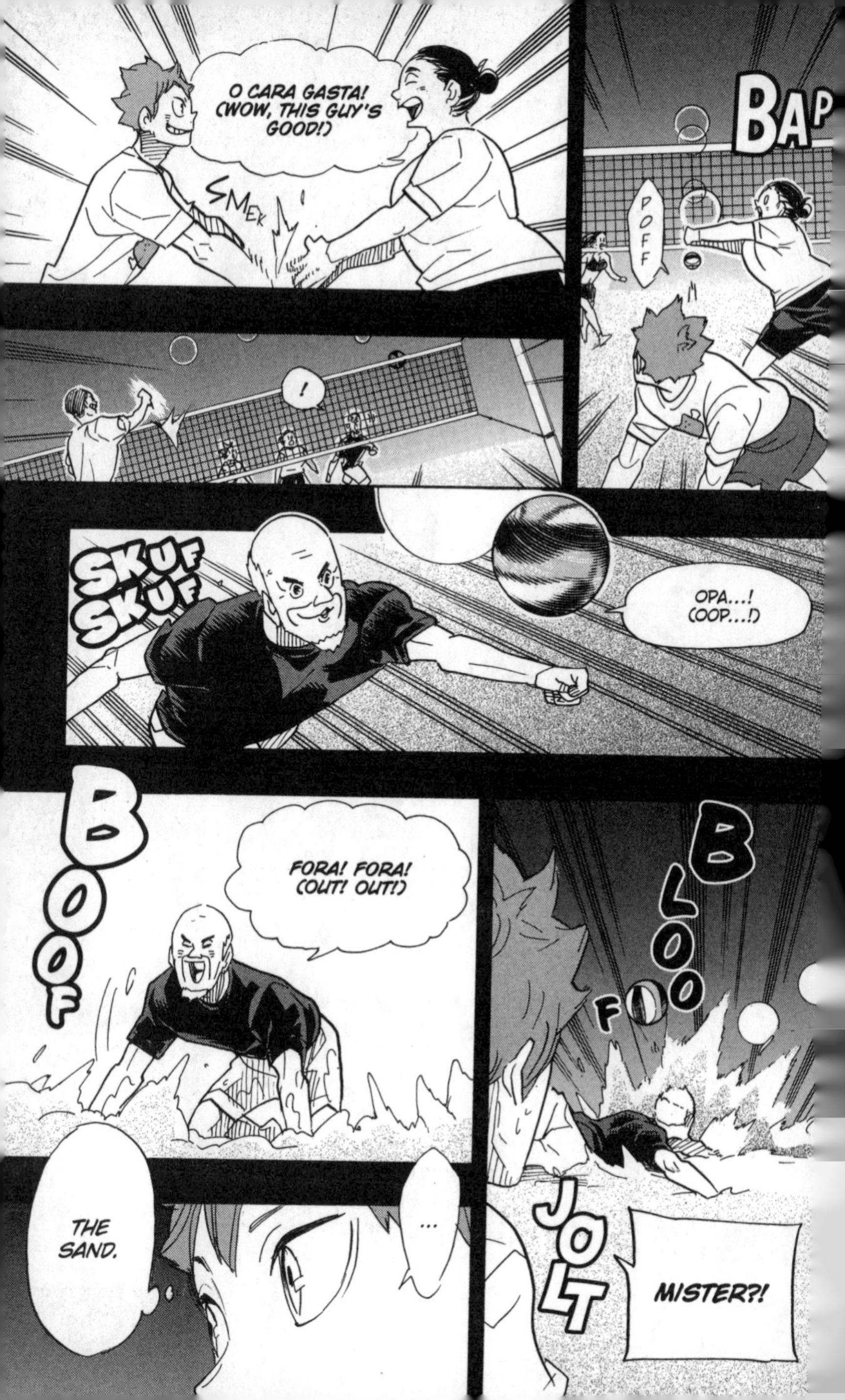
BAP
POFF
SMEK
O CARA GASTA! (WOW, THIS GUY'S GOOD!)
!
OPA...! (OOP...!)
SKUF SKUF
BLOOF
JOLT
MISTER?!
FORA! FORA! (OUT! OUT!)
BOOF
...
THE SAND.

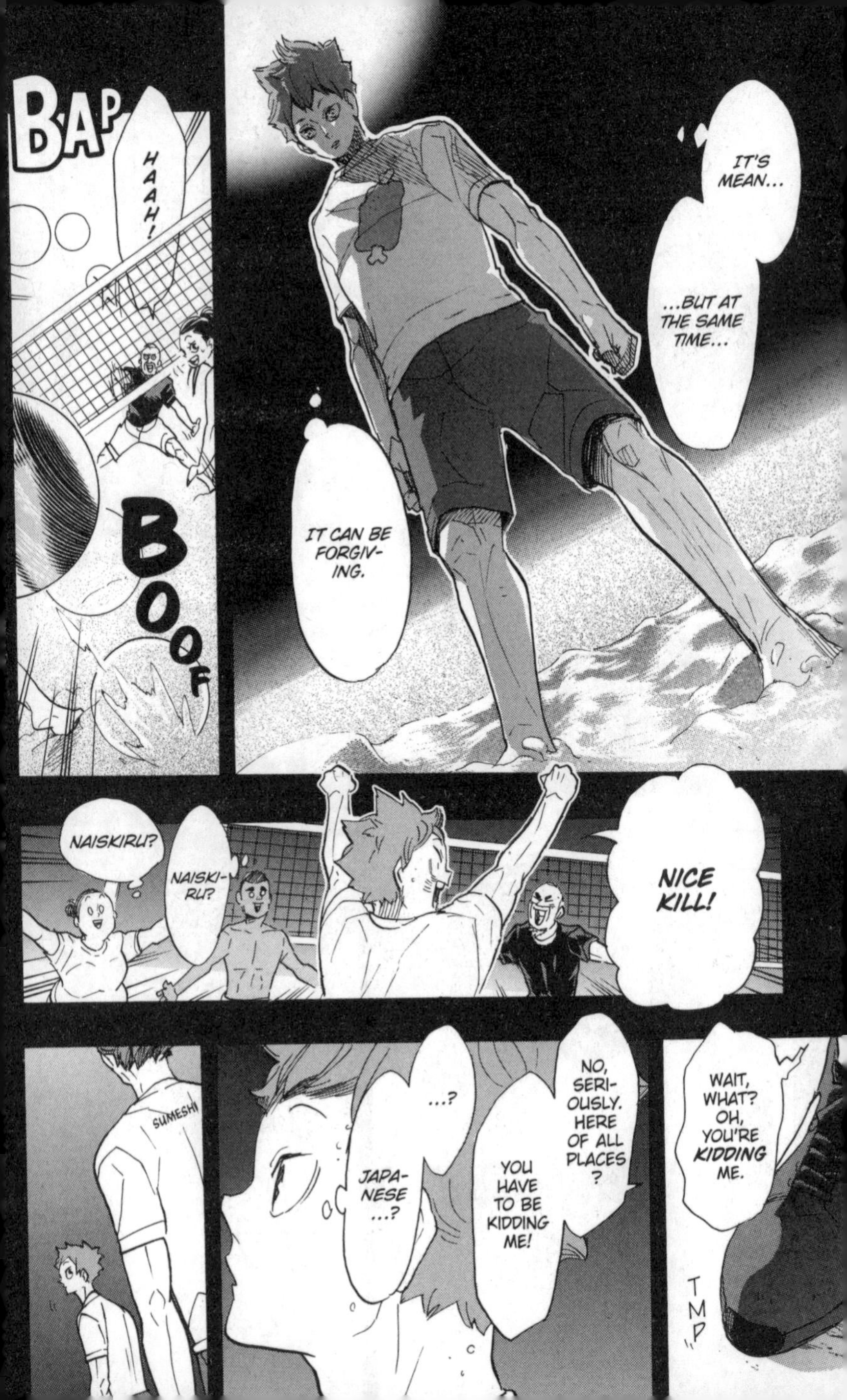

IT'S MEAN...
...BUT AT THE SAME TIME...
IT CAN BE FORGIV-ING.
BAP
HAAAH!
BOOF
NICE KILL!
NAISKI-RU?
NAISKIRU?
WAIT, WHAT? OH, YOU'RE *KIDDING* ME.
TMP
NO, SERI-OUSLY. HERE OF ALL PLACES?
YOU HAVE TO BE KIDDING ME!
...?
JAPA-NESE ...?
SUMESHI

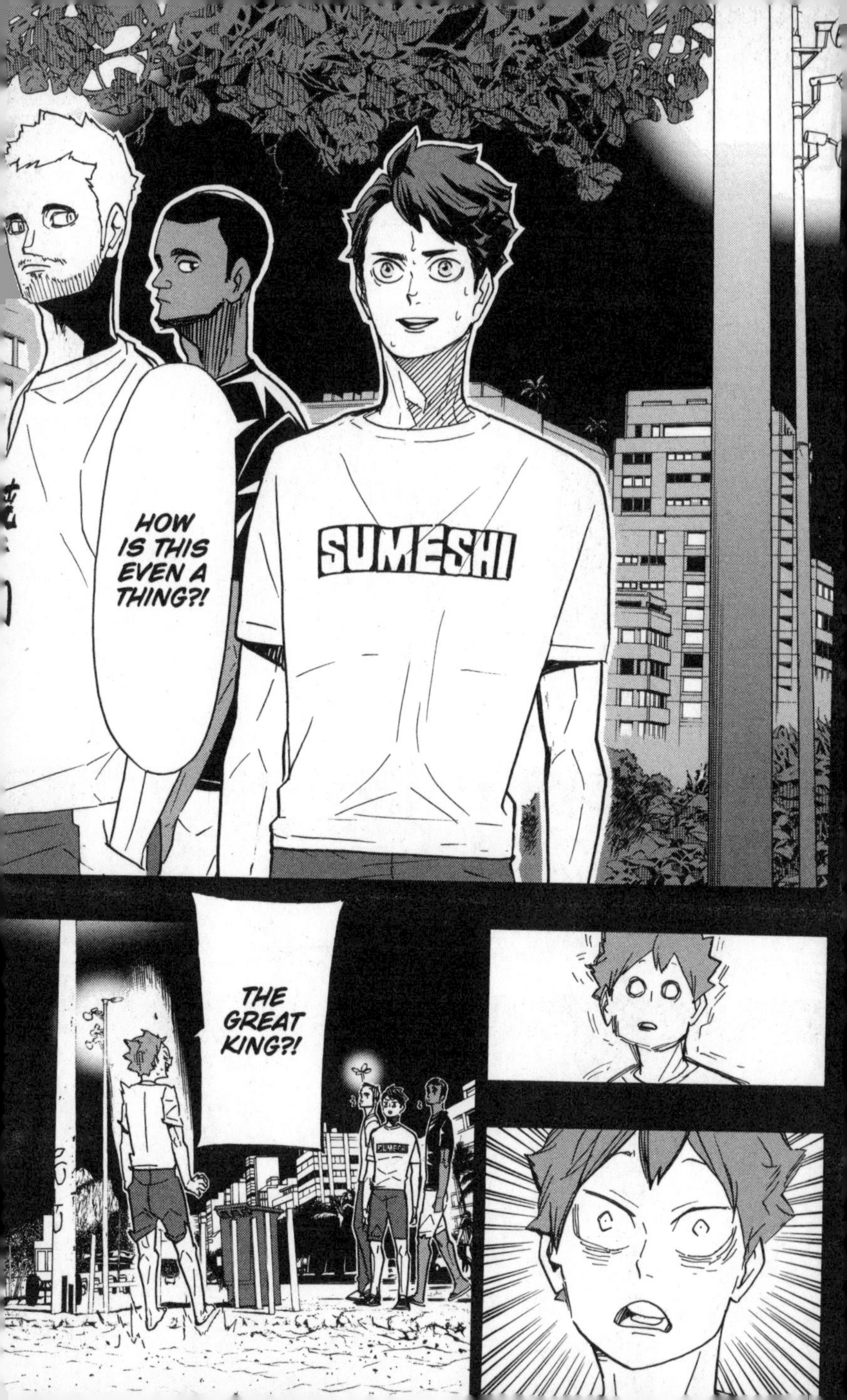
SUMESHI
HOW IS THIS EVEN A THING?!
THE GREAT KING?!
SUMESHI

CHAPTER 372

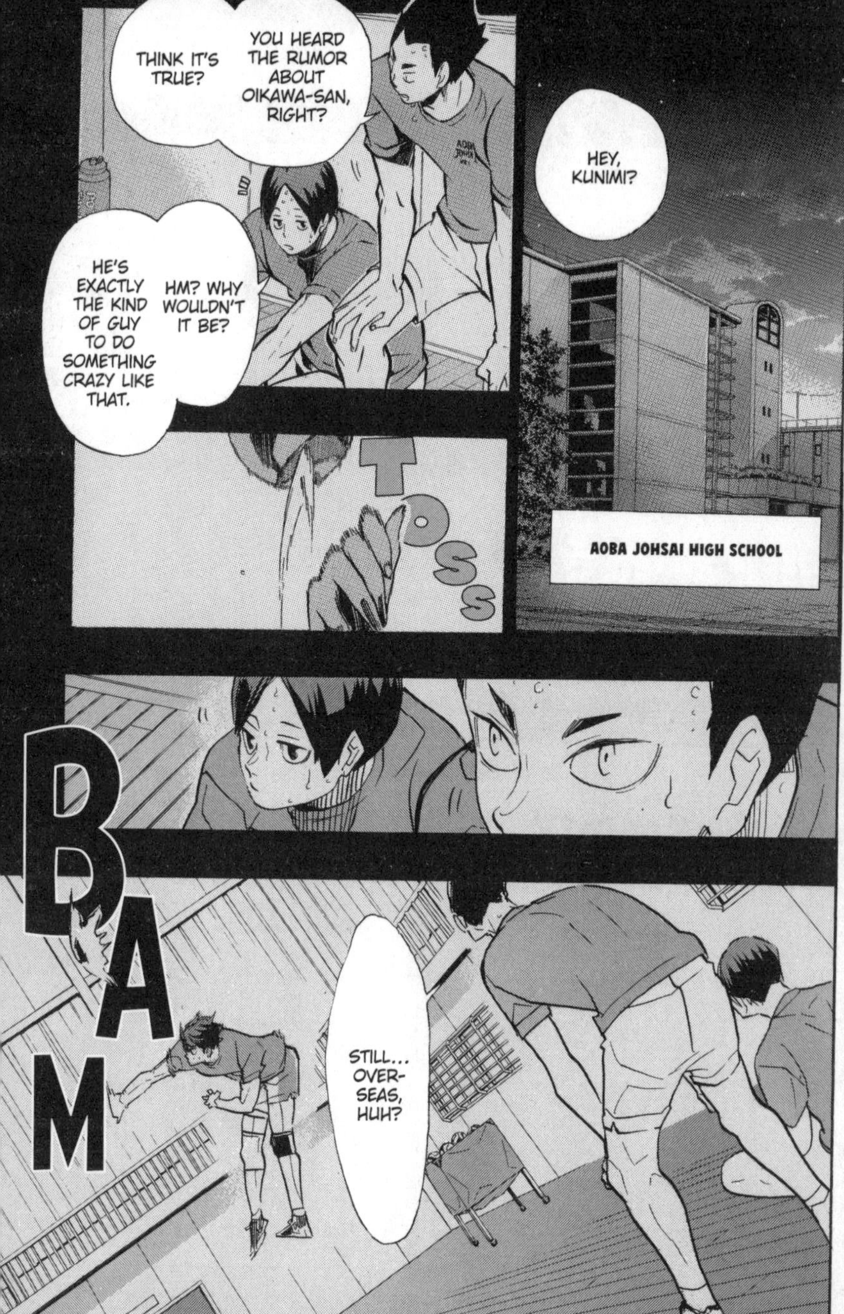
HEY, KUNIMI?
AOBA JOHSAI HIGH SCHOOL
YOU HEARD THE RUMOR ABOUT OIKAWA-SAN, RIGHT?
THINK IT'S TRUE?
HM? WHY WOULDN'T IT BE?
HE'S EXACTLY THE KIND OF GUY TO DO SOMETHING CRAZY LIKE THAT.
TOSS
STILL... OVER-SEAS, HUH?
BAM

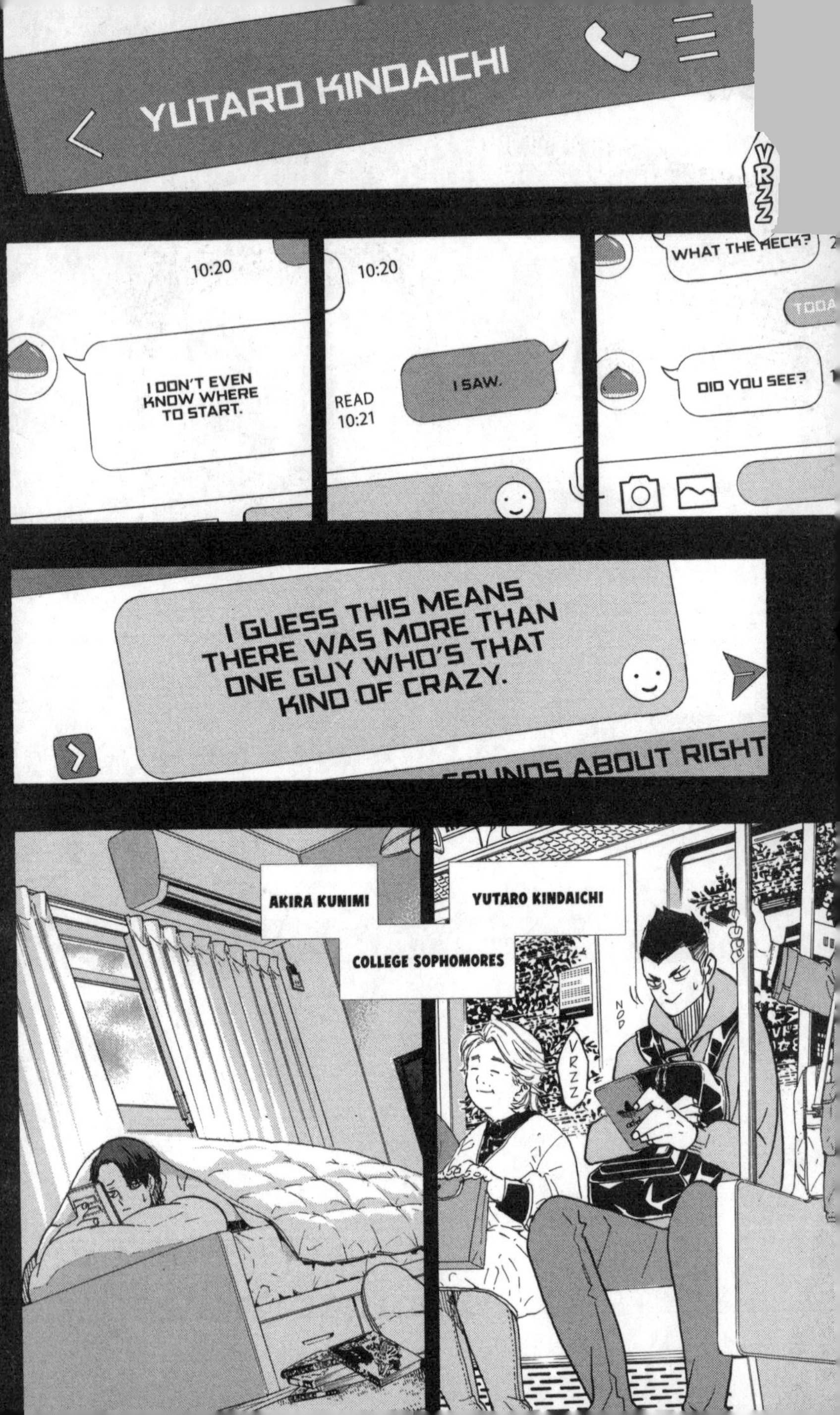
YUTARO KINDAICHI
VRZZ
WHAT THE HECK?
DID YOU SEE?
10:20
I SAW.
READ 10:21
10:20
I DON'T EVEN KNOW WHERE TO START.
I GUESS THIS MEANS THERE WAS MORE THAN ONE GUY WHO'S THAT KIND OF CRAZY.
SOUNDS ABOUT RIGHT
YUTARO KINDAICHI
COLLEGE SOPHOMORES
NOD
VRZZ
AKIRA KUNIMI

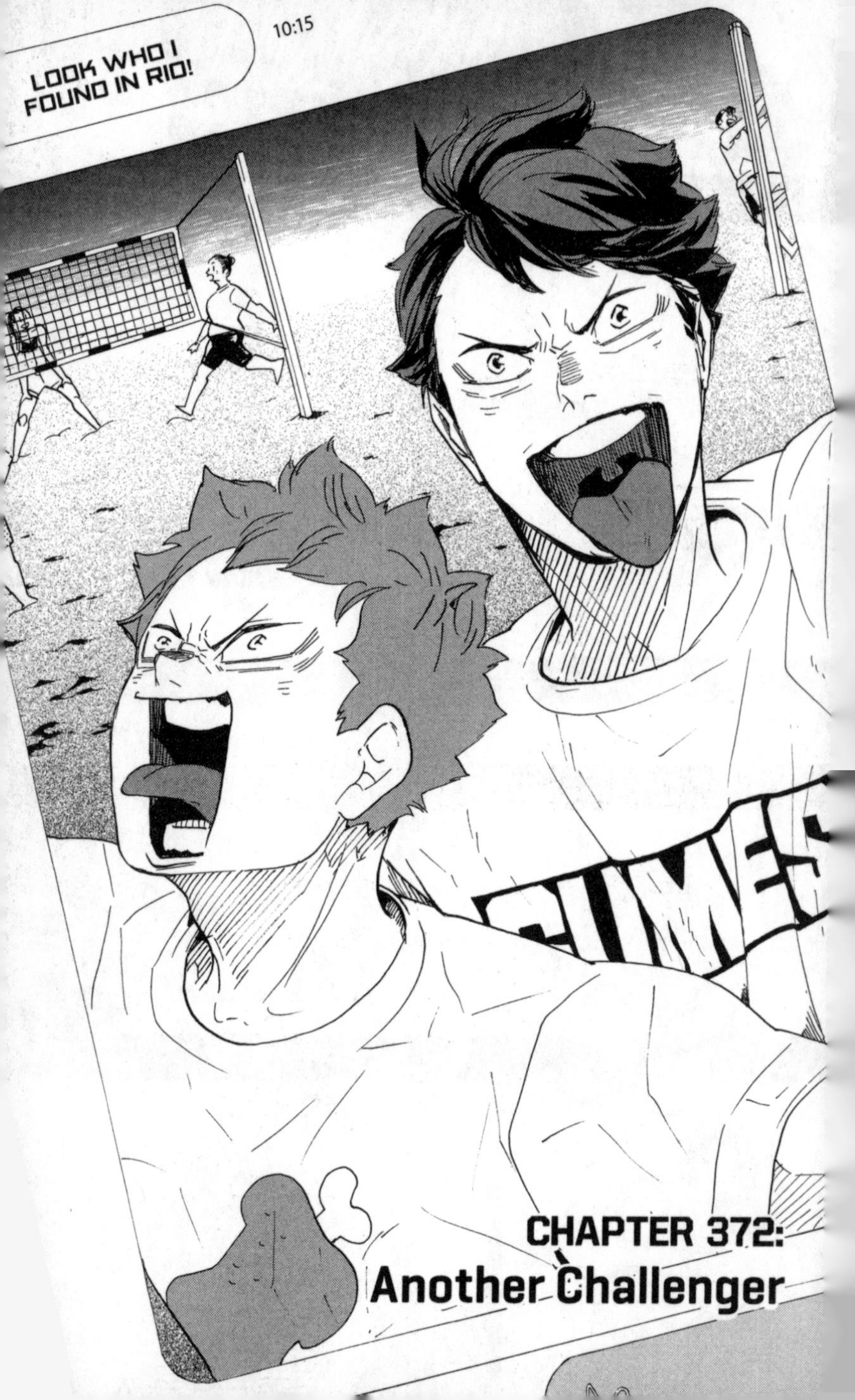
10:15
LOOK WHO I FOUND IN RIO!

CHAPTER 372: Another Challenger

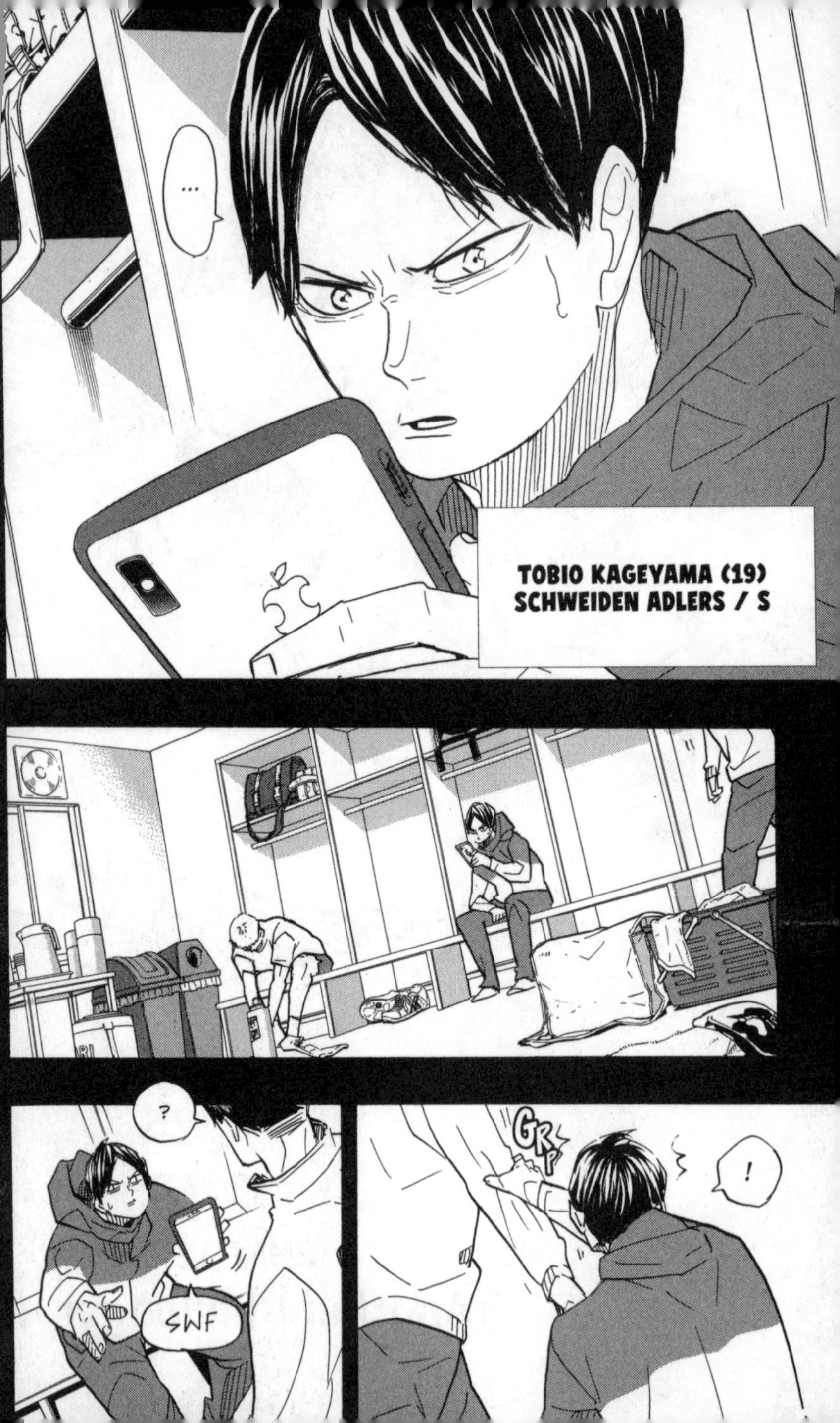
...
TOBIO KAGEYAMA (19)
SCHWEIDEN ADLERS / S
GRP
!
?
SWF

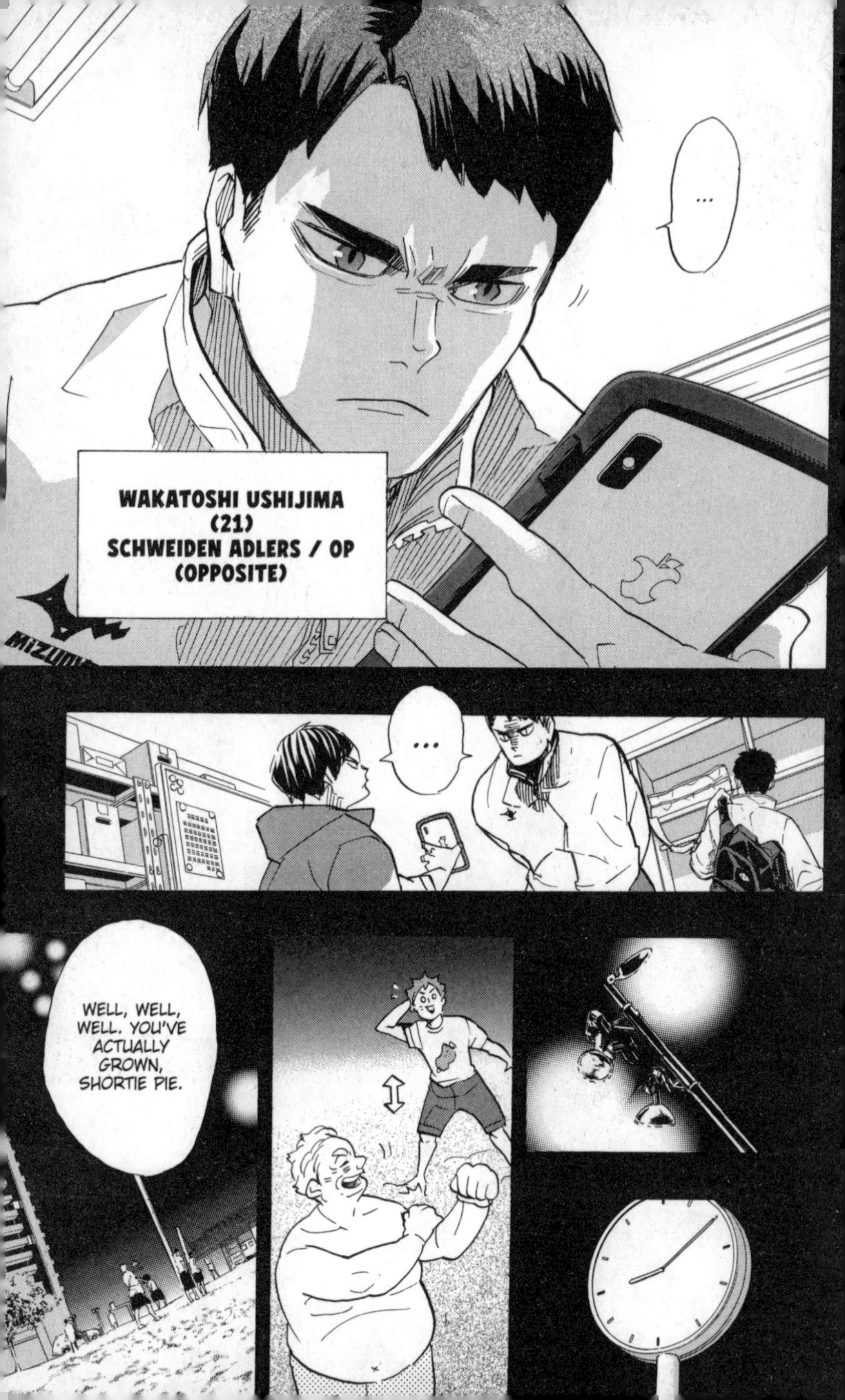
...
WAKATOSHI USHIJIMA
(21)
SCHWEIDEN ADLERS / OP
(OPPOSITE)
...
WELL, WELL, WELL. YOU'VE ACTUALLY GROWN, SHORTIE PIE.

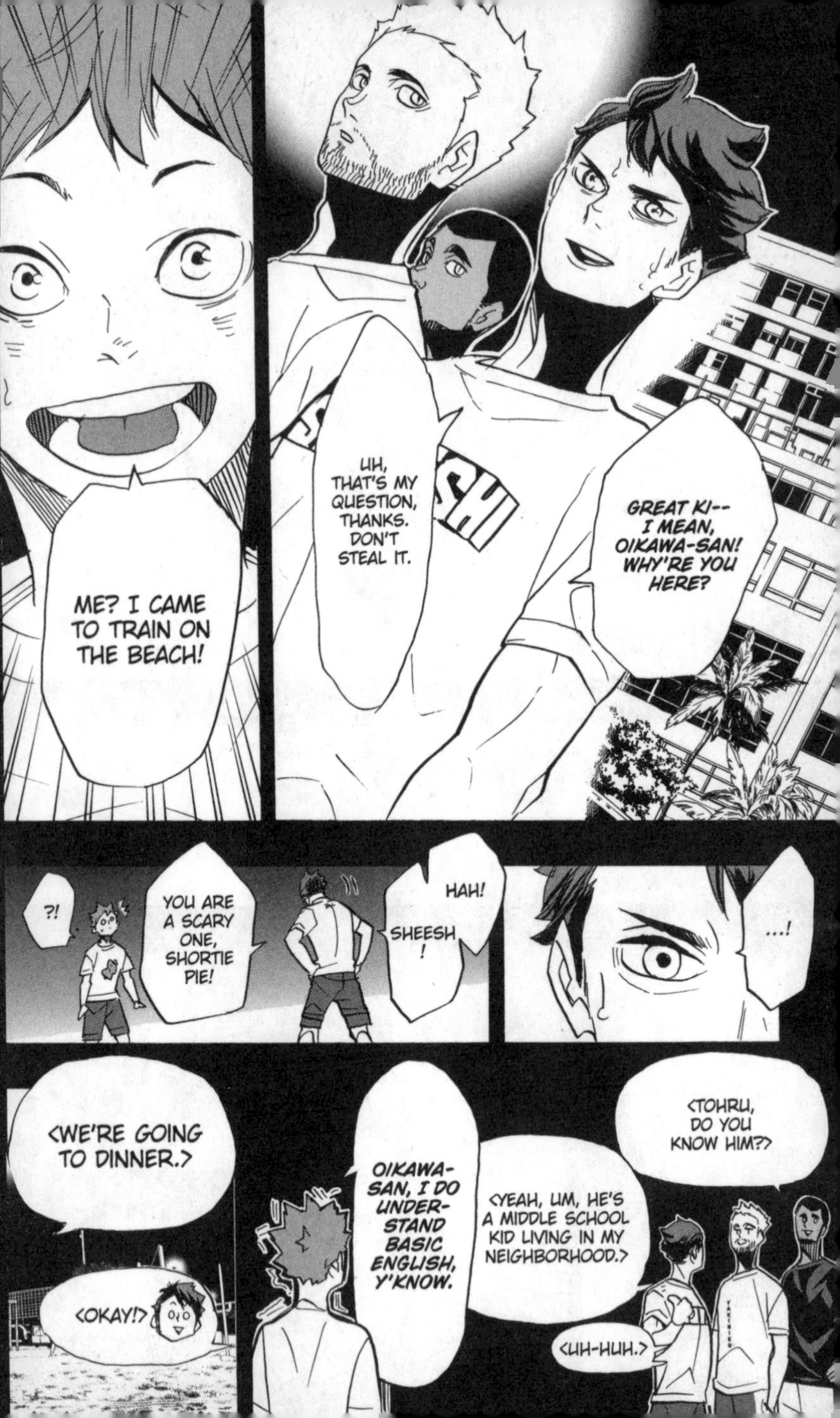
GREAT KI-- I MEAN, OIKAWA-SAN! WHY'RE YOU HERE?
UH, THAT'S MY QUESTION, THANKS. DON'T STEAL IT.
ME? I CAME TO TRAIN ON THE BEACH!
...!
HAH!
SHEESH!
YOU ARE A SCARY ONE, SHORTIE PIE!
?!
<TOHRU, DO YOU KNOW HIM?>
<YEAH, UM, HE'S A MIDDLE SCHOOL KID LIVING IN MY NEIGHBORHOOD.>
OIKAWA-SAN, I DO UNDERSTAND BASIC ENGLISH, Y'KNOW.
<UH-HUH.>
<WE'RE GOING TO DINNER.>
<OKAY!>

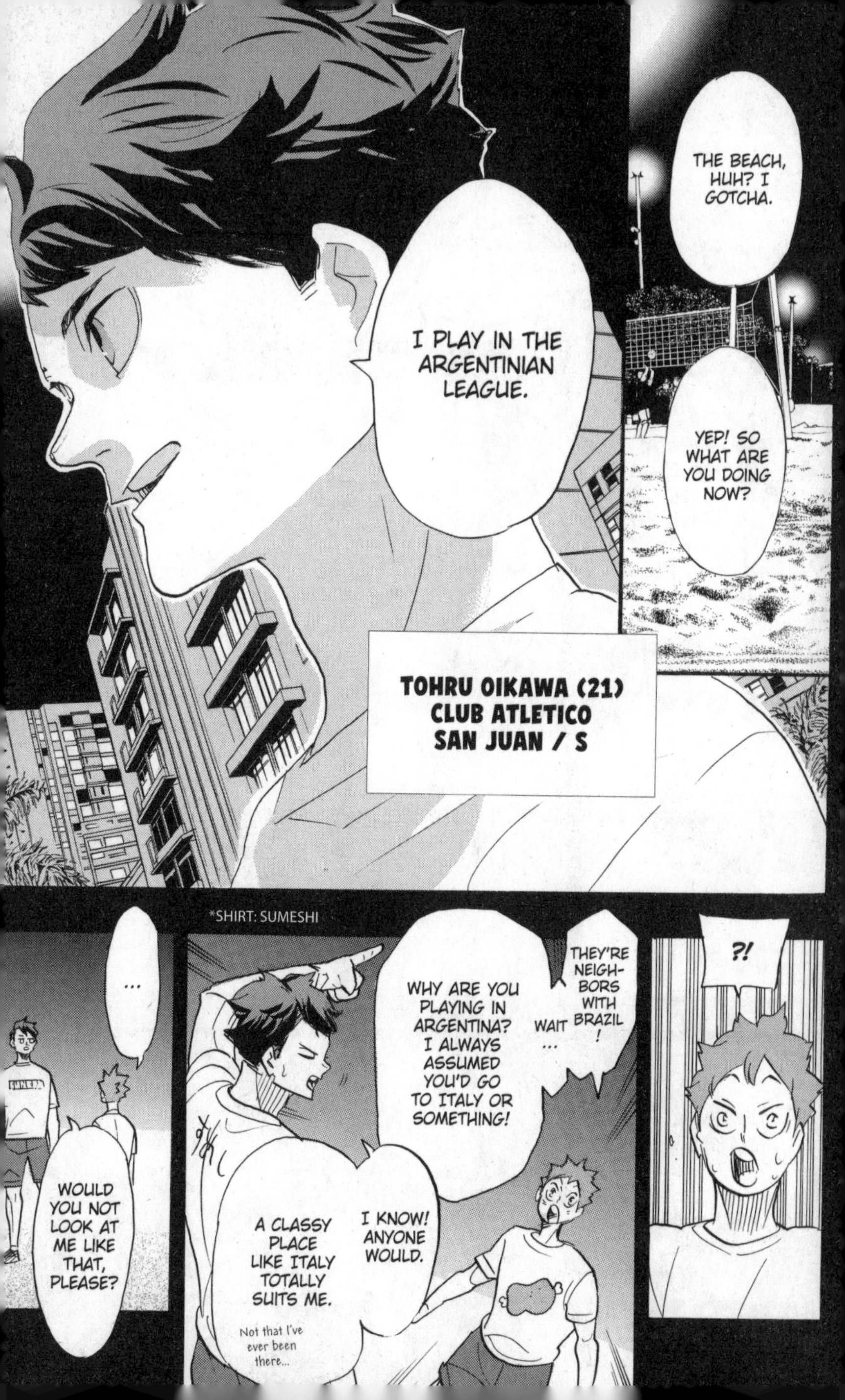
THE BEACH, HUH? I GOTCHA.
YEP! SO WHAT ARE YOU DOING NOW?
I PLAY IN THE ARGENTINIAN LEAGUE.
TOHRU OIKAWA (21)
CLUB ATLETICO
SAN JUAN / S
*SHIRT: SUMESHI
?!
THEY'RE NEIGHBORS WITH BRAZIL!
WAIT...
WHY ARE YOU PLAYING IN ARGENTINA? I ALWAYS ASSUMED YOU'D GO TO ITALY OR SOMETHING!
I KNOW! ANYONE WOULD.
A CLASSY PLACE LIKE ITALY TOTALLY SUITS ME.
Not that I've ever been there...
...
WOULD YOU NOT LOOK AT ME LIKE THAT, PLEASE?

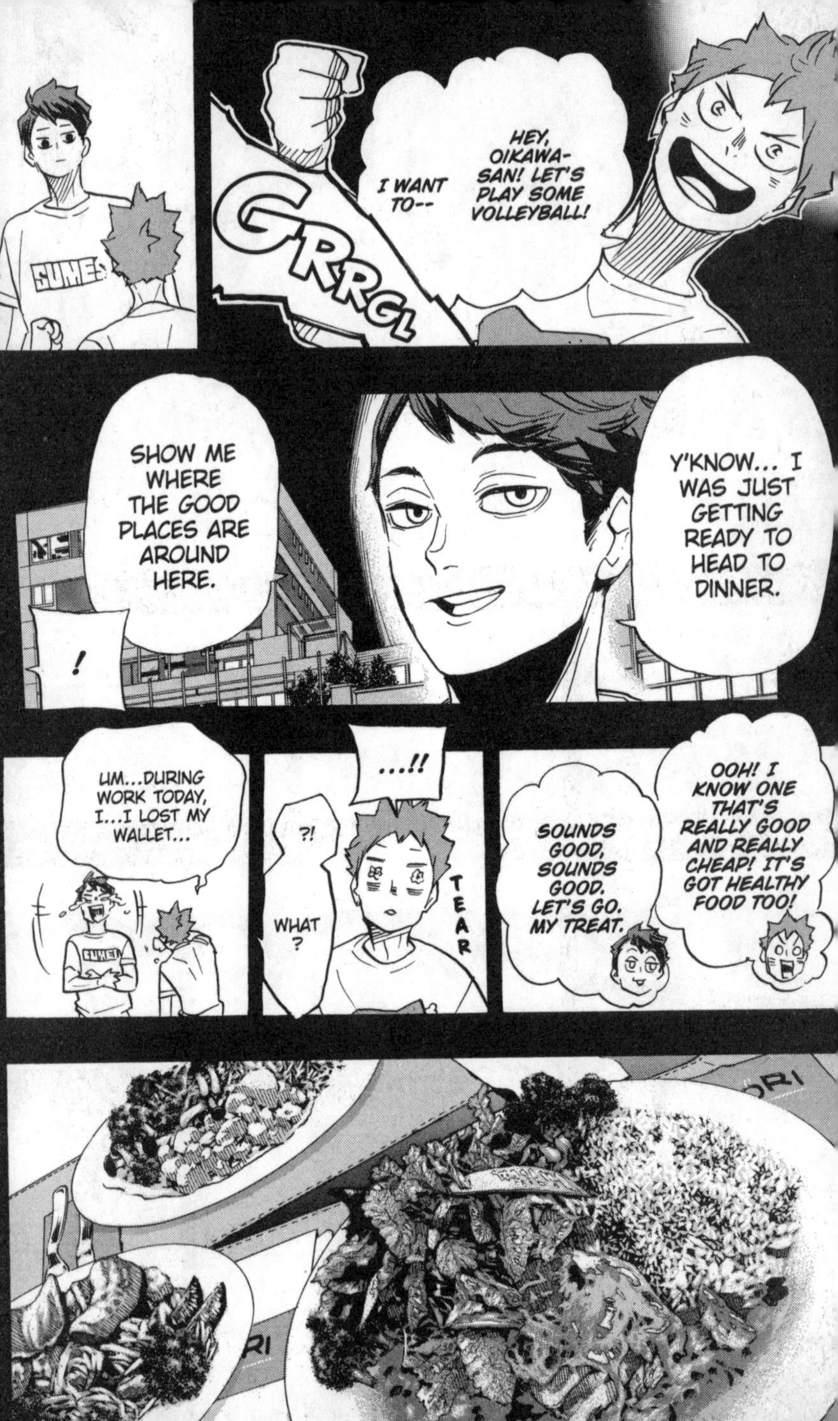
HEY, OIKAWA-SAN! LET'S PLAY SOME VOLLEYBALL!
I WANT TO--
GRRRGL
Y'KNOW... I WAS JUST GETTING READY TO HEAD TO DINNER.
SHOW ME WHERE THE GOOD PLACES ARE AROUND HERE.
!
OOH! I KNOW ONE THAT'S REALLY GOOD AND REALLY CHEAP! IT'S GOT HEALTHY FOOD TOO!
SOUNDS GOOD, SOUNDS GOOD. LET'S GO. MY TREAT.
...!!
?!
TEAR
WHAT?
UM...DURING WORK TODAY, I...I LOST MY WALLET...

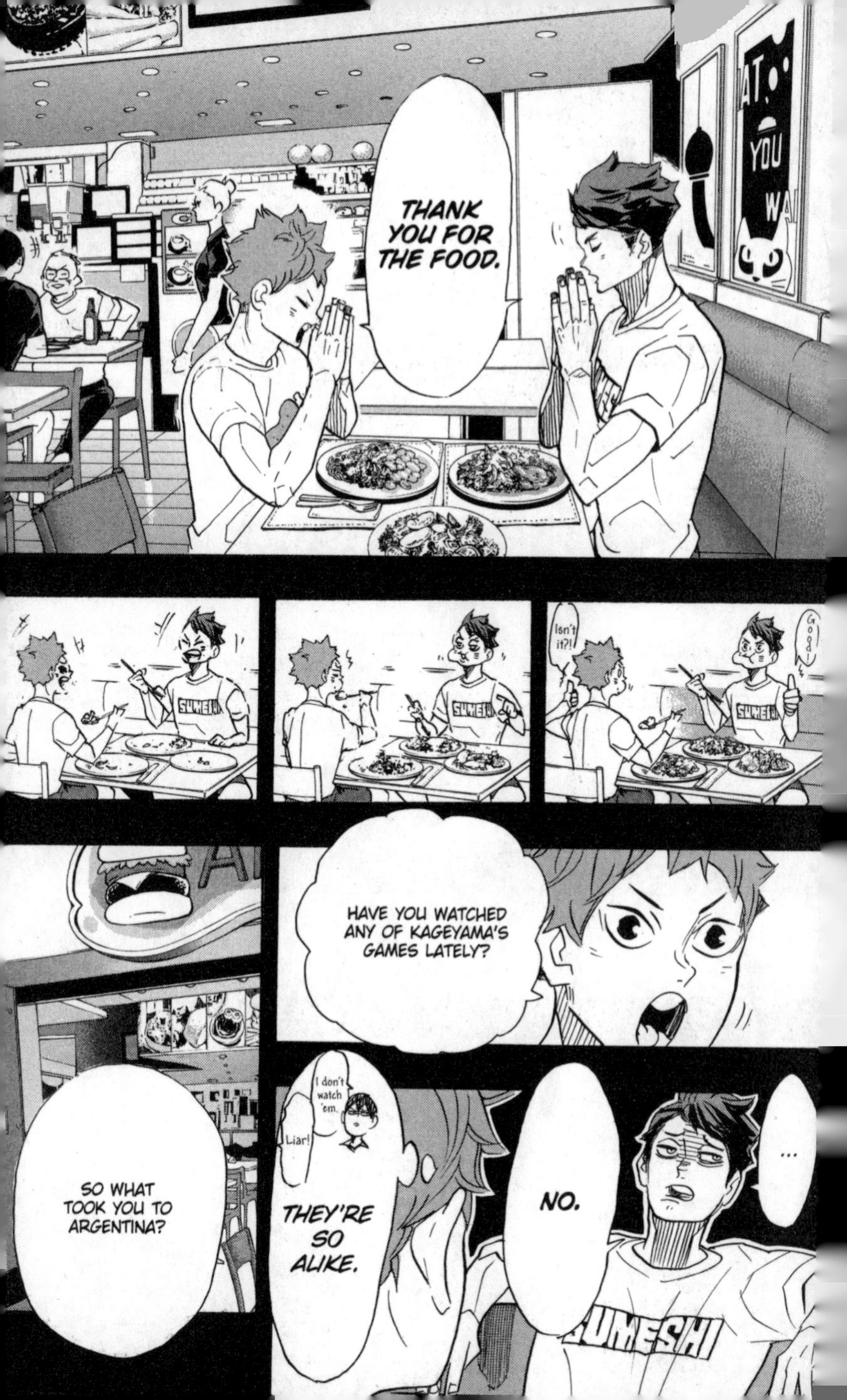
THANK YOU FOR THE FOOD.
Good!
Isn't it?!
HAVE YOU WATCHED ANY OF KAGEYAMA'S GAMES LATELY?
...
NO.
THEY'RE SO ALIKE.
I don't watch 'em.
Liar!
SO WHAT TOOK YOU TO ARGENTINA?

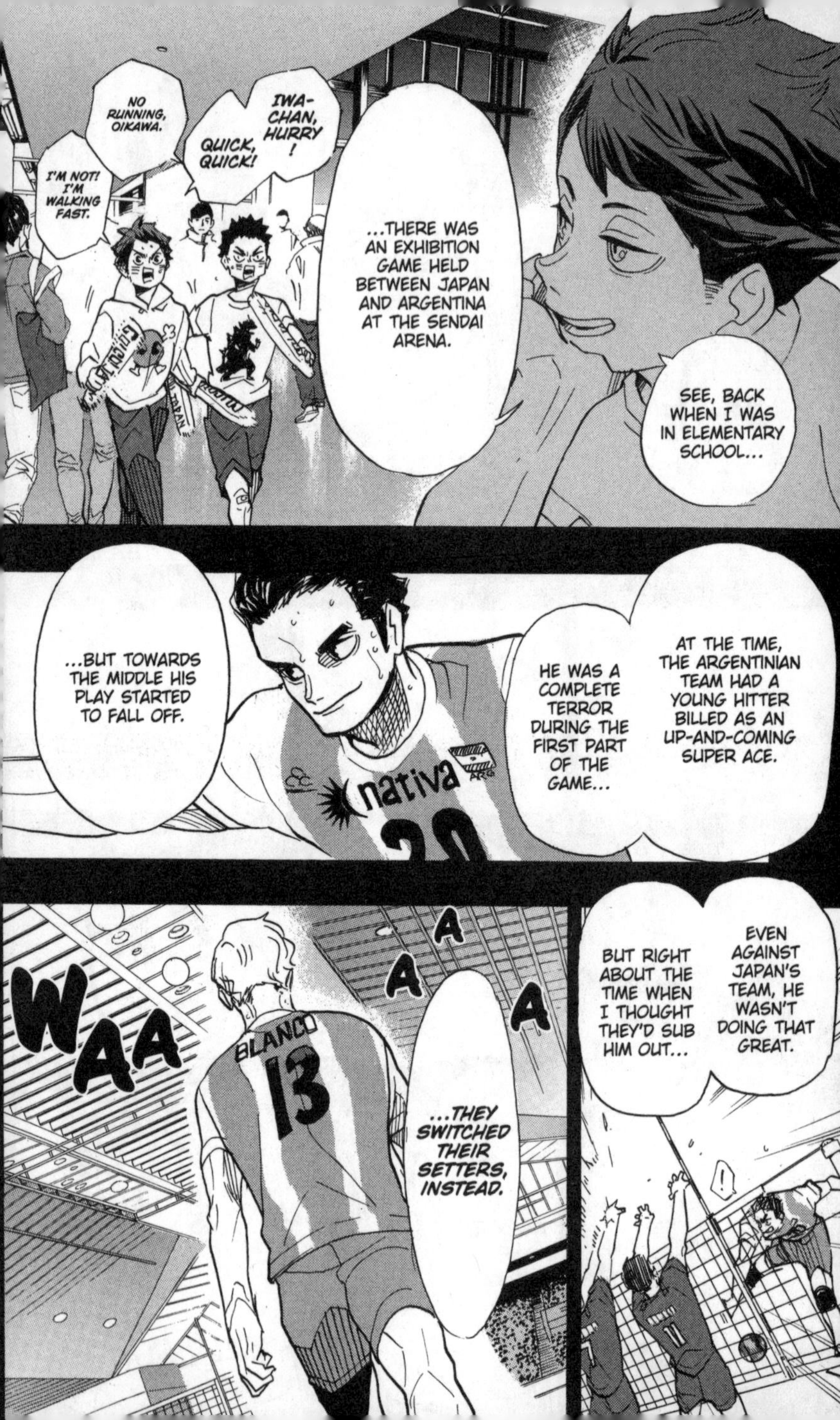
SEE, BACK WHEN I WAS IN ELEMENTARY SCHOOL...
...THERE WAS AN EXHIBITION GAME HELD BETWEEN JAPAN AND ARGENTINA AT THE SENDAI ARENA.
IWA-CHAN, HURRY!
QUICK, QUICK!
NO RUNNING, OIKAWA.
I'M NOT! I'M WALKING FAST.
AT THE TIME, THE ARGENTINIAN TEAM HAD A YOUNG HITTER BILLED AS AN UP-AND-COMING SUPER ACE.
HE WAS A COMPLETE TERROR DURING THE FIRST PART OF THE GAME...
...BUT TOWARDS THE MIDDLE HIS PLAY STARTED TO FALL OFF.
nativa
EVEN AGAINST JAPAN'S TEAM, HE WASN'T DOING THAT GREAT.
BUT RIGHT ABOUT THE TIME WHEN I THOUGHT THEY'D SUB HIM OUT...
WAA A A A
...THEY SWITCHED THEIR SETTERS, INSTEAD.
BLANCO
13

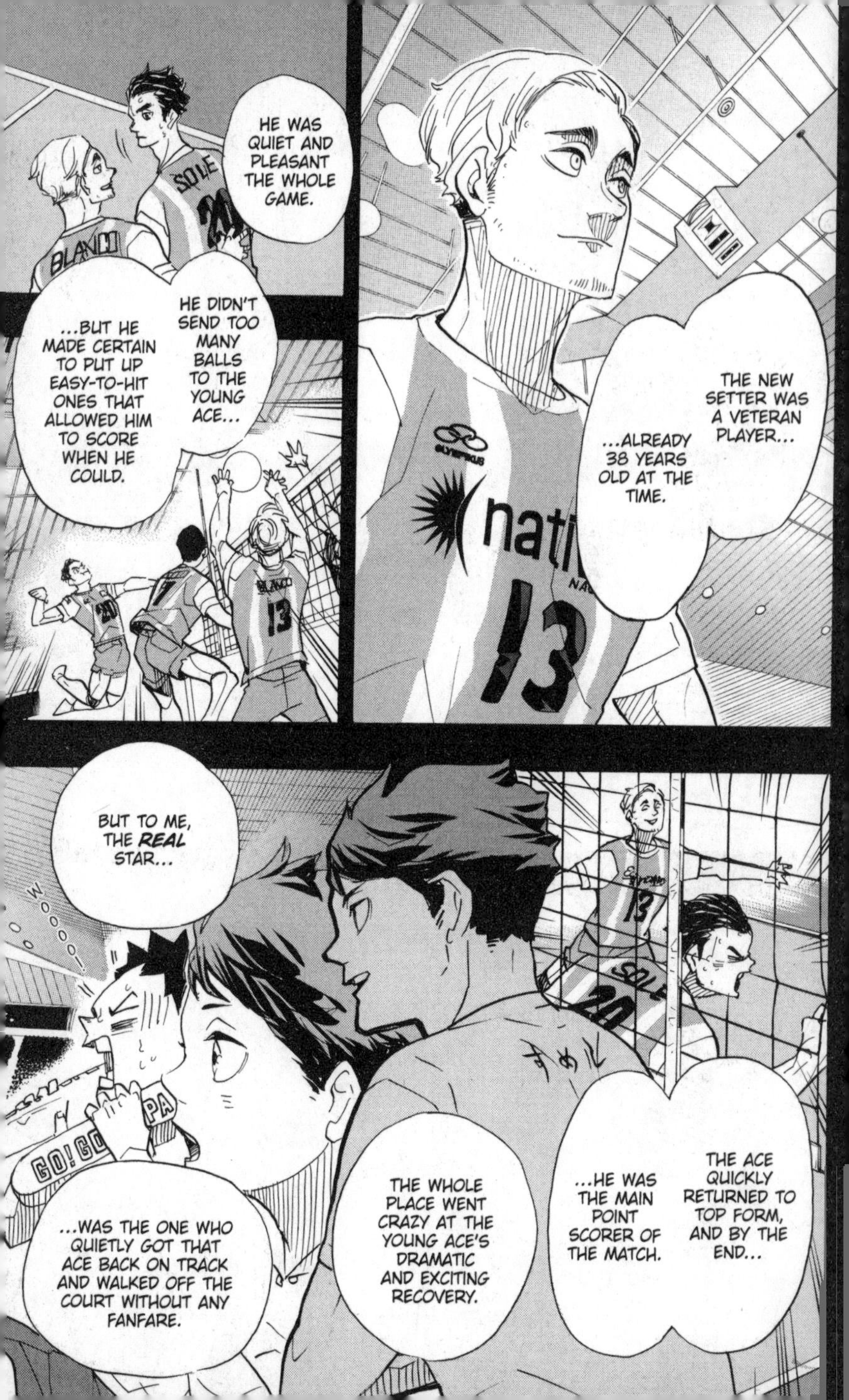
THE NEW SETTER WAS A VETERAN PLAYER...
...ALREADY 38 YEARS OLD AT THE TIME.
HE WAS QUIET AND PLEASANT THE WHOLE GAME.
HE DIDN'T SEND TOO MANY BALLS TO THE YOUNG ACE...
...BUT HE MADE CERTAIN TO PUT UP EASY-TO-HIT ONES THAT ALLOWED HIM TO SCORE WHEN HE COULD.
THE ACE QUICKLY RETURNED TO TOP FORM, AND BY THE END...
...HE WAS THE MAIN POINT SCORER OF THE MATCH.
THE WHOLE PLACE WENT CRAZY AT THE YOUNG ACE'S DRAMATIC AND EXCITING RECOVERY.
BUT TO ME, THE *REAL* STAR...
WOOOO!
...WAS THE ONE WHO QUIETLY GOT THAT ACE BACK ON TRACK AND WALKED OFF THE COURT WITHOUT ANY FANFARE.

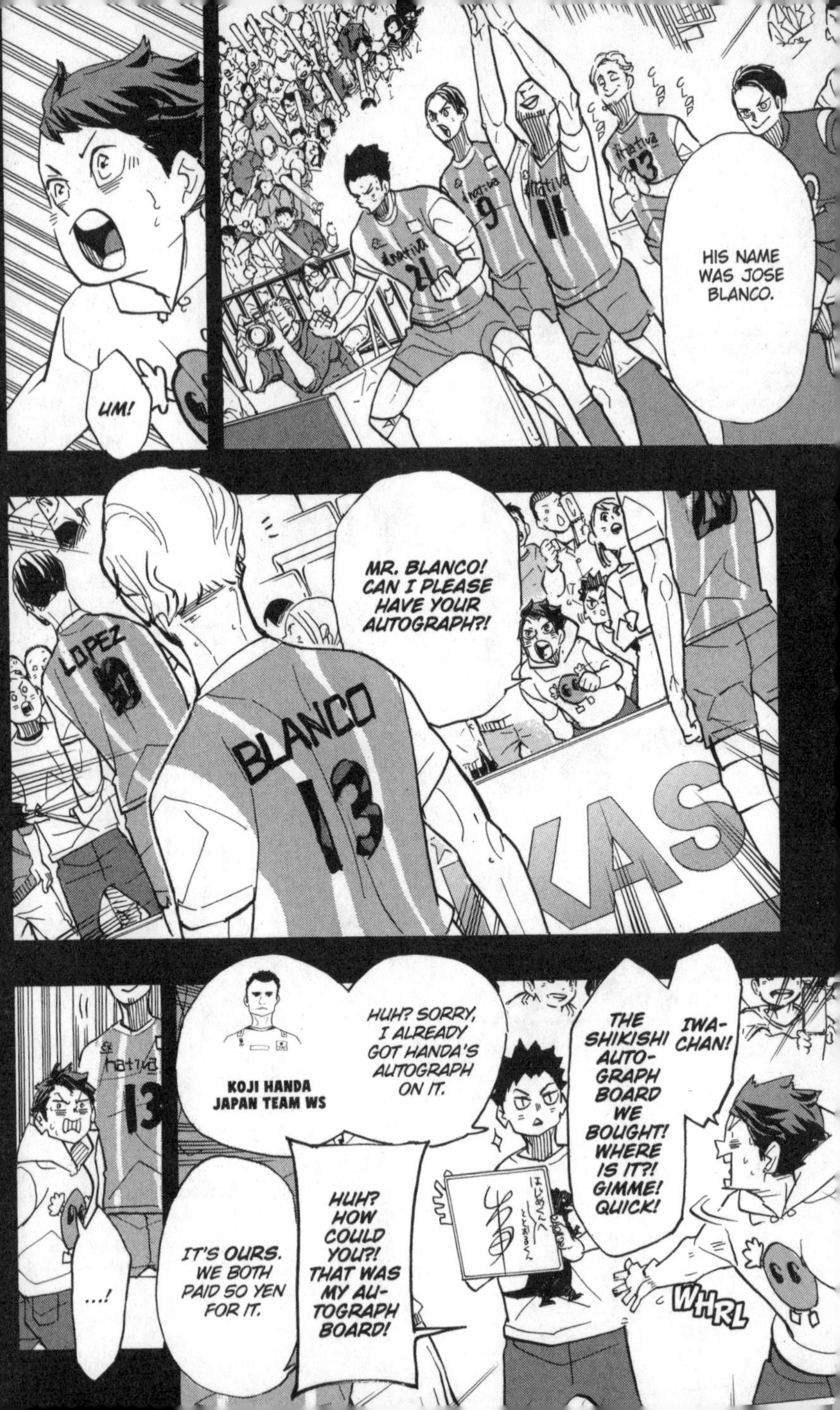
HIS NAME WAS JOSE BLANCO.
UM!
LOPEZ
BLANCO
MR. BLANCO! CAN I PLEASE HAVE YOUR AUTOGRAPH?!
IWA-CHAN!
THE SHIKISHI AUTO-GRAPH BOARD WE BOUGHT! WHERE IS IT?! GIMME! QUICK!
WHRL
HUH? SORRY, I ALREADY GOT HANDA'S AUTOGRAPH ON IT.
KOJI HANDA
JAPAN TEAM WS
HUH? HOW COULD YOU?! THAT WAS MY AU-TOGRAPH BOARD!
IT'S OURS. WE BOTH PAID 50 YEN FOR IT.
...!

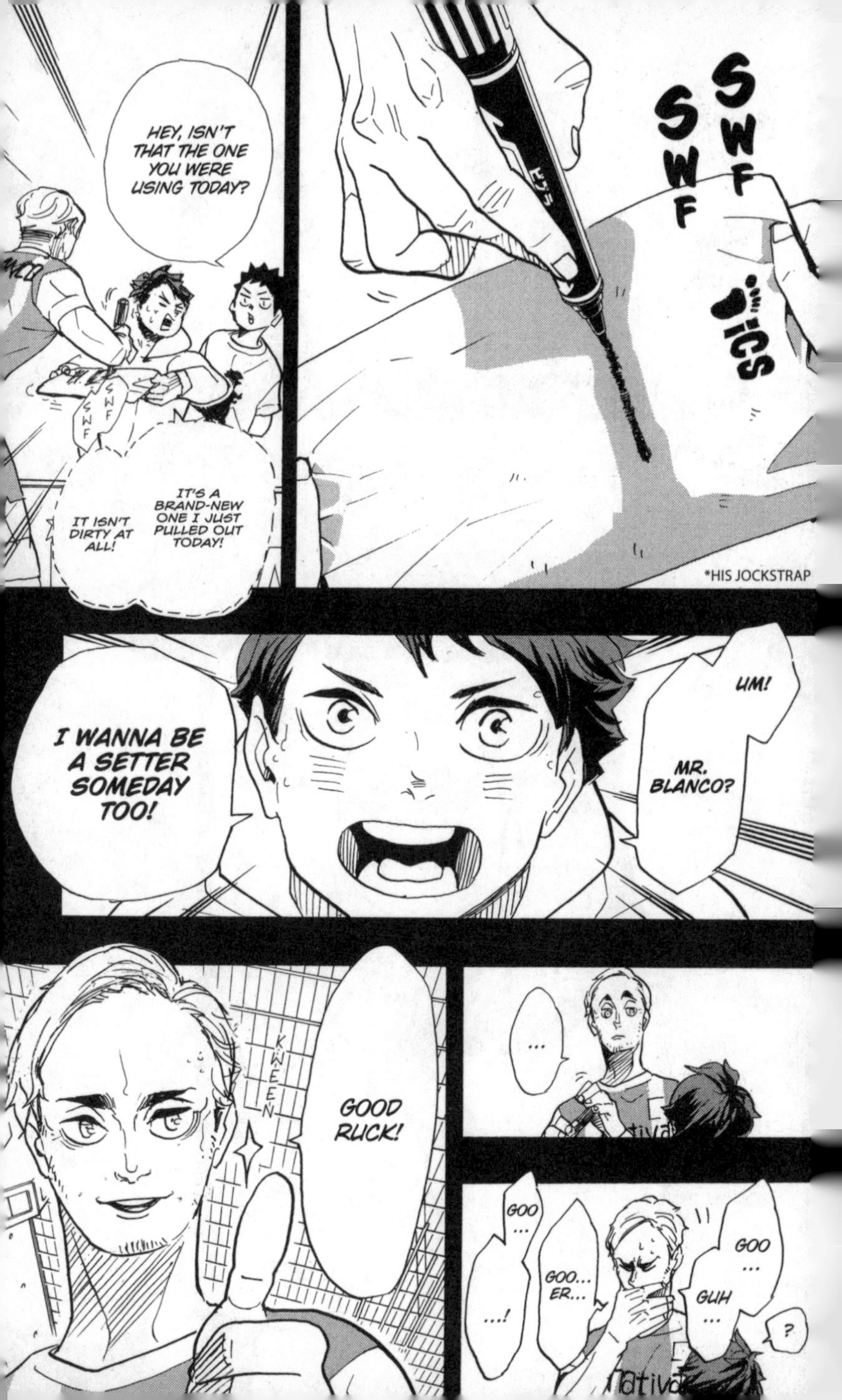
SWF SWF
SWF
*HIS JOCKSTRAP
HEY, ISN'T THAT THE ONE YOU WERE USING TODAY?
SWF SWF
IT'S A BRAND-NEW ONE I JUST PULLED OUT TODAY!
IT ISN'T DIRTY AT ALL!
UM!
MR. BLANCO?
I WANNA BE A SETTER SOMEDAY TOO!
...
GOO ...
GUH ...
?
GOO ...
GOO... ER...
...!
GOOD RUCK!
KWEEN

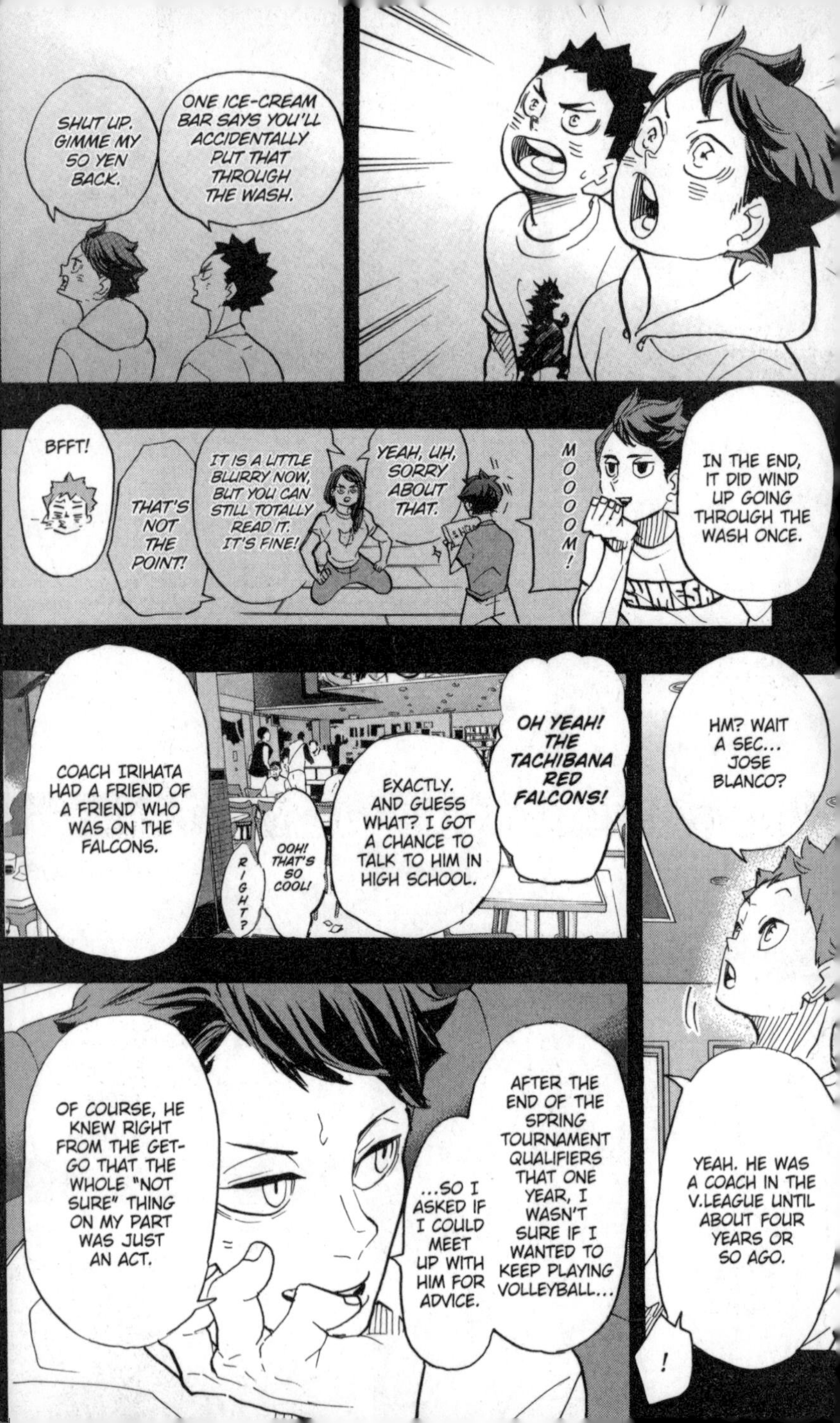
ONE ICE-CREAM BAR SAYS YOU'LL ACCIDENTALLY PUT THAT THROUGH THE WASH.
SHUT UP. GIMME MY 50 YEN BACK.
IN THE END, IT DID WIND UP GOING THROUGH THE WASH ONCE.
MOOOOOM!
YEAH, UH, SORRY ABOUT THAT.
IT IS A LITTLE BLURRY NOW, BUT YOU CAN STILL TOTALLY READ IT. IT'S FINE!
THAT'S NOT THE POINT!
BFFT!
HM? WAIT A SEC... JOSE BLANCO?
YEAH. HE WAS A COACH IN THE V.LEAGUE UNTIL ABOUT FOUR YEARS OR SO AGO.
!
OH YEAH! THE TACHIBANA RED FALCONS!
EXACTLY. AND GUESS WHAT? I GOT A CHANCE TO TALK TO HIM IN HIGH SCHOOL.
OOH! THAT'S SO COOL!
RIGHT?
COACH IRIHATA HAD A FRIEND OF A FRIEND WHO WAS ON THE FALCONS.
AFTER THE END OF THE SPRING TOURNAMENT QUALIFIERS THAT ONE YEAR, I WASN'T SURE IF I WANTED TO KEEP PLAYING VOLLEYBALL...
...SO I ASKED IF I COULD MEET UP WITH HIM FOR ADVICE.
OF COURSE, HE KNEW RIGHT FROM THE GET-GO THAT THE WHOLE "NOT SURE" THING ON MY PART WAS JUST AN ACT.

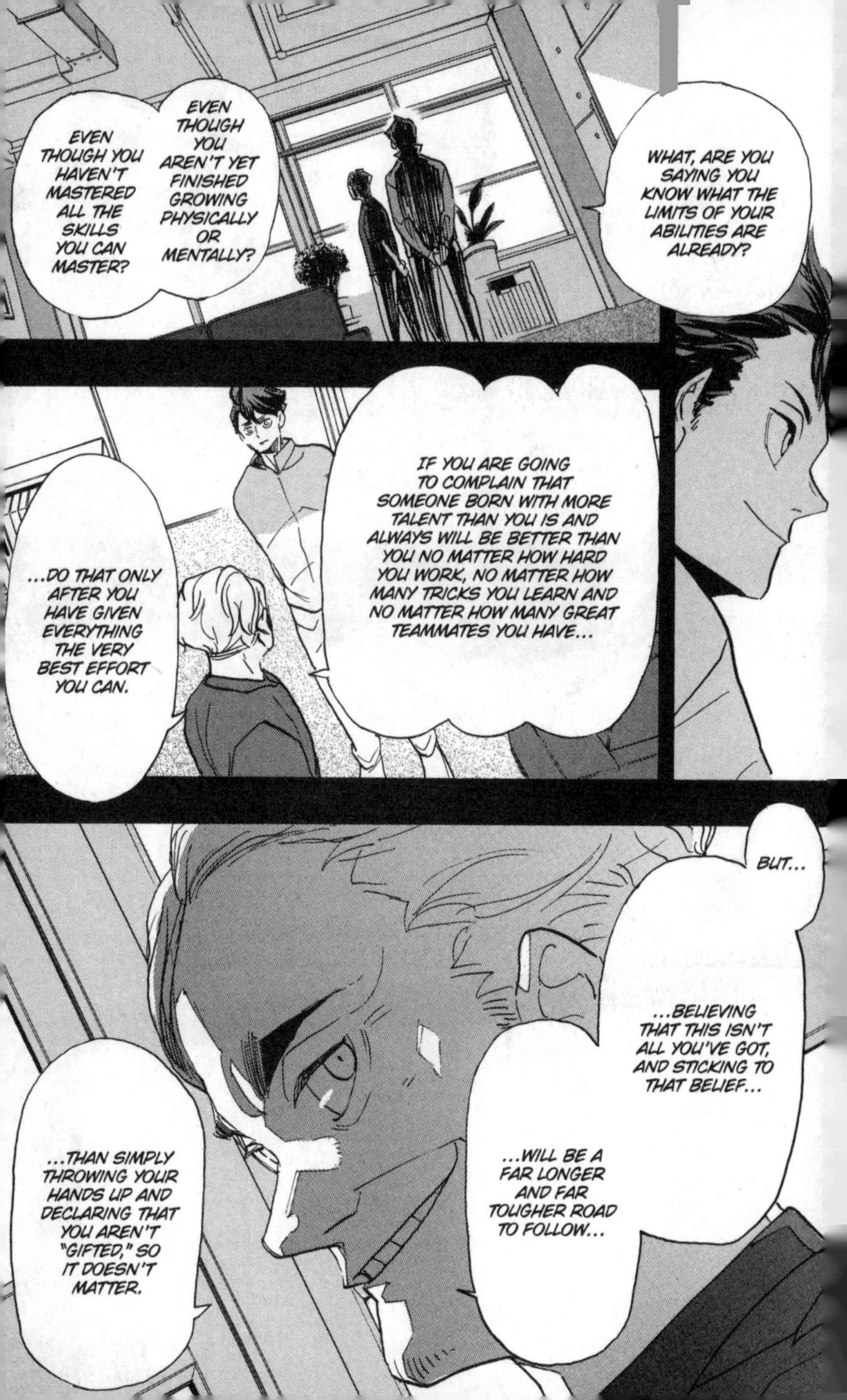
WHAT, ARE YOU SAYING YOU KNOW WHAT THE LIMITS OF YOUR ABILITIES ARE ALREADY?
EVEN THOUGH YOU AREN'T YET FINISHED GROWING PHYSICALLY OR MENTALLY?
EVEN THOUGH YOU HAVEN'T MASTERED ALL THE SKILLS YOU CAN MASTER?
IF YOU ARE GOING TO COMPLAIN THAT SOMEONE BORN WITH MORE TALENT THAN YOU IS AND ALWAYS WILL BE BETTER THAN YOU NO MATTER HOW HARD YOU WORK, NO MATTER HOW MANY TRICKS YOU LEARN AND NO MATTER HOW MANY GREAT TEAMMATES YOU HAVE...
...DO THAT ONLY AFTER YOU HAVE GIVEN EVERYTHING THE VERY BEST EFFORT YOU CAN.
BUT...
...BELIEVING THAT THIS ISN'T ALL YOU'VE GOT, AND STICKING TO THAT BELIEF...
...WILL BE A FAR LONGER AND FAR TOUGHER ROAD TO FOLLOW...
...THAN SIMPLY THROWING YOUR HANDS UP AND DECLARING THAT YOU AREN'T "GIFTED," SO IT DOESN'T MATTER.

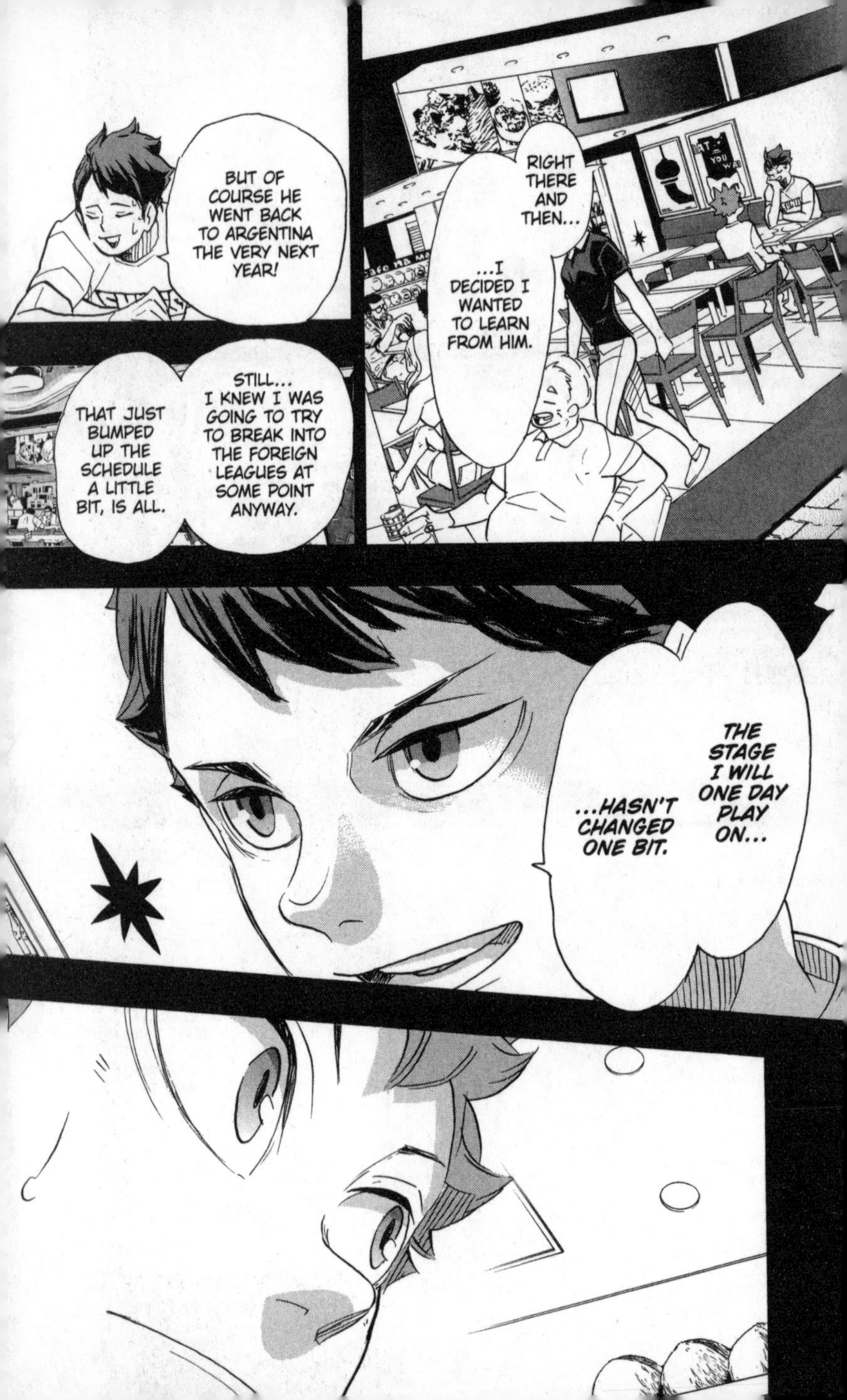
RIGHT THERE AND THEN...
...I DECIDED I WANTED TO LEARN FROM HIM.
BUT OF COURSE HE WENT BACK TO ARGENTINA THE VERY NEXT YEAR!
STILL... I KNEW I WAS GOING TO TRY TO BREAK INTO THE FOREIGN LEAGUES AT SOME POINT ANYWAY.
THAT JUST BUMPED UP THE SCHEDULE A LITTLE BIT, IS ALL.
THE STAGE I WILL ONE DAY PLAY ON...
...HASN'T CHANGED ONE BIT.

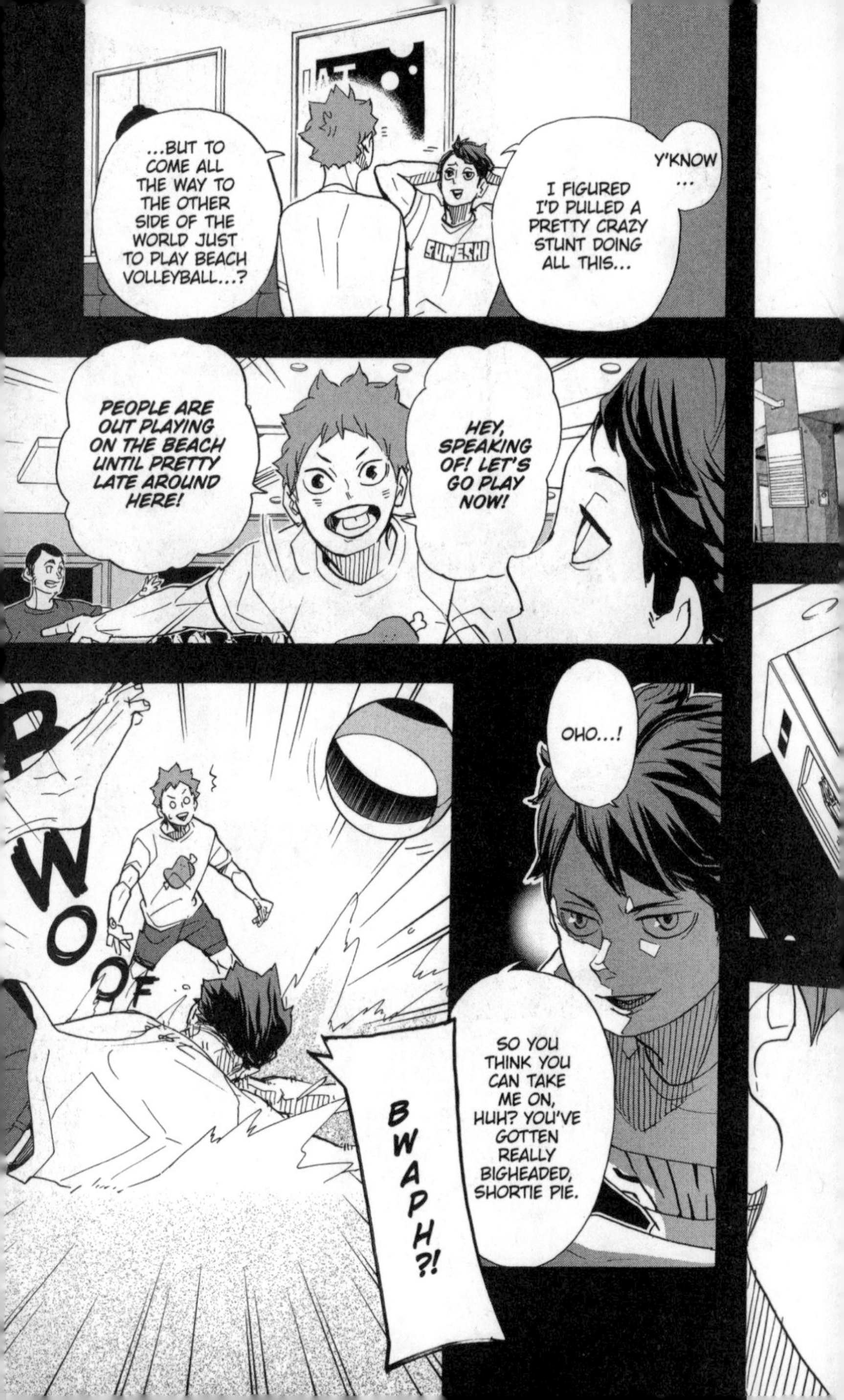
Y'KNOW...
I FIGURED I'D PULLED A PRETTY CRAZY STUNT DOING ALL THIS...
...BUT TO COME ALL THE WAY TO THE OTHER SIDE OF THE WORLD JUST TO PLAY BEACH VOLLEYBALL...?
PEOPLE ARE OUT PLAYING ON THE BEACH UNTIL PRETTY LATE AROUND HERE!
HEY, SPEAKING OF! LET'S GO PLAY NOW!
OHO...!
SO YOU THINK YOU CAN TAKE ME ON, HUH? YOU'VE GOTTEN REALLY BIGHEADED, SHORTIE PIE.
BWOOF
BWAPH?!

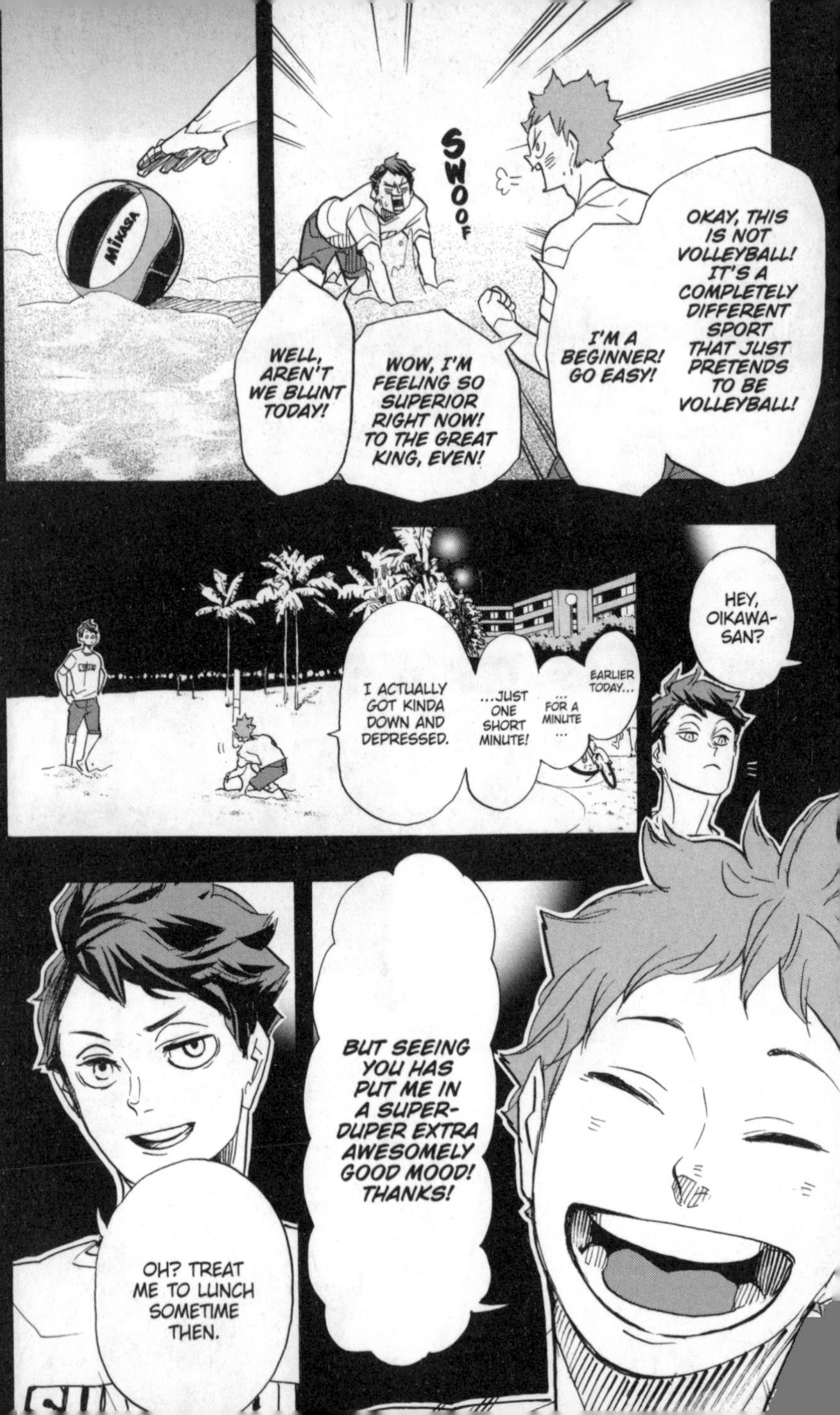
OKAY, THIS IS NOT VOLLEYBALL! IT'S A COMPLETELY DIFFERENT SPORT THAT JUST PRETENDS TO BE VOLLEYBALL!
SWOOF
I'M A BEGINNER! GO EASY!
WOW, I'M FEELING SO SUPERIOR RIGHT NOW! TO THE GREAT KING, EVEN!
WELL, AREN'T WE BLUNT TODAY!
HEY, OIKAWA-SAN?
EARLIER TODAY...
...FOR A MINUTE...
...JUST ONE SHORT MINUTE!
I ACTUALLY GOT KINDA DOWN AND DEPRESSED.
BUT SEEING YOU HAS PUT ME IN A SUPER-DUPER EXTRA AWESOMELY GOOD MOOD! THANKS!
OH? TREAT ME TO LUNCH SOMETIME THEN.

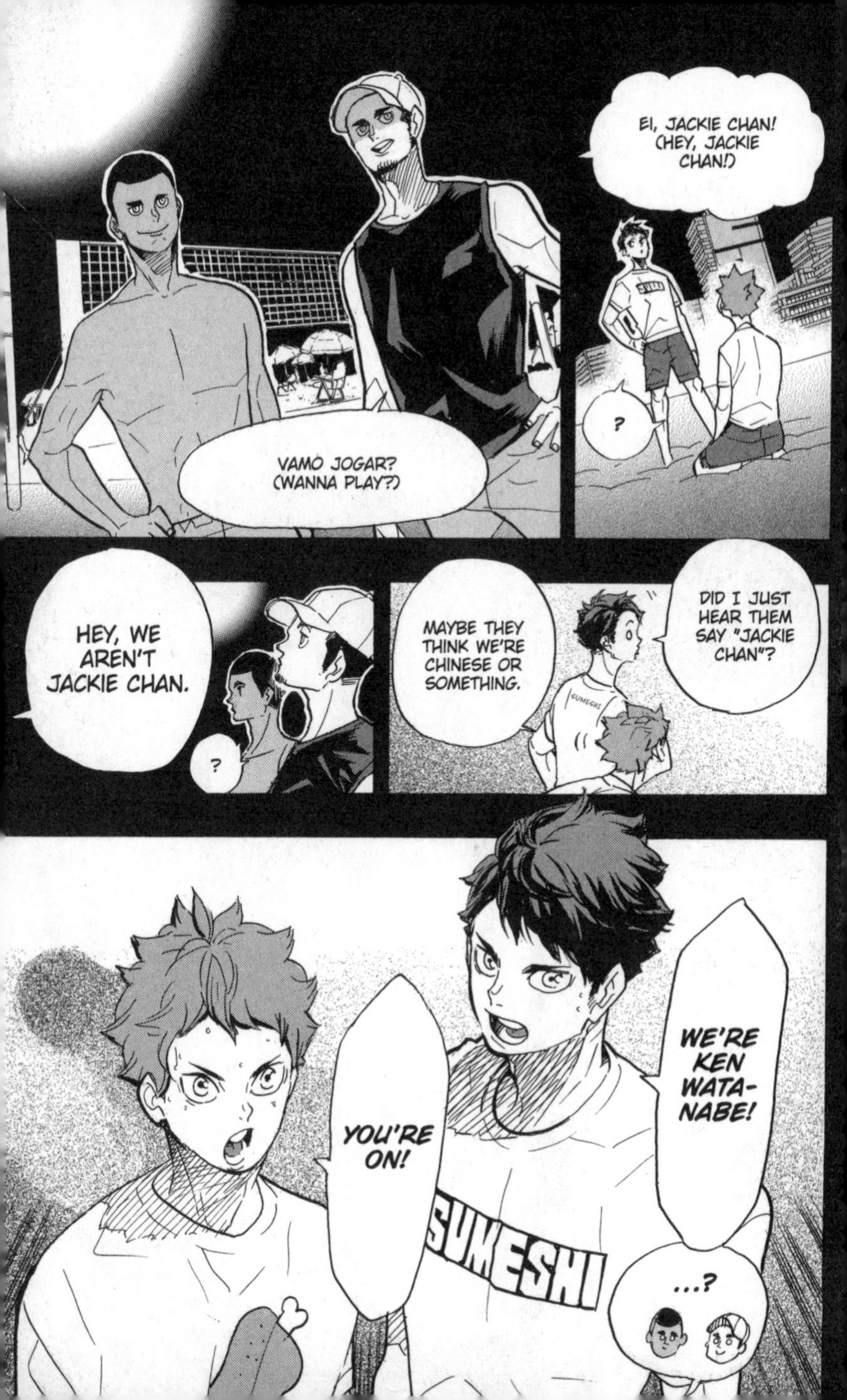
EI, JACKIE CHAN! (HEY, JACKIE CHAN!)
?
VAMO JOGAR? (WANNA PLAY?)
DID I JUST HEAR THEM SAY "JACKIE CHAN"?
MAYBE THEY THINK WE'RE CHINESE OR SOMETHING.
HEY, WE AREN'T JACKIE CHAN.
?
WE'RE KEN WATA-NABE!
YOU'RE ON!
SUMESHI
...?

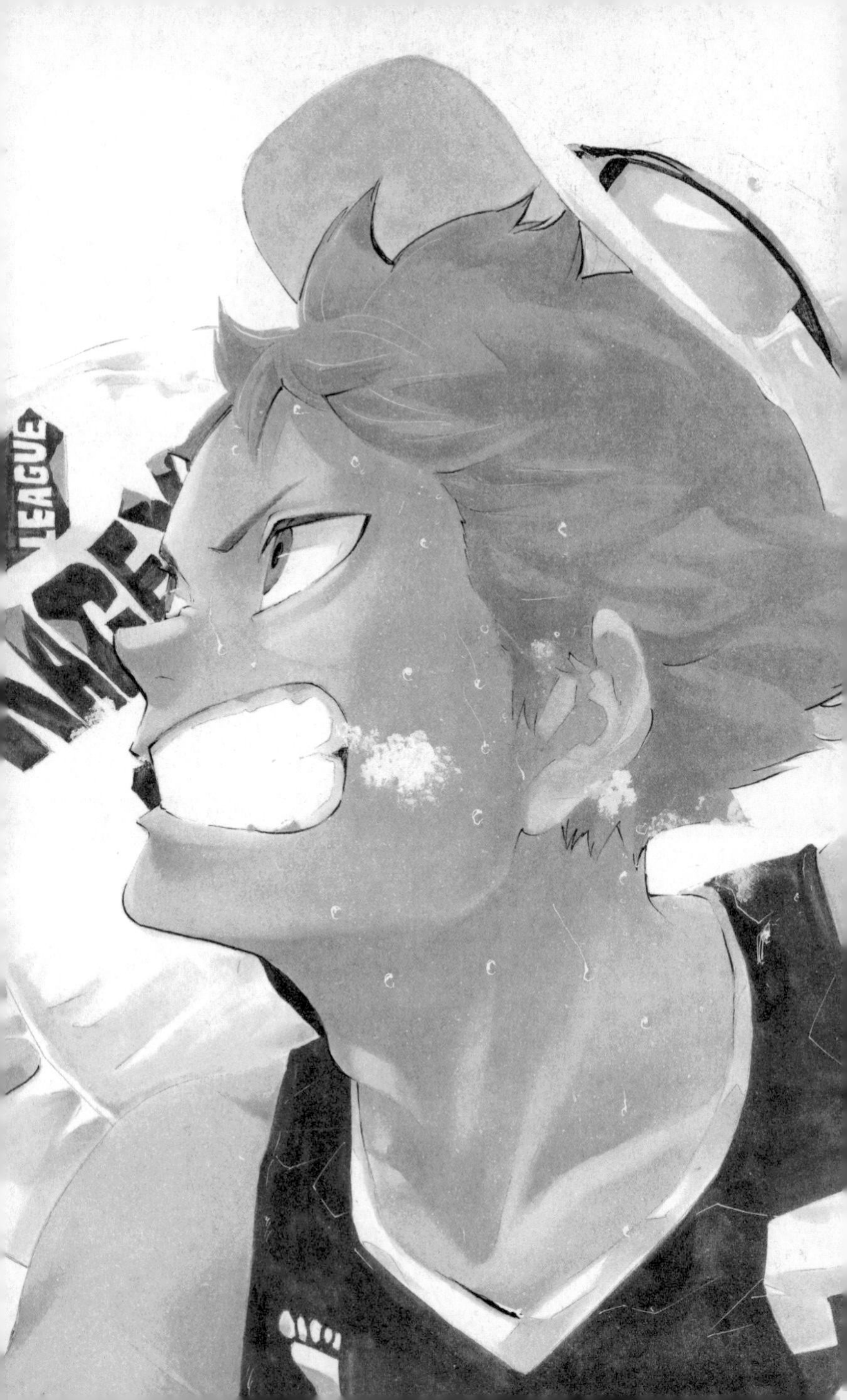
LEAGUE

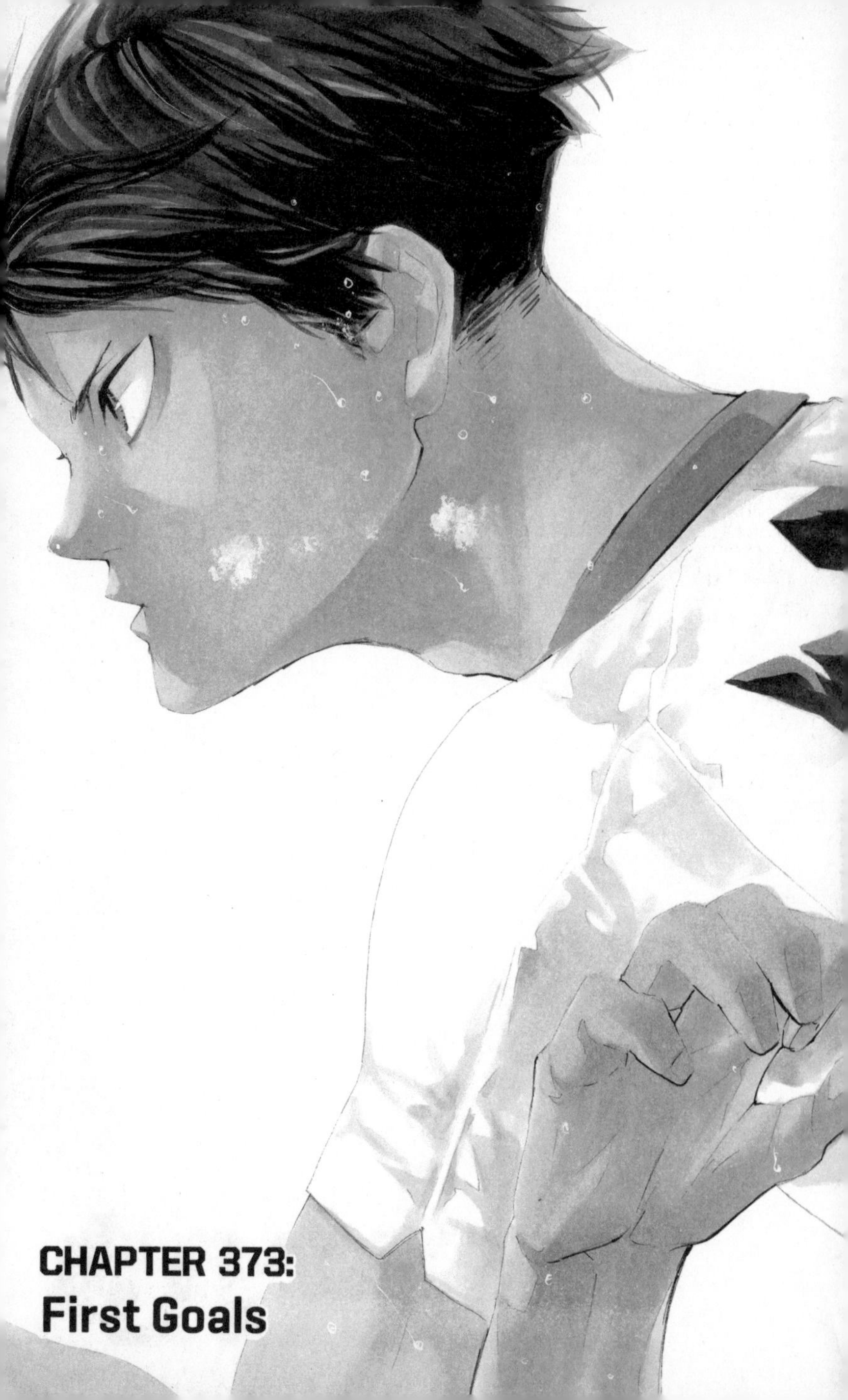

CHAPTER 373:
First Goals

HAIKYU!!

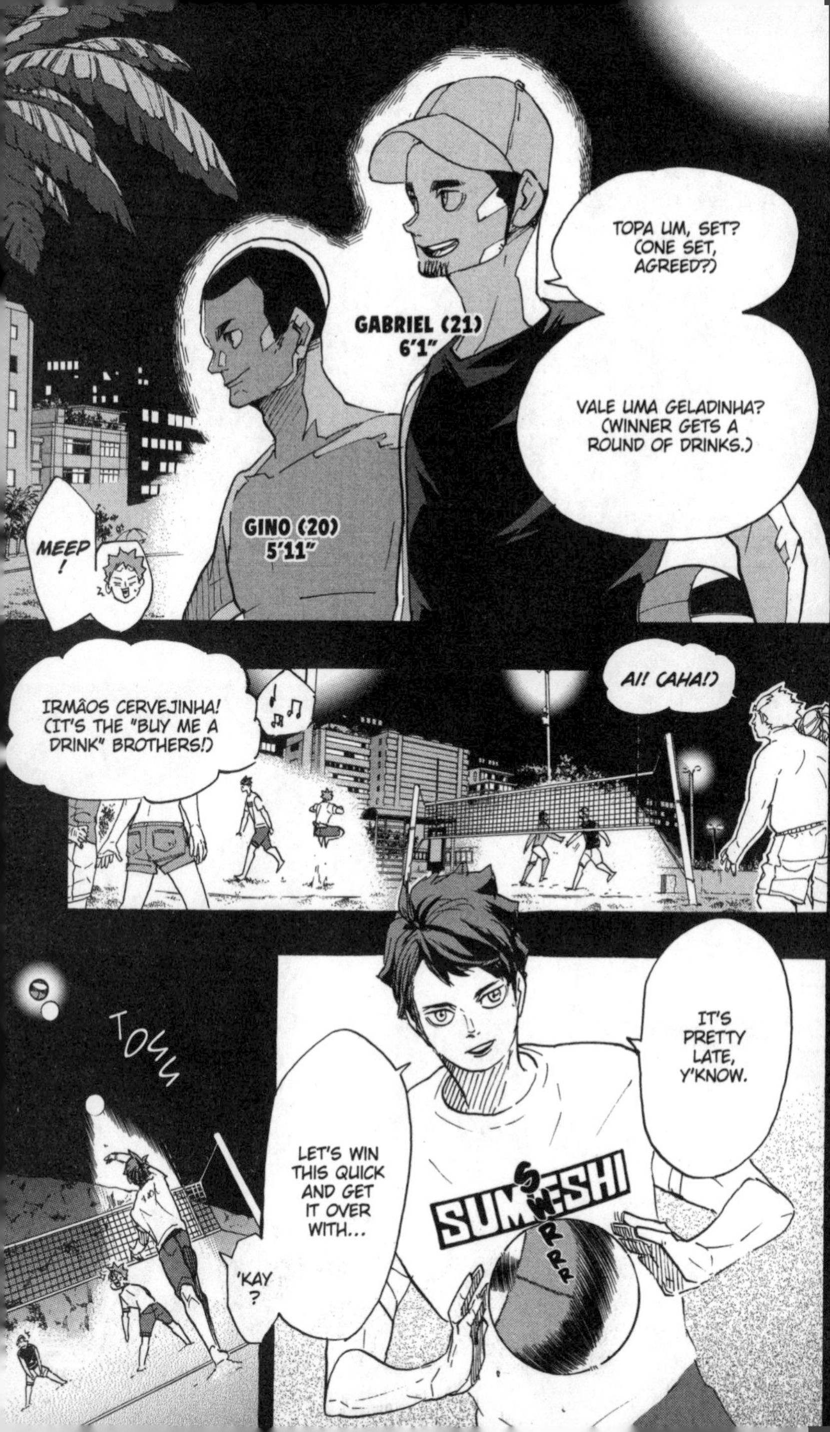

TOPA UM, SET? (ONE SET, AGREED?)
VALE UMA GELADINHA? (WINNER GETS A ROUND OF DRINKS.)
GABRIEL (21) 6'1"
GINO (20) 5'11"
MEEP!
AI! (AHA!)
IRMÂOS CERVEJINHA! (IT'S THE "BUY ME A DRINK" BROTHERS!)
IT'S PRETTY LATE, Y'KNOW.
SUMESHI
SWRRR
LET'S WIN THIS QUICK AND GET IT OVER WITH...
'KAY?
TOSS

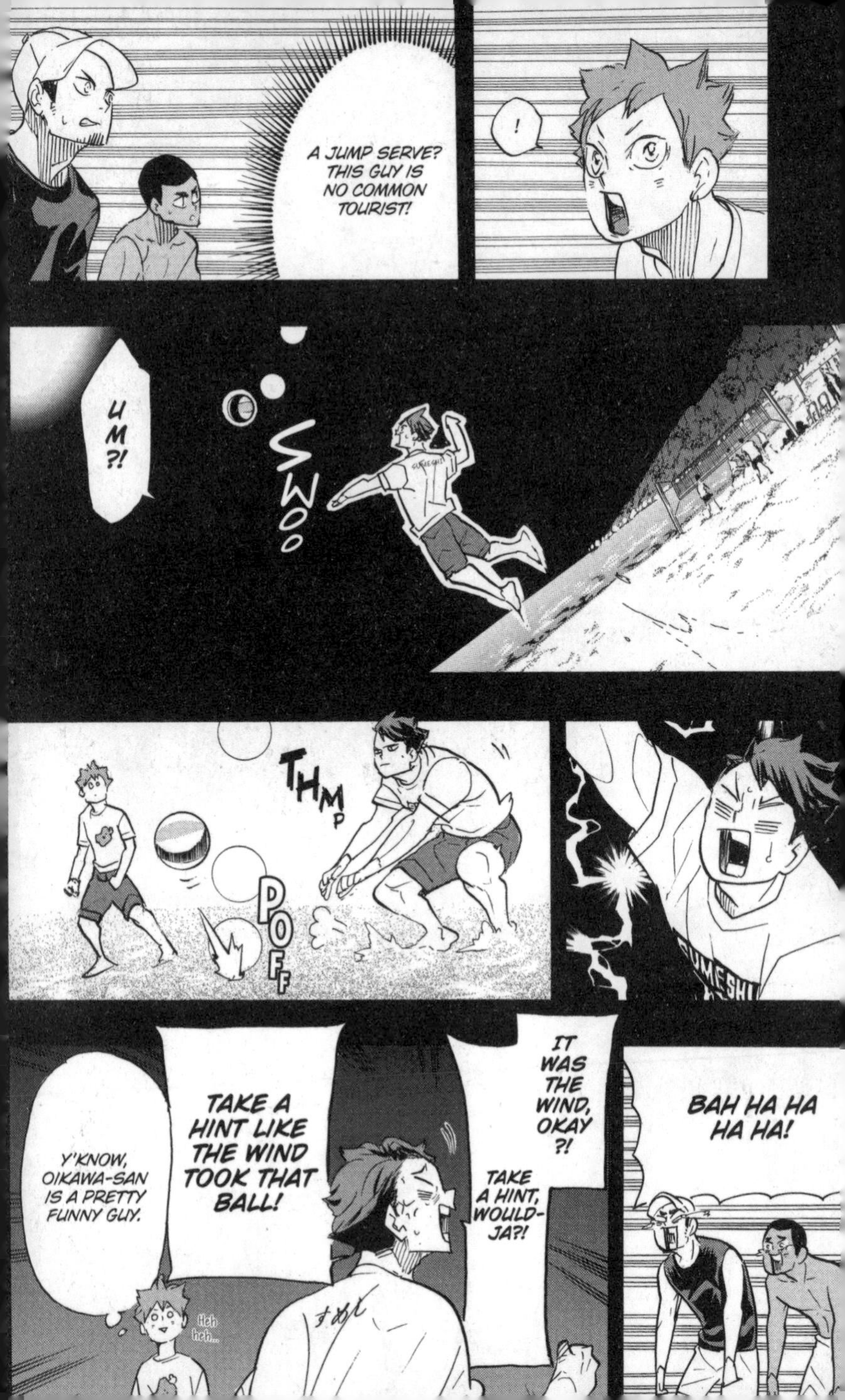
!
A JUMP SERVE? THIS GUY IS NO COMMON TOURIST!
UM ?!
SWOO
THMP
POFF
BAH HA HA HA HA!
IT WAS THE WIND, OKAY?!
TAKE A HINT, WOULD-JA?!
TAKE A HINT LIKE THE WIND TOOK THAT BALL!
Y'KNOW, OIKAWA-SAN IS A PRETTY FUNNY GUY.
Heh heh...

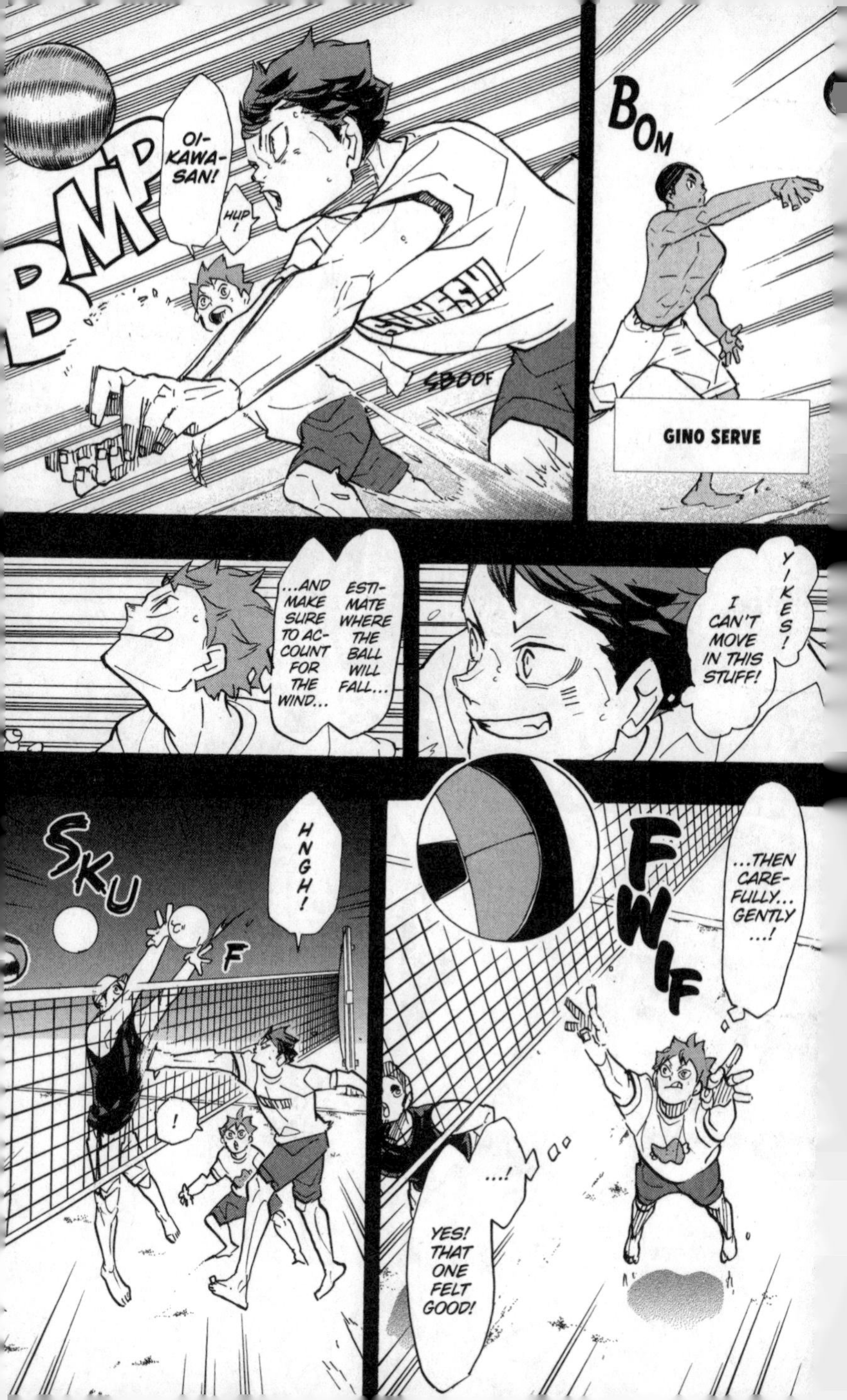
BOM
GINO SERVE
OI-KAWA-SAN!
HUP!
BMP
SBOOF
YIKES! I CAN'T MOVE IN THIS STUFF!
ESTI-MATE WHERE THE BALL WILL FALL...
...AND MAKE SURE TO AC-COUNT FOR THE WIND...
...THEN CARE-FULLY... GENTLY ...!
FWIF
...!
YES! THAT ONE FELT GOOD!
HNGH!
SKU
F
!

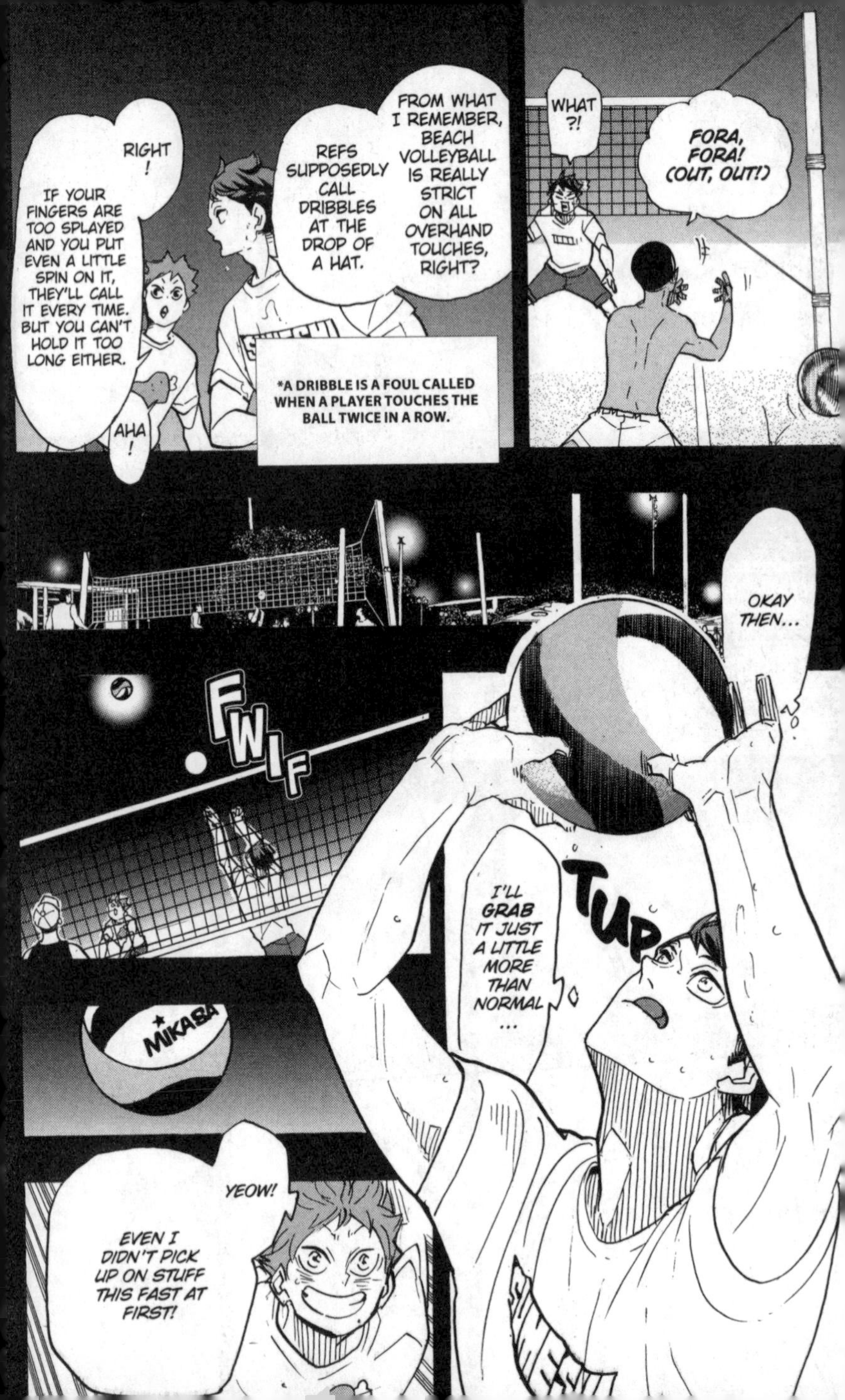
FORA, FORA! (OUT, OUT!)
WHAT?!
FROM WHAT I REMEMBER, BEACH VOLLEYBALL IS REALLY STRICT ON ALL OVERHAND TOUCHES, RIGHT?
REFS SUPPOSEDLY CALL DRIBBLES AT THE DROP OF A HAT.
*A DRIBBLE IS A FOUL CALLED WHEN A PLAYER TOUCHES THE BALL TWICE IN A ROW.
RIGHT!
IF YOUR FINGERS ARE TOO SPLAYED AND YOU PUT EVEN A LITTLE SPIN ON IT, THEY'LL CALL IT EVERY TIME. BUT YOU CAN'T HOLD IT TOO LONG EITHER.
AHA!
OKAY THEN...
I'LL GRAB IT JUST A LITTLE MORE THAN NORMAL...
TUP
FWIF
MIKASA
YEOW!
EVEN I DIDN'T PICK UP ON STUFF THIS FAST AT FIRST!

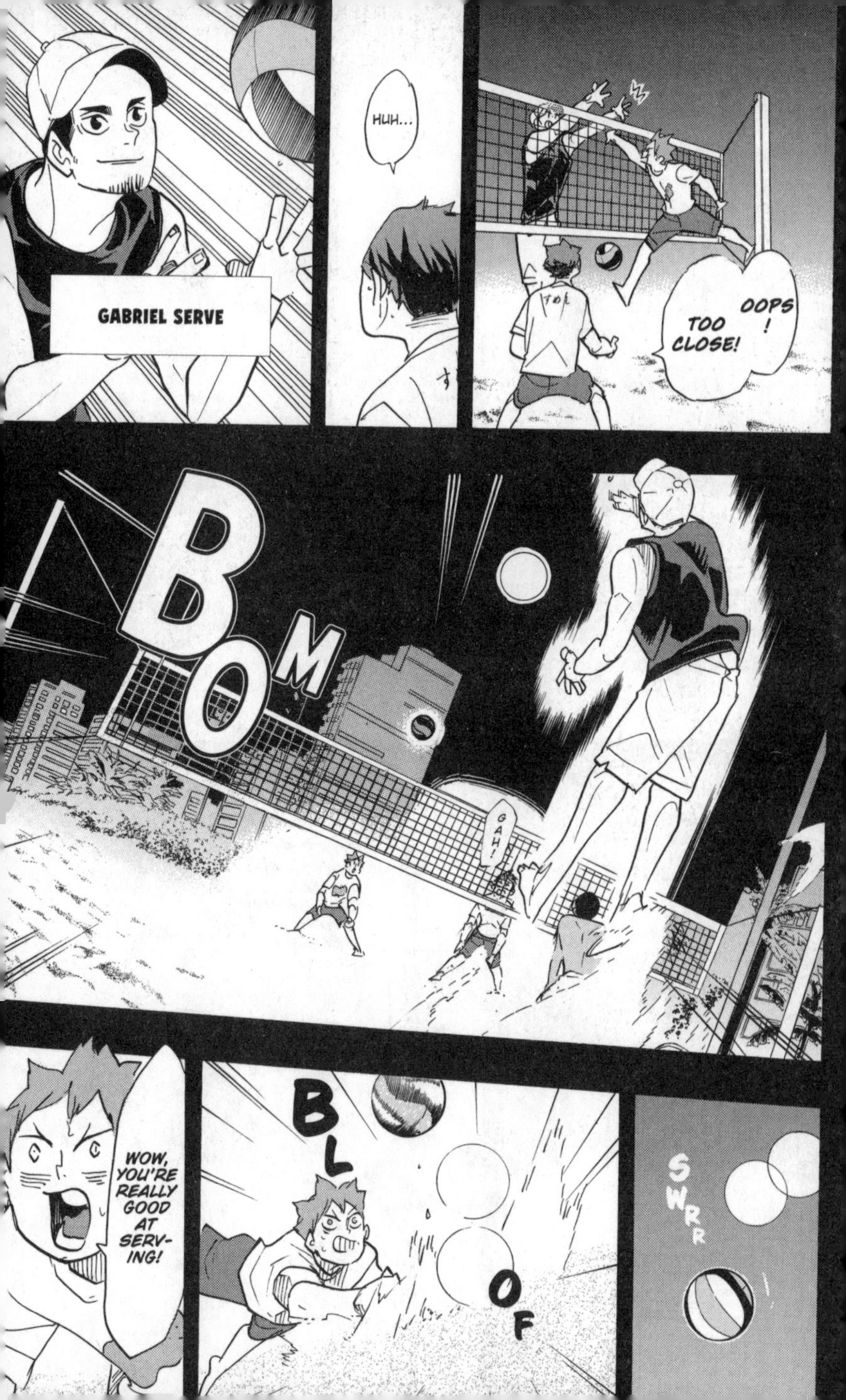
OOPS!
TOO CLOSE!
HUH...
GABRIEL SERVE
BOM
GAH!
SWRR
BLOF
WOW, YOU'RE REALLY GOOD AT SERV-ING!

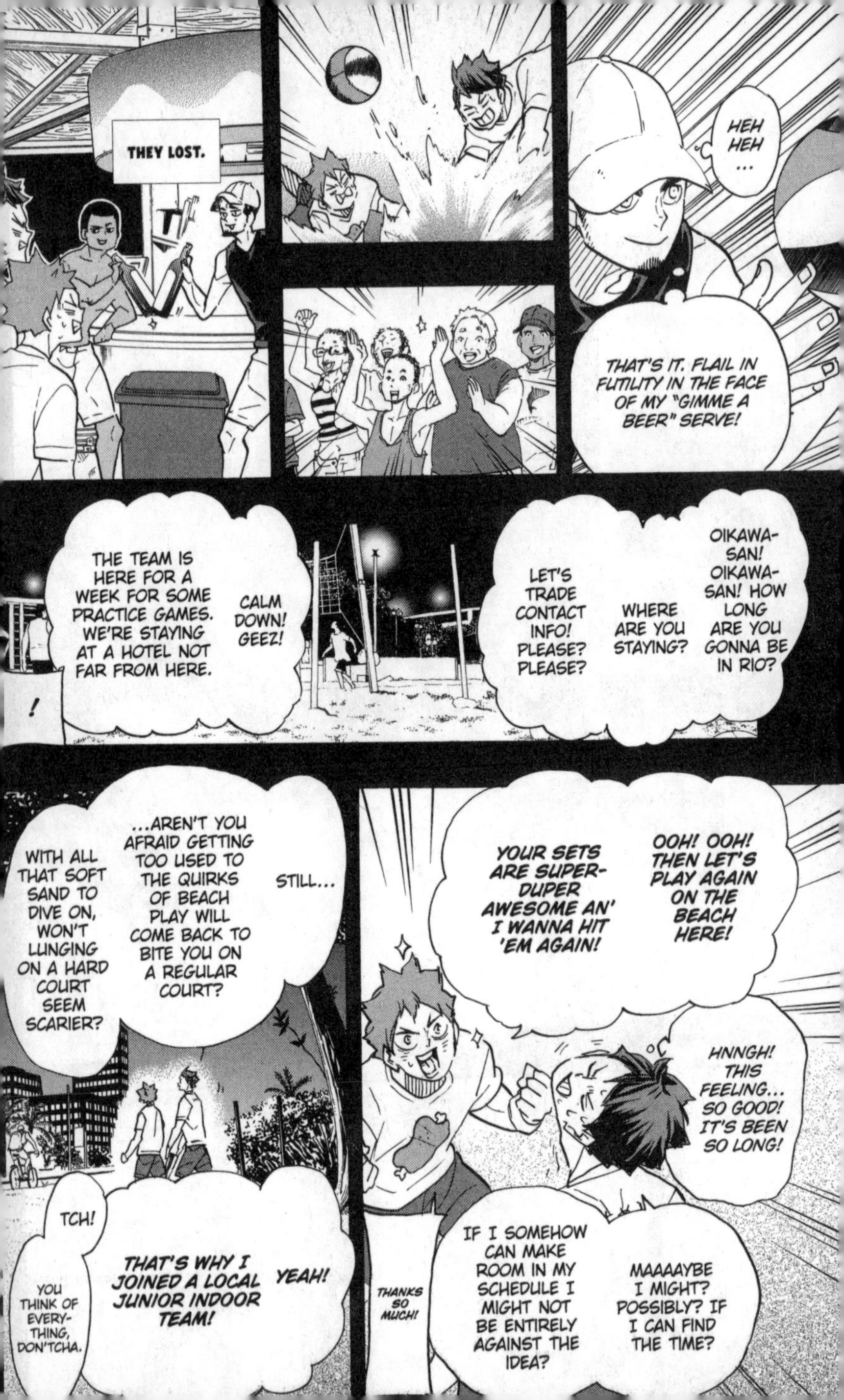
HEH HEH ...
THAT'S IT. FLAIL IN FUTILITY IN THE FACE OF MY "GIMME A BEER" SERVE!
THEY LOST.
OIKAWA-SAN! OIKAWA-SAN! HOW LONG ARE YOU GONNA BE IN RIO?
WHERE ARE YOU STAYING?
LET'S TRADE CONTACT INFO! PLEASE? PLEASE?
CALM DOWN! GEEZ!
THE TEAM IS HERE FOR A WEEK FOR SOME PRACTICE GAMES. WE'RE STAYING AT A HOTEL NOT FAR FROM HERE.
!
OOH! OOH! THEN LET'S PLAY AGAIN ON THE BEACH HERE!
YOUR SETS ARE SUPER-DUPER AWESOME AN' I WANNA HIT 'EM AGAIN!
HNNGH! THIS FEELING... SO GOOD! IT'S BEEN SO LONG!
MAAAAYBE I MIGHT? POSSIBLY? IF I CAN FIND THE TIME?
IF I SOMEHOW CAN MAKE ROOM IN MY SCHEDULE I MIGHT NOT BE ENTIRELY AGAINST THE IDEA?
THANKS SO MUCH!
STILL...
...AREN'T YOU AFRAID GETTING TOO USED TO THE QUIRKS OF BEACH PLAY WILL COME BACK TO BITE YOU ON A REGULAR COURT?
WITH ALL THAT SOFT SAND TO DIVE ON, WON'T LUNGING ON A HARD COURT SEEM SCARIER?
YEAH!
THAT'S WHY I JOINED A LOCAL JUNIOR INDOOR TEAM!
TCH!
YOU THINK OF EVERYTHING, DON'TCHA.

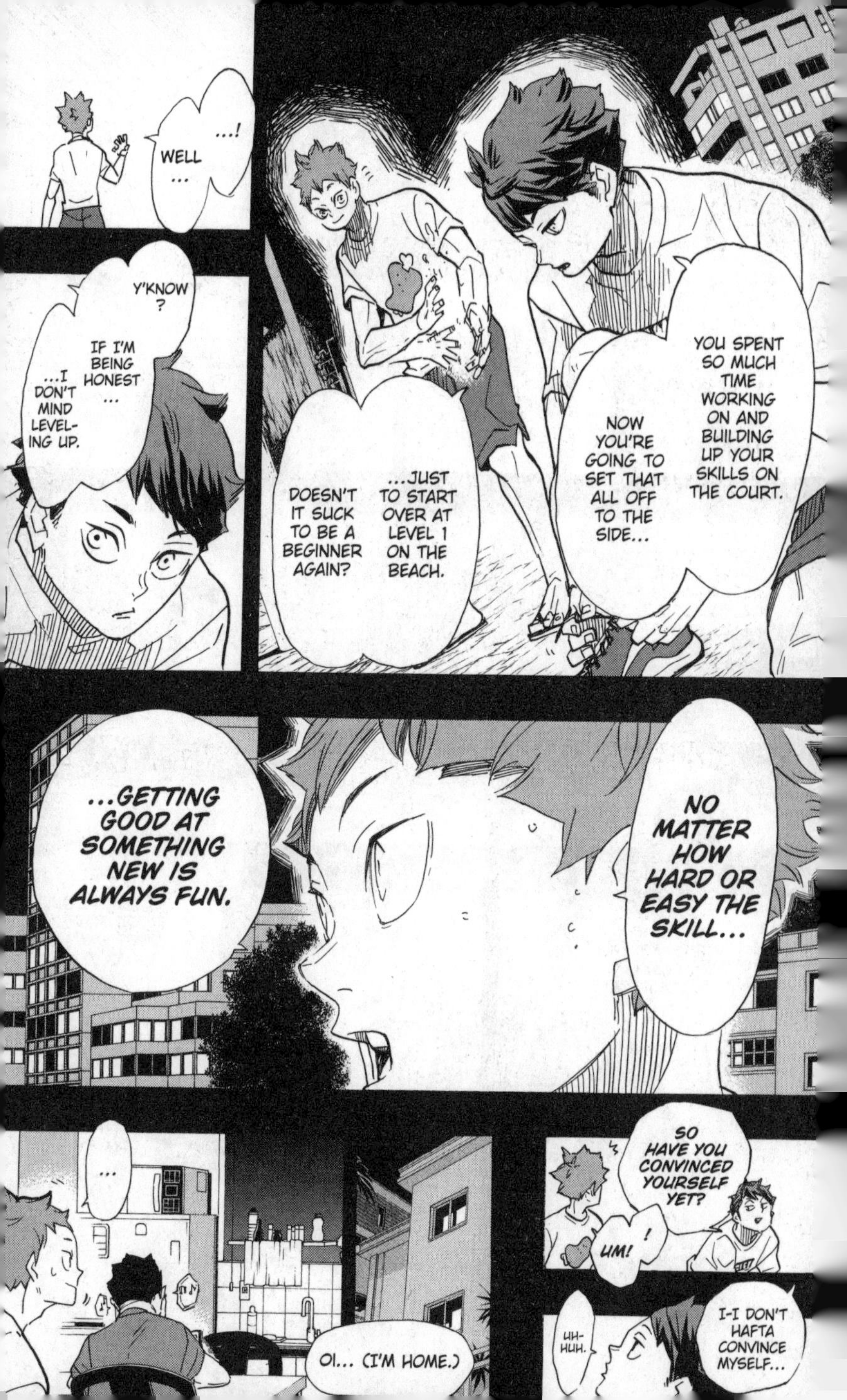
YOU SPENT SO MUCH TIME WORKING ON AND BUILDING UP YOUR SKILLS ON THE COURT.
NOW YOU'RE GOING TO SET THAT ALL OFF TO THE SIDE...
...JUST TO START OVER AT LEVEL 1 ON THE BEACH.
DOESN'T IT SUCK TO BE A BEGINNER AGAIN?
...! WELL...
Y'KNOW?
IF I'M BEING HONEST...
...I DON'T MIND LEVELING UP.
NO MATTER HOW HARD OR EASY THE SKILL...
...GETTING GOOD AT SOMETHING NEW IS ALWAYS FUN.
SO HAVE YOU CONVINCED YOURSELF YET?
! UM!
I-I DON'T HAFTA CONVINCE MYSELF...
UH-HUH.
OI... (I'M HOME.)
...

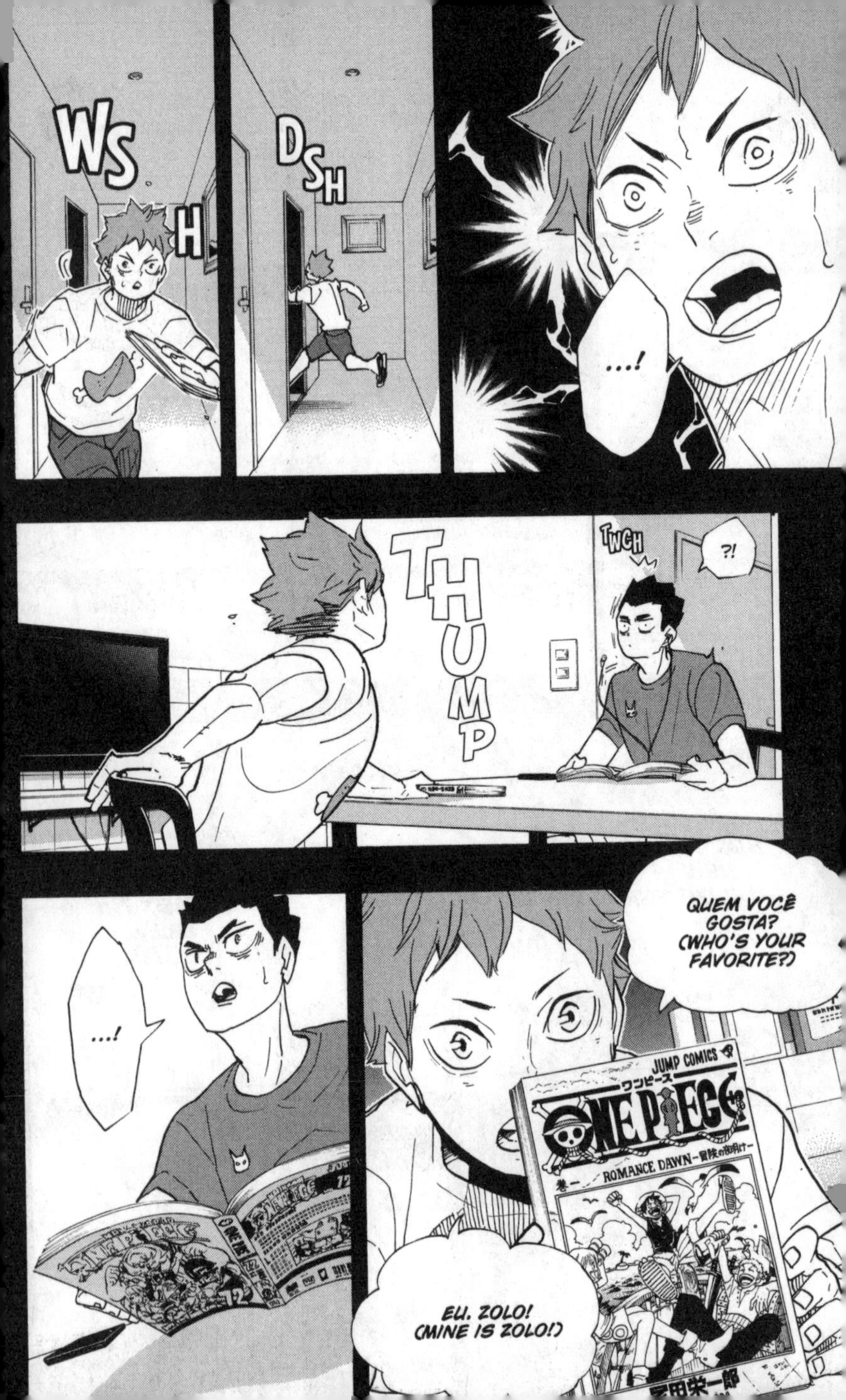
...!
DSH
WSH
TWCH
?!
THUMP
QUEM VOCÊ GOSTA? (WHO'S YOUR FAVORITE?)
JUMP COMICS
ワンピース
ONE PIECE
ROMANCE DAWN -冒険の夜明け-
巻一
EU. ZOLO! (MINE IS ZOLO!)
...!

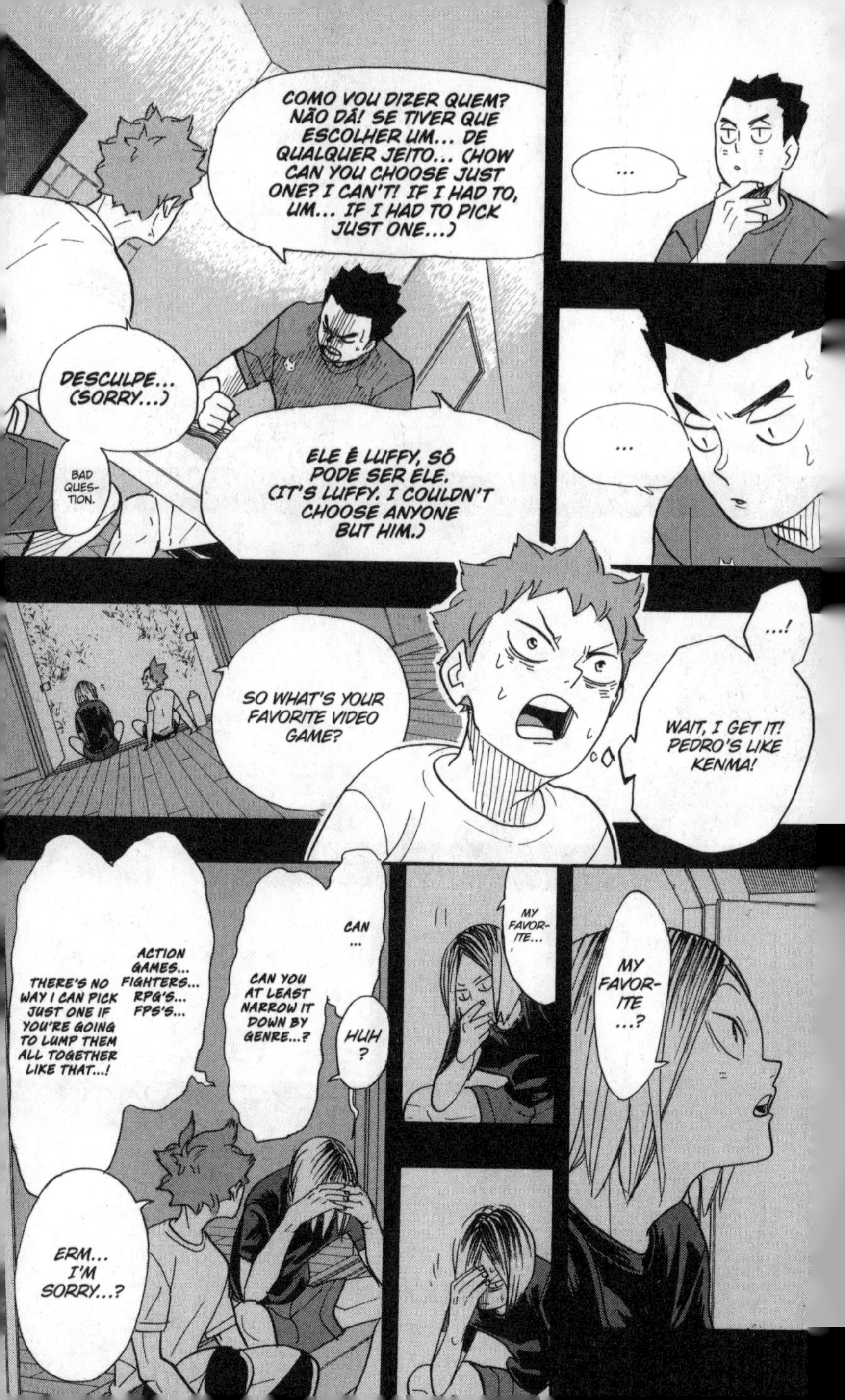
...
...
COMO VOU DIZER QUEM? NÃO DÁ! SE TIVER QUE ESCOLHER UM... DE QUALQUER JEITO... (HOW CAN YOU CHOOSE JUST ONE? I CAN'T! IF I HAD TO, UM... IF I HAD TO PICK JUST ONE...)
DESCULPE... (SORRY...)
BAD QUESTION.
ELE É LUFFY, SÓ PODE SER ELE. (IT'S LUFFY. I COULDN'T CHOOSE ANYONE BUT HIM.)
...!
WAIT, I GET IT! PEDRO'S LIKE KENMA!
SO WHAT'S YOUR FAVORITE VIDEO GAME?
MY FAVORITE...?
MY FAVORITE...
CAN...
HUH?
CAN YOU AT LEAST NARROW IT DOWN BY GENRE...?
ACTION GAMES... FIGHTERS... RPG'S... FPS'S...
THERE'S NO WAY I CAN PICK JUST ONE IF YOU'RE GOING TO LUMP THEM ALL TOGETHER LIKE THAT...!
ERM... I'M SORRY...?

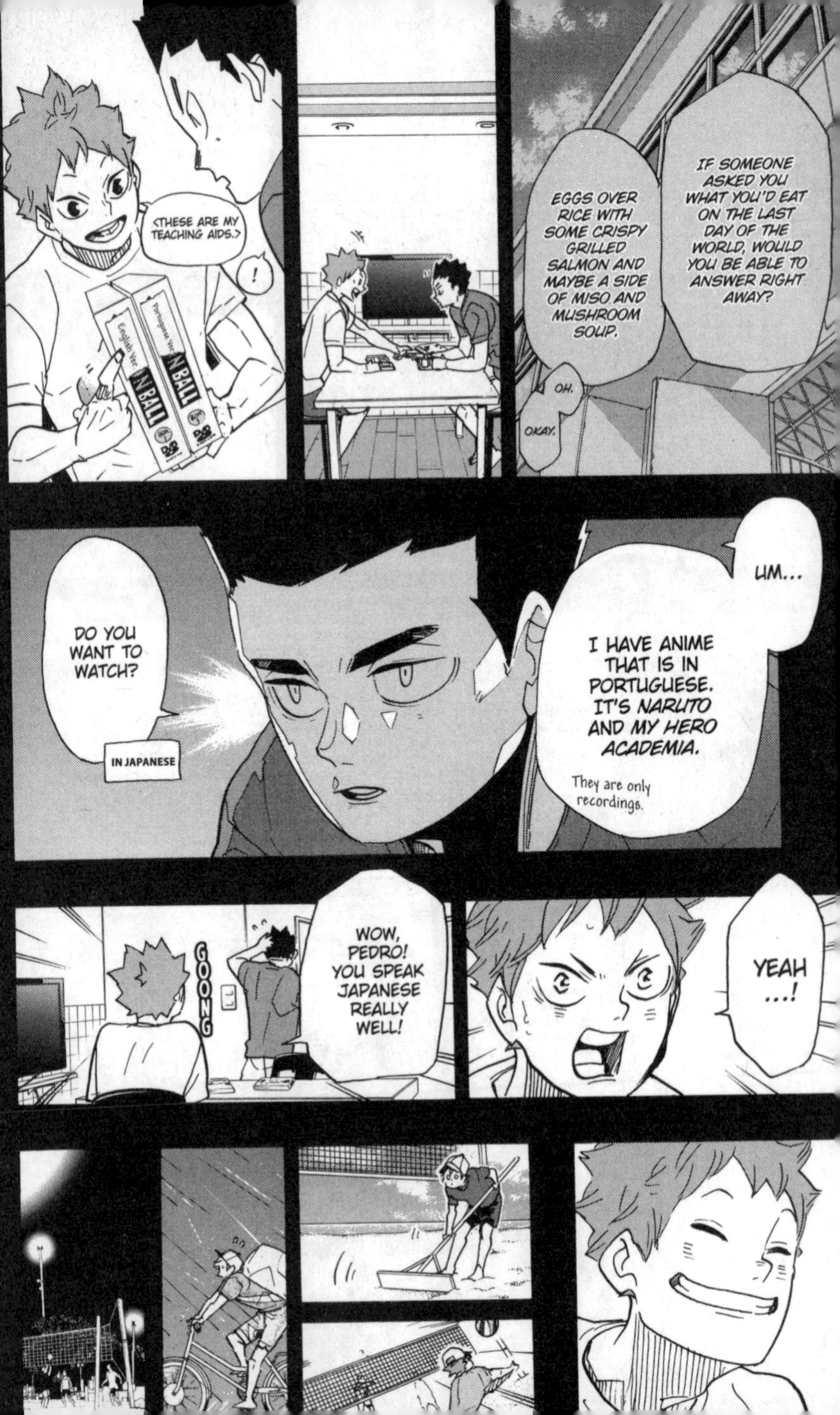
IF SOMEONE ASKED YOU WHAT YOU'D EAT ON THE LAST DAY OF THE WORLD, WOULD YOU BE ABLE TO ANSWER RIGHT AWAY?
EGGS OVER RICE WITH SOME CRISPY GRILLED SALMON AND MAYBE A SIDE OF MISO AND MUSHROOM SOUP.
OH.
OKAY.
<THESE ARE MY TEACHING AIDS.>
!
Portuguese Ver.
English Ver.
UM...
I HAVE ANIME THAT IS IN PORTUGUESE. IT'S *NARUTO* AND *MY HERO ACADEMIA.*
They are only recordings.
DO YOU WANT TO WATCH?
IN JAPANESE
YEAH ...!
WOW, PEDRO! YOU SPEAK JAPANESE REALLY WELL!
GOONG

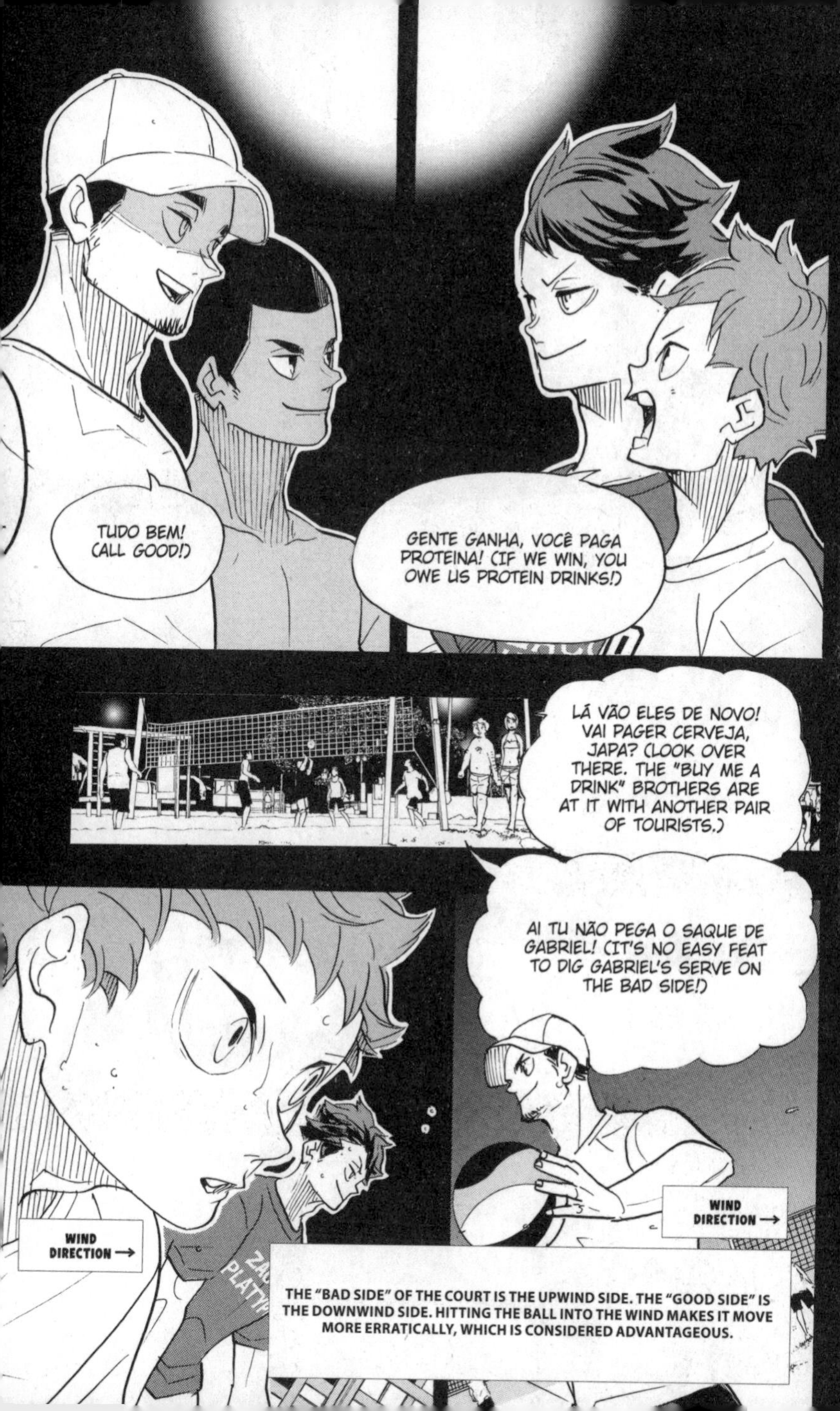
GENTE GANHA, VOCÊ PAGA PROTEINA! (IF WE WIN, YOU OWE US PROTEIN DRINKS!)
TUDO BEM! (ALL GOOD!)
LÁ VÃO ELES DE NOVO! VAI PAGER CERVEJA, JAPA? (LOOK OVER THERE. THE "BUY ME A DRINK" BROTHERS ARE AT IT WITH ANOTHER PAIR OF TOURISTS.)
AI TU NÃO PEGA O SAQUE DE GABRIEL! (IT'S NO EASY FEAT TO DIG GABRIEL'S SERVE ON THE BAD SIDE!)
WIND DIRECTION →
WIND DIRECTION →
THE "BAD SIDE" OF THE COURT IS THE UPWIND SIDE. THE "GOOD SIDE" IS THE DOWNWIND SIDE. HITTING THE BALL INTO THE WIND MAKES IT MOVE MORE ERRATICALLY, WHICH IS CONSIDERED ADVANTAGEOUS.

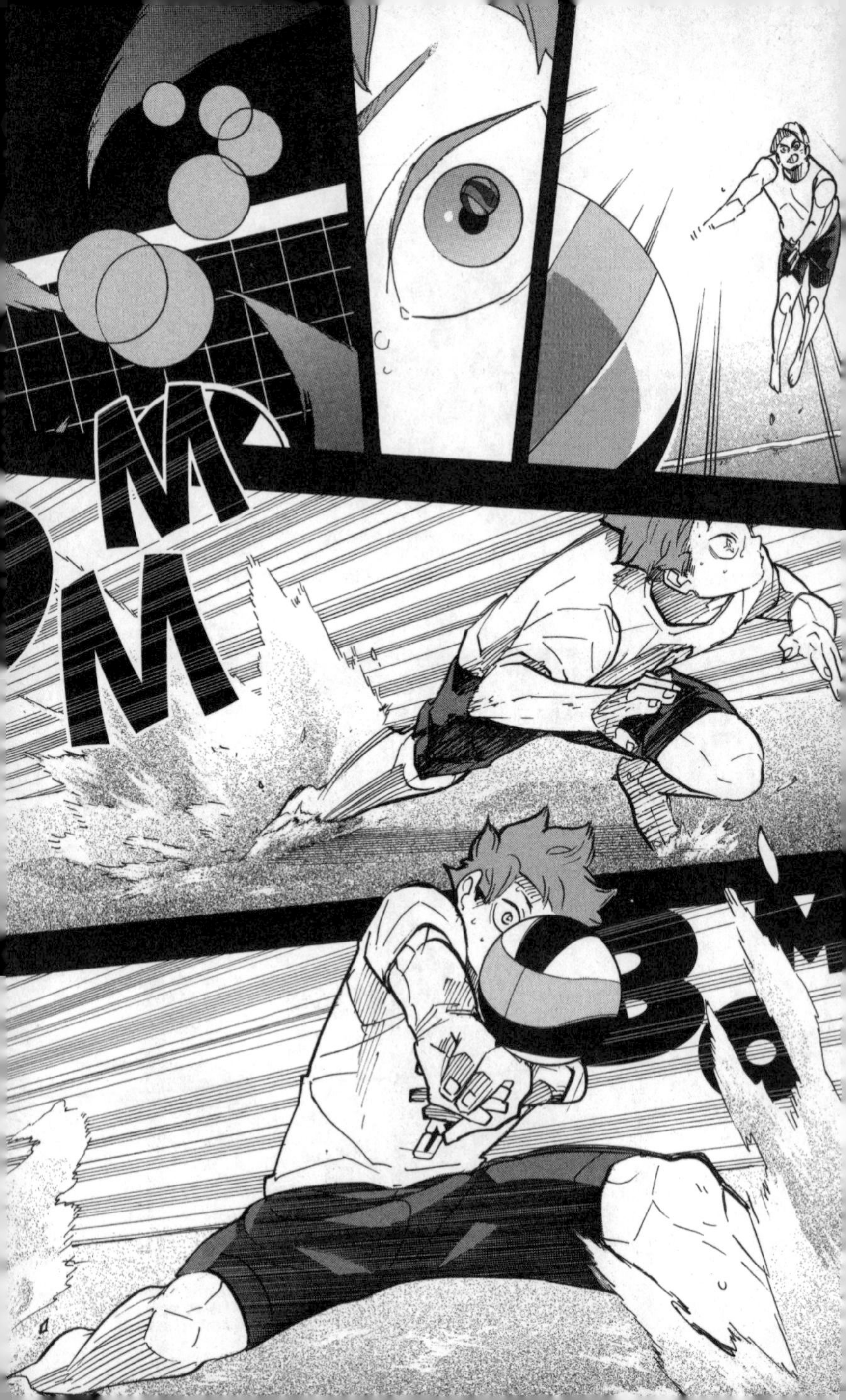
MM

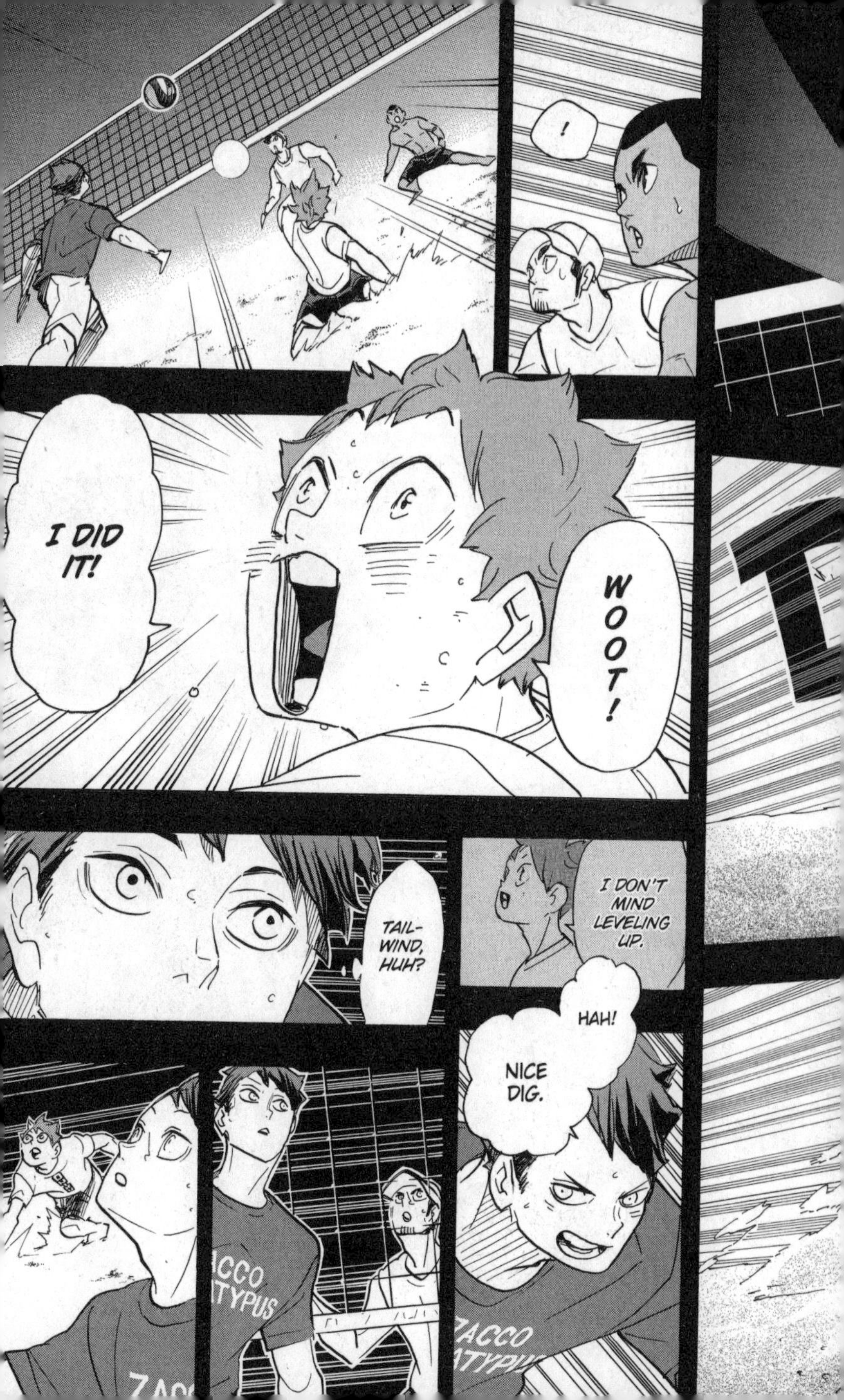
!
WOOT!
I DID IT!
I DON'T MIND LEVELING UP.
TAIL-WIND, HUH?
HAH!
NICE DIG.

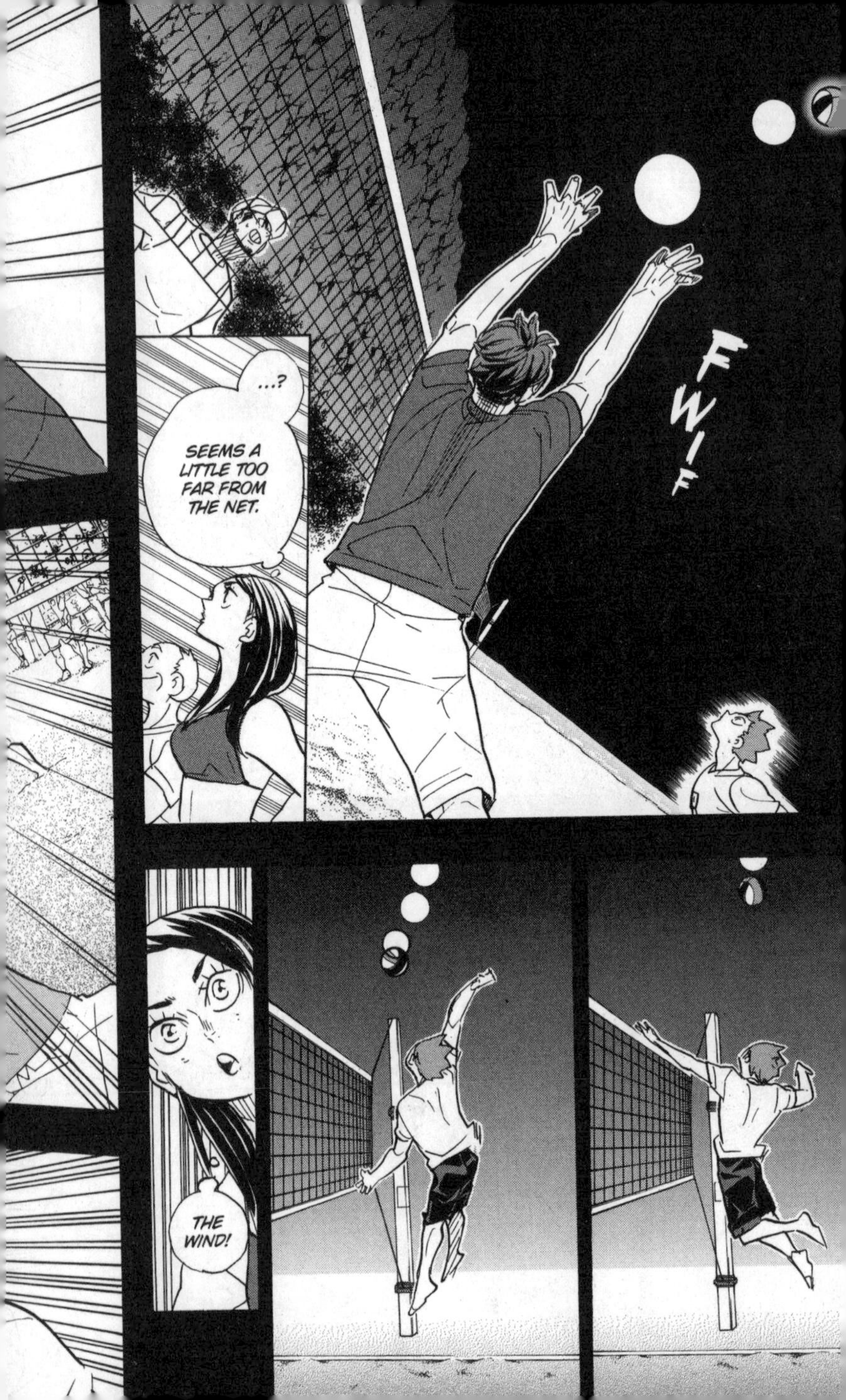
FWIF
...?
SEEMS A LITTLE TOO FAR FROM THE NET.
THE WIND!

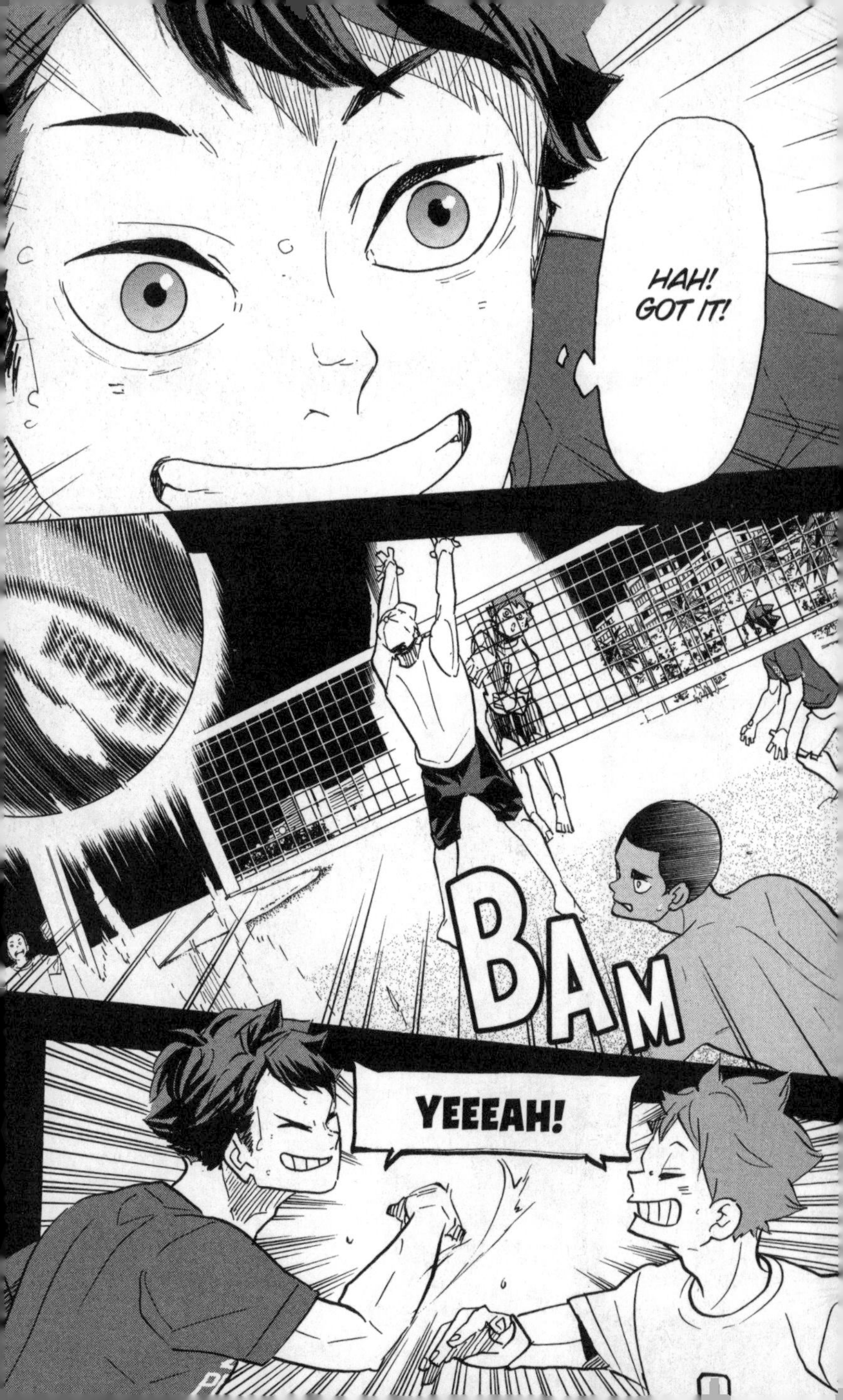
HAH! GOT IT!
BAM
YEEEAH!

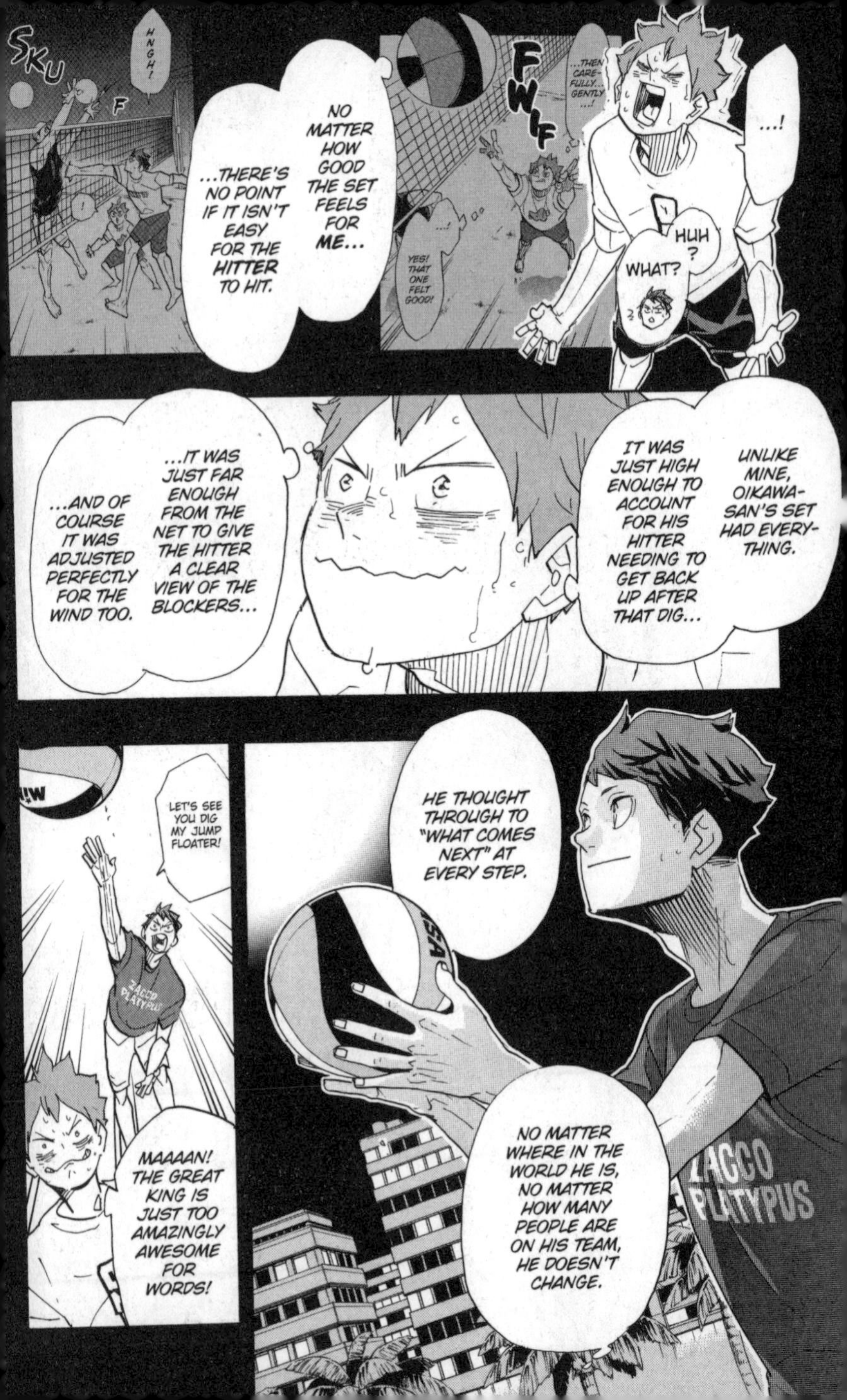
...THEN CAREFULLY... GENTLY...!
...!
HUH?
WHAT?
FWIF
NO MATTER HOW GOOD THE SET FEELS FOR ME...
...!
YES! THAT ONE FELT GOOD!
HNGH!
SKU
F
...THERE'S NO POINT IF IT ISN'T EASY FOR THE HITTER TO HIT.
UNLIKE MINE, OIKAWA-SAN'S SET HAD EVERYTHING.
IT WAS JUST HIGH ENOUGH TO ACCOUNT FOR HIS HITTER NEEDING TO GET BACK UP AFTER THAT DIG...
...IT WAS JUST FAR ENOUGH FROM THE NET TO GIVE THE HITTER A CLEAR VIEW OF THE BLOCKERS...
...AND OF COURSE IT WAS ADJUSTED PERFECTLY FOR THE WIND TOO.
HE THOUGHT THROUGH TO "WHAT COMES NEXT" AT EVERY STEP.
NO MATTER WHERE IN THE WORLD HE IS, NO MATTER HOW MANY PEOPLE ARE ON HIS TEAM, HE DOESN'T CHANGE.
ZACCO PLATYPUS
LET'S SEE YOU DIG MY JUMP FLOATER!
ZACCO PLATYPUS
MAAAAN! THE GREAT KING IS JUST TOO AMAZINGLY AWESOME FOR WORDS!

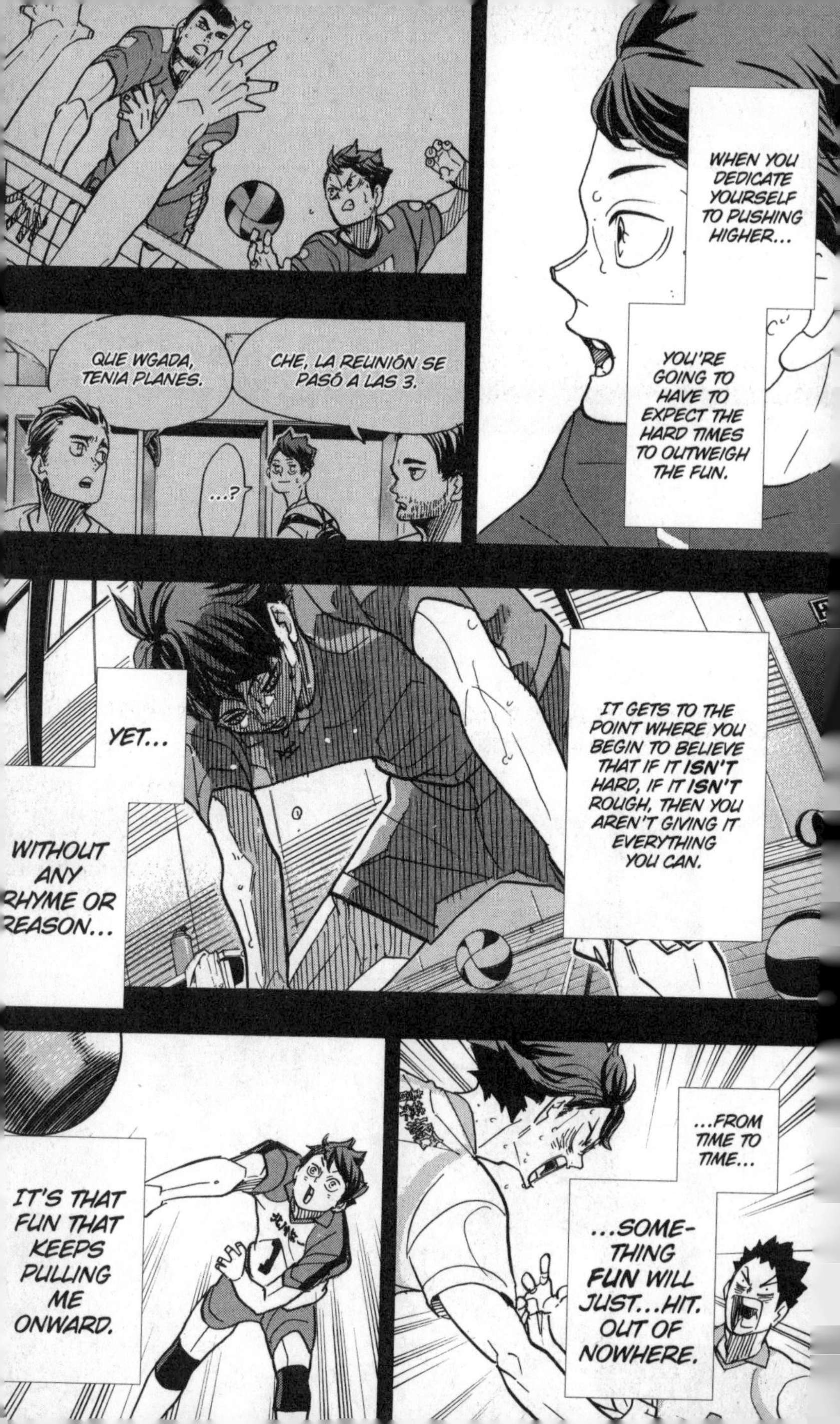
WHEN YOU DEDICATE YOURSELF TO PUSHING HIGHER...
YOU'RE GOING TO HAVE TO EXPECT THE HARD TIMES TO OUTWEIGH THE FUN.
CHE, LA REUNIÓN SE PASÓ A LAS 3.
QUE WGADA, TENIA PLANES.
...?
IT GETS TO THE POINT WHERE YOU BEGIN TO BELIEVE THAT IF IT **ISN'T** HARD, IF IT **ISN'T** ROUGH, THEN YOU AREN'T GIVING IT EVERYTHING YOU CAN.
YET...
WITHOUT ANY RHYME OR REASON...
...FROM TIME TO TIME...
...SOME-THING **FUN** WILL JUST...HIT. OUT OF NOWHERE.
IT'S THAT FUN THAT KEEPS PULLING ME ONWARD.

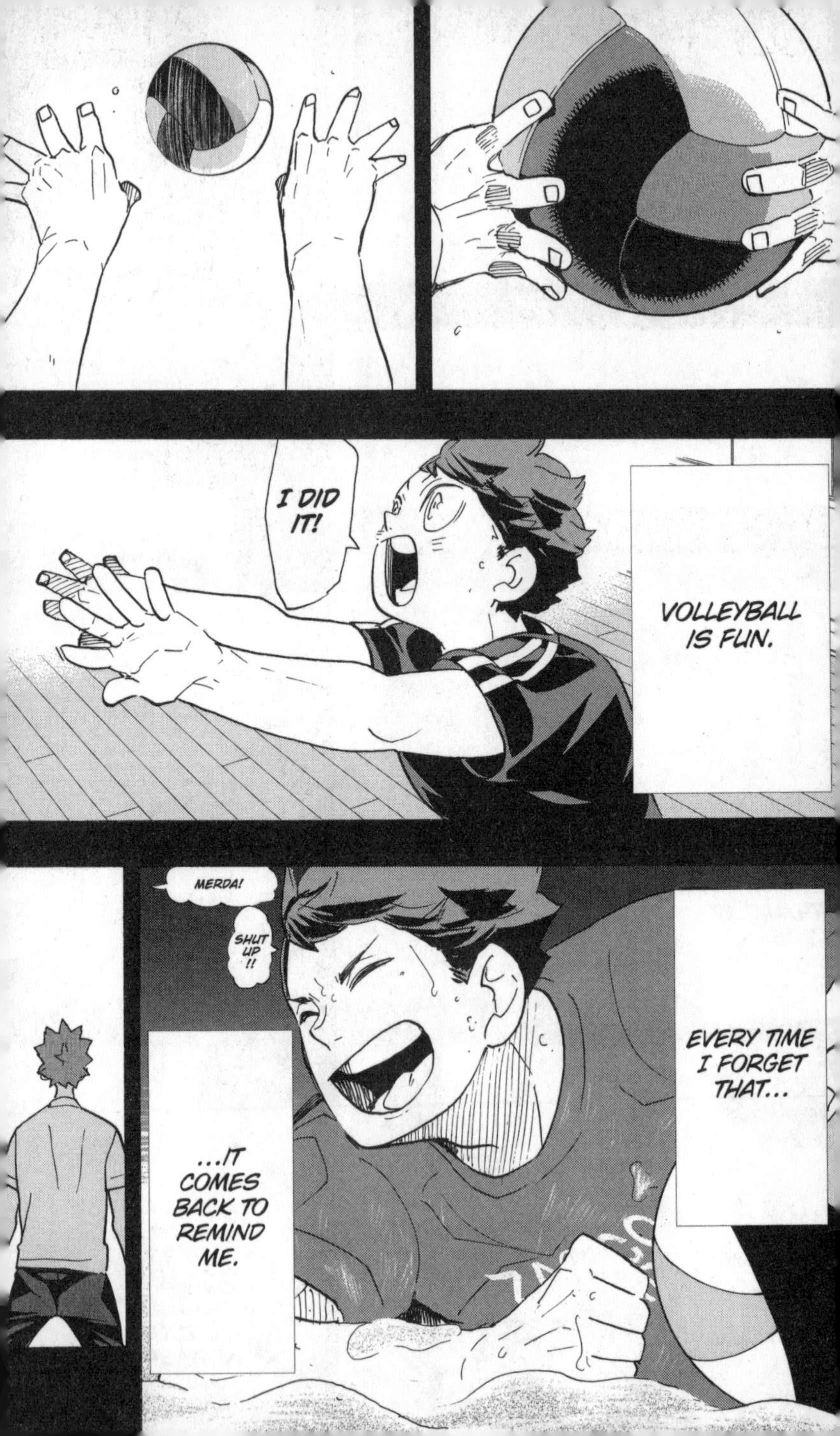
VOLLEYBALL IS FUN.
I DID IT!
EVERY TIME I FORGET THAT...
MERDA!
SHUT UP!!
...IT COMES BACK TO REMIND ME.

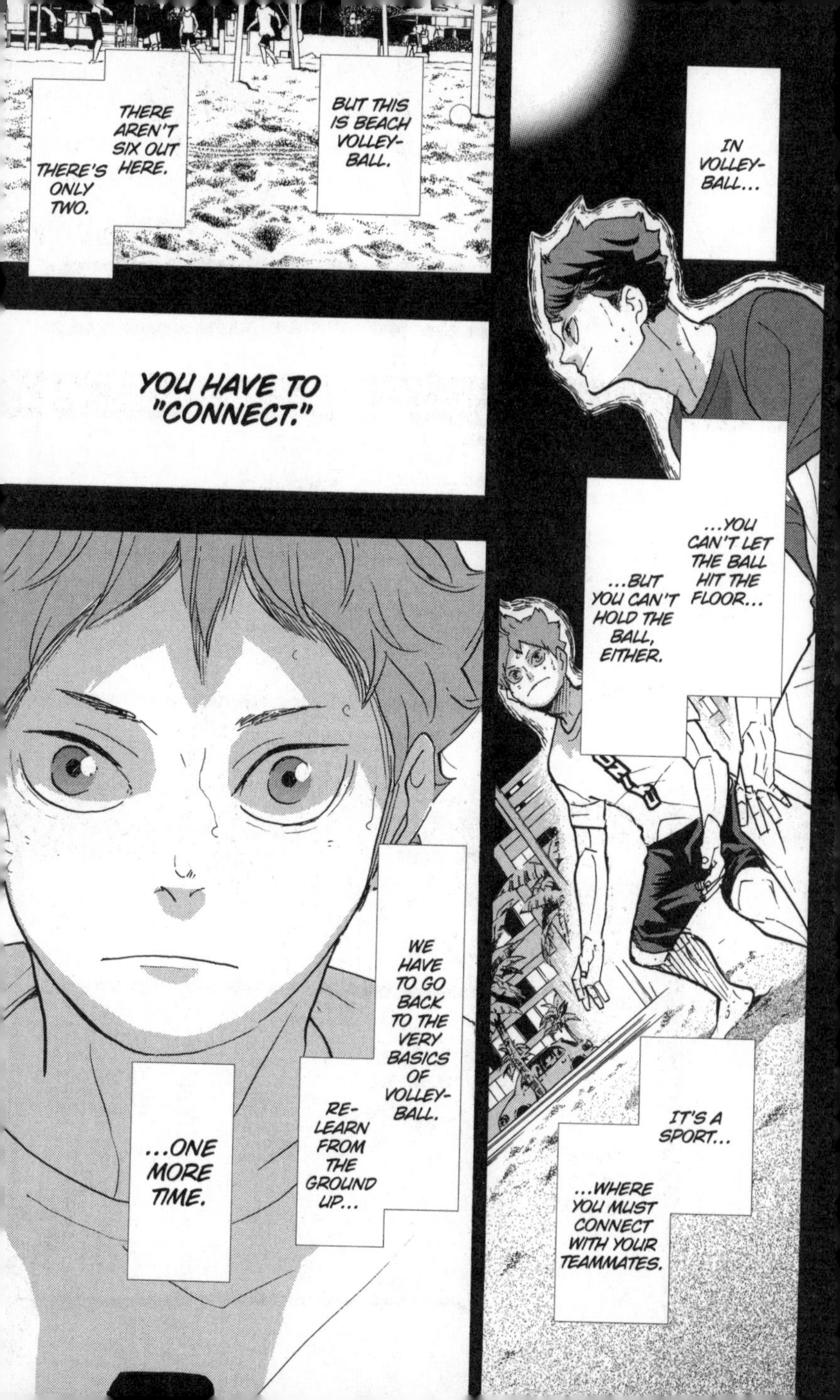
IN VOLLEY-BALL...
...YOU CAN'T LET THE BALL HIT THE FLOOR...
...BUT YOU CAN'T HOLD THE BALL, EITHER.
IT'S A SPORT...
...WHERE YOU MUST CONNECT WITH YOUR TEAMMATES.
BUT THIS IS BEACH VOLLEY-BALL.
THERE AREN'T SIX OUT HERE.
THERE'S ONLY TWO.
YOU HAVE TO "CONNECT."
WE HAVE TO GO BACK TO THE VERY BASICS OF VOLLEY-BALL.
RE-LEARN FROM THE GROUND UP...
...ONE MORE TIME.

PREPARATION

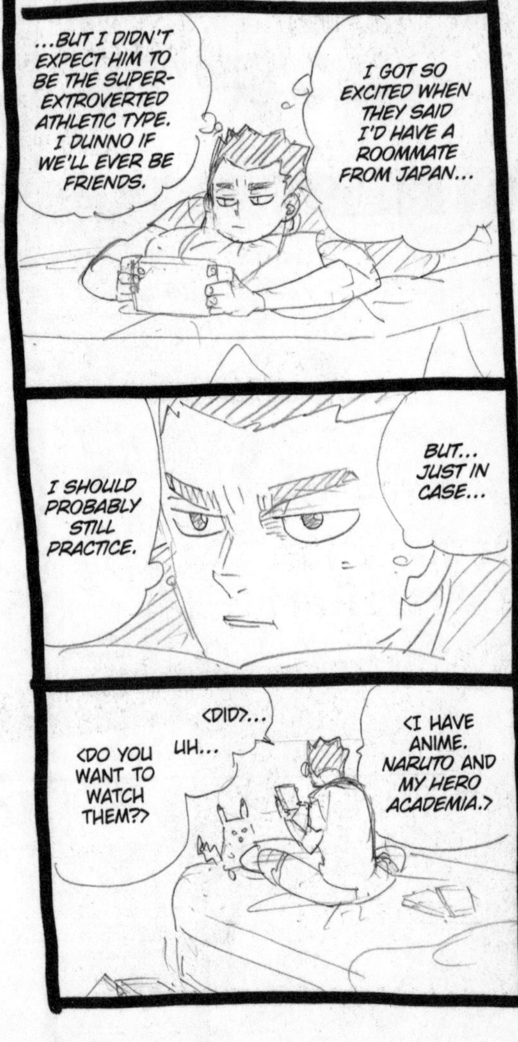
I GOT SO EXCITED WHEN THEY SAID I'D HAVE A ROOMMATE FROM JAPAN...
...BUT I DIDN'T EXPECT HIM TO BE THE SUPER-EXTROVERTED ATHLETIC TYPE. I DUNNO IF WE'LL EVER BE FRIENDS.
BUT... JUST IN CASE...
I SHOULD PROBABLY STILL PRACTICE.
<I HAVE ANIME. NARUTO AND MY HERO ACADEMIA.>
<DID>...
UH...
<DO YOU WANT TO WATCH THEM?>

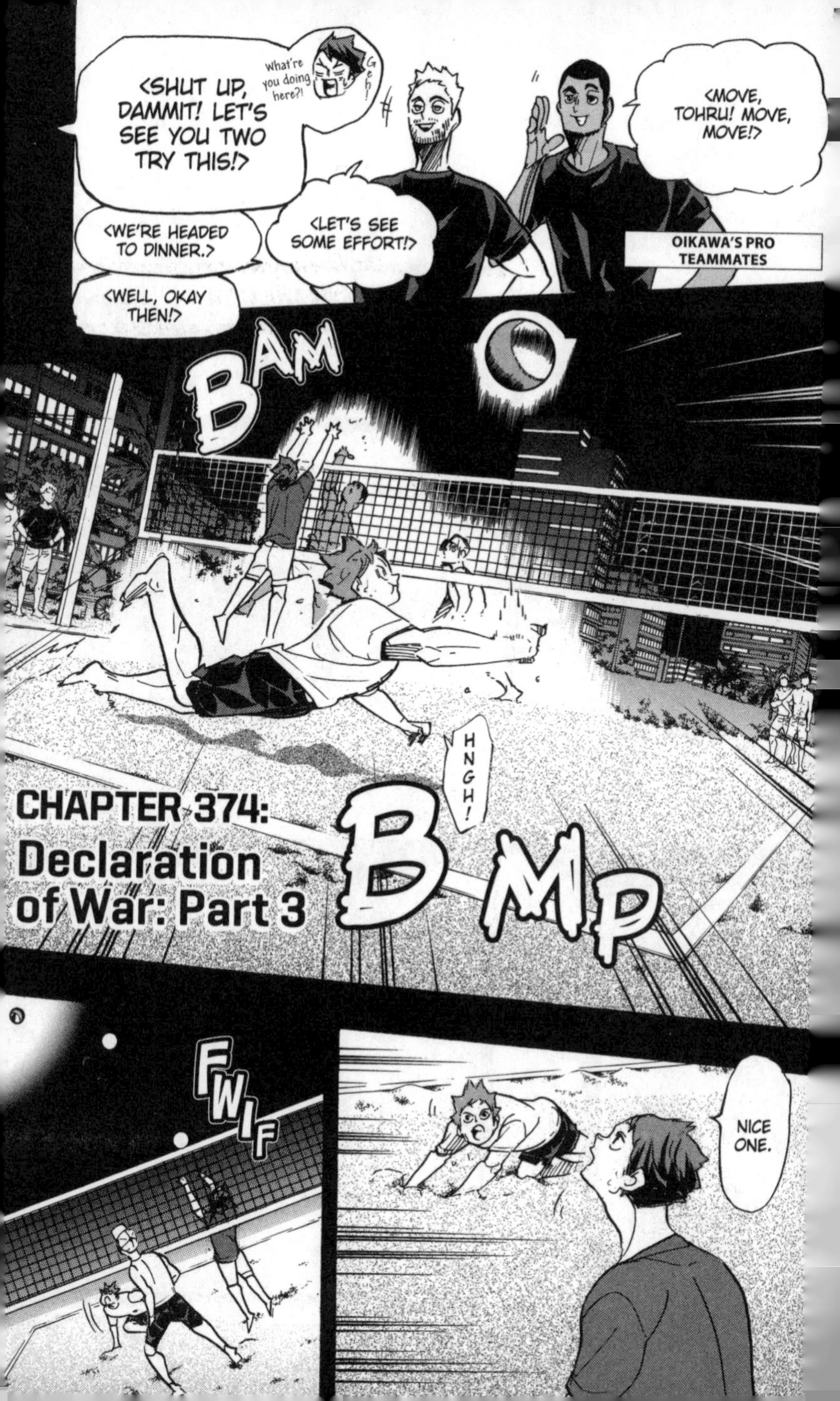

<MOVE, TOHRU! MOVE, MOVE!>
<SHUT UP, DAMMIT! LET'S SEE YOU TWO TRY THIS!>
What're you doing here?!
Geh!
OIKAWA'S PRO TEAMMATES
<LET'S SEE SOME EFFORT!>
<WE'RE HEADED TO DINNER.>
<WELL, OKAY THEN!>
BAM
HNGH!
CHAPTER 374:
Declaration of War: Part 3
BMP
NICE ONE.
FWIF

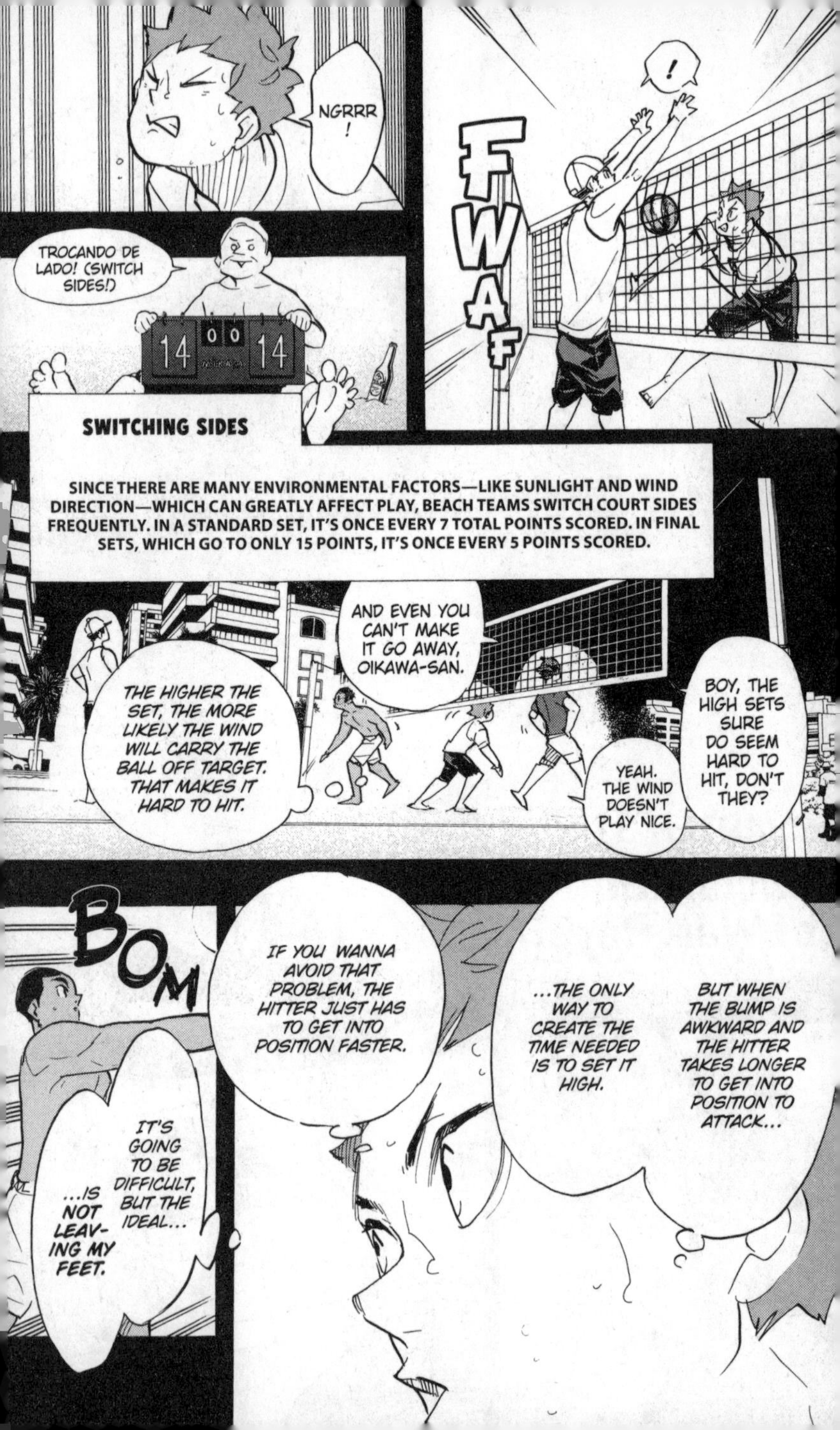
!
FWAF
NGRRR!
TROCANDO DE LADO! (SWITCH SIDES!)
14 00 14
SWITCHING SIDES
SINCE THERE ARE MANY ENVIRONMENTAL FACTORS—LIKE SUNLIGHT AND WIND DIRECTION—WHICH CAN GREATLY AFFECT PLAY, BEACH TEAMS SWITCH COURT SIDES FREQUENTLY. IN A STANDARD SET, IT'S ONCE EVERY 7 TOTAL POINTS SCORED. IN FINAL SETS, WHICH GO TO ONLY 15 POINTS, IT'S ONCE EVERY 5 POINTS SCORED.
BOY, THE HIGH SETS SURE DO SEEM HARD TO HIT, DON'T THEY?
YEAH. THE WIND DOESN'T PLAY NICE.
AND EVEN YOU CAN'T MAKE IT GO AWAY, OIKAWA-SAN.
THE HIGHER THE SET, THE MORE LIKELY THE WIND WILL CARRY THE BALL OFF TARGET. THAT MAKES IT HARD TO HIT.
BUT WHEN THE BUMP IS AWKWARD AND THE HITTER TAKES LONGER TO GET INTO POSITION TO ATTACK...
...THE ONLY WAY TO CREATE THE TIME NEEDED IS TO SET IT HIGH.
IF YOU WANNA AVOID THAT PROBLEM, THE HITTER JUST HAS TO GET INTO POSITION FASTER.
BOM
IT'S GOING TO BE DIFFICULT, BUT THE IDEAL...
...IS NOT LEAVING MY FEET.

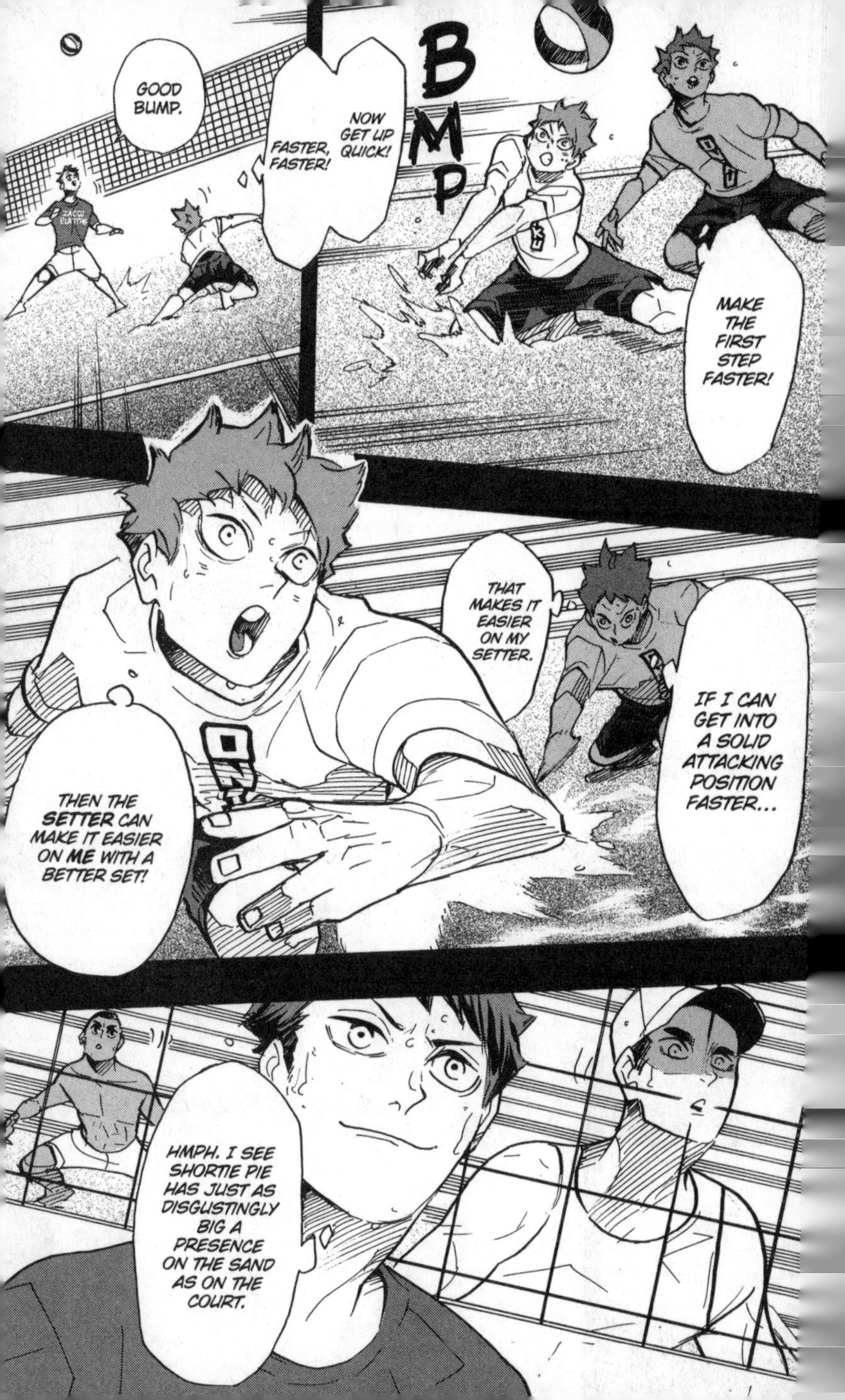
BMP
NOW GET UP QUICK!
FASTER, FASTER!
MAKE THE FIRST STEP FASTER!
GOOD BUMP.
IF I CAN GET INTO A SOLID ATTACKING POSITION FASTER...
THAT MAKES IT EASIER ON MY SETTER.
THEN THE SETTER CAN MAKE IT EASIER ON ME WITH A BETTER SET!
HMPH. I SEE SHORTIE PIE HAS JUST AS DISGUSTINGLY BIG A PRESENCE ON THE SAND AS ON THE COURT.

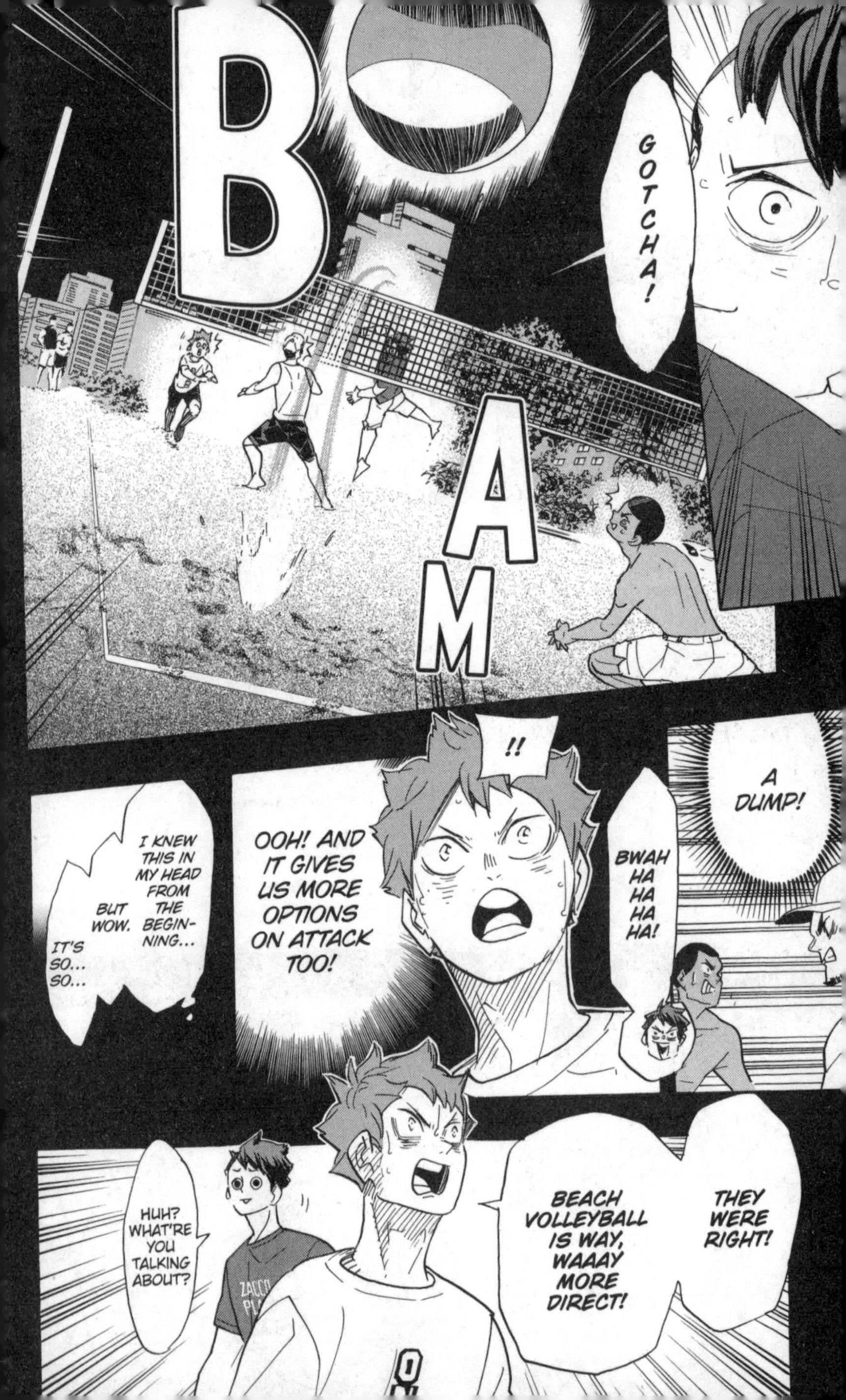
GOTCHA!
BAM
A DUMP!
BWAH HA HA HA HA!
!!
OOH! AND IT GIVES US MORE OPTIONS ON ATTACK TOO!
I KNEW THIS IN MY HEAD FROM THE BEGINNING...
BUT WOW.
IT'S SO... SO...
THEY WERE RIGHT!
BEACH VOLLEYBALL IS WAY, WAAAY MORE DIRECT!
HUH? WHAT'RE YOU TALKING ABOUT?

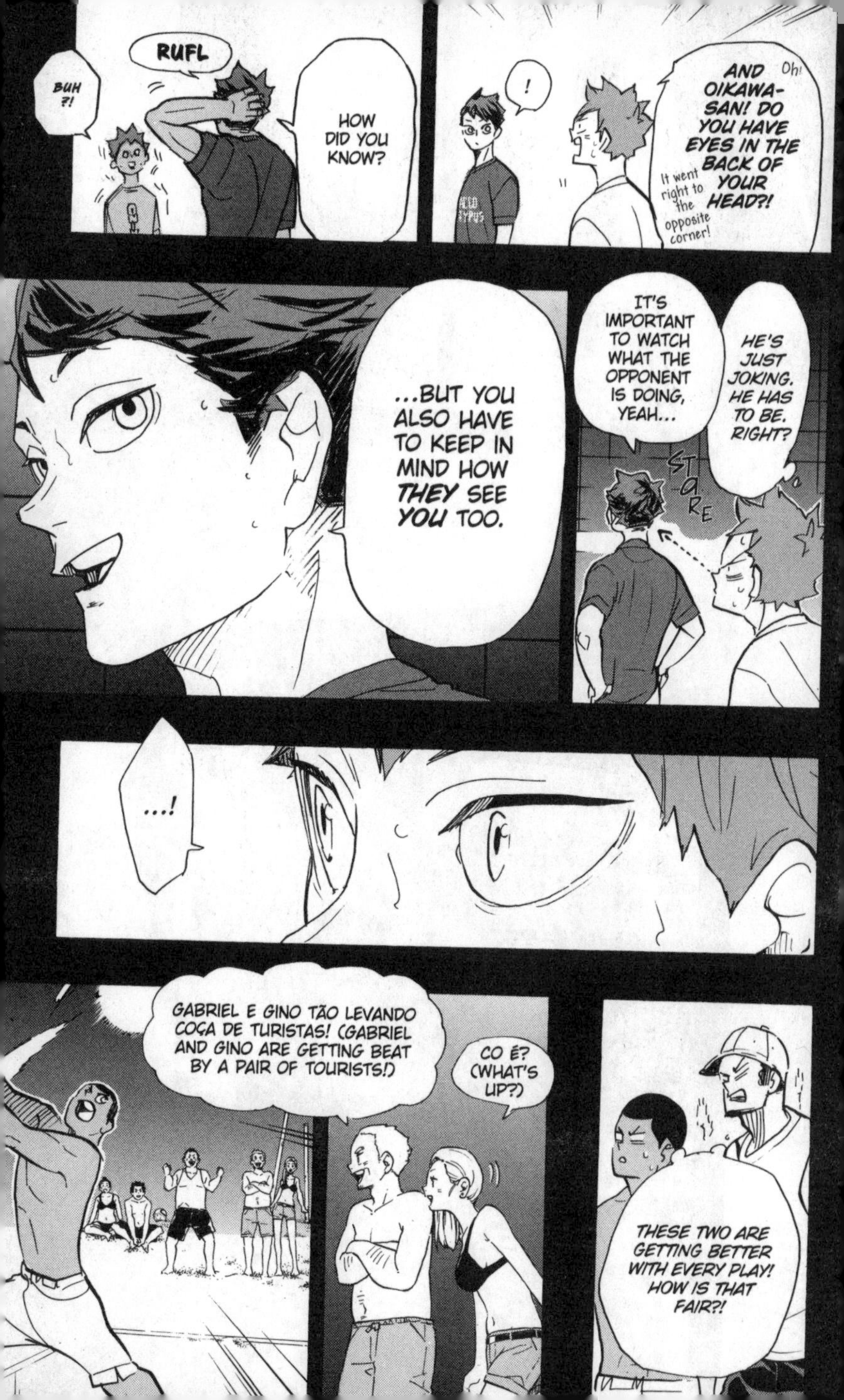
!
AND OIKAWA-SAN! DO YOU HAVE EYES IN THE BACK OF YOUR HEAD?!
Oh!
It went right to the opposite corner!
RUFL
HOW DID YOU KNOW?
BUH?!
HE'S JUST JOKING. HE HAS TO BE. RIGHT?
IT'S IMPORTANT TO WATCH WHAT THE OPPONENT IS DOING, YEAH...
STARE
...BUT YOU ALSO HAVE TO KEEP IN MIND HOW THEY SEE YOU TOO.
...!
THESE TWO ARE GETTING BETTER WITH EVERY PLAY! HOW IS THAT FAIR?!
CO É? (WHAT'S UP?)
GABRIEL E GINO TÃO LEVANDO COÇA DE TURISTAS! (GABRIEL AND GINO ARE GETTING BEAT BY A PAIR OF TOURISTS!)

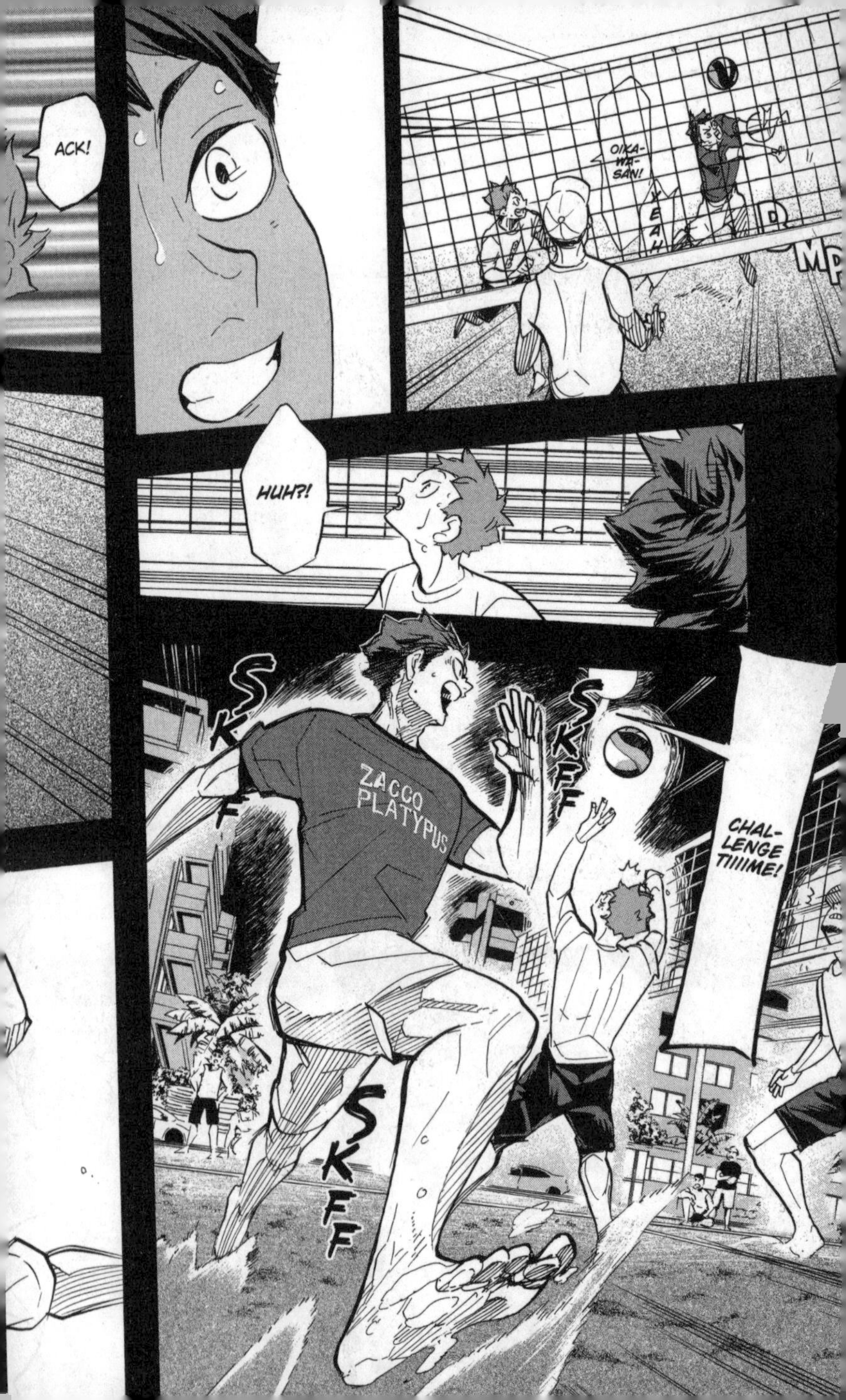

OIKA-WA-SAN!
YEAH
D
MP
ACK!
HUH?!
SKF
SKFF
CHAL-LENGE TIIIIME!
ZACCO PLATYPUS
SKFF

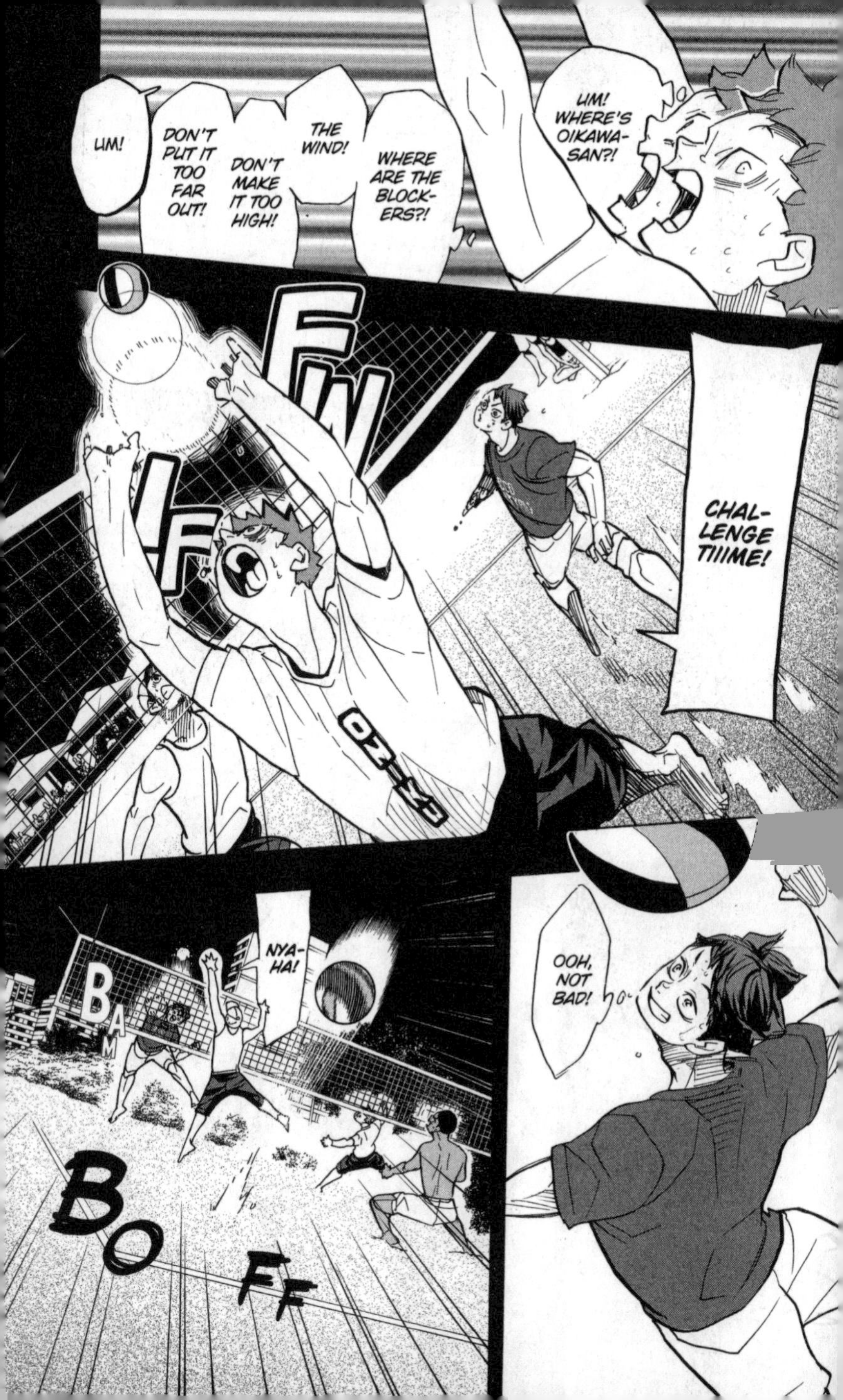
UM! WHERE'S OIKAWA-SAN?!
WHERE ARE THE BLOCKERS?!
THE WIND!
DON'T MAKE IT TOO HIGH!
DON'T PUT IT TOO FAR OUT!
UM!
CHAL-LENGE TIIIME!
OOH, NOT BAD!
NYA-HA!
BAM
BOFF

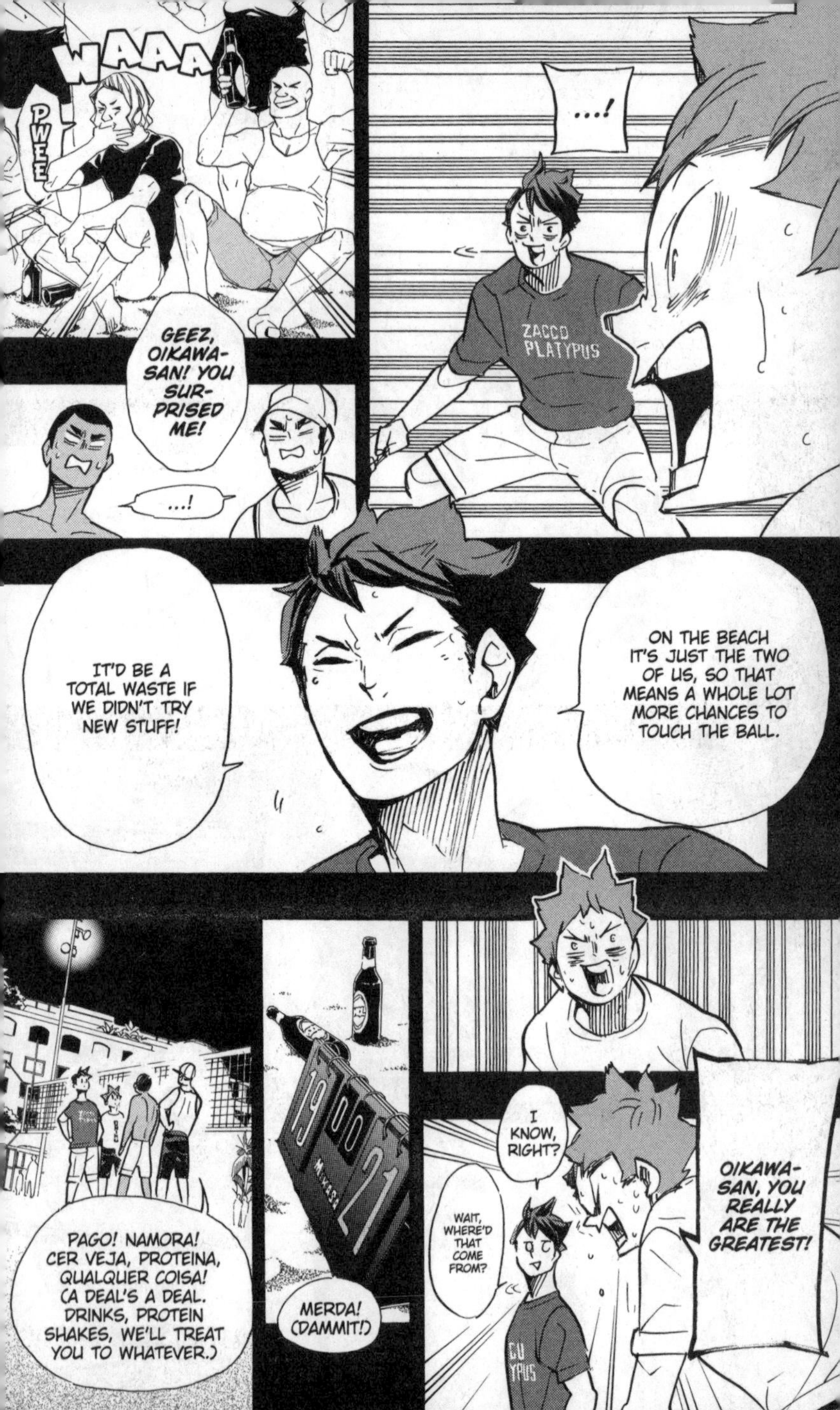
...!
ZACCO PLATYPUS
WAAA
PWEE
GEEZ, OIKAWA-SAN! YOU SUR-PRISED ME!
...!
ON THE BEACH IT'S JUST THE TWO OF US, SO THAT MEANS A WHOLE LOT MORE CHANCES TO TOUCH THE BALL.
IT'D BE A TOTAL WASTE IF WE DIDN'T TRY NEW STUFF!
OIKAWA-SAN, YOU REALLY ARE THE GREATEST!
I KNOW, RIGHT?
WAIT, WHERE'D THAT COME FROM?
MERDA! (DAMMIT!)
PAGO! NAMORA! CER VEJA, PROTEINA, QUALQUER COISA! (A DEAL'S A DEAL. DRINKS, PROTEIN SHAKES, WE'LL TREAT YOU TO WHATEVER.)

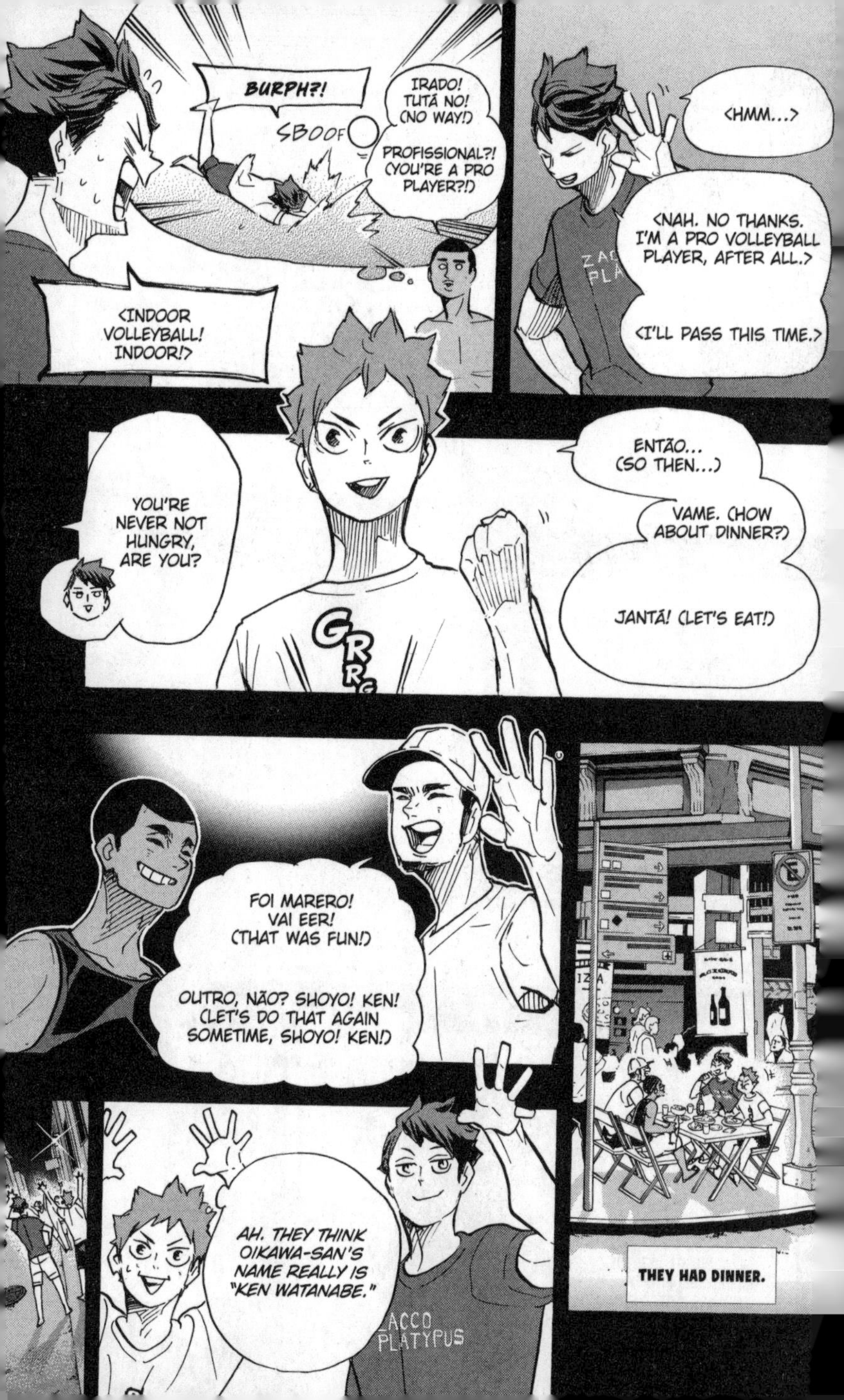

<HMM...>
<NAH. NO THANKS. I'M A PRO VOLLEYBALL PLAYER, AFTER ALL.>
<I'LL PASS THIS TIME.>
IRADO! TUTÁ NO! (NO WAY!)
BURPH?!
SBOOF
PROFISSIONAL?! (YOU'RE A PRO PLAYER?!)
<INDOOR VOLLEYBALL! INDOOR!>
ENTÃO... (SO THEN...)
VAME. (HOW ABOUT DINNER?)
JANTÁ! (LET'S EAT!)
YOU'RE NEVER NOT HUNGRY, ARE YOU?
THEY HAD DINNER.
FOI MARERO! VAI EER! (THAT WAS FUN!)
OUTRO, NÃO? SHOYO! KEN! (LET'S DO THAT AGAIN SOMETIME, SHOYO! KEN!)
AH. THEY THINK OIKAWA-SAN'S NAME REALLY IS "KEN WATANABE."
ZACCO PLATYPUS

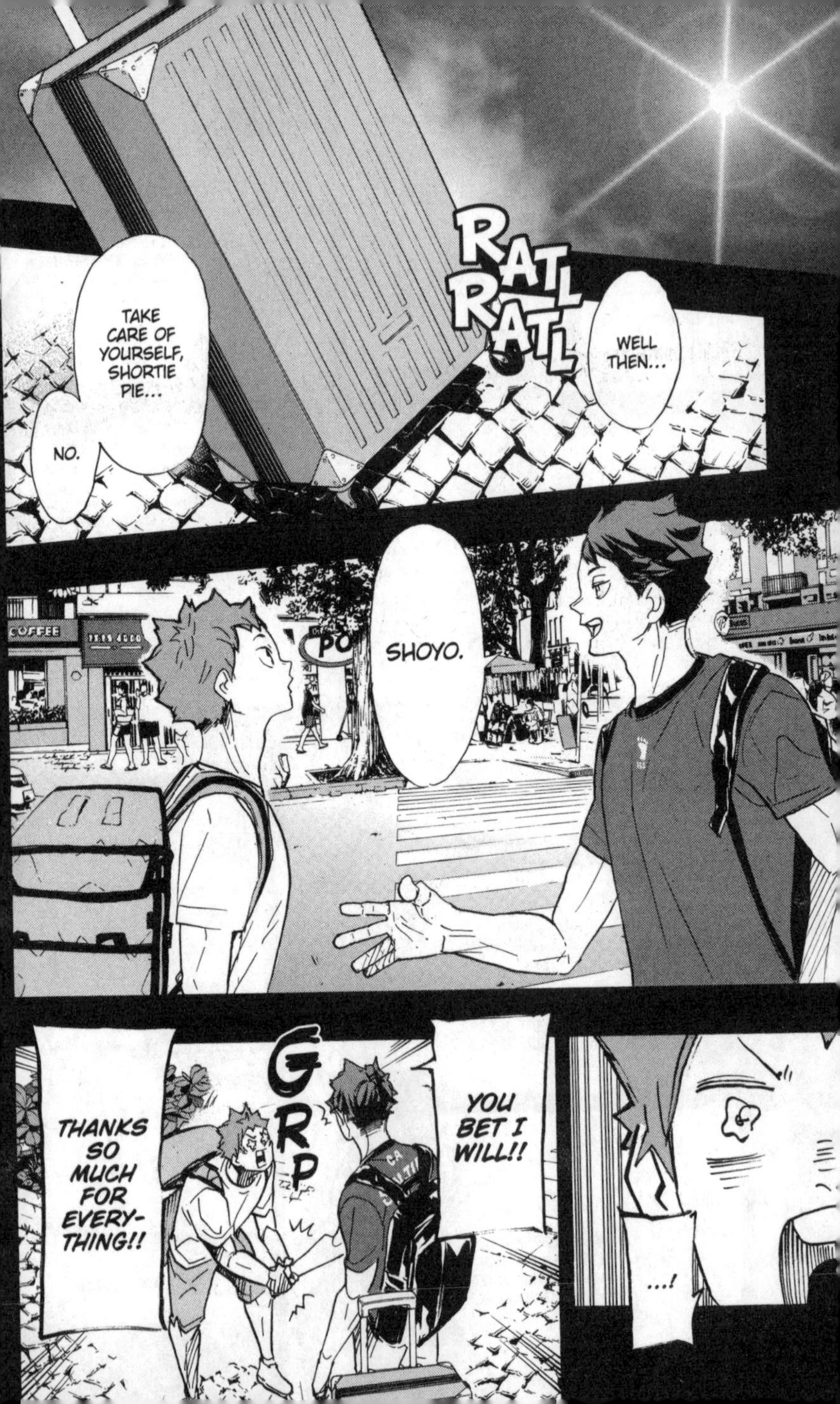
RATL RATL
WELL THEN...
TAKE CARE OF YOURSELF, SHORTIE PIE...
NO.
SHOYO.
...!
YOU BET I WILL!!
GRP
THANKS SO MUCH FOR EVERYTHING!!

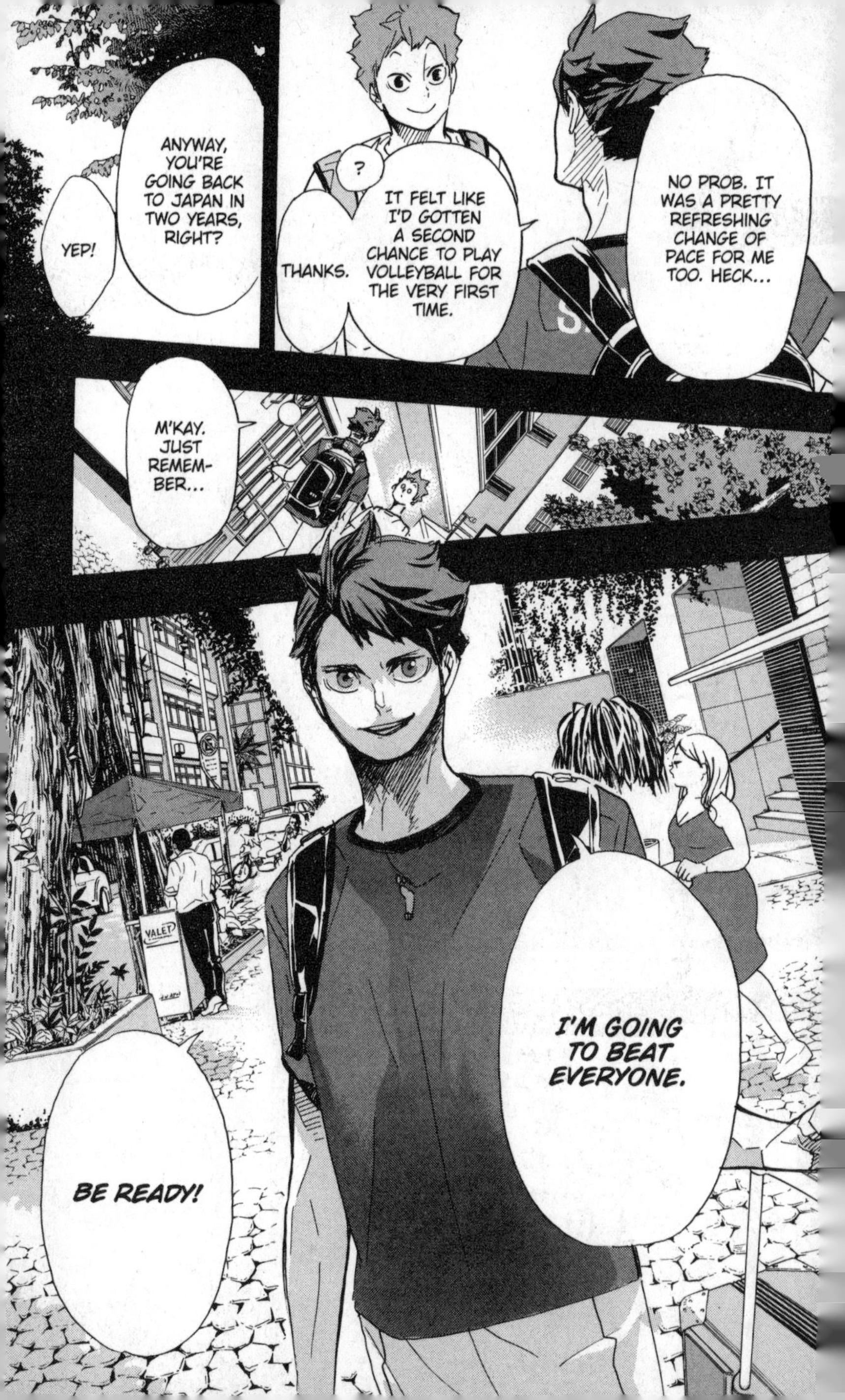

NO PROB. IT WAS A PRETTY REFRESHING CHANGE OF PACE FOR ME TOO. HECK...
?
IT FELT LIKE I'D GOTTEN A SECOND CHANCE TO PLAY VOLLEYBALL FOR THE VERY FIRST TIME.
THANKS.
ANYWAY, YOU'RE GOING BACK TO JAPAN IN TWO YEARS, RIGHT?
YEP!
M'KAY. JUST REMEMBER...
I'M GOING TO BEAT EVERYONE.
BE READY!
VALET

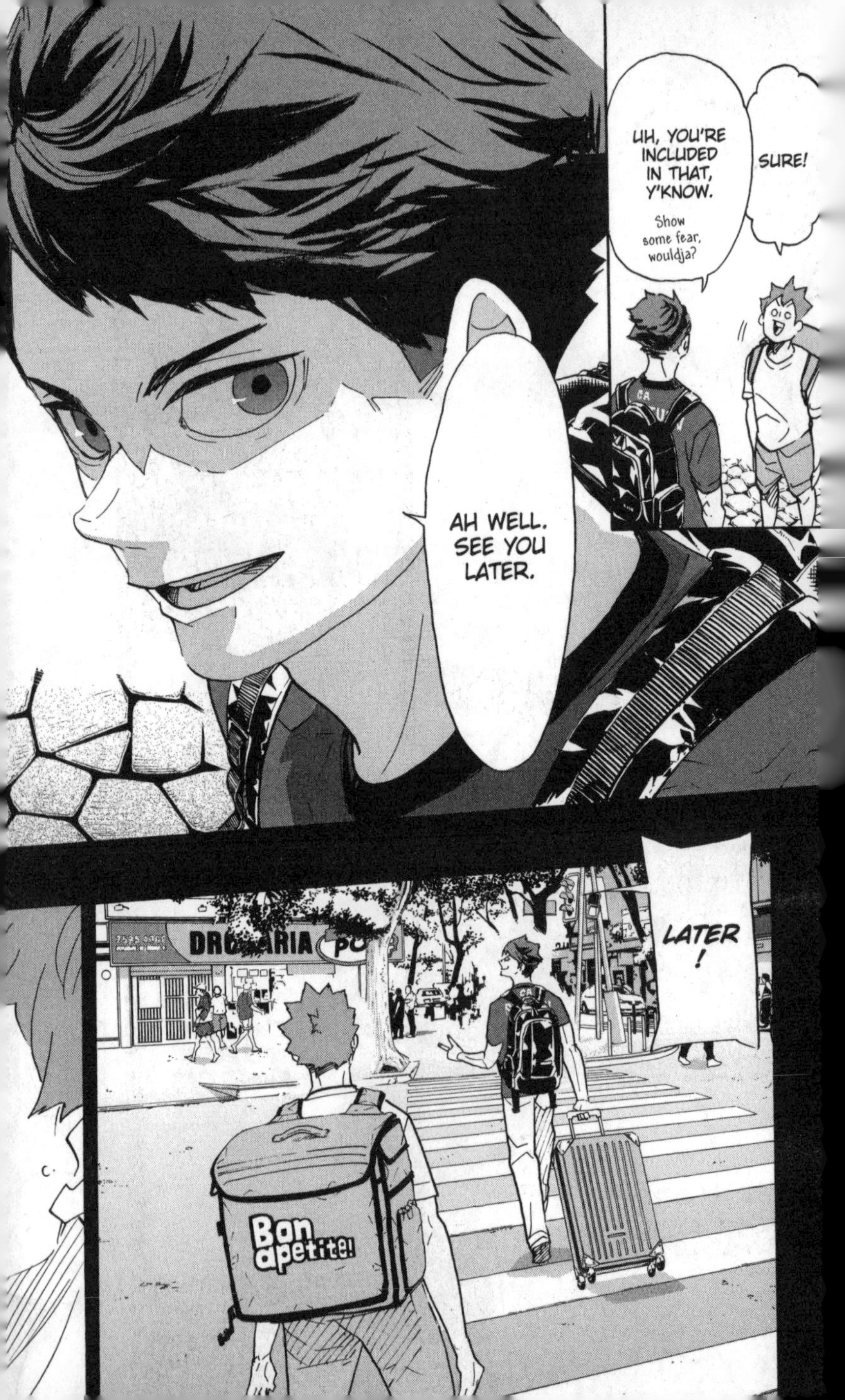
UH, YOU'RE INCLUDED IN THAT, Y'KNOW.
Show some fear, wouldja?
SURE!
AH WELL. SEE YOU LATER.
DROGARIA
LATER!
Bon apetite!

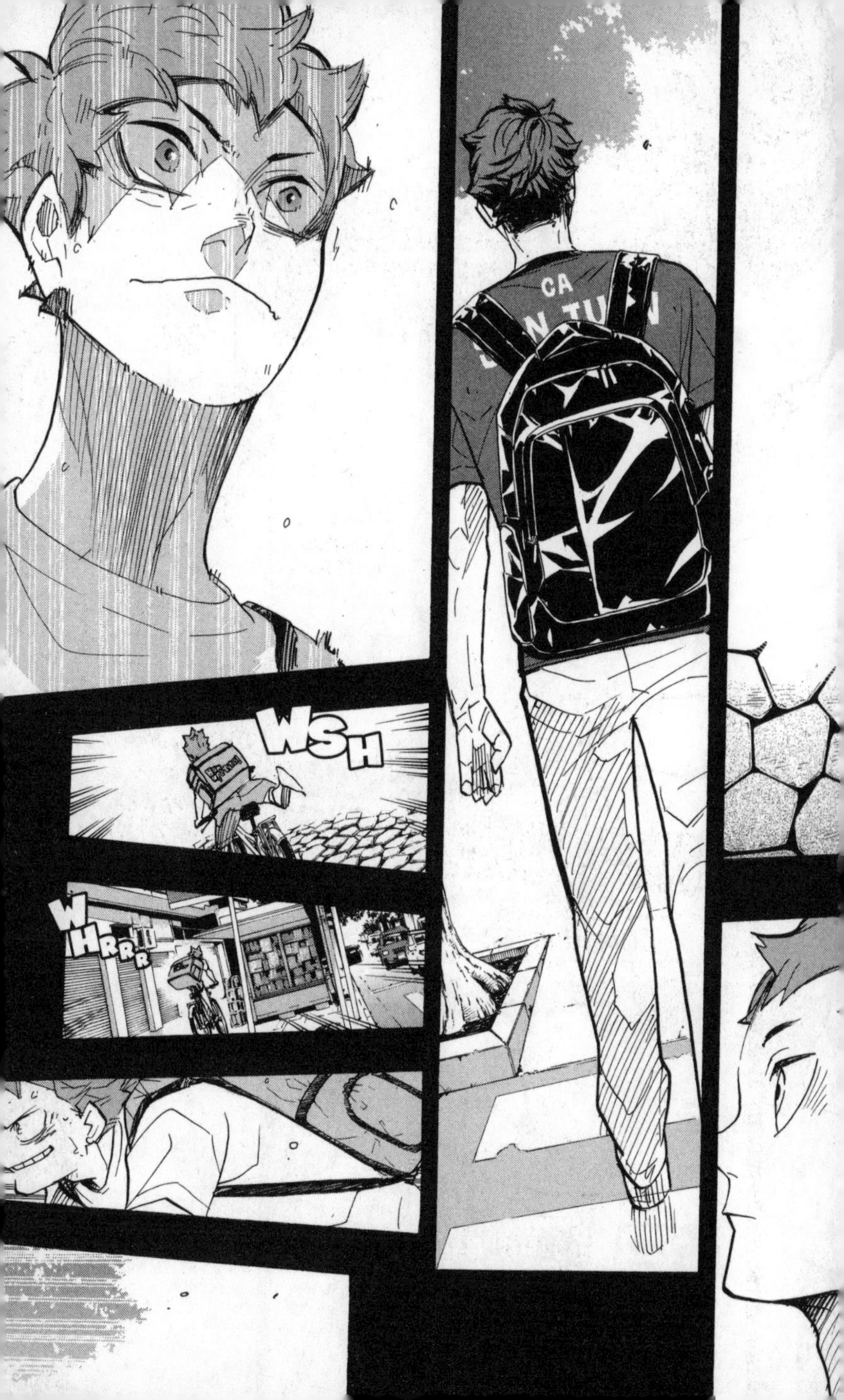
WSH
WHRRRR

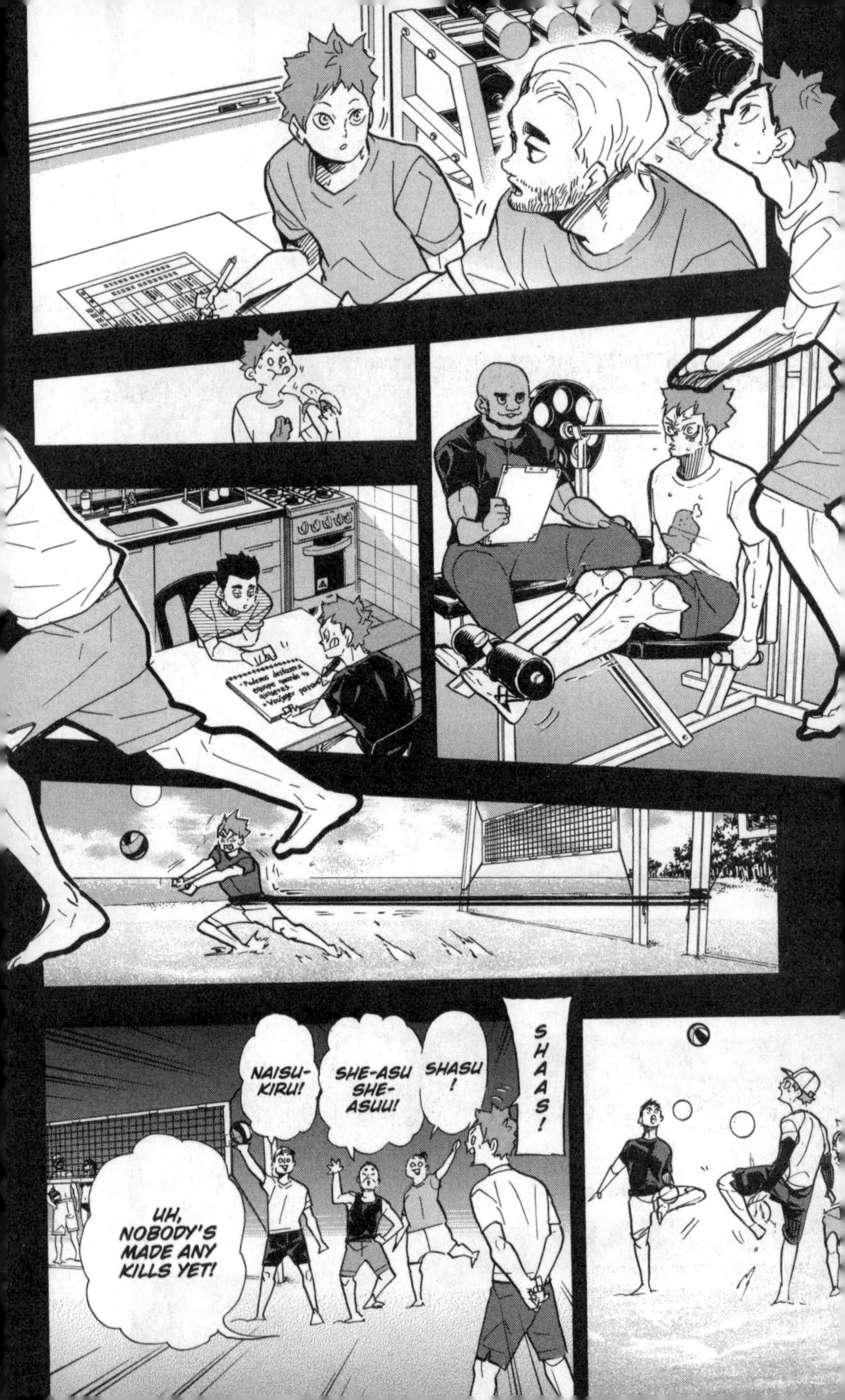
SHAAS!
SHASU!
SHE-ASU SHE-ASUU!
NAISU-KIRU!
UH, NOBODY'S MADE ANY KILLS YET!

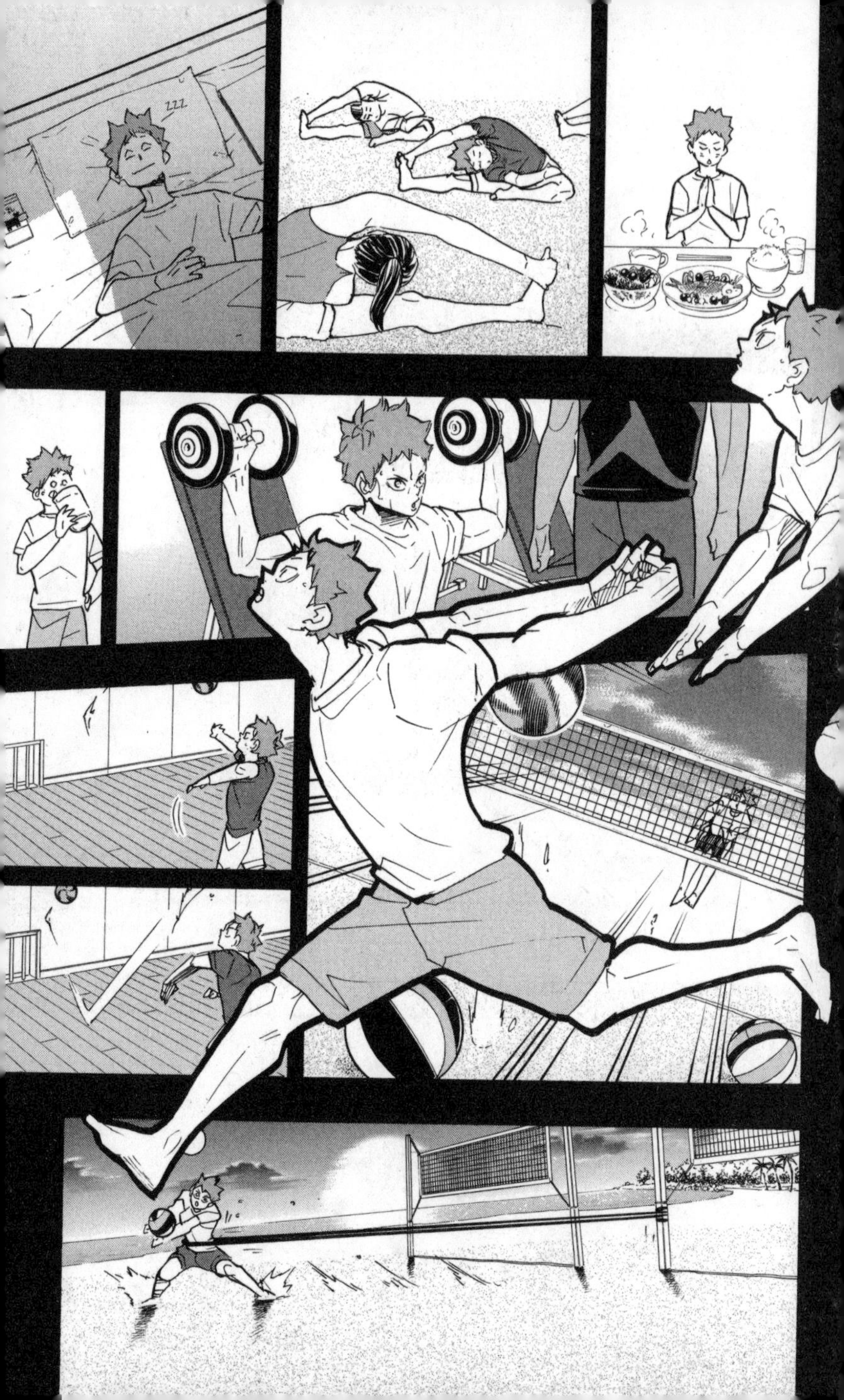
ZZZ

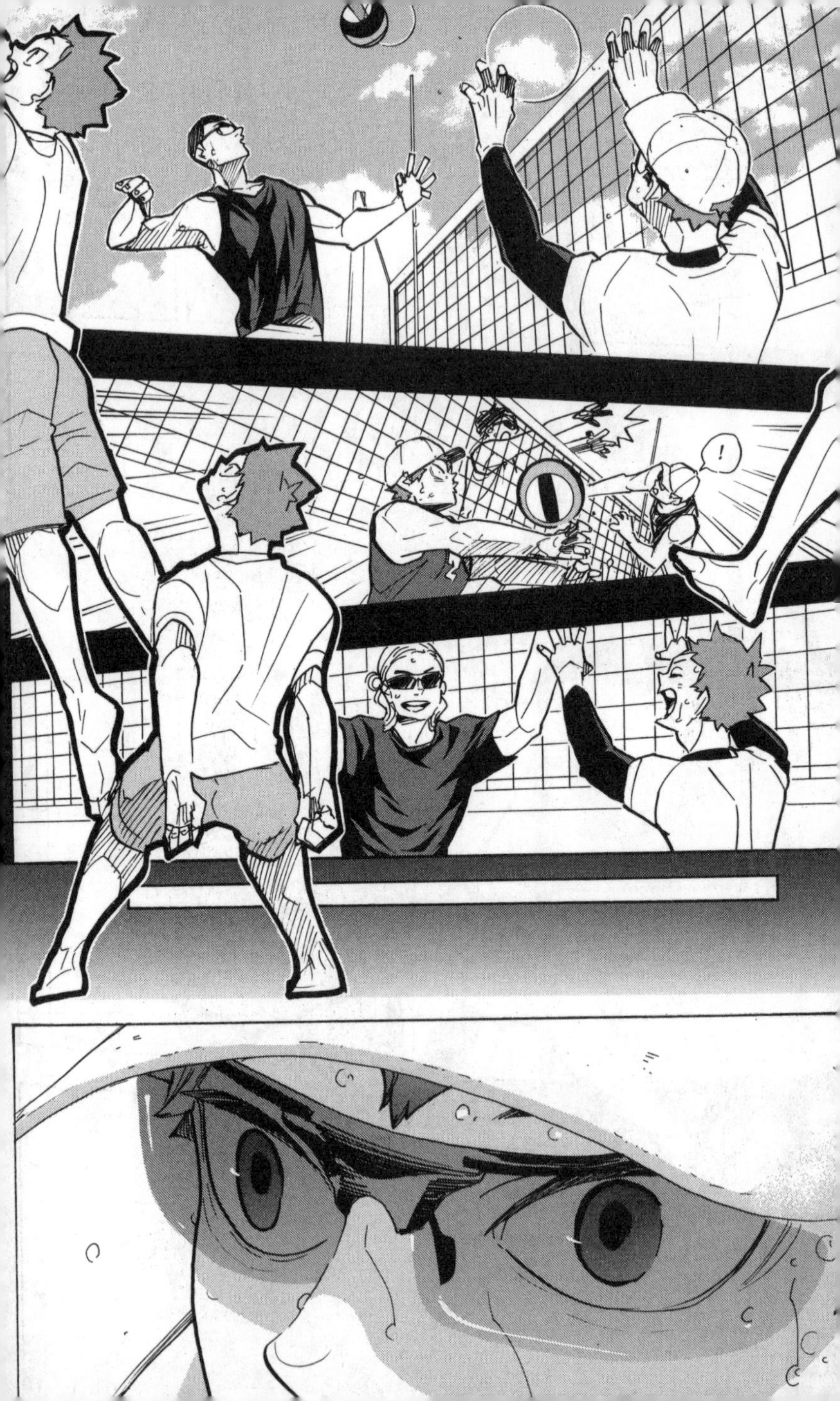
!

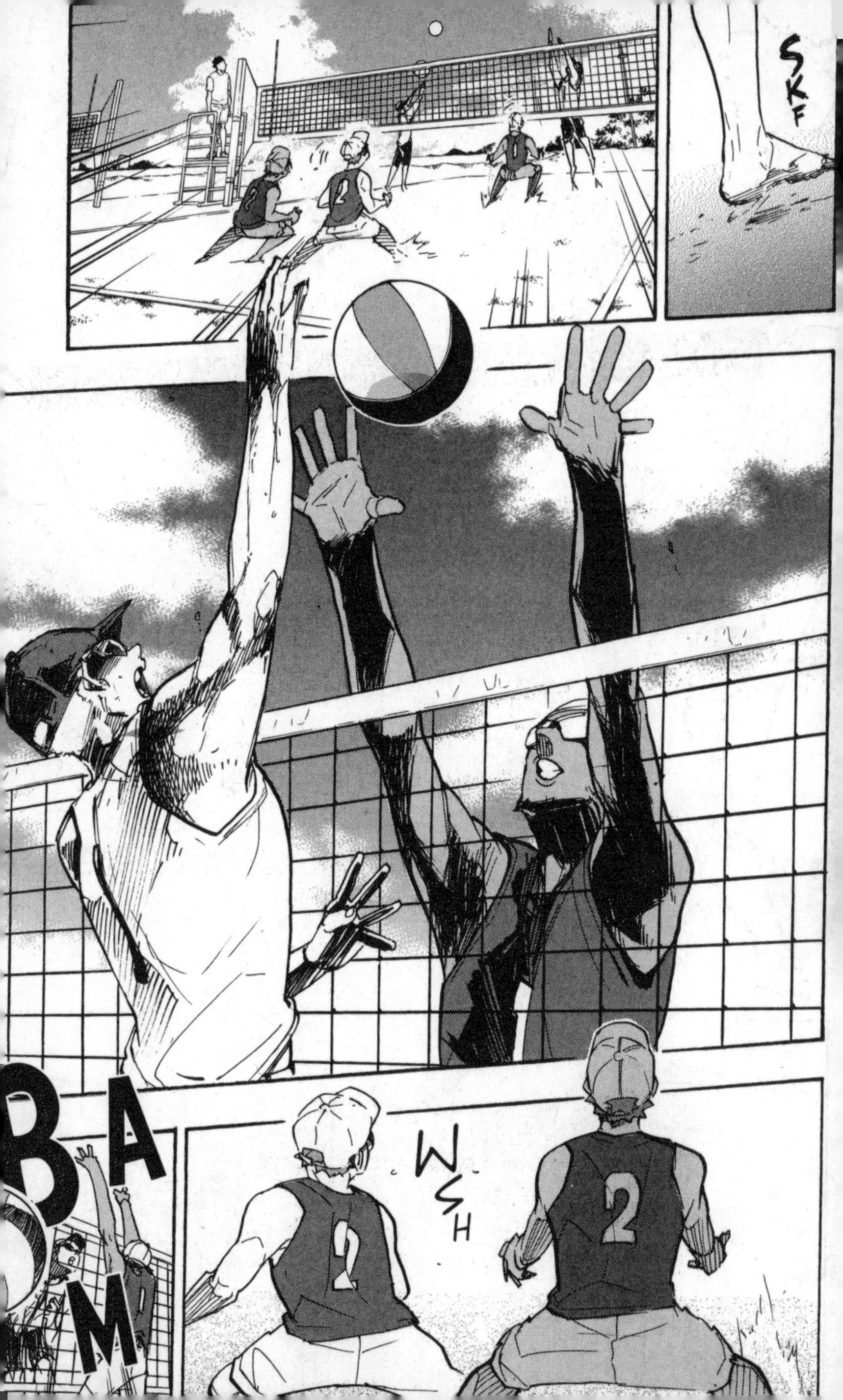
SKF
WSH
BAM

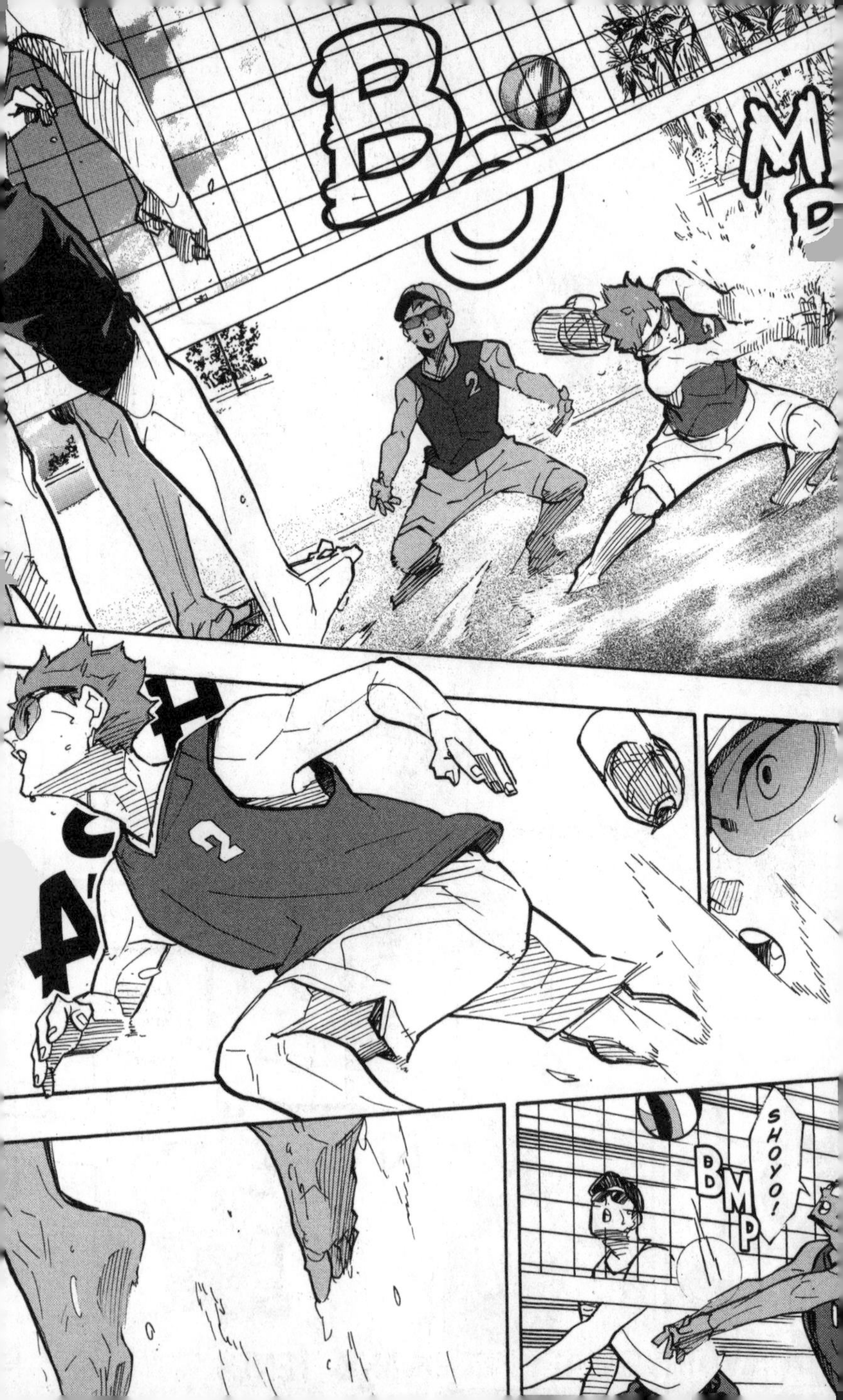
BMP
SHOYO!

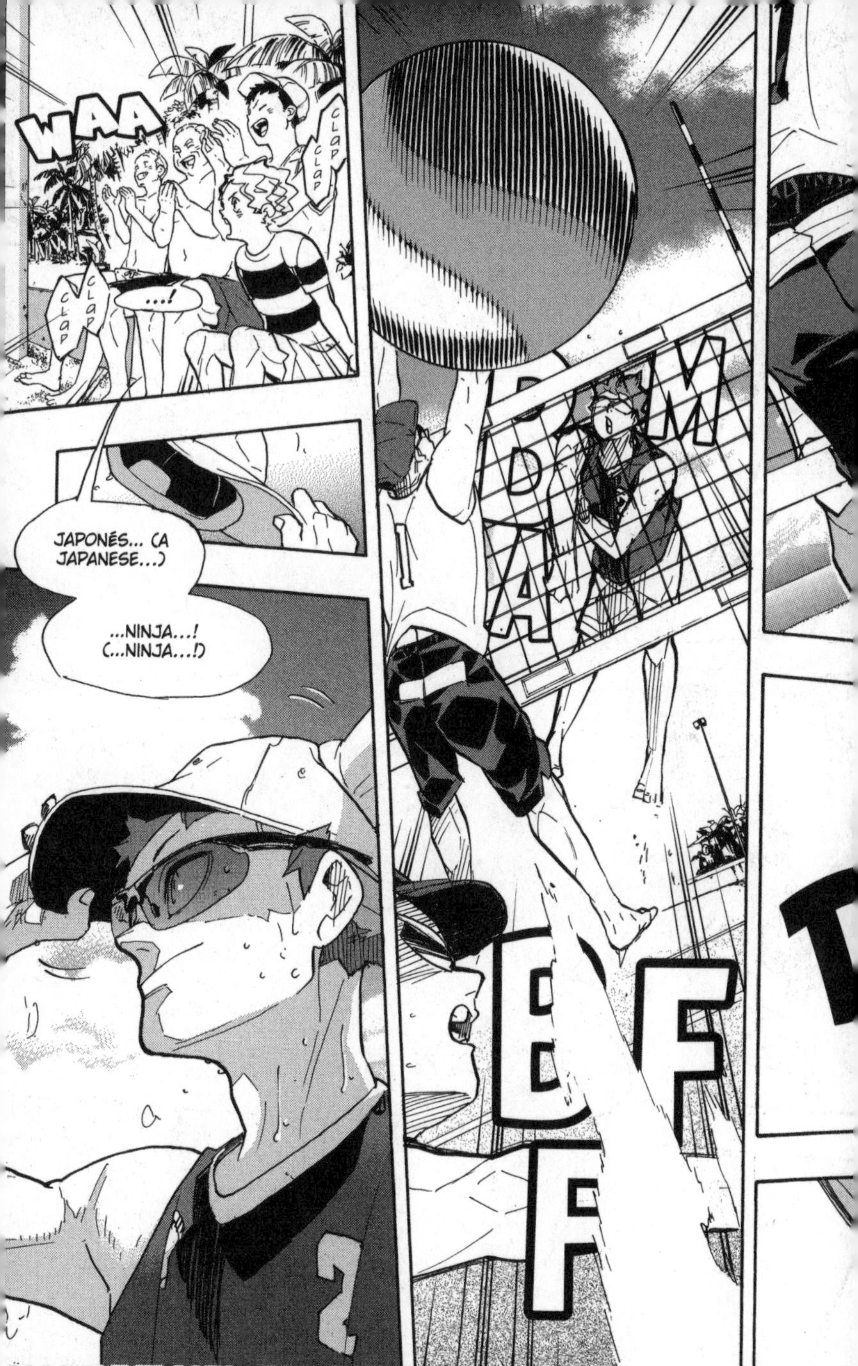
WAA
CLAP CLAP
CLAP CLAP
...!
JAPONÉS... (A JAPANESE...)
...NINJA...! (...NINJA...!)

HAIKYU!! VOL 42: BECOMING (END)

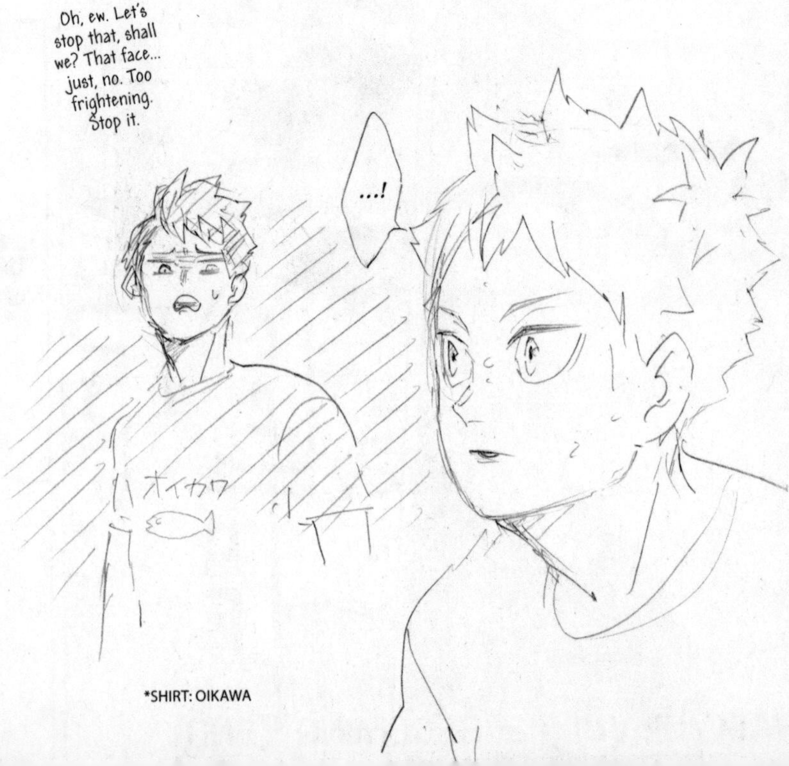
Oh, ew. Let's stop that, shall we? That face... just, no. Too frightening. Stop it.
...!
オイカワ

*SHIRT: OIKAWA

I WENT TO RIO DE JANEIRO IN MAY
2019 FOR RESEARCH PURPOSES. I
HOPE SOMEDAY I'LL GET TO WRITE
A TRAVEL JOURNAL ABOUT IT.

EDITOR'S NOTES

The English edition of *Haikyu!!* maintains the honorifics used in the original Japanese version. For those of you who are new to these terms, here's a brief explanation to help with your reading experience!

When saying someone's name in Japanese, a suffix is often attached to indicate how familiar the speaker is with the person. Some are more polite and respectful, while others are endearing.

1 *-kun* is often used for young men or boys, usually someone you are familiar with.

2 *-chan* is used for young children and can be used as a term of endearment.

3 *-san* is used for someone you respect or are not close to, or to be polite.

4 *Senpai* is used for someone who is older than you or in a higher position or grade in school.

5 *Kohai* is used for someone who is younger than you or in a lower position or grade in school.

6 *Sensei* means teacher.

Kuroko's BASKETBALL

TADATOSHI FUJIMAKI

When incoming first-year student Taiga Kagami joins the Seirin High basketball team, he meets Tetsuya Kuroko, a mysterious boy who's plain beyond words. But Kagami's in for the shock of his life when he learns that the practically invisible Kuroko was once a member of "the Miracle Generation"—the undefeated legendary team—and he wants Kagami's help taking down each of his old teammates!

Four-time consecutive U.S. Junior tournament champ Ryoma Echizen comes to Seishun Academy to further his reign as The Prince of Tennis.

His skill is matched only by his attitude—irking some but impressing all as he leads his team to the Nationals and beyond!

THE PRINCE Of TENNIS

STORY AND ART BY **Takeshi Konomi**

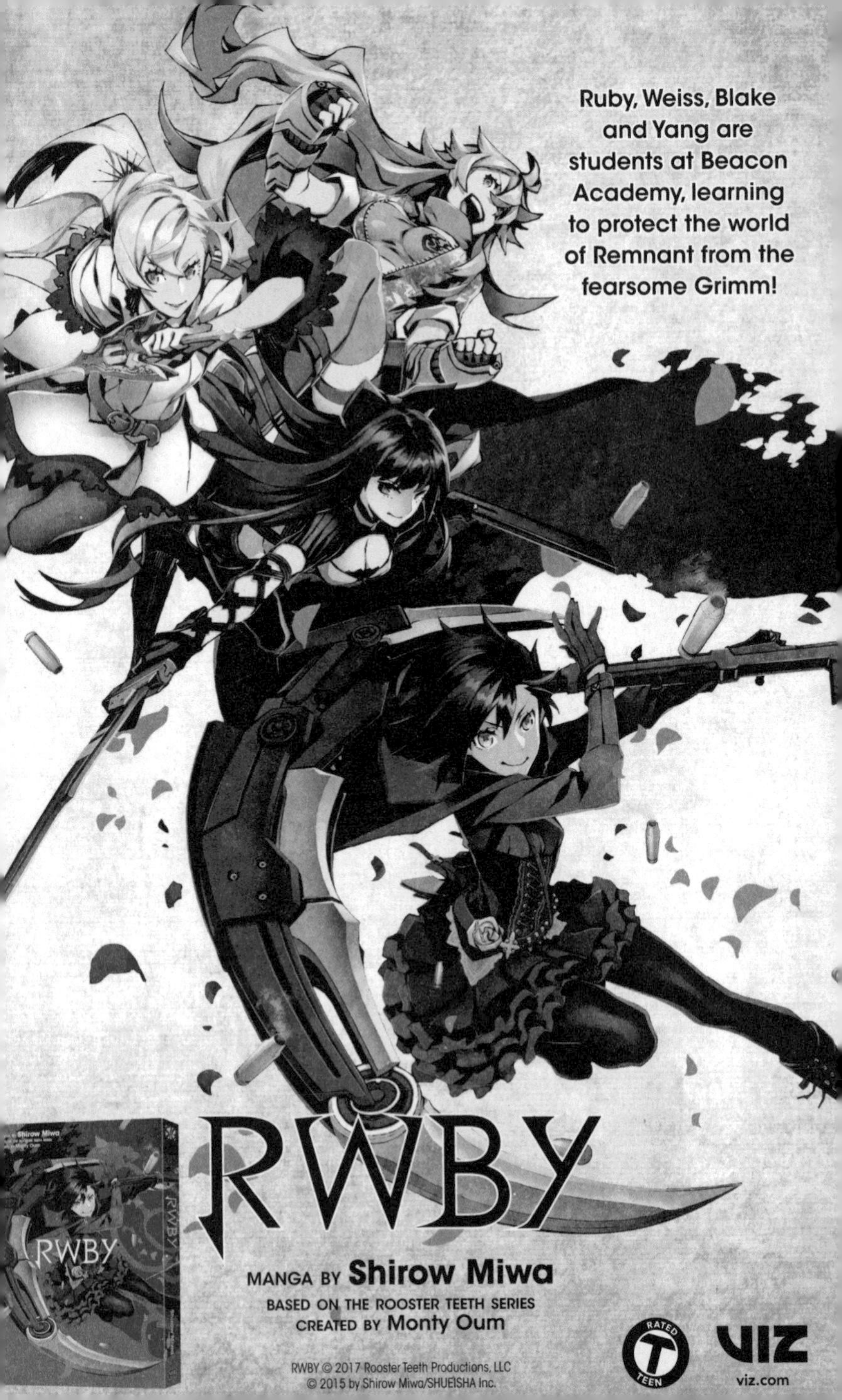
Ruby, Weiss, Blake and Yang are students at Beacon Academy, learning to protect the world of Remnant from the fearsome Grimm!
RWBY
RWBY
MANGA BY Shirow Miwa
BASED ON THE ROOSTER TEETH SERIES
CREATED BY Monty Oum
RATED T TEEN
VIZ
viz.com
RWBY © 2017 Rooster Teeth Productions, LLC
© 2015 by Shirow Miwa/SHUEISHA Inc.

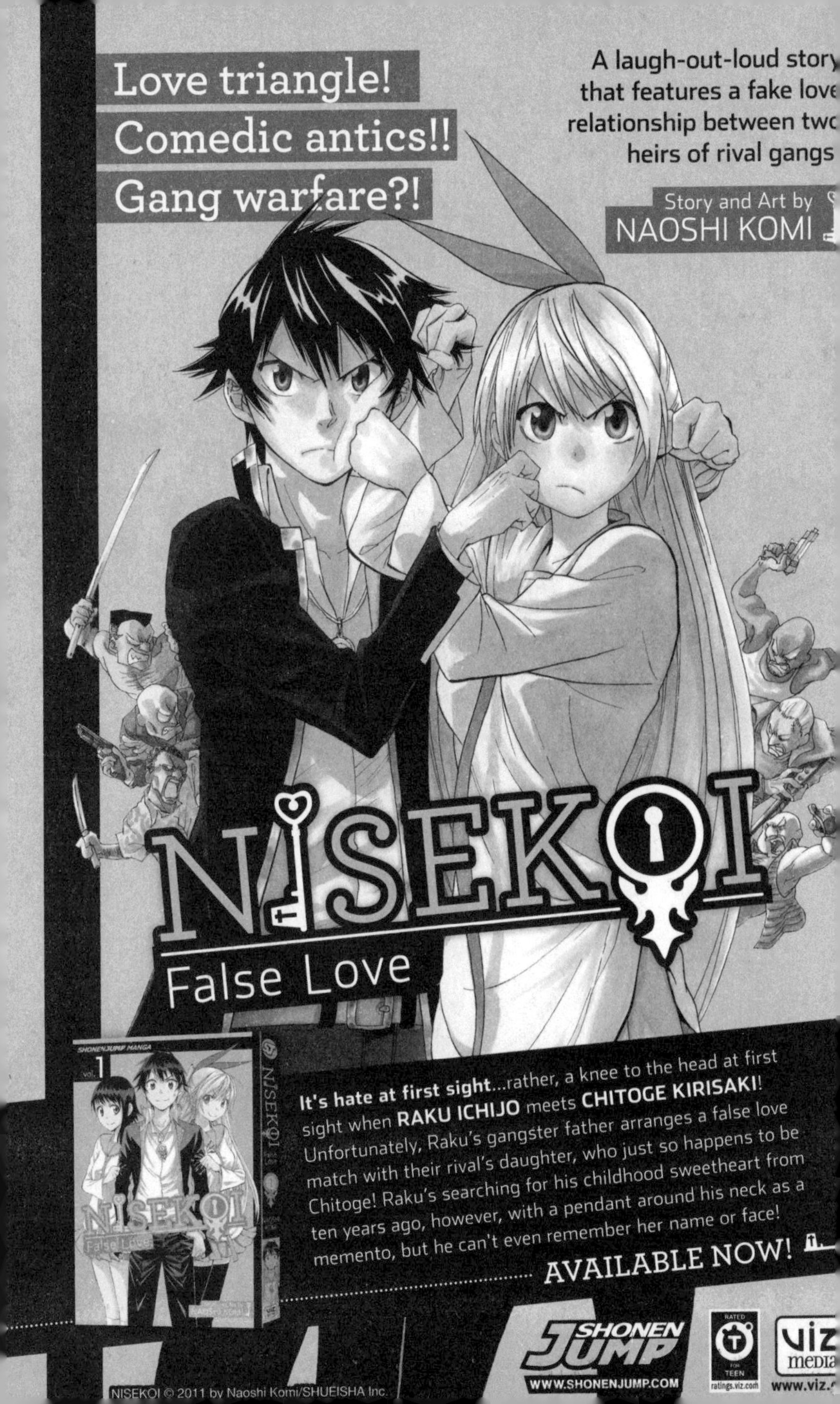

Love triangle!
Comedic antics!!
Gang warfare?!
A laugh-out-loud stor
that features a fake love
relationship between tw
heirs of rival gangs
Story and Art by
NAOSHI KOMI
NISEKOI
False Love
SHONEN JUMP MANGA
vol. 1
NISEKOI
False Love
It's hate at first sight...rather, a knee to the head at first sight when RAKU ICHIJO meets CHITOGE KIRISAKI! Unfortunately, Raku's gangster father arranges a false love match with their rival's daughter, who just so happens to be Chitoge! Raku's searching for his childhood sweetheart from ten years ago, however, with a pendant around his neck as a memento, but he can't even remember her name or face!
AVAILABLE NOW!
SHONEN JUMP
WWW.SHONENJUMP.COM
RATED T FOR TEEN
ratings.viz.com
viz media
www.viz.
NISEKOI © 2011 by Naoshi Komi/SHUEISHA Inc.

You're Reading the
WRONG WAY!

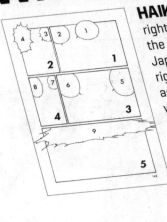

HAIKYU!! reads from right to left, starting in the upper-right corner. Japanese is read from right to left, meaning that action, sound effects and word-balloon order are completely reversed from English order.